Mega Cooking™

A REVOLUTIONARY
NEW PLAN FOR
QUANTITY COOKING

JILL PATRICE BOND

CUMBERLAND HOUSE PUBLISHING
NASHVILLE, TENNESSEE

Mega-cooking™ is a trademark of Jill Bond.
You can contact the author through the publisher or her website at www.megacooking.com

Published by Cumberland House Publishing, 431 Harding Industrial Drive, Nashville, Tennessee 37211-3160.

Cover design by Unlikely Suburban Design
Interior design and typesetting by Julie Pitkin

Library of Congress Cataloging-in-Publication Data

Bond, Jill.
Mega Cooking : a revolutionary new plan for quantity cooking / Jill Bond.
p. cm.
Includes bibliographical references and index.
ISBN 1-58182-096-8 (alk. paper)
1. Make ahead cookery. I. Title.

Tx652.B59 2000
641.5'55—dc21 00-022653

Printed in the United States of America
1 2 3 4 5 6 7 8 — 05 04 03 02 01 00

For Mom, Magah, Zoe White

No matter what we call you, we all know your love.

Some people invest in stocks, houses, banks, or luxuries.

But you chose a different path — you've spent your life investing in people.

Thank you, Mom, for investing yourself in my family and me.

Oh, and for teaching me how to cook . . .

Table of Contents

Acknowledgments

Throughout this book, I use the term "we" instead of "I" because that is exactly what I mean—"we". This book is the result of many people helping, advising, and instructing me.

To all the volunteer mega-testers: You have doubled the value of this book to any of its readers. Without your efforts, I couldn't have worked out the kinks in the recipes or known which ones needed more work. Your ideas and suggestions not only gave me the encouragement I needed, but provided very real tips for our readers. Each of you is special and I'm indebted to you for your support and work. As we read through the results, I kept telling my family how blessed I was that so many people would spend hours cooking and testing my recipes, and then take the time to write thorough reports. You are incredible people and I love you: Linda M. Bacon, Joanna Baker, Cheryl Beasley, Amy Beatty, Pam Bianco, Linda Bond, Christine Brincku, Helene Brock, Ruth Brown, Yanira Carter, Tracey Cavender, Debbie China, Judy Clark, Karen B. Collins, Tina W. Cook, Kellie Coombs, Sara Jane Dagen, Esther DeGeus, Jean Dominguez, Lauren M. Down, Pamela Evans, Sandy and Lacey Farrar, Paula Farris, Melanie Fierro, Colleen Finley, Cindy Fisher, Lisa Jeanne Fisher, Denna Flickner, Loralei Fox, Pam Geyer, Leslie Gipson, Jenny Goff, Tamara Grim, Diana Harrison, Sheryl Hartzell, Patricia Hastings, Marsha Hedges, Sarah Heggie, Sarah Hendrix, Jana Lee Hoffman, Terri Houchin, Mrs. Lynn Hoxmeier, Kristin Hulsey, Dorothy Hunsberger, Mrs. Fred O. Irby, Pam Jensen, Dee Kimmel, Mary Lu Kusk, Cheryl Lewis, Marcille Lytle, Jessica Mader, Michelle Manson, Cherry Martin, Joy McKelvey, Julie McWright, Janice Miller, Melinda Morgan, Kathleen Morse, Cindy Munger, Lynn Nelson, Michele Nielsen, Ward and Bretta Ogburn, Hieyoung Oh, Gina Pearcy, Patricia Peoples, Nancy Rasmussen, Linnea Rein, Suzy Richards, Cathy Robrock, Sandra Ross, Susan Rushing, Sherry Sartain, Cindi Sheahan, Leslie L. Smith, Nora St. Laurent, Melinda S. Stortenbecker, Lauri Swanbeck, Melanie Thurman, Becky Turner, Althea Underwood, Becky Valentine, Devin Vaughn, Suzi Walters, Tricia Watts, Bonnie Jean Wiebe, Deborah F. Wilson, Robin Wood, and Kathie Wright.

To all those who have asked intelligent questions, sent in valuable tips, and encouraged me and others with your testimonies: Thank you. When I wonder why I take the time to teach this, all I have to do is check my mail and there you are, telling me how mega-cooking has changed your life, and then asking, "Why do I have to dilute cornstarch in cold liquid first . . . ?" And to all the hostesses and coordinators who have organized my cooking workshops—thank you.

To Carol Severson, our computer problem-solver: You've battled with the lost-in-shipping monitor, the reformatting of the hard drive, and the modem fiasco—plus helped in so many ways with all the technical aspects of getting this book out. Thank you.

Kathy Ridpath has been such an answer to prayer for our family and ministry. She donated hundreds of hours setting up our website and helping us understand all the technical aspects of managing all that volume. Thank you, Kathy, you've been terrific.

To my secretary, Pat Jenkins: I don't know if you'll fully understand how your support and competence have helped me—not only in finishing this book, but with our entire ministry. If you hadn't come in to take over so much of the PREACCH workload, I would never have had time to write and invent new recipes. Thank you, Pat. And thank you David and Alan Jenkins for giving her that time to help with our ministry.

To my editor, Heather Armstrong: You must be the kindest editor in the business. Not only do you know your stuff about book production, but you know how to cook. You are always supportive, never demanding, and I thank you for who you are (and what you do).

To my spiritual sister, J. J. Howe: Thank you for your marvelous editing, recipe testing, wise advising, and powerful praying.

To my book designer, Julie Pitkin: Thank you for turning this manuscript into a lovely, readable format.

To our knee buddies: There are hundreds of people who regularly pray for our ministry and work. Without that supernatural touch, we would have nothing worth saying and no power to do it. Thank you.

To my family: Did any writer ever have a better pep-team? You are all amazing. Kay, you know just when to call to offer an encouraging word. Mom, I know I can call you 24-hours-a-day and you will lovingly answer my questions and give me a verbal hug—in addition to helping us stage so many of the photos in this book. Dad, thank you for having faith and never telling me I couldn't do something. You and Mom never put limits on what any of your children could accomplish. Thank you. Mark, Diane, Gary, and Jamie: thank you for being so supportive.

To my children, Reed, Stuart, Trent, and Bethany Kay: You are such blessings. I thank you for so patiently tasting everything I come up with, and then gently giving your comments. You have been wonderful by giving Mom time to write, participating in corrections, and scanning text and words for me. You four are the best assistants. Thank you for being good children while I write. I have been able to write knowing you are not sacking the house or watching garbage on television. I am so proud knowing I can trust you.

To my beloved, Alan: I am so blessed to be the woman God chose to wear your rib. I love you more than life itself. This book should have your name as author as much as mine. You've poured as many hours into this project as I have. Thank you.

Introduction

DEAR *DINNER'S IN THE FREEZER!* READERS

This book is different from *Dinner's in the Freezer!*™ (which I abbreviate as *DitF!*™). So, I'd recommend that you at least skim the front section (the how-to part). I've included things I've learned since I wrote *DitF!*™. Yes, some of the information will be covering the same topics like mega-shopping, assembly-line processing, and storage options—so treat it as a refresher course. But please, do not skip the explanations entirely.

What is different between this book and *DitF!*™?

- I'm older, so I've made more mistakes since I wrote *DitF!*™ (and am passing those findings on to you).
- We now have been mega-cooking™ for more than 17 years and are getting better at it each time.
- There are marvelous new appliances and techniques available and improvements in food handling.
- I've benefited from listening and learning from thousands of you who have called, faxed, e-mailed, written, and attended my presentations. You've given me suggestions, ideas, recipes, and testimonies.
- I've been blessed with a network of friends who are professional cooks, recipe-developers, appliance-mavens, and health-nuts. I listen and learn from them.
- I've experimented with hundreds of new recipes and after extensive testing from my wonderful mega-testers, the best ones are included here.
- I've expanded the book beyond dinner to include breakfast and lunch. I've also been testing and developing several styles of mega-cooking™ so that we can minister to families who are at different places in their lifestyles.
- This book features a Topics section that you can use to look up your specific interests and questions.

In this book, we are concentrating on the cooking. I'm developing more of the inspirational material for a separate book. Bookstores never knew whether to place *DitF!*™ with the cookbooks or with ladies' devotionals.

I also felt called to write this book to include more families. This book will relate to the inexperienced homemaker, as well as the "I-know-my-seasonings" professional ones. I have written it for the deeply committed and for those who are searching.

With anticipation,
Your friend,
Jill Bond

DEAR *MEGA COOKING™* READERS

How to use the book

It's different. I realize that. This isn't an ordinary cookbook. Not only do the recipes have a different format than any other cookbook, but there are a lot of pages dedicated to "How-to," not just "What-to."

With more than 15 years of mega-cooking™ and now more than 8 years of teaching the concept, I've learned a great deal. Each aspect of the book is written reflecting that experience. I listened to my students. I learned how they learned. I read their thankful comments, cooking concerns, and intelligent questions. In addition from learning from my students, I've been learning from the experts. I've been doing years of research into the science, history, and art of cooking, freezing, meal preparation, and storage techniques.

And you get the benefits.

Brand-new Mega-cooks

I recommend before you start that you invest the time and read the "how-to" section of this book. In those pages, I talk you through the concept and techniques so that you can maximize your time, energy, and food dollar. If at first glance the recipes appear complicated to you, don't worry. They will make sense. This system has been tested by thousands of cooks and they love it. You know your schedule, so pace yourself.

Experienced Mega-cooks

I realize you already know how to combine steps and mega-shop. I'd recommend you scan the opening sections as a review to pick up any techniques or concepts that you might have forgotten or haven't learned yet. Also, even "old-timers" need some encouragement now and then. With the improvements in automation, I've learned ways to make my work easier and less time consuming.

Topics Section

Please use the Topics Section. In it I've written explanations and procedures for selecting, maintaining, and using different ingredients. I've touched on some safety issues so that you will be aware of some of the risks of improper food handling. Without turning this book into a science lab, I have at certain times explained the premises behind cooking. Perhaps if you understand why a substance behaves like it does, you can avoid some common cooking mistakes.

Not Bossy or Bragging

I don't like it when people tell me what to do. I don't like it when they say, "Do this" and then if you don't do it their way, you are either "stupid" or "rude" and they get offended. I like it when friends give me ideas and tell me what worked for them. When I write, "We do this" or "I do it this way" I'm treating you as I would like to be treated. I've given you some ideas of what I've found that works for us and you can apply it or not. In fact, I applaud the mega-testers who customized the recipes in this book to their own family's preferences.

I'm also not saying, "I do it like this; look at me." This book is an adaptation of ideas—bulk cooking has been around for thousands of years—I'm not an inventor. So, when you read "I cut my bread with shears," you'll know it is friendly advice.

This Isn't a Competition

Don't feel you have to jump into this all at once. Some people do. Some people don't. Do what is right for you and your family. Adopting this program into your kitchen can have a drastic impact on your home—more quality time together, nicer-looking budgets, calmer and gentler meal times, healthier food, and increased peace of mind. We have never heard of anyone who regretted having invested the time to mega-cook—thousands of letters confirm that people are glad they did.

It is an effort, but it is well worth it.

Toward a more peaceful home . . .

Section One

Motivation

TELL ME AGAIN WHAT WE'RE DOING AND WHY

Mommy, what's for dinner?
Honey, do I need to bring something home?
Dad, do you want me to start looking for discount coupons on pizza?

If you have conversations like that in your home, do I have a suggestion for you. Welcome to "Mega-cooking™." This isn't a cure for everything that ails you, but it certainly can help you answer those three questions. The decision about what to eat will be solved, so you can then worry about more important things—like where do all those missing socks go …

Time

Time is one of our most precious assets. Deep down we know that we have exactly as much time as we need and the same 24-hour days as everyone else, but it still seems that we never have enough. Have you ever felt like you had "misplaced" a few hours each day? Where did it go? You never slowed down, but your To Do List looks identical to tomorrow's list (with nothing checked off as completed).

Then we review our day and realize that everything we planned to do lost out to all those little emergencies that we didn't plan for. We did accomplish some things, but we wonder if they were the best use of that precious gift called "today."

We have to spend our time carefully. For many of us it is more of a budgeting act to balance our time demands than it is to manage our money properly. The checkbook might balance, but the calendar never does.

Though all of you might not be familiar with an economics term, *opportunity cost,* you know of its reality. Here's what it boils down to: if you spend your time doing activity A, then you don't have that same hour to spend it doing activity B. So the cost of doing activity A is the price: activity B. Your *opportunity cost* is all those things you can't do, or had to give up to do A and not B, C, D, or Z.

In this society—never mind the fictional characters in print and film—we have 24 hours to get a day's worth of activities done. Yes, we do have helps with cellular phones, microwave ovens (and soon, flash ovens), minute rice, and instant oatmeal, but it seems we feel we have to do more, more, more.

Many of us have to choose A or B, because we can't possibly do both and stay sane.

So we reason: If I do volunteer to bake all the cupcakes for the Christmas party, will it cause more stress than the anxiety of knowing I should have but didn't, and that Joyce will do it and get all the glory? And if I do volunteer, which would cause more stress . . . doing it the day before and taking away my time to prepare that report . . . or rushing across town hoping that the store still has some "looks like you made them yourself" cupcakes available. And then we have the stress about worrying which would be more stressful.

I understand. I really do. Through my work I've now met thousands of women, and though your day isn't exactly like mine, your work is as important. In my attempt to be faithful to God, I spread my energy and minutes among being the *perfect* wife for my Alan, the *perfect* mother to my four children (one who has special needs), and being the *perfect* writer/speaker/counselor. Do I do it? No! Am I close? No! Then why in the world am I giving advice?

Only because I've made more mistakes than you. So, if you learn from my mistakes, you don't have to repeat them. In this book, I'm giving you some practical tools to help you with one area of your life: food.

Ah, Food!

Laundry, in theory, can wait for weeks . . . as long as you still have clothes to wear. Your children can wear their T-shirts inside out. You know you're getting behind when the "stack" outgrows the wicker hamper and you have to use the baby's playpen. So, laundry doesn't rank a "Code Blue" on the household triage scale.

And as far as I'm concerned, not decorating your house from one-end-to-the-other for every holiday is not life-threatening.

Now, dusting could be if you have an asthmatic child, but for most of us, we could go days without being terrorized by the thought of a white glove inspection.

The bathroom gets worse the longer you put it off, but with all these new miracle cleaners, the time is redeemable. And besides, you can buy a new shower curtain or even re-grout over the mildew with what you have learned from home improvement shows.

But . . . your family's tummies can't go more than a few hours without refueling. My "I-ate-three-times-as-much-as-you-did-at-lunch-but-that-was-two-hours-ago-so-what's-for-a-snack" sons don't let me forget that they need food or they will spontaneously wither away into nothingness.

Then you look at your children and your heart does a flip. After all you do love them. You "cave," giving them the key to the locked pantry. You give them the nod and they call the memorized number for "We Deliver Buffalo Wings," as you reach for your purse. That should tide them over for a few hours until dinner.

You've got so many things to do, but you are responsible to feed the family. "If they could only go into the kitchen and feed themselves" . . . but you reject that idea in stark terror. So, you have to pass sentence on dinner. You check all your alternatives, consider the look of utter despair on their faces, calculate how much time you have and how tired you are. Then you do a quick look-see in the refrigerator—persimmon yogurt (who bought that?), grated lemon rind, baloney, and grape jelly. (Ah, and you could squeeze some soy sauce out of those little packets you've been storing for just such an emergency). You realize you must either invent a new recipe or you could tell the kids to get dressed and all go meet your spouse at the "All-You-Can-Eat-Buffet on Tuesday nights" family restaurant.

Would you like an alternative? I figured you would or you wouldn't be reading this book.

I don't have my act together entirely, but we eat well. I don't have to waste energy thinking about what I'll fix for dinner. That's because I fixed most of dinner months ago when I mega-cooked.

Since the publication of my book, *Dinner's in the Freezer!™*, which introduced mega-cooking™, I've had a delightful time touring the country teaching these concepts to harried homemakers, hassled hubbies, and helpless hooligans (a.k.a. those beloved latch-key kids). On one television show the male host introduced me as a woman who only cooks twice a year. He didn't see what a big deal this was because he said he only cooked twice a year—Mother's Day and his wife's birthday. At that time I mega-cooked twice a year—putting up enough dinner entrees in my freezer to last our family six months. The very idea intrigued some, alarmed some, and intimidated others.

Intrigued

Some people wanted to know more. How could they learn to do this? They ordered my book and it changed their life. The mail that has come in could make me gloat, except for the fact that I have laundry stacked up, I don't have a decorator wreath on my door, I wonder if one of those allergy-collecting filters would eliminate the need to dust, and I have a living science experiment in the bathroom. But as far as food, my children eat healthy, delicious meals and snacks that fit within our budget. Thousands of families are now cooking this way and their testimonies are convincing.

Alarmed

What? Is she abusing her children? Is that some kind of a fast? They must eat out a lot! Her husband must be the cook.

Intimated

Thirty minutes into a radio interview, the host opened the phone lines, and a sweet lady caller started with, "I heard about you and thought you were some kind of a super woman. So, I thought I could never mega-cook. But after listening to you today, I figure that if *you* can do this, then anyone can."

Those who have met me understand when I say that I think people like Martha Stewart are proof that there are aliens among us. For all those people who don't believe in conspiracies, I challenge them to watch any of those "Suzy Homemaker" shows. They will soon see that it is a plot to make the rest of us feel inferior and stay up at nights wondering if the lady across the street really does make Christmas garlands out of last summer's grass clippings.

So, that sweet lady caller who declared me normal (I enjoyed the book, *Normal is Just a Setting on Your Dryer*) was right. If I can do this, you can. The concept is simple. This book will help you apply it. Don't feel like you have to be a rocket scientist or someone who can etch crystal goblets with pipe cleaners to make life in the kitchen easier.

Definitions

Mega-cooking™ is the term I invented to explain how I cook. My thinking goes like this: if I'm going to mess up my pans, bowls, and break a few eggs—why not mess up a few more pans, a bigger bowl, and take a few more minutes to crack a few more eggs—so I can make mega-batches and not have to cook this recipe again for months. Then, I'll have good food ready for those days when I can't or don't want to cook.

- **Mega-cooking™:** A method of cooking in which you duplicate as many repetitive steps as possible, purchase food at the best prices, streamline preparation, and make multiple batches of recipes.

  Any time you combine tasks, pre-prepare, make multiple batches, you're doing some mega-cooking™. You're working smart and maximizing your time and energy.

  There are all sorts of "levels" of mega-cooking™. And you can use any combination of them to help you master the hunger monster. I'll describe them briefly here and go into more detail in the Methods chapter (page 99).
- **Duplicating:** You might want to just bake two cakes the next time. Freeze one for later and serve one that day.
- **Multiple Batches:** Make dinner for tonight, but fix multiple batches and freeze the others.
- **Streamlining:** Prepare ingredients for the recipe you are currently making, and then save some for other recipes. You might go ahead and peel, chop, and bag extra onions to use in another recipe.
- **Mega-shopping:** Some people like to buy the ingredients for months' worth of meals ahead.
- **Assembly-line:** This technique makes you as efficient as some mechanized factories. You combine tasks that are similar, so you don't have to repeat them over and over for each separate recipe.

- **Some Assembly Required (SAR):** Not all meals are "pop-in-the-oven" types. But with almost everything I serve my family, I can have some of the ingredients qualify as "convenience food."
- **Mega-session:** In this "advanced" process, we combine all the other techniques to produce dozens of recipes in one block of time. My record is 86 meals in 6 hours for less than $200. (Aren't you impressed? Keep in mind that a lot of preparation when into that before we really started cooking—and we've been doing this now for more than 17 years.)

Don't let the idea of cooking a mega-session overwhelm you. You can get started on a small scale and build up as you realize the benefits of cooking this way.

Benefits

Some of the benefits are obvious. But I've learned that when you're in the middle of preparing spaghetti sauce in the largest pot you've ever seen, you might need some encouragement.

- **Time:** We've already looked at time, but consider how much more calm your life would be if you didn't have to worry about buying ingredients, chopping, dicing, sautéing, and mixing those ingredients into something your family will enjoy. It takes time to prepare a satisfying meal for your family. You love them and you want to do more than just flop a package dinner at them. I totaled the hours it would take to prepare meals the old-fashioned way (one meal at a time) versus my method. I compared apples to apples: the total time of getting the food to the table including the shopping (portal to portal and putting away), all the time

For those of you who are detail-oriented, here are my calculations. It would take me more than 780 hours in a six-month period to get the same quality of food to the table. That's averaging thirty hours a week in food purchase, preparation, and cleanup for three meals and two snacks a day. When I mega-cook for that same time-frame I spend twenty hours total mega-shopping and cooking, then about one hour each day in the kitchen getting those prepared meals to the table and cleaning up after the meal, a total of 200 hours. For the twenty hours of mega-cooking, I saved a total 700 hours of work. That's 700 hours divided by twenty, which equals thirty-five. I realize many people do not spend thirty-five hours a week on meal preparation and they might think that figure seems high. But think what it would take you to plan menus, travel to the various stores to get the quality ingredients I get, store all of those ingredients, and then make all the recipes you eat for a week yourself without using convenience products. You would also need to include any time you spend traveling to and eating in restaurants. Your calculations for your family will depend on what you eat, how you shop, and where you live. but I think you'll find that even if it was a 2:1 ratio, that's one extra hour you didn't have before. I figure I get a 5:1 savings on my time because I'm making mega-batches.

slicing and dicing, combining and mixing, sautéing and simmering. Plus consider that clean up is much easier—we dirtied all the pots months ago when we mega-cooked. All we have are the serving dishes and a few others to wash. I figure for every hour I spend mega-cooking™, I saved 30 hours! That is a great return on an investment! If I didn't mega-cook I wouldn't have any time to write, give Trent (my son who currently has autism) all the therapy he needs, or invest so much time with my husband and children. Now I spend about one hour a day in the kitchen. We like good food. If I didn't mega-cook, to get the same quality of food that we eat now, would take me about 2 hours just to prepare dinner.

- **Money:** One reason that convenience foods are doing so well in the market place is that we value our time more than we value our money. And that is something you'll have to figure out for your own family. Some families have to count every dollar that comes in and goes out. Some families have a little more flexibility, but they don't want to waste money. Why spend more money than you have to? If you could buy the same car for $30,000 or for $31,640, which would you choose? That difference of $1,640 is the average difference between mega-cooking™ and the daily method. The money savings come from bulk purchasing fresh food and cutting out as many middlemen (and their fees) as possible, as well as savings in energy costs (less electricity, etc.) and less time in stores.

We did a survey years ago among mega-cooks. It definitely was not a scientific study, we just wanted to know how they were doing. We asked them to estimate what they saved per year cooking this method as compared to their previous way.

- **Nutrition:** Because I cook my food from real ingredients, I don't have to battle with dyes, preservatives, and fillers. I buy my ingredients from the farmer or as close to him as I can get. I'm handling the food quickly so that it keeps as many nutrients as possible. The food is personalized to my family's tastes and dietary needs. I can use whole grains, real rice, and fresh vegetables. I can reduce or eliminate sugars, fat, and meat as we need to. I'm controlling what goes into our bodies, not just hoping that the manufacturers of "Dinner Supreme" know how red dye makes Trent bounce, or sugar drains me, or fat goes directly to my hips.

There are many other benefits to consider such as:

- **Helping those in need:** I now have the ability to minister to other families quickly. When Sally goes in for her surgery, you can provide meals quickly because you made them ahead and they are waiting in your freezer.

- **Better Stewardship of Our Resources:** This is more environmentally friendly. I make less garbage because I'm buying in bulk (less packaging) and buying produce directly from the farmer (no little foam trays and plastic wrapping for the landfills). I use less energy. It only takes about 10% more gas to bake eight loaves of bread as to bake one loaf. Compare that with the 700% more time it would have cost if I had baked each of those loaves one at a time. I use everything and have hardly any waste. Because I process the ingredients immediately, I'm not tossing old carrots or slimy beans away.
- **Happy Hour:** Instead of having the typical American mayhem—that hectic time when everyone is hungry and home and wanting attention, you'll be able to sit down and relax and talk to your mate and children, because you don't need to be in the kitchen. You put the thawed dinner in the oven, so go sit down for 30 minutes and catch up with each other.
- **Peace of Mind:** There is a lot to be said for peace of mind. Stress causes too much disease, injury, and illness. If you can reduce some of the stress in your life, do it. Mega-cooking™ takes a great deal of weight (and wait) off your mind. Food's done. It's a "no brainer" now. Just thaw, arrange, and heat. Don't you need some "easy" in your life? There's already enough things screaming for your full attention.
- **Teamwork:** Sometimes one member of the family feels "stuck" with all the food needs. It has stopped being a joy and has become drudgery. We mega-cook together. It takes teamwork and then everyone contributes to the meal. They had a say in what recipes we've selected and helped pick the ingredients. While one sliced, the others peeled and stir-fried. We're a family working together for the good of all of us.
- **Special Diets:** Do you have any family members who have to be on a special diet? With mega-cooking™ you can very easily customize portions just for them. I know one lady who used to make three different "meals" each meal-time. She and her husband would eat alike, but each child was allergic to different things. That is exhausting. She learned to mega-cook and her life was simplified dramatically.

I want you to get motivated enough to try mega-cooking™. Just reading this book isn't going to change your lifestyle, but starting to put some of these ideas into effect will. We haven't gotten a letter yet from anyone who regretted mega-cooking™. The results are in and they are positive and empowering.

So, let's get going on the how-to.

Section Two

Chapter 1: *The Process*

HOW DO WE DO THIS?

Like any cooking process, you'll gather ingredients, utilize your tools and appliances, combine and process the ingredients, and then consume them. It's just that with mega-cooking™ you'll be gathering *lots* of ingredients; utilizing almost every kitchen gadget, dish, and appliance you own; combining processes; and consuming the food over a period of time.

The concept is simple and the process is basic. If you just take it one step at a time, you'll see there is a logical flow. The next parts of the book will walk you through these topics. In addition to these "step-by-step" instructions, the Topics section is filled with more explanations and definitions about specific ingredients, methods, and equipment.

Planning
We start with planning, selecting recipes, scheduling tasks, and adapting our tastes to streamline our cooking.

Equipment
We consider our equipment and collect, borrow, or rent good tools.

Ingredients
We procure our ingredients, competing with restaurants and grocery stores for quality and price. We evaluate quality and rethink storage and processing.

Methods
We process and cook the ingredients on a much larger scale than single servings.

Storage
Storage is a major consideration, as we want our food to be delicious when we do eat it months later.

Serving
With mega-cooking™, you'll have to consider thawing time, reheating, and serving quite differently than when you prepared, cooked, and served a dish all on the same day.

If you follow this system step-by-step, you'll soon see that it is something you can do.

Chapter 2: Planning

HOW DO WE DO THIS?

One of the most critical aspects of mega-cooking™ is planning.

That comes naturally to my husband. He is a list maker. I'll never forget coming home from a five-day publicity trip and seeing a Gantt chart down the length of the hallway. He had planned the children's activities in 15-minute blocks. It was a work of art with the intricacy of a shuttle launch. If that isn't amazing enough, they did it. They stayed on schedule including meeting me at the airport with a bouquet of roses. I laugh now because he never did that again. He learned his lesson and decided it wasn't worth it. Now when I travel he just makes rough home schedules with alternatives figured in, or we travel together as a family.

But for me, planning is work. I've had to force myself to become somewhat organized. If I didn't, I would have to call the dentist's office and say something like, "Oh, yes, this is Mrs. Bond, Stuart's mother. I was just calling to reconfirm his next appointment. Would you mind verifying the date and time for me?" That's how we word it when we've lost that little business card they gave us six months ago . . .

If Alan was at one end of the Likert organizational scale, I was at the other. Now, I've learned to inch more toward the middle.

And you'll also need to get a little bit organized to mega-cook as well. Not too much, but just enough. If you're inclined toward that scientist approach to life, then you will love mega-cooking™ because you can organize and plan and make Gantt charts to your heart's content.

In other words, the meals don't just jump out of your freezer—no matter how much you want them to. You have to sow some before you can reap.

> Now, I do plan Trent's therapies in 15-minute blocks, but Alan had planned days in advance when he was going to bathe the children and change their diapers (two in diapers at the time). I don't think he understood that at that stage of our lives, I didn't plan baths—they just happened. Such as when they went "swimming" in a grape jelly jar or washed the dog with toothpaste, or ate dirt, or . . . I bathed them when they needed it, and even when they didn't (or so they thought). I'm not against planning, I have learned that some aspects of life just happen and no amount of scheduling can predict when it's time to change a diaper.

As someone who enjoys cooking and writes cookbooks, I read recipes like most people read novels—for enjoyment. I have a collection of cookbooks from the 30s, 40s, and 50s that I enjoy and get many ideas from. I'm always searching for, and then "improving," recipes.

Menu List

My first step is developing my menus (a list of the recipes I'll use). For me it is a rough draft. I've never stuck with one completely, but it's a start. I fantasize about what I'd like my family to eat (all things being equal)—and then I face reality and consider what they like, what I'll accept, what's available, and what the checkbook will bare. I'll search through my recipe books, I'll go through my recipe cards, I'll read the back of boxes, and I'll sift through my stacks of magazines (filled with recipes I'll cut out some day and organize). You have your own style and preferences. This is when you take control of what *you* eat.

There are some recipes that we cook every time we have a Mega-Weekend. My children love them and they fit well into our "menu matrix." Those are spaghetti sauce (I'll then use it for many recipes), chili, meat loaf, and hamburger patties. About everything else is up for grabs.

Things you need to consider:

- How large of a mega-cook do you want to tackle?
- Do you want all your meals to come from the plan?
- Do you want to still cook some meals from scratch during that time frame?
- How often will you be eating meals away from home?
- How many meals do you want available for hospitality (ones to take to sick friends or to use for hosting others in your home)?
- How much storage space do you have (freezer size)?

Recipe Selection

Choose your recipes carefully. I've learned from years of experience what combinations will freeze well and what won't.

- Fat doesn't freeze well.
- Butter works much better than margarine in freezing.
- Porous foods will absorb the flavors of the other ingredients. (That's why spaghetti and noodles are better the second time around). Sometimes this is great and gives you a good blend, but sometimes it makes everything taste the same.

- The more moist a recipe (in contrast to dry) the better it freezes.
- Mis-handling of high water-content ingredients will change textures. (More about proper handling throughout the book.)
- Always consider your family's preferences. Freezing doesn't make something they don't like taste any better.
- Always use the freshest, highest quality ingredients available.
- Never scrimp on safety and food hygiene.

Jill's First Law of Mega-Cooking™:
ALWAYS TEST A RECIPE FIRST BEFORE YOU MAKE MEGA-BATCHES.

If you read a recipe and think your family might like it, then cook it. Before you serve it, save one portion and freeze it. If your family likes the recipe cooked and served the same day—good. After a few weeks, thaw the frozen portion and warm it up. Have a taste test. If it works, then add it to your menu list. (With three hungry sons, if I don't save some *before* it goes to the table, there won't be any left to test freeze afterwards.)

Believe me, you don't want to make 12 meals worth of a recipe to find out your family doesn't like it. It is well worth the time to test recipes. Sometimes it is just a matter of adapting the ingredients a little or changing processing steps slightly. We've found that families have various levels of tolerance to sweets. One family will say a recipe is too sweet, while another wants more honey in it. I've varied recipes just a little (less garlic, more spices, and a different type of cheese) and transformed a "I-love-you-BUT" recipe into a "Mom-let's-come-up-with-a-good-name-for-it-to-put-in-your-next-book" recipe.

(*Note:* all the recipes in this book have been tested by other families. In some recipes, I've given suggestions for variations of a particular ingredient that won't substantially change the recipe (it will still rise, congeal, or work.) In some recipes, I'll indicate [mol], which means "more or less"—you can adapt it to your family's tastes.

Sometimes I'll vary the same recipe as we batch cook to give us variety. We'll take the same base recipe and then add additional ingredients as we divide it. An example would be meat loaves. I vary the basic recipe to make seven different flavored loaves. Suggestions are listed with the recipes.

Rewriting Your Favorite Recipes

There are enough recipes in this book to keep your freezer stocked for the biggest of mega-cooks, but I fully expect you to adapt and rewrite your own recipes to fit your tastes.

If you haven't looked at the recipes in this book, please, take time and review a few. You'll notice they aren't written in a format like other cookbooks. That's because we're mega-cooking™. I rewrite recipes I use into a new format. It makes my life so much easier when it is time to mega-cook. Sometimes, in another cookbook, I'll just jot down notes in the margin next to the recipes about multiple amounts and then number and write in additional steps for preparation.

I wrote this cookbook the way I like to cook and to be instructed. I like it when a friend gives me a recipe and writes down that she uses 2 cartons of sour cream instead of only the one the original recipe called for. I like it when she tells me how she got the recipe or a story about it. I like to be "walked" through a recipe. So, I'm treating you with the same respect and friendship.

Here is an explanation of each of the aspects of the recipes in this book. As you write your own, use any of these features you feel would make your work easier and more enjoyable.

- **Title:** I see no point in giving my recipes boring titles. I market my recipes to my family. Who can get excited about "Lima Bean Casserole?" I changed that recipe around and then renamed it Chuckwagon. When I serve it, we use bandanas for napkins and do a cowboy theme for dinner. My sons have third helpings. Have fun with recipe names. Make it something that the family wants to eat, that sounds delicious, or evokes a memory. We like to name recipes after the person who gave us the recipe, for example, Aunt Kay's Lunch. One of the all-time favorite name change of a recipe is what I used to call black bean soup: Feature from the Black Legume. (Chuckwagon and Feature from the Black Legume are in *Dinner's in the Freezer!™*.) My children have been asking me to name a recipe "I Don't Know" so that we can have a "Who's on First" type of conversation when they ask what's for dinner. They are your recipes, call them what ever you want.
- **Background:** This is where I chat with you and give you some history about the recipe, some suggestions for preparation or serving, or some encouragement concerning this recipe. You might want to jot down some notes about how you created a recipe, who gave it to you, when you first served it, or any ideas you have as to how to make it more appealing to your family.
- **Ingredients:** This is one aspect that is critical to mega-cooking™: listing ingredients and their amounts in a useable format. (For a detailed explanation about Ingredients, see page 67.)
- **Pre-steps:** Here I draw attention to those aspects of the recipe that I do ahead of time, do to save money, or incorporate with other recipes.
- **Steps:** In the Methods section, I give details about preparing food and developing steps to incorporate with other recipes, thus making the whole process user-

friendly. You'll notice most recipes start with common steps that can be completed no matter what your mega-cooking™ style. Then I offer options depending on if you are doing a mega-session, duplicating, or multi-batching.

- **Additional Suggestion, Tips, or Comments:** Here I cover anything else I think will prove helpful in preparing this recipe. I suggest you make notes on your recipes as to what side dishes you like with this, which option works best for your family, and any particular brand of ingredients, flavor, or variation. I've also included suggestions and comments from the mega-testers.
- **Ratings:** I like to know what I'm getting into before I start a recipe. Here is where you'll want to judge how difficult a recipe is to make, how time consuming, how expensive, etc. For the recipes in this book, these ratings are a result of years of mega-testing and responses from other cooks. Your actual results will vary. Use these figures for comparing recipes with each other.
- **Equipment:** Here we list any special equipment that we'll need to make this recipe easier to prepare. Of course, we'll need measuring spoons and cups, mixing bowls, etc. (standard kitchen equipment) for every recipe, so I don't waste space mentioning those. I only add equipment that I consider specialized, or something that isn't basic to common recipe preparation. It is only a suggestion of how to make the best use of your time. For those of you who have not started collecting extra kitchen equipment, you can do these recipes by hand, plus each recipe features alternatives. (See chapter about Equipment on page 51.)

Don't make extra work for yourself. Only include information you need. If you know you'll always make "x6" of a recipe, don't bother to calculate three other multiples. If you'll always prepare it using one particular option, don't write two other methods of preparation. Of course, I give several options because so many different people are reading and using this system. You can write your recipes on index cards as data-files on your computer, or on plain notepaper using the example in this book.

Abbreviations are useful for those cooks who do mega-sessions and are coordinating many recipes at one time. You'll want to code your recipes. There is no need to write a title out each time on ingredient lists. Designate a number code or a 3 letter to simplify your planning. This really isn't making more work for you, it is cutting out duplication of effort.

Scheduling

People fascinate me and I enjoy them immensely. I appreciate how everyone has their own style and way of doing things. One place you can really notice the different styles of people is at a club swimming pool. There are the bold ones who don't test the water but immediately exit the locker room, climb the tall ladder to the platform diving board and dive head first. Then some walk to the steps and carefully dip one toe into the water. They shudder. Think about it. Then they slowly submerge one foot. They work slowly inch by inch until it has taken them an entire hour to get their waist wet. And then there is every variation between. Neither one is right or has mastered the best way to get into a pool. It is a matter of preference, and sometimes health concerns.

Likewise with mega-cooking™. There were some who opted for the high-diver approach and some who inched their way in. We received quite a few letters from ladies who, upon reading *Dinner's in the Freezer!™*, bought ingredients for six-months worth of meals, cooked it, and ran with it—they were thrilled. We also have many letters from those who started with one recipe, doubled it and then tripled it, and then added another recipe to their repertoire. The system works for each of them and a hundred variations in between.

Let's look at some of your options. You know what you can handle, your cooking level, your storage space, your schedule, and your budget.

Don't live someone else's life. Live your own. Don't worry or even concern yourself with what your neighbor is doing. I can't imagine anyone calling you to compare if you have as many meals in your freezer as they do—and if you do have a friend like that, pray for her. There are bigger things in life to spend our energy on. Even if you have only one extra meal ready to heat in your freezer, that's one meal you didn't have before and it is progress.

When I started mega-cooking™, I first fixed a huge pot of spaghetti. I was pregnant with my first child and had 24-hour "morning" sickness. So, when I had a "good day" I made up a mega-batch of whatever I was cooking because I didn't know when I'd have another "good day." At that same time, I was pursuing my Master's degree in industrial engineering, majoring in systems management. Our need for decent meals within our budget and the systems design work I was studying blended wonderfully. I thought, why not apply all that expertise producing widgets into producing meals. So, my husband and I began mega-cooking™. The more we mega-cooked the more we learned. I made lots of mistakes, but now that we've been at this for more than 17 years, we have it down to a science.

As you read the Methods section, you'll note a variety of ways you can add mega-cooking™ to your meal preparation. Pick and choose as you like. Depending on what is going on in my life, I pick and choose also. For instance, I might double a recipe, serve it with one dish I cooked during a mega-session months ago, duplicate my effort on the bread, and streamline the preparation of the fresh fruit.

I use a calendar program to estimate blocks of times and schedule each person's activities—when I feel like being that organized. Or, I just "bark" out orders as the steps occur to me. In other words, you might want to plan each phase of mega-cooking™—while Mom is cooking hamburger meat and Dad is peeling onions, Junior should core and slice apples, and Sister should be making meatballs. Or, you might make rough notes, like "First we process the produce, then we cook the meat, then we make sauces, then we assemble recipes." You can schedule actual steps with as much detail you want.

Ingredient List

One form I use every time I mega-cook is the Ingredients List. This is much more than a shopping list—I use it more when I'm cooking than I did when I was shopping. It helps me not only list what I need to buy and how much, but it serves to keep track of how to use the ingredients.

Duplicating and Multi-batching Ingredient Lists: If you are duplicating or multi-batching by making only one mega-recipe per shopping trip, then you could incorporate the ingredients for that recipe onto your regular list, but please continue reading for the other options, because some of the ways we apply and use this list will help you also.

Mega-sessions (All Sizes): No matter if you are planning to do a large or a small mega-session of cooking, you need to plan out the ingredient list. Believe me, it will pay off. First, I'll tell you what we're doing and why, then I'll give you several methods answering how to do it.

What We Need to Include: Whichever method you choose, you need to keep a running list of the ingredients, then add the amounts for each recipe separately. Once you have the amounts listed, you can total for the shopping list.

Why We Isolate Amounts: Normally when people shop, they don't have to coordinate ingredients used in several recipes. They're buying in such small quantities that mega-shopping isn't an issue. They can make quick substitutes, and when at home, it is relatively easy to know which recipe the stew meat goes in—the stew.

STRATEGIC COST REDUCTION PLANNING

By pooling all the amounts of each ingredient into a master list, I then have a tool to bargain with. I can then mega-shop for the best prices on large amounts. Mega-shopping has so many advantages I've dedicated an entire chapter to the concept. (See page 67.) By preparing a good Ingredients List, you can plan your attack at the market.

ADJUSTMENTS WHILE SHOPPING

If you have "ground beef—2 pounds" on your list, you know that meat is for hamburgers for Saturday's lunch. If you don't like the quality or price of the ground beef that week, you can simply change your menu to personal pizza and buy pepperoni instead of ground beef. But when you are planning anywhere from 5 to 50 different recipes, it would take the mental equivalency of juggling elephants to remember every ingredient in every recipe and the amount. If I can't find good (quality and price) acorn squash for the Harvest Chicken recipe, I can review my Ingredients List and make an intelligent choice:

1. Scrub the recipe entirely—reduce the amount of chicken quarters by 20 pounds and scratch one of the #10 can of peaches and . . .
2. Invent a new recipe—acorn squash doesn't look good, but since I need them for Harvest Chicken, I could try butternut squash instead.
3. Reschedule that recipe—if the prices for the non-perishable ingredients are great or I'm bulk purchasing any of the ingredients to qualify for special discounts, I can go ahead and buy the other ingredients, process them to some extent and wait until acorn squashes are reasonable (in a few weeks or so). Note that this works when there will only be a short delay until the needed ingredient will be available or in season. For example, I just freeze the extra chicken, store the can of peaches, and either freeze or store the other ingredients until my supplier can get the squash—then I'll simply multi-batch that one recipe.

If I had just printed totals for all the ingredients I wanted to buy, I could not have made an informed decision if there was a change of availability. Here's another example: All Susie writes on a shopping list is 10 cans of tomato sauce (she had calculated the figure "remembering" the sauce came in 12-ounce cans), but at the store she finds the cans are 16-ounces. If Susie had made a thorough Ingredients List, she could quickly make the adjustment, she might find out that she can go ahead and get two #10 cans for less money and then supplement with a few of the small cans. (If Susie knows the recipes, she'll know that most of the tomato sauce would be used during the mega-session. She really only needs a few small cans for use on some SAR—some assembly required—recipes.)

USE OF INGREDIENTS

The benefits of the Ingredients List extend beyond planning and shopping to cooking. Normally, it is very easy to know how to use the food you've purchased. The roast is for the roast dinner on Thursday. The head of lettuce is for Taco Night on Tuesday.

But when you are mega-shopping and processing large amounts of food and those same ingredients are going in half-a-dozen different recipes, you need a plan. Though we cover this in detail in the Methods chapter (see page 99), let me give you three examples:

- We cook all the ground meat for the appropriate recipes ahead of time and store it in one large container in the refrigerator. When I start assembling recipes, I look on my Ingredients List to refresh my memory about all the recipes that call for cooked, crumbled ground meat. I then "pace" my use of that meat. If I'm not careful, I'll be over-generous on the first few recipes I assemble. It looks like so much meat, after all. But then when I prepare the last recipes, I won't have the meat I need—either I have to be sparse with the meat, or go buy and cook more. But if I consider all the recipes I've planned for that meat, the balance comes out right.
- Or I won't forget that half of the mushrooms need to go into the Count Stroganov Beef and not accidentally put them all into the spaghetti sauce.
- By looking at the row on the list for lemons, I won't mistakenly juice them all, forgetting that I need the zest from a dozen before I squeeze them. I can quickly see on my Ingredients List just how I should process my produce. I'll know that half my apples need to be peeled and sliced, and half should be sliced only.

I use the Ingredients List to manage how I actually process and use the ingredients.

How to Make a Useful Ingredients List

Now that you know the Ingredients List is important and have a rough idea of how we use it, let's look at options for producing one that works for you. There are several methods. Choose a method that makes the most sense to you, and is cost and time-effective. Don't make extra work for yourself.

PAPER AND PENCIL VERSION

In the Form section, there is a sample that you can use, or you can apply the design on plain paper if that is easier. I suggest you use pencil, so you can make changes easily.

1. Top each recipe column with a heading indicating what recipe that column's ingredients are for. You might want to use either the 3-digit or 3-letter coding provided in this book. Or use your own designation so that you can identify what belongs to what.
2. Review your first recipe (recipe column 1).
3. Start with the first ingredient. Write it down as the ingredient 1, then go to recipe column 1 and write in the amount. *Note:* You might want to make two amount columns, one for shopping amount and one for assembling amount (see page 41).

4. On the second line for ingredients, write down the second ingredient of your first recipe. Write the amount needed for recipe 1 on the second row in recipe column 1.
5. Proceed with step 4 for each of the ingredients on the first recipe.
6. Review your second recipe (recipe column 2); start with its first ingredient.
   a. If it is an ingredient already on the list, then just trace across that row and write the amount in column 2.
   b. If it is a new ingredient (not already on the list), add it in the next available row and the amount needed in column 2.
7. Proceed through all the ingredients for recipe 2, repeating step 6 as often as needed.
8. Continue working through each new recipe, adding a row for each new ingredient or using the row for any previously listed ingredient.
9. Once you have all the ingredients logged, add the rows and print your totals in the last column.

Concerns and Additional Ideas

What if you are using more recipes than you can make columns across the paper?

1. Use the paper sideways (landscape instead of portrait) OR
2. Tape additional sheets side-by-side for the width you need OR
3. Double or Triple use each recipe column. For example:
   a. make recipe column 1 for 3 recipes: #1 write in blue, #2 write in green, #3 write in red
   b. Use slash marks to separate the different amounts
   c. Use highlighter pens to distinguish the amounts for the two or three different recipes.
4. Or use one of the next three methods.

What can you do to make the ingredients easier to find on the list?

1. Plan on using several sheets of paper and head the sheets with:
   a. an alphabetical system (page 1 would be for ingredients that start with the letters A-D; page 2 for those E-H, etc. OR
   b. a type group system (page 1 would be for meats, page 2 for produce, page 3 for condiments, etc.) OR
   c. a supplier grouping system (page 1 for ingredients you'll buy directly

from the farmer, page 2 for those you'll buy from the grocery wholesaler, etc.) OR

d. any other grouping system that makes sense to you.

2. Use highlighter pens or colored pens to distinguish between ingredients either by type, or supplier, or any grouping you choose.
3. Plan on the first time through as your "rough draft." Then re-do the form, using whatever grouping system works best for you. Some might want to organize it according to the layout of their favorite store, by food type, by supplier, or by alphabetical order. The column "group" is for you to use to designate any type of grouping.

Done	Supplier	Ingredient	Group	#1	#2	#3
				AKL	CDM	SPS
		Meat, ground	Meat	8 lbs	15 lbs	20 lbs
		Corn, kernels	Can	1-#10		
		Taco seasoning	Con	1 cup		
		Tortilla chips	Dry	1-large		
		Sausage, ground	Meat		3 lbs	
		Onion, chopped	Pro		1 cup	5 cups
		Garlic	Pro		5 cloves	20 cloves

Legend:

Meat—any meat products
Can—any canned goods
Con—any condiment, spice, or other extra items
Dry—any dry goods
Pro—any produce

You can use any system that makes sense to you. This matrix will serve you well as you plan, shop, and cook.

Index Cards

You will basically be doing similar steps as with the paper and pencil method, but you'll be using a separate index card for each ingredient. Here's how you would use this system.

1. Purchase a stack of index cards. You may want to buy divider cards and a box, but that is optional. (You can color-code this system if you want to. See below.)
2. Review your first recipe.
3. Start with the first ingredient. Write it down on the first index card. On the first line of the card, write in the name or code of your first recipe. Then start a column for the amount. Write down the amount of that ingredient for that recipe. (*Note:* You might want to make two amount columns, one for shopping amount and one for assembling amount; see page 41.)
4. On the second card, write down the second ingredient of your first recipe. On the first line of the card, write in the name or code of your first recipe. Then start a column for the amount. Write down the amount of that ingredient for that recipe.
5. Proceed with step 4 for each of the ingredients on the first recipe. At this point you might want to alphabetize them so you can find them quickly.
6. Review your second recipe (recipe column 2); start with its first ingredient.
   a. If it is an ingredient already on the list, then below the listing for the previous recipe, write the name or coding of the second recipe and the amount.
   b. If it is a new ingredient (not already on the list), start a new card and follow the same procedure.
7. Proceed through all the ingredients for recipe 2, repeating step 6 as often as needed.
8. Continue working through each new recipe, adding a new card for each new ingredient or using the card already made for any previously listed ingredient.
9. Once you have all the ingredients logged, you can add the amount columns and write in your totals.

Concerns and Additional Ideas

How can you use these cards differently than a list?

1. Bidwork—You can use the space on the back of the card to write notes when you call for bids on certain ingredients.

For those of you who really want to be mega-organized, you can color-code the cards for quick reference. Here's a suggestion: red cards for meat products, green cards for produce, tan cards for staples, pink cards for condiments, etc. Then you can quickly work through them as you call for the best prices and shop the store.

2. Shuffling the cards—You can sort the cards one way when you call for bids (all meat recipes together), organize them later by supplier (all Farmer's Market cards together), and then reorganize the cards in order according to each store's layout—or just keep them in alphabetical order. You also can move the cards to a pocket or container as you buy the ingredients (where as with a shopping list you'd check off the ingredients as you buy them). You also can make any notations on that ingredient's card as you shop (e.g., substituting yogurt for mayonnaise in recipe "X").

Can you use these cards again, or do you have start with blank cards each mega-session?

You can use these same ingredient cards over and over again.

1. Give them a permanent storage case once the mega-session is over. File them in alphabetical order for quick retrieval next time.

Bell Peppers

Recipe		**Shop**	**Assemble**	**Current Session**
CLS	chopped	5	5 cups	5
GRM	chopped	4	4 cups	0
HON	strips or rings	20	20 cups	20
SPS	chopped	5	5 cups	5
Current total for this session:		30		30

2. Then you can write in the amounts for the recipes that you'll be repeating and add the new recipes. Total the amounts for the current session. (See sample card above.) You'll have to make new cards for the new ingredients that you haven't used before.
3. Use the cards to keep a personal "history" of that ingredient. Write on the back of the card the date you purchased the ingredient, the price you paid for a specified amount, the supplier, and any comments about the quality. You can notice seasonal pricing, inflation, or suppliers' pricing. This will help when you shop next time. You also might want to note any safety precautions or how to select the best quality.
4. You also can keep track of that ingredient as "inventory." If you had extra bell peppers, you might want to note on the card "froze 16 cups—stored on 3rd shelf" or "dehydrated 10 peppers—jars on left side of pantry 4th shelf."

Are there any other ideas that can make your work easier?

1. *Note about processing:* You might want to note how you process the ingredient. (Of course this is only applicable to certain ingredients like produce.) But this will help as you make choices about quality and selection when you are shopping and processing the ingredients. On the sample card, I wrote in "chopped" or "slices." (If I was going to use them for a stuffed pepper recipe, I would select top quality, well-shaped peppers, but if they are going to be chopped, I can save money by purchasing a lower grade.)
2. *Note about assembly:* Some ingredients are shape-shifters. You buy them in one form of measurement, but in cooking, you use another form of measurement. For example, you buy ground beef in pounds, but once you've mega-processed it and have a bin full of cooked meat, how do you convert pounds to cups? I've supplied you with my conversions in the appendix. You'll have to make adjustments for how your ingredients actually work. You might want to include those conversion amounts on the ingredient cards and on the recipes (I've done some for you.) On the sample card you'll note I made two columns: column number 1 for the shopping amount, and column number 2 for the assembling amount when the ingredient is processed.
3. Again, you can organize these cards as much as you want. You can use different colored cards, or use colored pencils and make a stripe across the top. Use stickers or magic markers to make these cards work for you.
4. To keep cards from getting mixed up, punch a hole in one corner and use a ring (available at most office supply stores) to keep them in your order. Then work your way through as you shop. Or keep the cards in a little plastic box and work through as you shop, moving the card to the back of the box when you've purchased that ingredient.
5. If you will be changing the number of batches you'll be making in the future, you'll want to note that on the ingredient card. Add another column that says "multiple," then you can change it next time. We always make the maximum of a recipe, so I don't do this step. This is important, if you forget that the last time you made a recipe you only made "x2," and this time you plan on "x8." So, as you reuse cards, double-check your work.
6. Note any changes for your family's preferences on the cards. If you decide you don't need so much cheese, make the change on the index card, so from then on, the card is done correctly according to how your family likes the recipe.

What are the drawbacks of the Index System?

1. Scrubbing recipes on location: Since the ingredients for a given recipe are written on several cards, it takes more than a quick look to make any changes if you scrub a recipe. (With the table method, the ingredients were all in one column.) You can solve this by taking a complete set of your recipes with you, planning ahead, and only using recipes for which you know you can get all the ingredients. Or plan to have extras of some ingredients to use another time. Or go through the cards and make your changes.
2. The first time is the most time consuming. But once done, each additional mega-cooking™ session takes less and less planning.

Computer Database

Nowadays I'm using my computer more and more. Sometimes it saves time. Sometimes it takes as much time as handwriting information. Usually, the information on the computer is more readily available and easy to manipulate. Since I don't know your particular computer programs, I give generic directions. You'll have to adapt these models according to the parameters of your programs. In other words, I won't tell you to use F4, or Alt+space+6. I will tell you to tab to the proper column.

SPREADSHEET

Similar to the paper and pencil method, using a computer spreadsheet will give you a matrix. Just as an accountant would delegate certain columns in a matrix to certain types of data, we're doing the same thing.

1. Set headings for your columns according to the sample form.
2. Top each recipe column with a heading indicating to you what recipe that column's ingredients are for. You might want to use either the 3-digit or 3-letter coding provided in this book. Or use your own designation so that you can identify what belongs to what.
3. Review your first recipe (recipe column 1).
4. Start with the first ingredient. Type it in the column for ingredients on the first available line. If you already know where you'll purchase it, type that in the column headed "supplier." Type in some coding of a grouping (if desired). Tab over to the column for recipe 1 and type in the amount. If you want the computer program to compute totals for you, then only enter a number. Don't enter the letters for "lbs" or "cans." That confuses the programming. If you

realize that the increments change greatly, you'll want to add a column for "standards." In that column, you'll write "lbs" or "cups" or whatever you are using as standard increments. Then be careful to enter each ingredient amount in that same form. You'll have to convert in some cases. For instance, if you use "cups" as your standard, and a recipe calls for 4 ounces, don't write "4" because the computer will calculate 4 cups. You'll need to type in "½." *(Note:* You might want to make two amount columns, one for shopping amount and one for assembling amount; see page 41.)

5. Move your cursor to the next row. Type in the second ingredient of your first recipe. Fill in the grouping and supplier column, if desired. Write the amount needed for recipe 1 on the second row in recipe column 1.
6. Proceed with step 4 for each of the ingredients on the first recipe.
7. You can then use the "sort" feature of the recipe and either alphabetize the ingredients or sort them by group. That way you can find the ingredients more quickly as you work your way through the different recipes. You can sort as often as you like.
8. Review your second recipe (recipe column 2); start with its first ingredient.
   a. If it is an ingredient already on the list, then just trace across that row and write the amount in column 2
   b. If it is a new ingredient (not already on the list), add it in the next available row and the amount needed in column 2.
9. Proceed through all the ingredients for recipe 2, repeating steps 7 & 8 as often as needed.
10. Continue working through each new recipe, adding a row for each new ingredient or using the row for any previously listed ingredient.
11. Once you have all the ingredients logged, the computer can generate the totals for you. It will do all the math. Follow the instructions for "sum" or "summation" with your particular program.

Concerns and Additional Ideas

But it's on your computer, what good is that in the store?

I'll be the first to admit that computers are not completely reliable. Mine has crashed many times. One year, I lost a total of three months work to computer problems. Without the computer I was high and dry. We do make back-ups of everything. We also have learned to print out much of the information, so we have a hard copy if the computer decides to take a "vacation."

You can print it onto several sheets of paper. You can sort easily. You can have the computer print all the meat ingredients on one page, all the produce on another. Or you can sort to print all the ingredients you'll buy from Supplier X on one sheet, and from Supplier Y on another. You also can quickly mark those ingredients that you have on hand and, by sorting and then doing subtotals, separate out the list.

Can you use the work again the next time you mega-cook?

Yes! By simply cutting and pasting, you can duplicate your list, delete recipes you won't use this time and add a few columns for those you are now including. Most of your work is done already, you just need to make a few changes and then calculate the totals.

What are the drawbacks to the Spreadsheet Method?

If you aren't already familiar with your spreadsheet program and how it will total and do other functions, you may spend extra time learning computer-ese. But once learned (some programs have instant "HELP" features), you can use it over and over again.

Also, if you are doing many recipes, the columns can go on and on, making it complicated to print. You can "remove from view" or "hide" certain columns. So, as you are adding amounts, your current recipe column is right next to the ingredient column—you don't waste time tabbing twenty columns over. When you are finished, you tell the computer to show (or whatever your program command is) all the columns.

DATA FILES

Similar to the index cards is a computer database. Basically, you make a "file" for each ingredient, just as you made an index card. You would set your fields like you would on the index card. Then fill in the fields. You could have fields for history, prices, and bids, as well as the ones for recipe, processing comments, shopping amount, assembling amount, and whether you are using it currently or not. You could also write up any information about safety and quality selection.

Follow the same steps for the Index Cards, except use data fields instead of lines and columns.

Let the computer sort, print reports, and do all calculations.

Concerns and Additional Ideas

But it's on your computer, what good is that in the store?

Depending on how you set up the files and your printer, you can have it print 3 x 5 (or 4 x 8, or . . .) cards. Or you can print the information on regular 8½ x 11 inch paper and organize in a notebook using standard dividers.

Or you can print the information in list form. Of course, while you are home cooking, you can make changes and notes directly to the data file.

Can you use the work again the next time you mega-cook?

Yes! All you do is add the ingredients to any new recipes, designate which recipes you'll be using, generate printouts of any of the changes, and print totals. The work you invested the first time pays off, as each time is easier and easier.

What are the drawbacks to the Data File Method?

As with the Data Sheet Method, it might take extra time to learn how to use your computer's database program. But for those familiar with these programs, it is quick work. As with any computer program, you run the risk of corrupted files and system crashes. Make backups of all your work.

A Few Points About All of the Methods and About the Ingredients List

- **Ingredients:** Write all ingredients, even if you have them on hand. If they are already on hand, check off as done, move the card, or sort the list that way. You want to have an accurate listing of all ingredients so you won't have any surprises. For instance, you might think you have plenty of salt. But once you total all the recipes, and find you need a whole cup of salt—you can check your supply to see if you need to buy more.
- **Not that complicated:** I know some readers are feeling bogged down with a mind full of rows and columns. I'm not worried. Thousands and thousands have made Ingredients Lists, and once you start working the system, it will make sense. I don't need extra work and I figure you don't either. I try never to waste time on needless tasks. So, I purposely made this step as stripped-down, no-frills as I could. Each thing I write down serves a purpose or it is trash. Each comment or column I use serves in making my mega-sessions flow smoothly.

- **Grow with it:** You can start slowly. Don't let the idea of a couple hundred index cards frighten you. You may start by making 5 index cards for one recipe that you will multi-batch. Use those five cards along with your regular shopping list. Then when you are ready to make another multi-batch, make 5 new index cards, using 3 you already made (they both call for the same three ingredients). Make 4 new cards for the third recipe you add to your repertoire. By the time you're ready for your first mega-session, most of your cards, data files, or spreadsheets will be done.

Tasks List

When I first started mega-cooking™, I had to think through the tasks to be done. I'd log the steps of the recipes and combine them, then schedule them. Now that we have been mega-cooking™ for so long, I don't make tasks lists anymore. I just keep that information in my head and then refer back to specific recipes as I need to. You'll understand more about how we work the routine in the "Methods" chapter. For now, realize that it is fine to jot down notes about which tasks have to be done.

I used a form with headings for:

- **Check:** to mark as we completed each task.
- **Task:** to briefly describe what needed to be done (e.g., peel, quarter, chop onions).
- **Priority:** to rank order the tasks, as to which had to be done before I could go on to another task (e.g., if I made peel onions a task, and quarter onions a separate task, I'd have to peel the onions before I would quarter them). I used a 1 to 10 rating, to sort them. A "#1" would be the first task that I would need to do during a mega-session, then down to a "#10", representing a task which the timing didn't matter.
- **Delegate:** who would do it. Now with older children, I'm able to delegate more and more tasks.
- **Recipe:** I'd note that a particular recipe would be on "hold" until this task was done.
- **Timeframe:** estimation of how long the task will take. This will help you schedule. Remember it is only an estimate.
- **Note:** room for additional comments.

You can prepare this task list using the form as a master or as a guide, or use a computer. Even a basic "word processing" program with a "table" feature would work. You could make your own columns, and then sort by priority, who would do it, or timeframe. You also could use a spreadsheet program, or a data file program. I like to use an actual "tasks" program that is tied in with my calendar. I can coordinate the whole weekend and use the built-in priority functions. It allows for assigning tasks, monitoring progress, and giving reminders. Also, as in the "scheduling" section, I can integrate time blocks onto a computer calendar that then will give friendly reminders, like, "Don't forget the turkeys need to bake for four hours . . ."

Whatever level of detail you choose to plan the tasks, allow for "down time" and "slow progress." Remember children (and parents) get tired. Everyone needs breaks. Some things just don't go right. And some things work like a charm. Build in flexibility. We watch videos or listen to books on tape or music as we work.

Timing List

This list may seem superfluous. But you'll be glad you made some kind of notation. I realize that if you bake only one roast, you easily can time it for 2 hours. Put it on at 5 P.M., it will be ready for dinner at 7 P.M. But when you mega-cook, you work anywhere from 2 to a dozen recipes at one time. And unless you can play 5 games of blind-chess at one time and win, I suggest you either invest in lots of timers or jot down reminders.

- **Timers:** I use 4 timers to screech at me when I need to check something. I have to note though which timer goes to what appliance. I move them around the kitchen. I also will pay extra for any appliance that has a built-in timer feature. They are worth their weight in pennies—most definitely. I especially enjoy appliances with an automatic shut-down feature when the timer goes off.
- **Sticky Notes:** How did mankind ever survive before the invention of sticky notes? As I look around at my desk, I have 25+ posted, including my reminder to include a section about sticky notes in this part of the book. I can stick a note on an appliance, or on the oven to remind me I put the casserole in at 4:30 and need to check it at 5:15.
- **Superwatches:** My son had a watch that had more features than my first computer. Some of these watches are amazing. My sons will time processes for me. They can set buzzers to go off. And they are still young . . . they can remember which buzzer goes to which food.

Blind chess is played without looking at the board. Opponents must keep the position of each piece in their minds. Moves are announced to a gamesman, who moves the pieces. It isn't for the scatterbrained at all.

- **Timing Form:** In the back of the book is a timing chart from. You are welcome to use it as a master form (for copying) or as a guideline, or a running list. Abbreviate as much as possible. Fill in the item that you are working on, the start time, the approximate cooking time, time you need to check it, the estimated ending time, and any other notations, like actual cooking time. (Make notes on the actual recipe so you'll know next time you cook it.)
- **Chalkboard:** Make notes on your kitchen write-and-wipe board, chalkboard, or clipboard about when to check certain items.
- **Computer Reminders:** If you have a computer near your kitchen and a schedule program, the computer will buzz reminders of when to check what.

Again, it may seem silly to do all this work keeping track of time, but once you are into your 25th recipe, you might not know if it is morning or afternoon, Friday or Saturday. And you certainly can't remember if you put the broccoli on 30 minutes or an hour ago. This will also pay off as you make adjustments to recipes according to your pots and pans, and appliance performances.

Other Lists You Might Want to Keep

- **Comparison Pricing:** There are other forms and lists that will benefit some of you. A Price Comparison List will track the prices different suppliers charge. This is helpful for future reference. If you are working with index cards or data files, you can keep this information with the ingredient.
- **Pricing Chart for the Farmer's Market:** A form for the farmer's market is helpful. I could then note the vendor's stall number, his quote and any information about quality. With this information, I could shop on paper, then go back to the chosen vendors for my purchases.
- **After-action Reports:** Early in our marriage, I was active in the Officers' Wives' Club. We, in true military fashion, had to write up after-action reports for everything. The idea was that the person who held our post the next year would benefit from our mistakes. In a way, this book is my "after-action report" from my years of mega-cooking™. I don't think you need to go into this much detail. But once your head is clear and your feet feel real again, take the time to write down what you've learned. Make any notes on recipes. Annotate your phone book. Scribble through ideas that didn't work or "X-out" any vendors that didn't deal fairly with you. Write down any changes in time or temperature on a recipe. Add any suggestions or ideas you have for varying it next time. Do it as soon as you can, because with time we forget. I know if I don't write it down, I'm prone to make the same mistake six months later.

Planning Chapter Summary

I estimate that I spent about 10 to 25% of my mega-session time in planning. It depends on how many new recipes I'm adding and how many old-favorites I'm falling back on. But I have never regretted any time I've spent in the planning stage. It reaps benefits when I'm later running an eight-burner, two-oven circus. Following are examples of charts you may wish to use.

Now that you are really scared, let's look at that equipment.

Pricing Chart for Comparison Shopping

Item	Store			Store			Store		
	Size	Price	Compare	Size	Price	Compare	Size	Price	Compare

Shopping List

Done	Place	Ingredient	1-	2-	3-	4-	5-	6-	7-	Totals
			8-	9-	10-	11-	12-	13-	14-	

Timing Chart

Item	Start Time	Approx. Cooking Time	Check Progress At	Estimated Ending Time	Comment/ Done

Tasks

Done	Task	Priority	Who?	Before Recipe	Note

Chapter 3: Equipment

WHAT TOOLS DO I NEED?

Don't bemoan what you do have. Don't covet what you don't have. Just get on with it. That sounds good and easy, but I know it is work for some of us. Our attitude is our biggest problem.

What did me a world of good was to live in a third-world country for two years. Alan was stationed in the Republic of Panama. When I saw how whole families lived in refrigerator boxes and my maid could feed her family off of my throw-aways, I soon realized how rich and spoiled I was.

You can begin to mega-cook with what you have and then as you have funds, you can purchase more or better equipment.

Your Kitchen

Through nineteen years of marriage, I've had seventeen different kitchens. They ranged from camper-sized (dorm-housing) to luxury (complete with maid's quarters). And I've mega-cooked in all of them. We've lived where the wiring was so bad, I could only use one appliance at a time or the refrigerator fuse would blow (that was the "luxury" apartment in Panama); where the refrigerator was so old that it had the metal freezer door inside the refrigerator (shades of June Cleaver) and the oven was so small I couldn't bake anything larger than an 8x8-inch pan; where the oven didn't have a working thermostat and was whimsical about which temperature it would produce; and the list could go on, but I think you realize that I understand your circumstances might be less than ideal. No situation is perfect: that gives us room to be creative, practice patience, and to laugh a lot.

WORK SMART WITH WHAT YOU HAVE

There are only a few stores that Alan fears having me go into: card shops, bookstores, restaurant supply centers, and stores that sell organization equipment. He has to give me a maximum to spend because I always see just one more thing to buy. I like gadgets, gizmos, bins, racks, shelves, dividers, etc. These items give me such a feeling of hope that if I have a place for something, I'll be able to find it again. Okay. It is just a hope. But . . .

I do recommend that you organize what you have. Put the most used items within reach. Store the once-a-year stuff in the dark, back corners. Clean out. Give away things you haven't used in a while. Sort. Shift. Settle. Home supply centers have wonderful shelf organizers and spinning trays and drawer dividers. Use them. Stacking dividers can double your storage space. Use hooks. Hang as much as you can from the ceiling or on the walls. Have you ever seen a professional's kitchen? They have whisks on hooks by their stove. Why not treat yourself as a professional?

When we mega-cook we use the whole house. We do not entertain that weekend. We'll have one child making meatballs on her play table (after it has been sanitized), or another browning meat in a skillet on a card table in the living room, and Alan will have the dining room table covered with bags and boxes as he prepares food for the freezer. I was delighted to find that worktables (a.k.a. buffet tables or folding tables) are inexpensive. They are sturdy enough to roll out pastry. The smaller ones can fold up and slide under your bed. After your mega-cooking™ session when you're ready to entertain, use it as a buffet table or as an extra table for dining. They are so portable; they also travel outside very well. (More on how to use what you have in other sections.)

EASY NON-PERMANENT IMPROVEMENTS

Alan and I have only owned two homes. Otherwise it has been rentals or government housing (military bases). And when someone else owns the house, you can't tear down walls and add new cabinets. So, we had to get creative. If where we've lived had too small of a kitchen (according to me), we expanded the kitchen into the breakfast room. To give you an idea, in one house we had a dining room off the kitchen and a breakfast room. I didn't need both a breakfast room and full dining room. So, we moved in the refrigerator we brought from our old house, a work table, the microwave and its table, and two sets of book shelves into the breakfast room—and doubled the size of that kitchen. When we moved, it looked just as it did when we moved in, yet I had the advantage of a nice big kitchen with two refrigerators.

Even when we lived in the family-dorm housing, we used a bookcase as a pantry and room-divider blocking off part of the dining room corner to make space for a full freezer that was given to us.

Remember it is your home. You shouldn't be decorating it or living for the pleasure of what someone else thinks a home should be. I'm not out to impress anyone. Are you?

REMODELING

This isn't a primer on how to improve your kitchen (I'll leave that to Bob Vila and Tim Taylor), but I want to encourage you with the possibilities.

A friend just remodeled her kitchen and, by spending around $2,000, increased the value of her home by more than $20,000 (according to the appraisal). Wow! They shopped around and did all the work themselves. She chose beautiful tile that was discontinued and available at very low prices. She now has exactly what she wants, and she does appreciate it.

In her case, they gutted her old kitchen and re-did everything, including the flooring, walls, electrical wiring, and appliances.

If you own your home, you could start small and work your way around your kitchen with a good plan. Find out what you really want. As you figure and compare, you'll grow to appreciate what you have now and adjust your standards. Don't forget that some simple carpeting can expand kitchen space.

Knocking out the soffits (some older homes have the area between the top of the cabinets and ceiling boxed in) will free a great deal of space for baskets, canisters, and big pots. What about adding in "typing drawers?" Wooden shelves that slide in and out above your drawers will give added counter space.

Any hidden space in the corners? Could you saw through the side of a cabinet to access that lost space or square area? Add shelves and you have room for more items.

There are several publications that will give you ideas. Check out your friends' kitchens. Make friends with your local hardware man.

COOK SOMEWHERE ELSE

Some churches, garden clubs, or other community buildings have wonderful commercial kitchens. For a small fee, you can use the facility for a few days, as long as you leave it cleaner than you found it. This could work well for several families to team-cook using professional equipment, and then divide the food.

Or if you have a friend with a lovely kitchen, team up with her and ask your husbands to take the kids to the park that day.

> Christine Crawford of Ohio teams up with a friend every three months. They select recipes, divide shopping and cooking preparation. In their own homes, one cooks and debones chicken and the other browns ground meat. Then they get together for a team cooking day. They assemble 4 to 6 pans of each entrée and divide it.

Acquisition of Appliances

- **Borrow or Rent:** Just as you can rent a church kitchen, sometimes you can borrow the large pots, etc. from a commercial kitchen, church, or community center kitchen—as long as you have them back by Wednesday night's covered dish dinner. If your church doesn't have such a program, set one up like a library. What a ministry that would be to your community.

  What about borrowing extra mixing bowls or a food processor from your friends, and then loaning yours when it is time for their cooking session?
  Does your community have a "We Rent Everything" business. You might be pleasantly surprised at how inexpensively you can rent heavy-duty mixers, etc.

- **Purchase:** *Pre-Owned Goods.* Check out garage sales. I've picked up some great bargains.

  Look in the classified and thrifty-shopper newspapers. Someone else might have purchased a wonderful new flour mill, but doesn't need it now. You could buy one for one-fourth the price of new. Look at bulletin boards. Does your club have something like that? What about the employee newsletter at work? Use the want-to-buy section. Someone might have a bread-machine that she received as a Christmas present and never used, but doesn't want to go through the trouble of having a garage sale.

  Word-of-mouth. I told everyone I knew that I wanted a heavy-duty kitchen center and the word got around. One day a lady called. She had a friend who had more than $800 worth of equipment, but had found she was allergic to wheat. She sold it to me for $350.
- **Blessings:** Don't be surprised at how God wants to bless you. One of my delights through my travels is hearing so many testimonies of how families have received free equipment. A sweet lady in Texas mentioned to her next door neighbor that she was attending one of my cooking classes and said, "Now we just have to save up for a freezer." Her neighbor said, "Well, we have one in the garage that we never use. You can have it." A friend's crockpot died, but the large ceramic dish was intact. She gave it to me as an extra large mixing bowl. Ask friends to save their butter tubs for you. My mother gives me her coffee jars (plastic and air-tight) to use as freezing containers. You'd be surprised at how much use you can get out of other people's unwanted items.

Items

There are several specific items you'll want to start collecting or borrowing. This section will focus on purchasing (or renting) and maintenance, the detailed use or application will be presented in recipes, in the Topics section, and in the Preparing section. My husband, Alan, an engineer, has added information on the science involved with some of the equipment, so you'll be a more educated consumer (a salesman won't pull one over on you), use the equipment to its full capability, and maintain it well.

FREEZER

You have a freezer now, but what's in it? Instead of that food you still have to process, wouldn't it be great if it was stocked with your own homemade dinners? Of course, if all you have is the "above the fridge" size freezer, you can't mega-cook six months worth of dinners. But you could do one month's worth. Or at least have a few fast meals ready to go.

Get the best freezer you can afford. Freezers are very economical to run. You want to keep your freezer stocked full, even if that means freezing jugs of water. A full freezer works better than one that is half full.

Maintain it. Check the gaskets. Keep them clean so you have a tight seal. Regularly dust or vacuum the coils (dust just loves to cling to those puppies). It will take less energy if coils are fully exposed to the air.

If you lose power, don't open the freezer. Your food should stay frozen for a few days. If your power will be out for more than that, make arrangements. Either add dry ice (follow all safety precautions) or move your items to another freezer. Cook any seafood at once. Don't ever refreeze thawed seafood.

For those who live in colder regions, the great outdoors works great. Ladies have told me how they plan their mega-cooking™ when the high of the day will be well below freezing. They use their back porch as a second freezer. They lay out their dishes to freeze solid, then they are loaded into the freezer.

ALAN: Heat is energy. Cold is not. Cold is actually the absence of heat. As heat leaves, molecules slow down, draw nearer to each other, and start to solidify. Ultimately, at about -460°F, there is no heat energy in the molecule and the atoms stop moving. So, a freezer, at 0°F is balmy by comparison. A freezer passes a liquid through an orifice that makes (by use of pressures) the liquid change phase into a vapor. In doing so, it absorbs heat—from the food in the freezer section. The heat is dumped behind the unit by reversing the vapor phase process. The goal is to freeze the food solid and keep bacteria from being active. Chemical processes that are water dependent virtually cease as the water freezes. Some processes will continue, though very, very slowly. Sometimes you only need to remove enough heat to keep foods cool. Food spoilage is reduced at temperatures below 40°F, compared to sitting out at room temperature. It doesn't cease, but it is much slower. So most refrigerators regulate interior temperature—much the same way as freezers—between 35° and 40°F.

DEHYDRATORS

Dehydrating is one of the oldest forms of food preservation.

How did I ever manage in the years before I had a dehydrator? If I have any extra fruits and vegetables after a mega-session I dehydrate them. Dehydration is the technique of removing the moisture from your produce so the food will last longer and not ruin. It has been done for generations without our present day electric dehydrators. Raisins are a prime example. Grapes go bad in the matter of a week, but properly stored raisins will last for years. To give you an idea of how long dehydrating techniques have been around, the Holy Bible tells us that Abigail served (soon-to-be) King David and his men raisin cakes.

It is possible to use the sun (depending on your location) or low set ovens for some dehydrating. For instance, some companies carry the "Food Pantrie"—a natural, non-electric food drier and seed sprouter . Several ladies who lived through the depression have told me about how they would use window screens spread out between two lawn chairs to dry their produce. With the growing popularity of dehydrating, the electric machines are very economical. They make the work so easy anyone can dehydrate with success.

ALAN: The science of dehydrating is simple—dehydrating uses the principle of evaporation to remove water from the food. Warm air is blown across the food, which gains the heat out of the air to help evaporate. The moving air entrains water vapor as it passes. Soon the content of water diminishes and the food dries.

Buy the largest, most professional unit you can afford. My personal favorites are the Magic Mill Magic Aire™ II, which comes with eight rectangular trays (expandable to ten), has a quiet motor, and has very efficient drying potential; the Air Preserve II (Professional Model), which comes with eight round trays (expandable to thirty) and has an adjustable temperature control, and the Excalibur (from Back to Basics), which comes in three sizes and has an adjustable thermostat. Shop around and get the best price.

Also, think about renting one or teaming up with several other families to co-own one. I find I use my dehydrator in spurts. It'll go months collecting dust, then after a trip to a farm or the farmer's market, or the weekend all the tomatoes ripen, I dream of owning several. Team up with friends to share a machine and schedule your dehydrating sessions. One alternative that works extremely well is to combine using your dehydrator and your freezer—see page 124 for instructions.

Here are some points to consider when choosing a dehydrator:

- **Drying capacity:** The actual area available to spread out your food. This is a major concern when you're processing your garden harvest or trying to dehydrate lots of fresh produce. I use ours 24-hours a day for about 3-weeks during harvest time. Remember there is a lot of wasted space in a circular design.
- **Drying potential:** It pays in the short-run to get a good motor that can speed up the process. If its motor is weak, you'll be doubling or tripling your drying time—wasting electricity while some of your produce is ruining waiting to go in the next cycle.
- **Center Core:** This should be large enough to guarantee good air circulation. A small one will give you more area, but will cut down on the drying potential.
- **Trays (or racks):** These are the "shelves" that stack. You can lay large pieces of food directly on the trays, though I prefer to always use mesh sheets for easier removal and clean-up. The trays should have a very open weave so that air can

pass easily. Too dense of a weave won't allow air to circulate as well. [Too much food will do the same thing.] Check to see if you can add more trays and their cost. Some companies sell the dehydrator at a low price, but only provide one or two trays, and then charge an inflated sum for extra trays. If you can add more trays, figure out the maximum.

- **Mesh sheets:** You can make these, but a good dehydrator should come with custom-made mesh sheets. These have a tighter weave than the trays. I use them every time to make my work easier. They don't impede the airflow too much. You can make these using plastic (e.g., plastic needlepoint canvas) and cutting to fit. I like to have several sets of these, so I can have a clean set to load the next cycle of food and not waste any time. I then can wash the other set and have it ready. This way I alternate the sheets (in a round-robin style) and the dehydrator is continually running.
- **Leather trays:** These are plastic trays that you can pour in pureed fruit to make your own fruit roll-up snacks. They are made of a suitable plastic for the dehydrator—just the right ply as to allow drying and yet sturdy enough to avoid spills.

Claudia Tiefenback and her family built their own dehydrator. She sent me a copy of the plans from The University of California (Leaflet 2785): "Drying Foods at Home" and "How to Build a Portable Electric Food Dehydrator (Oregon State University Extension Service Circular 855). The U.C. publication was dated 1978, so I don't know if you can get that same exact leaflet, but do contact your local university and your county agent. Check out the Internet for do-it-yourself designs. The design she sent appears very doable and the instructions were simple. She wrote that they spent less than $20 on that unit because they were able to salvage some of the parts. There are other do-it-yourself plans on the market.

When processing a large amount of vegetables, I use some immediately in the recipes I'm preparing, freeze some, and dehydrate the rest. I super-dehydrate some and then blend the pieces into a powder for use as a spice, flavoring, or soup base. Some dry a little for chewy snacks. Some vegetables or fruits are dehydrated in bite-sized pieces for rehydration in muffins, soups, or other recipes.

When considering a dehydrator, keep in mind that quality is worth the price. One lady who bought a cheap unit found that after five days her apples were still soggy. Because the motor and airflow was minimal on her machine, it took too long to dehydrate and she lost food. I wouldn't trust food that took days to dehydrate. Remember that when dehydrating, we're beating the spoilage factor by removing moisture quickly. If it takes days to do that, there is too much time for bacteria to grow.

STOVES/OVENS

Not all ovens are the same. I've used dozens of ovens (from my own kitchens, host-kitchens, friend's kitchens and commercial kitchens) and I've found ovens have their own "personalities." Some have "sweet spots" and temperature glitches.

Replacement: Replacing your stove, oven, or cooktop is usually a costly investment and not one we do on an annual basis. Ovens can last for thirty to forty years, so we want to purchase wisely. Of course, shop around for the best price. Don't let a "pushy salesperson" disrupt your plan. Go with exact measurements of the space available. Figure out what your precise needs are. I need the largest capacity of oven space available (I bake multiple loaves at one time).

- **Gas:** I used to dislike gas appliances. They always seemed to trigger my asthma. We insisted on electric appliances. That is until we moved into one particular house. The main kitchen was equipped with both a gas cooktop and a gas wall oven. They were both circa early sixties. In an old magazine, I noticed an ad for such an oven: "Mom"—a model with a bouffant hairdo, a chiffon full-skirt, and a string of pearls—is pulling out hors d'oeuvres, as "Dad" comes in the door in his black suit, skinny black tie and white shirt carrying his briefcase. I was skeptical, remembering my previous experience with an old oven, but I tried it. I soon knew why so many professional chefs prefer gas ovens. I could control the temperature better than with electric. When you turn the heat down, it is immediate, while with electric you have to wait for the coils to cool. There are some dangers using gas, but with careful maintenance, those dangers can be minimized. We monitored the pilot and were on "watch" whenever the flame was on (especially when the little ones were nearby).
- **Electric:** Electric ovens are more common. They work by passing electric current through an element (shaped in a loop or coil) that glows from the energy going through it. The heat radiates into the oven body and ultimately into the food.
- **Convection:** Convection ovens have been used by professionals for decades. They are known for cooking more evenly, often more quickly, and at less heat than conventional ovens (especially electric ovens). The principle of convection is similar to conduction, like in a regular oven, in that the heat transfers from a source to the air surrounding the food. But it differs in that the heat doesn't "bathe" the food. Instead a blower passes the hot air over the food, much like a whirlpool. This does two things: it passes heat to the food and more importantly, it blows away the thin layer of cool air around the food rather than having to conduct through like a regular oven.

When Replacement Isn't an Option: Most of us are "stuck" with the ovens we have, so we have to learn to make adjustments. A useful device is an oven thermometer. Test your own oven. Test the temperature in your oven at different places (according to the directions). Often just the practice of rotating pans during the baking process will make for more even baking. Rotate back to front and shelf to shelf. Whatever your situation, be content. Aren't you glad you don't have to chop down a tree, split logs, and kindle your own fire to be able to cook dinner?

STEAMER

My steamer is one of my favorite appliances. I think I'd give up my microwave oven before I'd give up my steamer. I use it for all rice cooking, most vegetable cooking, and for quite a bit of the reheating of frozen foods. The unit I have has stackable trays and a timer. It automatically cuts off. For a busy cook, that feature is great. It is wonderful for cooking because food retains color, it puts in moisture instead of taking it out, and it is quick and very efficient. Steamers are very inexpensive. Before I had an electric steamer, I rigged my own with a metal colander and Dutch oven. The food went into the colander over the boiling water in the Dutch oven, with the pan lid fitting snuggly. Caution: monitor the amount of water often. If the "mock-system" isn't air tight, you'll lose water in the form of vapor. If you don't continue to add water to the Dutch oven, you'll have a mess and a safety hazard. I've also used a similarly-rigged system with plastic dishes in the microwave oven.

MICROWAVE

I know there is a great deal of controversy about microwave ovens. There are purists who refuse to use them, and others who "swear" by them. We use ours for everything from defrosting to heating to actually cooking. It isn't my favorite mode of cooking, but it can be quite useful. I use it frequently for defrosting frozen food. Always keep your microwave in clean order. Wipe all seals regularly.

HEAVY-DUTY MIXER

For mega-cooking™ I like my heavy-duty mixers. I have both a Bosch Universal and a Magic Mill Assistent® (formally known as a DLX). These are multi-functional units with options for blender and food processor, as well as a mixer. I like them because they can take a lot of handling. Some of the standard mixers aren't made for the extreme amounts we handle in mega-cooking™. Their motors would fail with that much use. Also, with the heavy–duty units, you can mix very large amounts. For instance, in the stainless steel bowl of my DLX I can mix enough bread dough for 8 loaves at one time, including kneading. These can be major purchases, so do your homework first. Look for quality workmanship, versatility of attachments, service, warranties, and expense.

FOOD PROCESSOR

When I first started mega-cooking™, I had the old-fashioned food processor: a knife and cutting board. Then came a standard food processor unit, but we wore out the motor on it very quickly. When we had saved enough money, I purchased a used Bosch. It was up to the challenge and worked well. The only drawback was having to stop too often to dump the bowl of cut vegetables, then restack the unit to continue. It was a slight drawback, but was an improvement over manual slicing. When my DLX arrived, I was thrilled. It has a different design and I could process a whole bushel of carrots without stopping. I just aimed the drum over a clean bucket and kept feeding in the carrots. When I'm processing bushels of a vegetable, that feature is great. It does save time. You need to determine how you're going to use your processor. If it will see use only once in a while, then a standard model might be fine. But if you plan on buying vegetables in bulk from the farmer's market, you'll want to spend the extra $100 or so and get the quality food processors. There are hand-crank products available also that work quite well.

VACUUM SEALER

I purchased an electric vacuum sealer on sale. I used it to seal my Mason jar lids. I rarely used the bag option because the plastic is so expensive and the vacuuming process can ruin some of the food, especially casserole-types. The bags work well for raw meats and other more solid (dense) items. But for anything with a light texture, the compacting squeezes the ingredients too much. The machine I have has an attachment to vacuum seal Mason jar lids. I later purchased a PUMP-N-SEAL™ system, and it is becoming one of the most used appliances in my home. At about one-tenth the price of an electric model, the PUMP-N-SEAL™ works better and quicker. This handy apparatus allows me to vacuum seal in ordinary jars (in addition to my quality canning jars) and off-the-shelf freezer bags. I use it almost daily to reseal all my dehydrated food and mixes, and just regular everyday use items—it is so easy, we vacuum seal most of the jars in the refrigerator to keep them extra fresh. This method works well for long-term storage of dehydrated food. Here's an example: One day my sister forgot her lunch when she came over to help with our ministry, so I offered her some of my salad, apologizing that it wasn't as fresh as I'd like but I had been in a hurry. She guessed that it was from our supper the night before. I laughed because it was more than ten days old. I now make a huge salad (without the really wet items like tomatoes) and seal it in a glass jar with the PUMP-N-SEAL™. It keeps in the refrigerator for a week, and will still be reasonably fresh after ten days. It saves time on fixing a tossed salad each evening. This idea works for many other steps in mega-cooking™.

FLOUR MILL

You don't have to have a flour mill, but if you can, I highly recommend a mill. The health benefits are worth every penny. There are quite a few good electric models available in the $200-$300 range and good hand-crank mills from $65 on up. Look for a good motor (or crank system) and milling blades or stones. My unit can grind not only wheat berries, but corn (popcorn), and beans. Once you start using fresh-ground flour, you'll be hooked. Before I had a mill, a friend would grind flour for me. Until you can afford your own mill, check around. Some health food stores, quality grocery stores, co-ops, and private dealers, sell freshly ground flour. There is a big difference between freshly ground whole-wheat and packaged flour from the store. There is more information about wheat in the Topics section.

HAND CRANK

My all time favorite mill is my Whisper Mill by Grain Master. Compared to a previous mill we used, this one is the difference between Mozart and being under the Concorde taking off. The noise level is a definite consideration. It also works very quickly. To me it is worth every penny (about $260.00). However, that is out of some pocketbook ranges, so there is the option of using hand-crank mills. There are some that do a passable job for as low as $65. My favorite in this category is the Marga Mulino by Marcato. Not only does it grind flour, but you can use it to flake your oat groats.

GRILL

We do about 30% of our cooking on the grill. Not only do we like the flavor, but it is a very healthful way to cook. I know it is a great deal of work to fire up your grill. So whenever we have it going, we cook and cook and cook. We will grill dozens of chicken breasts, dozens of hamburger patties, a pack of steaks, and/or some fish or roasts. That smoked flavor goes in deep. We freeze the items and then can reheat them in the oven. It isn't as good as fresh-grilled, but it is a hundred times better than pan-fried. There are several new indoor grills available now in many sizes, as well.

I know this may sound extreme, but as you become more aware of the difference between fresh and processed, you will be amazed at the difference between fresh flaked oats and store-bought varieties. Often in my classes I'll flake some groats and have the students taste them. They can't believe the flavor and color in the fresh oats—very indicative of the nutrients. Everything I make with fresh oats is better: granola, cookies, or oatmeal. The cost of 50 pounds of oat groats is about $25. For comparison, I almost double the volume when I flake groats to meal—one cup of groats will yield a smidgen less than two cups. My Magic Mill Assistent® has an electric attachment that flakes the groats in 2 to 3 minutes (by the time the water starts to boil).

BLENDER

I know someone who thinks blenders are only for bartenders, but we use ours for making everything from Better Butter to Smoothie Frothies to homemade dressings. It is wonderful for smoothing out sauces and roux for gravies. Depending on the quality of your blender, you can even grate carrots and other vegetables. My blender is an attachment to my Kitchen Assistent®, so the motor is quality. One feature that I appreciate in this model is that the blades are part of the pitcher. With some units, washers and rings hold the blades in place to the pitcher. I've found that the more parts there are the more I have to clean and the more there is to break. The DLX pitcher is a breeze to clean. We use our blender for pulverizing dehydrated food into powder.

CROCK-POTS

I treat my crock-pot as an extra Dutch oven. It has a setting for high (can boil water) and low (for all day stewing). I use it to make sauces and soups during a mega-session. I also use the crock-pot on my buffet table to keep things hot, especially apple cider. Another way you can pre-assemble meals is to pre-assemble all the ingredients for a crock pot recipe, divide into meal-size amounts, and freeze in labeled bags. Then on those mornings when you're rushing out, you can simply grab a bag marked "crock-pot," add the necessary amount of water, and let it cook all day. Dinner's ready when you come back through the door. Depending on which recipe you use, you might need to thaw the bag out a day ahead of time. With some recipes, you can thaw and then cook all in the same day in the crock-pot. It seems obvious, but buy a crock-pot with the size "bowl" that would work best for your family. Too big and you're wasting electricity and not getting as thorough a cooking for smaller amounts. But always, try to get one that has adjustable heat settings.

ELECTRIC SKILLETS, PIE MAKERS, AND SANDWICH GRILLERS

Okay, I admit it. I'm Jill and I am a gadget addict. I can justify it, though, as "doing research" for you. I like tools that make my life easier. Some of these are just "nice-to-haves" and some are pretty basic. I can't imagine cooking through a mega-session without an electric skillet. Because my children help in the kitchen, invariably one of them would scratch the surface and we'd have to replace the skillet. Now they are older and are doing better. We also realized that soaking the skillet was not a good idea. After we use it we immediately pour in water to cover any food residues, but only let it sit for ten minutes and then clean it out. That will make the protective coating last much longer. When we were letting it soak like our pots, the water was undermining the coating. We used to think if a skillet lasted one year we were doing well; this current skillet has lasted for almost two. I appreciate other electric appliances, though I realize that they aren't necessities. When "pie-makers" went on sale I bought two. These devices are similar to a waffle iron except shaped like a "tart." We use these two machines during a mega-session to stock our freezer with homemade personal pies (dessert and meat). We also use our sandwich grill for not only sandwiches, but also turnovers, and our own hot sandwiches. We can make dozens of sandwiches, freeze them, and then they are ready for picnics, road-trips, or busy days. Because the sandwich maker seals the edges of the bread, they are great for road-trips—less mess in the car. It takes only minutes per pie or sandwich. We mega-make the ingredients and either the pastry or bread. Then, while we're doing something else, we load a pie or sandwich. While it is cooking, we are busy with other recipes. When the timer goes off, we repeat the process. It takes very little extra effort. It is a delight to have dozens of these homemade treats in the freezer, ready to thaw or heat for a fraction of the cost of the store-bought varieties. We can also customize them to our family's taste.

CREPE PAN

I like good engineering, and my crepe pan is well designed. It makes crepe-making fun. In fact, we've staged parties around the crepe making. This device looks like a small racket with a coated surface. It couldn't be easier. I simply make a batch of crepe batter (5 to 6 times the basic recipe) using the blender. I pour some of the mix into a regular 9-inch pie pan and store the rest of the mix in an airtight container in the refrigerator. Guests then have fun dipping the crepe maker upside down into the batter. They flip it and let the crepe cook in about a minute's time. Then they help themselves to a variety of fillings (everything from flavored cream-cheeses, to meats and sauces, to fruit or pudding fillings.) Everyone is amazed at how easy the process is. Our daughter, Bethany Kay, could make crepes when she was six-years old. Crepes freeze wonderfully. There are dozens of ways to use them. If you like crepes, using a crepe pan seems the only reasonable way to go. I tried doing it the old-fashioned way with a regular pan and they were too tricky. You had to monitor it constantly. A German woman I know told me that in the old days they would dip the pan's bottom into the batter and cook them in the fire. This electric crepe pan is quite an improvement.

WAFFLE IRON

I learned a good lesson about waffle irons. I was trying to save money, so I bought an iron at a swap meet. We started making waffles, but it was taking twenty minutes for each waffle. I finally bought a new waffle iron. With the new iron, we made a waffle in about four minutes. It really changed things around here. Though I do like to buy "pre-owned" things, I'm much more careful about what I'll tolerate. For the $15 I paid for the new iron, it more than made up in saved electricity and time. Like so much other work we do, we make a mega-batch of batter and make enough waffles for 5 to 6 breakfasts. We eat some as we make them and then freeze the rest for other mornings. Then all we have to do is pop the frozen ones into a toaster for those mornings when I don't have time to cook. Waffles also make for a great shortcake-type dessert with fruit and topping.

PASTA MAKER

Have you ever had fresh homemade pasta? It is so delicious and not that difficult to make when you have good equipment. But for me trying to make pasta during a mega-cooking™ session would be too much. So, here are some options: make your own pasta days ahead of the mega-cook to use in upcoming recipes, or just compromise and use store-bought pasta. When using meals out of the freezer that call for fresh pasta, you'll have time to make it then. I have a hand-crank pasta maker (Atlas, by Marcato) that has an optional motor and dozens of attachments to make many varieties of pasta. A basic pasta recipe is: crack one egg per person into a bowl (there are six in our family, so I use six eggs), add enough flour (seminola is ideal) to absorb the egg. Then knead this dough through the machine until it is ready for cutting. Cut into the size/shape you desire and allow to dry or cook immediately in boiling water. There are dozens of variations in flour, wetting ingredients, and processes.

POTS AND PANS

All pots and pans are not alike. I learned that the hard way. I'm a bargain hunter, but buying cheap pans is not a bargain. It will cost you more in wasted food and time than buying good ones. As I can afford it I'm replacing my pots with quality cookware, one piece at a time. The difference between cooking with the good-stuff and the cheap-stuff is amazing. For instance, cooking the *same recipe* in two different pans: with the quality pan I can cook at medium heat and it will cook twice as fast as the old pan does on high heat. With the quality pan the heat is better dispersed, I don't have to stir as often, and the sauce comes out creamy. With the old pan, I have to stir constantly and it still might have lumps. When we were mega-testing, I investigated why the same recipe could get different comments (drastically different comments), and found that the cookware did make a difference. Also, you must adjust your temperature or cooking time if you're switching from glass to metal or metal to glass. They conduct heat differently. The required temperature can vary as much as 25°F. Learn your cookware and make adjustments. If every time you make a recipe, and you have to bake longer than the recipe, realize that the recipe isn't "at fault." It could be either your oven or the quality of the pan you are using. There was a time when pots and pans were common and there was quite a bit of uniformity in their design and use. With constant improvements in the industry, we have a wide variety of qualities available. When your pan doesn't match exactly with the one suggested in a recipe, please adjust your oven's temperature and cooking time accordingly. Think of the mass involved. If I take the batter that would make a tube cake, but pour into a jellyroll pan, it will take about half the cooking time, and a lower temperature (25°). I'd also cover the corners with foil to prevent the edges from over-browning. The same idea applies to casseroles. If the recipe calls for an 11 x 15-inch pan and you bake it in an 8-inch soufflé dish, realize that it won't heat the same. The inside may still be cool while the top is crusty. Make allowances. You'll notice many of the recipes in this cookbook can be prepared in a variety of shapes. That is why there is a "range" for cooking times. The more spread-out the ingredients, the less time to heat. The more dense the ingredients, the longer. There is a fairly new product on the market that I endorse—the new Teflon® sheets. They turn any pan into a coated pan. We use them for everything. They are great for freezing—ingredients just lift out for rewrapping. They are great for baking—casseroles, cakes, breads, roasts, or whatever lift out of their pans beautifully. And clean up is a snap! What a blessing those sheets of Teflon® are. I don't have to pre-grease or pre-spray anymore, so it has to be much healthier than my old methods. These sheets are relatively inexpensive and can be reused indefinitely. They come in a variety of sizes to fit many standard pans. At this time, they aren't great for molds (they can't detail intricate shapes and grooves), but for a good deal of my cooking, they work perfectly. Move them to #1 on your birthday list.

SPOONS, UTENSILS, AND KNIVES

One of the few "must haves" for mega-cooking™ is a heavy-duty spoon. Go to a restaurant supply store for these. For about one dollar more than you would have paid at your local grocery store, you can get a spoon that won't bend on you. Whenever I give my cooking classes, I carry two spoons, one I bought at the state-of-the-art grocery store and one I paid about a dollar more for at a restaurant supply store. I can bend the grocery store version quite easily. No one in any of my classes has been able to bend the restaurant supply store version. When you're mixing large amounts, you need a sturdy spoon. I think you'll be very pleased with the quality at these stores. And remember you don't have to own a restaurant to shop there. Some warehouse stores carry a line of restaurant equipment, also. A good set of knives should last you all your adult life—definitely worth the investment (or a good hint on your bridal registry). Just keep them in good shape and sharpen regularly. A dull knife is more dangerous than a sharp one. A sharp knife cuts with ease, so you can control it. But you have to fight with a dull knife to get it to cut—and it can hurt you when you lose control of it. There are all sorts of utensils you can purchase. I have a growing collection of bent wires on handles and scoops and spoons. Some of them are a curiosity; some are quite useful, especially for tasks other than what they were designed for. For instance, I use an old-fashioned pastry knife (blade) for chopping boiled eggs. It is perfect. A food processor turns them into pate', and a knife takes all day. A few up and down strokes with the pastry knife and the egg is just right for salads or garnishes. I use strainers for "basket shapes," and melon-ball scoops for meatballs. A potato masher works great for batter dips (makes a really interesting shape), and cookie cutters for sandwiches, shaping cheese, and French toast.

BOWLS, BINS, AND TUBS

If you haven't ever mega-cooked, be forewarned—you'll be working with a lot of batter, mix, or globs of ingredients. You'll need mixing bowls, lots of big mixing bowls. I joke in my classes about washing out the sink really well and using it as a big mixing bowl, and if you have a really large family, use your bathtub. Then ladies nodded and told me they did. We've used our bathtub to wash what seemed to be an acre's worth of strawberries. We also use the bathtub to wash out big pots and bowls. They won't fit in my sink. We use dish-pans—those pans that are made to line your sink and sell for a dollar. They are clean and they work great for mixing up ingredients. We also store ingredients in them for temporary storage. We've used punch bowls (might as well get some use out of them), canner's pots (those huge pots for boiling canning jars), blanchers, crock pots, upside down cake covers, and even the vegetable crispers from the refrigerator. As long as it is clean, why not?

GADGETS

There are dozens of items I haven't mentioned and each of you has your favorite items. I understand. Some items I use occasionally, like dumpling makers (plastic presses that form dumplings) and a mortar and pestle set for grinding my own herbs. Some items I use more often, like good rolling pins. One of my favorites has a set of rings that can be placed near the handle. For instance, I can set it at ⅛" to roll out my dough exactly to that height.

As I said at the beginning of this section, don't go invest hundreds of dollars into gadgets and gizmos. Much of my equipment has been given to me as gifts or purchased either at a good sale price or at a garage sale. While I was working on this manuscript, I needed some more molds to stage photos. We went shopping and I was disheartened by the prices. So, I prayed about it and on my way home from the store (where I refused to pay that much) I happened upon an estate sale. I purchased eight molds, six pie pans, and quite a few other dishes for the whopping price of $5 (and that included twenty-seven videotapes).

In summary, the only things you need to buy that you might not already have are some heavy-duty spoons. You can make do with what you have to get started. Then as your savings mount and you can afford it, purchase some appliances, pans, or tools at the best prices you can get. Or borrow. Or rent.

If you are blessed with a well-equipped kitchen, are you willing to share? Maybe you could provide the kitchen and a friend could help you cook. Then you can split the food afterwards. Would you be willing to loan out some of your equipment?

Chapter 4: Ingredients and Mega-shopping

WHAT ARE WE COOKING AND HOW DO WE GET IT?

Though many of us are taught that "cooking" is something we do in the kitchen, meal preparation involves much work out of the kitchen—procuring good ingredients. If you think of all the work you do in getting a meal to the table, about 15% of that work was in acquiring the food. The same applies to mega-cooking™. It's just that now much of that time is going to be spent on the phone, not cruising store aisles.

Let's First Talk about Nutrition and Quality

Before we get into marketing strategies, let me invite you to consider the nutritional content of your food. There are dozens of excellent books on the subject, so I will only briefly discuss. Alan and I have been studying nutrition in depth for more than ten years and we find we've barely scratched the surface. Yet, I can say we are healthier now than we were ten years ago. Alan's cholesterol level was 130 the last time it was tested and mine sometimes breaks 100. (See below. Anything less than 170 in our age group is considered excellent.) I know that isn't a true reading of one's health, but it is a popular index. Though I have a string of medical conditions that would warrant a medical alert-type bracelet, I'm not on any medication. I can't claim any credit for my recovery. God gets all the glory for that. But I know He is blessing our faithfulness in trying to lead a healthy lifestyle. That goes well beyond what we eat and includes stress management, exercise, sleep, and spiritual health.

Since we have a special-needs child and had a ministry to the special needs community, we've been immersed into a whole sub-culture about this issue. We've been dismayed to see the links between diet and learning disabilities. We've seen a child who was diagnosed as autistic who is practically symptom-free when all preservatives, dyes, and additives are

Alan's cholesterol was tested the day I wrote that sentence: February 13, 1998.

The medical conditions I referred to include: Deep venal thrombosis, vascular damage, nerve damage, asthma, hypothyroidism, hypoglycemia, vertigo, medication sensitivities, allergies, IBS, GPC...well, you get the idea.

removed from his diet. They visited a friend's house and the hostess had tried to adhere to all of this boy's dietary restrictions. She knew to serve real butter on the table. But she didn't realize that using margarine in the muffins would be a problem. Naryan ate one muffin. There were only trace elements of the additives in margarine, but for three days all his autistic-like symptoms reappeared. He is that sensitive.

We are concerned about this issue and we work with it on a daily basis. Maybe that will be our next book, but in this book, I want to draw nutrition to your attention.

Please consider the quality and nutritional content of the food you're feeding yourself and your family. There is a definite link between some serious medical conditions and diet. Please be careful. Read labels. (More on translating label jargon in the Topics section.) We've heard the adage: if you can't pronounce it, don't eat it. I like what one nutritionist that we've worked with told us: if it has a label, don't eat it. I know that is a great ideal. But for many of us that is impossible at this stage of our lives. But when you think about it, it is a move in the right direction. An apple doesn't need a label. It contains apple. Wheat berries contain wheat berries. And so on . . .

The recipes in this book are about mid-level on the healthy eating spectrum. There will be many families who are eating healthier than some of these recipes suggest. But my experience has been that for most people these recipes are a positive step—a move toward better nutrition. If you are way ahead of us, then use what you like and adapt your own recipes. We want to cover a few points about nutrition:

Diversity

The perfect diet for one person may not be the best for another. There are factors that determine our dietary needs:

- **Heritage:** Our genetic makeup can affect how our body handles certain foods. Some nationalities (or in the case of Americans, our ancestors' nationalities) need more or less protein than others. A total vegetarian regime may work for some, but for others it is not their best option.
- **Lifestyle:** I think everyone would agree that someone with an active lifestyle needs more calories than someone with a sedentary lifestyle. That is obvious. But there's more to it than that. How do you handle stress? Do you ball it up inside, or let it explode and injury those you love? Can you say "no" when others try to talk you into volunteering for one more "good deed"? So much of our health depends on how we manage our time, not just our forks.
- **Age:** Obviously a three-month old is going to need a different diet than an octogenarian. But consider the differences between what you could handle when you were 18, with what affects you now that you are 38. My sons need three-to-four

times the calories that I need. I'm also trying to instill in them the habits of good eating for their whole life.

Digestion

The more we study how marvelously our bodies are designed, we're awed by the recuperative abilities God gave us. Some of us are downright cruel to our bodies. We take for granted that we'll bounce right back as we always have. This attitude can build up bad habits. Let's take a quick look at some important aspects of our digestive system.

- **Mastication:** If you won't do anything else to improve your diet, please chew more. That one thing can improve your body's ability to use the nutrients you eat. Chew. I know it sounds almost un-American, not to inhale our food as our society goes rushing through lunch. But as often as possible, we actually sit down at a table and chew our food before swallowing it. Please teach your children by example to slow down and completely masticate their food before they swallow. Our stomachs weren't designed to process the huge chunks of food we're sending it. Also, wonderful enzymes are released in the mouth that aid digestion. When we gulp and swallow, we rob the process of that enzyme reaction—creating more problems along the way. So, if you'll do nothing else, start chewing your food.
- **Water:** As important as chewing is, drinking water is even more important. Somehow as a society we don't honor drinking water as we should. When I counsel about diet, one of the first questions I ask is when was the last time you drank 8 ounces of water. I'm amazed that some people will count the time in days, not minutes. "Ah, let's see that would have been Tuesday at lunch." The problem is that today is Friday. They've been drinking, but it hasn't been water. Pure water. They start the day with coffee, have more at work, and then have sodas for lunch and snacks. They have cocktails or wine at dinner. Do you remember when in every restaurant, the waiter automatically gave everyone a glass of water? Now, in almost every restaurant we eat in (including some multi-star establishments) we have to ask for water to drink. Of course, they would rather we spend more money ordering "costly" beverages, but we stick with water. It is the healthy option. Not to mention that it can save $10 to $20 off our total bill, if the whole family has water instead of sodas.

  Water is marvelous. Our body needs it desperately. It will help your complexion in addition to aid in digestion. We need to stay lubricated. Men who would never think of letting their cars get low on oil will fail to maintain their own bodies that well.

Drink the best water you can. Invest in filtering systems. We think that distilled water is the best. Distilling is a means of boiling and separating based on vapor phase of the solutes. We had a full-house filtering (reverse-osmosis) unit and it did help with everything from bathing to cooking. The quality of water does affect taste and nutritional content. A great deal of cooking involves water. The particle density (hardness) of the water will affect how well recipes come out. For instance, when we use pure water, I can dilute recipes more and get the same flavor. Likewise, in laundry, with good water it takes about ⅓ the amount of soap as with hard water.

- **Organ Work:** No wonder we see so many degenerative diseases affecting organs. Too many of us are straining them beyond their design. It's as if we take a 1-ton truck and make it haul 2-tons everyday up a steep hill without giving it as viscous an oil as its engine needs. Then we're dismayed when parts start breaking down. Respect your organs and let them do their work. Avoid toxins, though it is almost impossible today. Even if you grow vegetables organically, your neighbor could be spreading pesticides on his lawn or the water table can be damaged, affecting your garden. But, at least you can avoid using those toxins that you have control over.
- **Enzyme Work:** Enzyme production by the digestive system is crucial to being able to draw nutrients out of the food for the body to use. Mastication helps break down the rough food to increase surface area for enzyme activity; organ work provides the place where food can be processed and digested; but without the chemicals produced by the digestive organs—starting with salivary glands through the stomach, liver (bile), and into the small intestine—the food will not be effectively exploited for its worth. Enzymes themselves are chemicals which attack certain complex molecules and reduce them to a digestible form. For instance, lactase reduces milk sugars (lactose) sugars into short chain hydrocarbons.
- **Bowel Work:** Some people rob themselves of health because they have no respect for their bowels. Their bowels are clogged and ruinous. When the bowels aren't working properly, then we lose nutrients and set ourselves up for all sorts of complications. Read about bowel care. I know I had to learn my lesson. When I was in college, I abused myself by trying to do it all. I averaged 4 hours of sleep per night, worked a full time "career-climbing" job, drove 3 to 4 hours a day between home, work, and the university, and maintained a dean's list, full-course load. I was hospitalized and the diagnosis was IBS: Irritable Bowel Syndrome. The main cure was to reduce the stress in my life, to rest, and to eat properly. I

had to drastically change some things. I went to part-time work, wasn't so "straight A's or nothing" minded, moved back with my parents (good food!), and tried to get more sleep. My health improved. Though I was young, I was making my body perform more than it was able. It rebelled. The way my system works, my bowel is my "thermostat." When I get my life out of order and take on more than I'm designed to bear, it starts acting up. I make changes.

I've gone through bowel cleansing regimes that helped to rid my body of years of built-up improper eating. Check with a good doctor or a nutritional consultant about this. Don't just try something on your own. When your bowel is working properly you'll be amazed at how it affects your whole health. Your skin, your disposition, your energy level, and, of course, your figure will all benefit.

Food Content

- **Supplementation:** I agree with many of the experts that we should be able to get all the nutrients we need from our food. We should. Unfortunately, for most people I know, that is impossible. All the vitamins, minerals, and glyco-proteins we need are no longer in the food chain or aren't available to many of us. I can't grow all my own food. I can't even ascertain where all my food is grown and how it is grown. For some of our diet, though I'm very careful, we rely on market quality.

  So, we supplement. We don't supplement to "justify" bad eating. We supplement to augment what we are eating. In other words, I don't say "Eat what you like, it doesn't matter, as long as you swallow this mega-vitamin." Rather, do all you can to get your nutrients from your food, and then supplement for the gaps in your food.

  Though some consider herbs to be part of their "food," some consider it supplemental. It depends. When we're facing cold season or have been exposed to contagions, we supplement with echinacea and other immune-building herbals. There are some wonderful natural alternatives to alleviate suffering with symptoms, instead of loading up with pharmaceuticals, and their side effects. Read more about herbs and consult a trusted herbal counselor.
- **Organic:** A farm has to go through inspections and soil analyses and continued investigations to be approved as organic—not an easy task. It takes quite a commitment on the farmer's part. Not only does he have the added labor of organic farming, he has to contend with all the bureaucratic red tape. I applaud farmers that go through that hassle, because I appreciate their produce. When you evalu-

ate all the work they go through and sometime additional costs in fertilizers and pest control, you can understand why you have to pay a premium price for certified organic produce. Also, states have different requirements. Organic means different things in different areas of the country. We've made friends with an organic farmer and "pick-our-own." When we aren't able to get what we need from them, we buy locally.

If you can't afford certified organic produce, the next best alternative is to work with a farmer who is doing his best to grow organic produce. He might not have everything it takes to qualify, or he might be waiting on certification. You can buy good produce at decent prices.

If you are buying "off the shelf," please wash your produce well. Clean it and then clean it again. And know that you're eating fresh produce, which is much healthier than processed.

The more popular organic produce becomes, the more available it will be. And then market forces come into play that bring the price down for all of us. It's worth asking your green grocer about.

People spend a whole lifetime studying nutrition. These brief few paragraphs only are to remind you of a few concepts and to encourage you to read more.

By far the best book we've ever read on the topic is the Holy Bible. That may seem odd, but it's true. We highly recommend you check for good sound nutritional guidance and healthy living guidelines. It's all true.

Let's Talk Mega-shopping

I don't know how many of you have or are currently working outside of the home. But most likely many of us had some business or volunteer experience in which we had to work with someone else's money. Either as chairman of the band boosters or an account executive, we've had to work with budgets, get bids, and/or report to someone else about our spending decisions.

What I want you to do is use that same financial skill when it comes to groceries. I realize it isn't as glamorous, but if you'd get half-a-dozen bids from vendors for team T-shirts that go *on* your child, why wouldn't you compare prices and quality for the food that is going *in* your child.

I realize this isn't the way many of us were taught. We shop like Mom did, driving to the local grocery and walking the aisles. We choose to eat according to what the grocer has on sale. Call me radical, but I think I know more about my family's dietary needs than a market representative somewhere else does. Though they might not have thought about it this way, some people are allowing some advertising agent somewhere to determine what their children will be eating each week. More on this later.

For some of you, what I'm proposing is a radical change; and for some of you it is a confirmation about what you are already doing. I realize it might take a while to change your shopping paradigm. But you can do this. And as I've been hearing from shoppers everywhere—it is fun.

After a mega-cooking™ seminar class in Texas, I received a call from one of the hostesses. She was thrilled as she reported some of the responses. One lady said to herself, "Well, I'll give Jill's idea a try." She called around for prices and she doubled her buying power. She calculated it out and she was able to buy twice the amount of food for the same budgeted amount. As exciting as that is—to double your food buying power in one week without adding one cent to your budget—think of all the weeks, months and years of money she could have saved had she been doing this all along. Sadly, you can't undo what's been done, but start now and look what you can do in the future.

My undergraduate degree is in marketing. Since you are dealing with marketers every time you walk in a store, read an advertisement, or purchase an item, I think you need an "Avoid a Crash" course in marketing.

Let's look at some marketing concepts:

The "Four P's of Marketing" Plus Two

If you think you are spending your money on a product when you purchase something, you're partially right. The product is part of what you're buying. You are also "buying" the place, the promotion, and the packaging. Those are the four basic "P's" of marketing:

PRODUCT

The actual food, item, or useable part. Example: the actual toothpaste, an apple, the raw meat. The product is what you really want, or should care about. It's the real ingredient that you're going to cook with. The rest you can't eat. Whenever possible I try to pay for just the product—just the calories, not the plastic, promo, or place.

PLACE

Each time you buy food from the local grocery store, you are also paying for the grocery *store.* It's called overhead. You are paying for the "right" to shop there, for the convenience of their location, for the smiling clerks, for the electricity to run the big freezers, and for all the produce that the stores buys—whether it's sold or thrown out.

During my cooking classes, I ask how many of the attendees have freezers. Hands go up. Then I tell them that all but the young should raise their hands because they all own a freezer, a lovely commercial freezer (or a percentage of it). It's just that their grocer has been kind enough all these years to keep it down at his store for them. Though it's not the most common way to look at it:

I figure that if I'm going to buy a freezer, I should keep it and control what goes in it, determine how I'm going to use it, and make it more convenient by storing it in my house with food I like and own.

Through the years with all the money you've paid for groceries, you were really paying for overhead. It paid for either a full or a good part of one of those freezers in the store.

The neat part of spending my money on my own freezer is I don't have to keep doing it. Some families through the years have paid for one freezer at the store and are buying another—each time they shop. I paid for my freezer the one time with savings from mega-cooking™, and then it is paid for. The savings from then on can go for other things.

Think of "place" as rent. You are "renting" part of the store. It's like a time-share. A portion of your total bill pays for that hour a week that you shop.

I don't begrudge business managers charging for overhead. They have to. It is a fact of accounting. Without the built-in overhead charges, they couldn't provide you with the food. Simple.

I'm proposing that you think about it. Then, as much as possible, pay yourself the "overhead" instead. You don't have to "rent" their facilities so much. When you do need to "rent" their "show room," be aware of what you're doing and shop smart.

Having had a full-time ministry, I have great compassion on businessmen. Sometimes I wonder how some of them stay in business. When you calculate what they are paying for rent (some malls charge astronomical per-square-foot rates), staff, insurance, utilities, and taxes, you realize they have to cover those expenses and sell a lot of merchandise or service to make a reasonable profit. We held our overhead down drastically, and still it seemed overwhelming at times to cover all the operating costs. So, I appreciate what those who provide these "places" do. They do deserve their "rent."

I just try, as best as I can, not to "rent" stores very often.

Also, you pay for the freight of moving the product to the place. Each time a part is shipped that fee is added in. In our experience, some of the items we shipped cost less than the shipping did. We had to pay for the item to be shipped to us and then for that item to

We feel it is honest to pay for services rendered. When we travel we sometimes stop at a fast food restaurant to use their facilities. Though we are under no "law" to purchase anything, we buy something. Sometimes we'll all get juice or a snack. It is our way of compensating and thanking the business for providing public bathrooms that are clean and much better than some at gas stations. We like to treat others as we want to be treated.

Actually, we "rent" a store about once a week. But for us it is a bargain. We take Trent, our son who currently has autism, shopping. He enjoys grocery stores. We go to one locally where he has made friends with several of the clerks. Dear Josie goes out of her way to make Trent feel special. We buy some of our weekly fresh produce and some other products. I figure for the effect it has on Trent, the rent is a small price to pay for the privilege of blessing him. Trent loves to eat cucumbers, and he eats them like some children eat candy bars. Ah, if you could see his face light up when he sees a huge stack of cucumbers and he gets to count them and put them in a bag. Yes, I'm paying full price then, but I've weighed the cost and it's not found lacking.

be shipped to the purchaser. No wonder shipping is big business. (More on this idea when we talk about mail-order.)

PROMOTION

When you buy a product that is advertised, you are paying for part of that ad. Those large advertising budgets are added to the cost of the goods sold.

Quite a bit of the price of an item is its promotion. When you buy an item you're paying for the advertising budget, the marketing surveys, commissions, brokerage fees, and the positioning of the product in the marketplace.

- **Advertising Budget:** I know we've been talking about food, but let's look at the make-up industry. The actual "goo" doesn't cost that much to produce. What you're paying for is the "image" created by the advertising—the hope that if you use lipstick shade #5436 you'll look as lovely as the supermodel does. When you buy lipstick shade #5436 you're paying part of the salaries for the supermodel, photographers, set designers, artists, and idea people—and part of their overhead. You're paying for print space in the magazine or airtime on television. Lipstick shade #5436 costs very little, it's that "image" you're buying and you are getting all the rest as part of the deal. If advertising didn't work, no one would pay for it. You have alternatives:

    1. Appreciate your money's worth as you pay a "royalty" to the advertisers. Look at it as "the price of admission" to view their ad. And continue to pay the high prices of these heavily advertised items, doing exactly what they want you to do, OR
    2. Evaluate your choices. Test for quality. Consider an off-brand that doesn't advertise, so their costs are lower. Don't pay for ads you don't like. Don't support things you don't want to support.

In a way, it's like voting. Vote for your favorite advertising campaigns by purchasing their products. Vote against the ones you don't like by buying from their competition. Or abstain from voting all together, by opting out and buying what you want to—disregarding the high-priced ads.

Some advertising does provide a service. There is some education involved. You learn about what is available. But very little of some advertisements tell you anything about the product. They instead try to confuse the issue and create an image. The image supercedes the product. Think about some of those silly perfume commercials. What are they really selling? One key to "good" advertising is to create a "need." You have to convince satisfied people that they aren't as happy as they think they are. They have problems that your product can solve. They might have continued very happily with their life until you told them that their neighbor's toilet bowl is cleaner than theirs.

I encourage you to watch out for "invented" needs. Watch out for hype. Do your homework and don't buy a product because of some clever ad campaign. Buy because you do need it and because it is the best value for the money. We aren't as dumb as they think we are. We aren't little white rats running through their maze. We are smart, savvy shoppers who can discern value. Go assert yourself in the marketplace!

- **Marketing Surveys and Research:** There are grown adults whose life work is determining if "Mrs. Average-Housewife" will be more attracted to a label printed in olive green or lemon green ink. They run tests with focus groups. They plant cameras in stores and monitor eye flicker rates. They run pilot studies. Then when they can prove statistically that 3 out of 4 women choose the lemon green ink, they have "earned" their extreme fees. I praise God I have more fulfilling things to do with my time.

You're paying for "human rat tests" when you purchase some products. I'm hesitant to even mention all the R&D costs from that side of the house. You're also paying for all the "products" that never came to market. R&D has to be paid for somehow. So the products that do make it have to bear the cost of all those that didn't—and the research involved in proving they wouldn't make it.

I think you get the idea. You can better appreciate all the costs that go into a product—and why you are paying the price you're paying. Now that you are wiser, you can make a more educated choice.

Depending on which marketing professor you listen to, Research and Development (R&D) can be figured as part of "product," but for this discussion I think you get the idea. Let the accountants and budget analysts figure out how to bill R&D.

POSITIONING

This is sometimes a tough concept to understand. Do you know part of what you pay for is the "position" of that product in the market place? You pay for the "idea" of its worth. Do you really think that a luxury car costs ten times as much to produce as the budget-model one? No. You're paying for the image of luxury. There are people who will pay top dollar for "the idea of quality," not for quality. Now, I'm the first to admit that some cars are made better than other cars—they have safety features that all cars should have. But I know it doesn't cost an extra $50,000 to put those safety features in. It's the illusion of worth. It also plays into our "snob" gene. We want to think we're "rich" or are driving what "rich" people drive. It's what the market will bear. It's perception. (Of course, there are levels of quality that include selection of materials, designs, fabrication processes, appointments, and options, but still a good chunk of that price is "perception.")

I find the longer I live, the less I'm impressed with perception. We were the victims of a hit-and-run driver who was eventually tracked down, but had no insurance. We had to pay for the repairs on our mini-van. While it was in the shop, our insurance picked up the tab for a rental car. The only vehicle they had that would seat my whole tribe was a luxury car. We drove it for one week. The first day was fun as the children "rode" the electric seats and maneuvered them into hundreds of possible positions. But I realized that we still got from point A to point B. I was cleansed. I thought of the difference between owning that car and our "free-and-clear" van: $50,000. All I could think of was waste. What a waste of money to spend it on "image" when all I really needed was transportation. That automatic seat was not worth $50,000 to me. There was a time I liked cars. I knew something about them. Some of our closest friends growing up were car dealers' kids—so we talked cars. We knew models. We knew years. Now, I have no idea what people drive. It just isn't important to me. If you like what you drive and it fits within your budget, what difference does it make what other people think? Ask yourself if you could still get from point A to point B with the same degree of safety in a less expensive vehicle. Ask yourself if your self-worth is so precarious that it teeters on the "perception" of others about what car you drive. Calculate the money difference. Think about what else you could do with that money. Is it worth it? If it is, then be happy and go in peace. If it isn't, do something about it. Sell the "image," buy transportation, and invest the difference in something more worthwhile like your children's future, a charity, paying off your credit cards, or your own retirement.

I used the example of cars because I think we can all relate to that. Most of us either drive or need transportation of some sort. But apply these same ideas to other purchases. Don't let any smooth-talking salesman con you into spending more than you can afford for a fleeting image. I'm working on that myself. But I feel good when I'm rock solid about getting a good buy without even considering where this particular brand is positioned in the marketplace.

PACKAGING

Packaging costs money. I'm appalled at how much we spend on stuff that gets trashed. I'm talking about the plastic bottle, the cardboard box, the Styrofoam inserts, the case, the packing peanuts, and the bubble wrap. Inking, printing, folding, molding, adhering, inserting, shrink-wrapping all cost money. There are good people working assembly lines doing this. They earn their pay for their labor. It's added into the price of the goods sold.

Try to shop to avoid paying those fees. You can minimize the packaging costs by buying in bulk and choosing products with minimal packaging. When I do buy commercial packaging, I try to reuse the containers. I buy detergent in 5 gallon pails or buckets. That saves the environment from extra plastic bottles. We then use the drums to store dry dog food, and other products I buy in bulk. I buy window cleaner concentrate in small plastic bags directly from a janitor supply company, or make my own using basic ingredients—I add my own water and use the same spray bottle again and again.

Realize that, for many of you, when you buy a tube of toothpaste, you're paying more for the tube and the box than you are for the paste. And the paste is what you use.

When you buy food, think about packaging. Much of what I buy doesn't come packaged. I have to either take my bag, crate, or box. Or it comes in bulk packaging—one bag with 50 pounds of onions, one roll of 10 pounds of meat, one can with 6-pounds of beans. To give you perspective on this: we reduce by 233% the amount of metal used when I buy a big can of tuna instead of the same amount of meat in smaller cans. That impacts the price and our environment—we produce less landfill fodder.

Please start thinking about how much you spend on packaging. The last time I bought strawberries, I only paid for strawberries. We picked our own from an organic farm using our own labor and our own boxes. We didn't pay for any hidden costs of advertising or packaging. We did pay some overhead—the farmer's profit. Yet, we paid less than 10% of the price of what organic strawberries cost at the local store. And we got some of the freshest, healthiest strawberries we've ever eaten. Well worth it!

A note about long-term packaging: I appreciate having some "emergency rations" on hand. That's my long-term storage of grains and some dehydrated food in case of a power failure or "An Act of God." We package our grains, beans, etc. in nitrogen-packed food-grade buckets. This protects the grain for years and years. You might come across a variety of storage methods—some companies use oxygen absorbers (be careful—it could do too much and actually pull oxygen through the bucket and you end up with a worse situation

I have learned about making my own cleaning products, especially because of Trent, my son with special needs. A book that has been very helpful is *Clean and Green: Complete Guide to Nontoxic and Environmentally Safe Housekeeping,* by Berthold-Bond.

than before you started—we don't opt for this method), dry-ice (if you do this yourself, be very, very careful), CO_2 (leave this to the professionals), and Super Pails (this method seems like overkill to us—you could pay as much as $10 more for this method and it doesn't do that much better).

AND AN EXTRA ONE: PIZZAZZ

In addition to the textbook marketing considerations, I think another "P" figures into the purchase: the intangibles—the *pizzazz.*

- **Self-Actualization:** Some people actually feel better about themselves when they buy something. Some people enjoy shopping. My grandmother did. If shopping was ever an Olympic sport, she would have been the team's coach. They like the "rush" that purchasing gives them: those few minutes of being in control, of being served, of being the "boss." Unfortunately, that "high" is very short lived. It's the "sense of being a good parent" that some have when they see the smiles and hear the "ohhhs" from their children on Christmas morning—it only lasts until the batteries run low and the bills start coming. It is the old lie—believing that providing things will make up for not being there—things instead of time.

  There are shop-aholics, and they need help. I pray you aren't one of them. But even for the rest of us, we have to battle this temptation of shopping for pleasure. Our self-worth doesn't come from buying things.

  It does feel wonderful when sales clerks make you feel like royalty. Before we know it, we're agreeing with them that we do look great in that dress and we do "deserve it." We use the plastic genie and receive their, "Very nice choice, Ma'am." Few will even remember us ten minutes after we sign the ticket.

  Marketers even have a name for this idea: it's called post-purchase dissonance. It's that sick feeling you get after you've bought something and are stuck with it. It's what makes you continue to "shop" for the same item to see if you could have gotten it for a better price after all, somewhere else.

  Don't fall for any attempts of salesmen, clerks, or marketers to tie your self-esteem into a thing. *You* are worth far more than that.

  Are there some legitimate perks to shopping? Yes, especially when you shop for proper motives. It does feel good to know you've done well to live within your means, provided quality for your family, and have no regrets. That's the "pizzazz" I like—and then I put my feet up and rest.
- **Convenience:** I like convenience. I like that I don't have to rent a boat and sail down to Honduras every time I want to eat a banana. I like not having to pick

my own cotton, spin, weave, cut, and sew to have clothes for my children. I don't mind paying for those wonderful kinds of conveniences. And I'll do it again.

Evaluate how much convenience you're willing to pay for. I draw the line at certain points. I won't pay for the convenience of shopping one mile from my home at a quick mart. It is worth while to drive more miles for better prices.

I don't like paying for the "convenience" of someone else cooking for me. That is where I draw the line. I'll make my own convenience meals . . .Thank you very much though, for cooking for others.

AND IF I'M COMPLETELY HONEST, YOU'RE ALSO PAYING THE SIXTH "P"—POLITICS

Through the manufacturing process taxes are added. With a quick look, you might think only sales tax is added at the final sale; but with closer inspection you'll realize that percentages are sent to the government at all levels. For example, think about every time any part or ingredient was transported. For that shipping, there were taxes on gasoline, licenses, transit fees, tolls, employment taxes, etc. Now apply that example to every aspect of the manufacturing process, and you'll see that the 6% sales tax paid (or whatever it is in your area) is only a part of the total amount of taxes paid. The real amount of taxes paid is actually much higher—but you don't realize how much because it is built into the price of the item. In some areas, you might think you aren't paying any tax on food items. Think again. You are—you just don't get an itemized receipt. All those "hidden taxes" are included in the price.

At each level—manufacturer, distributor, retailer—there are income taxes, payroll taxes, as well as ad valorum-type taxes. It's in there.

One way to lower that tax bill is to buy items with the least amount of manufacturing processing and transit. And amazingly enough, usually you'll find the food is healthier. The less it is processed and hauled around—the fresher and more nutritious it is. You win on both sides of the issue.

From the Accountant's Perspective

My cost accounting classes were tedious, but enlightening. Though we "role-played" as the manager determining what cost we would finally attach to a product, I thought of it from the consumer's perspective: all the things one pays for when he buys a product. In addition to the marketing four P's, accountants have complicated formulas for adding such things as:

Depreciation of equipment, taxes, time value of money, replacement of equipment, return on investment, worker's compensation, payroll taxes, retirement plans, perks, travel and entertainment involved with the product. The list goes on and on . . .

And all you wanted was some toothpaste to brush your teeth. When you follow that one tube back through the maze of shopkeepers, marketers, distributors, accountants, assembly-line personnel, truckers, tax agencies, farmers, and chemists—you realize you paid for a lot more than just toothpaste.

Alternatives to the Local Grocer

GARDENING AND FARMING

I think we'd agree that gardening is the best source for produce. It isn't feasible for some of us. We've grown a little bit in our side-yard garden, not even 1% of what we ingest yearly. It is a good feeling though, to dig in the dirt for potatoes, wash, cook, and then eat them. There's a deep satisfaction there. I like the feeling. I'm not the great gardener my parents and in-laws are. Yet, I do heartily encourage any one to raise as much food from their own garden as possible. Not only is it usually cost effective, but the quality should be outstanding. You can eat food that is minutes off the vine—full of every possible nutrient.

One of the big problems with our current food supply is "green harvesting." Fruits and vegetables are picked while still green. They finish ripening in transient to the store—away from the soil, sun, and nutrients. They lack the full complement of chemicals that our bodies need. That's why I like to work with my own produce or directly with a farmer.

Make friends with farmers in your area. If you don't garden, does anyone you know have this hobby? I know of friends whose gardens produce more than they need, so they take the extra and sell it at their job sites. Check out the "you-can-pick" places.

Consider gleaning. It isn't shameful. It's actually Biblical. Once professional crews have gone through a field, ask if you can glean. Some of the fruits, beans, or berries will have ripened since the crews went through, and you'll have plumb delicious food for a fraction of the cost—and sometimes free. You're doing the farmer a favor.

Also, if you can't plant a full or even a box garden, you might be able to grow some herbs. It really does make a difference in recipes when you use fresh-cut herbs instead of processed ones.

FARMER'S MARKETS

As I travel around the country, I take "busman's holidays"—I visit farmer's markets and check out grocery stores. I continue to be impressed with farmer's markets. I'm not talking

Do you remember the story of Ruth and Boaz? She went to glean in his fields. What a story! They were the great-grandparents of King David, the giant killer. In the book of Leviticus, the Hebrews were admonished not to harvest the corners of their fields as to leave some for their gleaners.

about every roadside stand that calls itself a farmer's market. I'm referring to the markets, usually one or maybe two in a state, where the farmers take their produce to sell to restaurants and grocery store chains.

Call around. When we moved to Florida I kept asking each green grocer where he got his produce. I'd ask his supplier. Then his supplier. Then his supplier, until I ended up on the loading docks in Tampa. The Tampa market is quite different from the one in Dallas and different from the Amish one in Pennsylvania, but the principles still hold. Farmer's bring their produce in on trucks and sell it for the best price they can get. Even at the market there are the true farmers and distributors. I get my best prices from the farmers, but sometimes they don't want to sell one box, they want to sell the whole truckload. I then turn to the distributors. With my trusty clipboard and wearing a jacket (those bays are cold, even in summer, because of the huge refrigerators), I start negotiating. Here's my advice:

1. Have a good shopping list. Know exactly how much you need and what quality. For example, do you need perfect bell peppers for a stuffed pepper recipe, or will a lower grade work because you'll be cutting them up?
2. Take the cash you can afford to spend. Usually cash is the only means of payment, though there are some exceptions. Don't take more than you can afford. I find I spend every cent I take. There are so many great buys that I get as much as I can afford each time.
3. Get bids before buying. I cruise the entire market, writing down locations, prices, and quality.
4. Be honest. When I shop there's a man on the left of me buying for a chain of restaurants, on my right, a lady buying for a chain of grocery stores, and there I am buying for my chain of children. I get my best buys because I'm not a restaurateur or a chain-store shopper. It's obvious I'm buying for my family. Bethany Kay is with me. She's a big help because with her "cute" is a verb. Let me give you some examples:

    - **Plums:** Because my children are with me, we get quality. There is one distributor who likes Bethany Kay and asks if the fruit is for this sweet little girl. Normally, these jobbers display "gift-quality" fruit. The buyer places an order. Then a clerk goes into the room-sized refrigerators and brings out a box to load in your car. Of course, the display box is the best fruit and the box you get might not be as prime. This distributor gives us the display box and says he'll make another display. He wants Bethany Kay to get his best fruit.

- **Grapes:** Sometimes I have to keep reminding the distributors that the produce is for us, and not for resale. Remember 95%+ of their customers are retailers and commercial buyers. I don't care about the boxes or crates. I'm going to move it to my own containers. We were offered some seedless white grapes at only $8 a flat because the crates were crushed and they couldn't get their normal $14 a flat from the commercial buyers. A flat's worth of grapes would have cost us more than $50 at the local grocery store.
- **Onions:** The jobber asked again, "Now these are for you and you're going to process them today?" I replied, "Yes." 'Well, then I'll sell you this bag over here. They're fine as you can see, but they'll be bad within the week and I can't sell them to any of my commercial buyers because they need more lead-time. (Gives you an idea of how old the produce is in some grocery stores.) If you want it, I'll sell it to you for $4." I took it. That sack of onions contained 50 huge beauties that sell for $1 a piece at the state-of-the-art grocery store. With that product alone, I saved $46.

5. Try to shop the last period of time before a three-day weekend.

We were just about finished shopping and the car was full. I negotiated a man down to $2 a flat for strawberries and spent my last $6. As the clerk was loading them for me, he asked me how much I had paid. I puffed up like a peacock because $2 was my best price to date. The lowest price previously was $4 a flat. He said, "You got taken." "What?" My pride had to calm down to reason. I was about to learn something. "Ma'am, it's a three-day weekend." "I know that. That's why I'm here so my husband can help me for three days to process all this produce." "Ma'am, what I mean is that I'm hauling all this food out to be trashed. It won't last for three days. We're throwing all this away. If you drive your car around, I could fill it full of vegetables and fruits." I learned something. It cost me $6, but it was worth it. We pulled the already fully-stocked car around and *stuffed* it with more strawberries, hands (not bunches, but *hands)* of bananas, boxes of tomatoes.

We handed Bethany Kay a watermelon to keep in her lap. The boys all held boxes of fruit. Alan just didn't understand the situation, and insisted on leaving windshield room. He said he needed to see to drive. Men!

We had food to spare. We gave away flats of strawberries to friends. We had plenty of food. A nice clerk told me the same thing happens every three-day weekend. I'm not saying you can get all your produce for free, but it's worth considering.

CO-OPS

Co-ops or cooperatives vary one from another. But basically, it is a group of individuals who pool their resources to get competitive prices. There are produce co-ops, meat co-ops, and everything-you-can-imagine co-ops. I managed a food co-op for more than a year. We then realized we could do better for our family on our own. That year was invaluable to me because I learned quite a bit about quality and marketing. Though I no longer use a co-op, for some of you, a co-op is an excellent alternative. Before you join, check out the requirements. With some you have to volunteer for certain hours or duties. There may be minimums and forced orders. Sometimes you have no say on what is purchased. You might agree to three fruits, three vegetables, and three salad ingredients, but you don't know if you'll get broccoli or turnip greens. With some you get exactly what you order. That has it advantages and disadvantages. If you had done the shopping you would have passed on the cucumbers (they didn't meet your standards) and chosen sprouts instead. But since someone else is shopping for you, they get cucumbers—exactly what you ordered.

Co-ops are great because you can buy in more family-sized quantities and yet still get "army-sized" discounts. How does it work? If I want two heads of lettuce and so does Joan's family, and Bill's, and . . . we can buy box of lettuce and get the bulk rate. So everyone saves.

Check it out. Make sure you agree and are comfortable with all the requirements before you sign up. Then follow through. If you say you'll sort and bag every first Saturday, then do it. Dozens of other families are counting on you.

There are also commercial co-ops that carry lines of foodstuffs. Some have the same products you pay so much for at health food stores. If you can reach their minimum order amount, then their truck will stop at your assigned location. Again, they fill your order and you have to trust them to get the quality you want. It is an excellent option for some families, and some co-ops combine their order for this group-drop.

How do you find a co-op? Check bulletin boards at churches, community centers, and your local grocer. Some have listings in the advertising section of the phone book. Some health food stores will pass on the information. Some won't because they believe co-ops rob them of customers. Ask your local county agent if he knows of any co-ops in your area. Ask everyone you know. Some home education families are involved in co-op programs, so considering asking homeschoolers you know.

As co-oping grows in popularity, they will offer more services, with some having professional managers, not just volunteer staffing.

CATALOGUE OR ON-LINE OPTIONS

You can order food from catalogues and even online. This online option will grow as more and more people tap in. My local area just opened up to accept "Priceline" transactions. And as more people feel safe with this "new" way of buying food, it will bring costs down and increase availability. If you do shop online, please make sure the site is secure—otherwise, don't give out personal information. And as with all vendors, both online and direct, never give out your social security number unless it has a mandated link to your taxes. Identity theft is not fun. The catalogue companies can provide everything from picture-perfect oranges to taste-free cookies (oops, I mean fat, sugar, salt-free). You can order everything from gift hams, fruitcake, and nuts, to kosher steaks and vegetarian meat substitutes.

No matter which companies you choose, triple check for quality and price. Look at the full price. Sometimes the item price is great, but when you add in the shipping, you could have done better locally. Sometimes not.

Some products are great to order this way. I think spices are a prime example. I have been pleased with all the spices I've ordered from a Watkins dealer and from Frontier Natural Products Co-op. There are other companies.

Since companies change so often, by the time this book is off the presses, half of the companies I might list would have either moved or closed down and another dozen or so would have gone into business.

Don't depend on me: learn how to get information yourself. If you aren't already getting catalogues in the mail, wait; they appear somehow. You can always write to companies (for listings, check the Internet, the Thomas Registry, or other such listings in the reference section of your library). To find the ones on the Internet, use your search engines to do the work.

MIDDLEMEN

Middlemen are nice people. I happen to love two dearly. My husband's parents are marketers. They work hard and earn their fees. I believe workmen are worthy of their hire, and should be paid for the service they provide. If it weren't for them—and others like them—our grocery shelves would not be so well stocked. People have different gifts, skills, and abilities. I rejoice about that. This world would be a pretty miserable place if we were all the same. There are good businessmen who make good products. But, they either lack the skill, manpower, or desire to do the legwork of getting their products to the consumer. They "hire" marketing firms to get their products on the shelf, so we can buy it.

My idea is to do some of that work. I like to become the "middleman." I go directly to the producer as much as possible. When possible, I go directly to the farmer, the packer, or the rancher.

When it is impossible or impractical, I go directly to the middleman and save the mark-up in the store. For instance, we work with a grocery supply firm. They are great people. I call my agent days before a cook and get prices. According to what they can get within my price allowance, I adjust my recipes. Then I call back, place my order, and go pick it up. Their complex is about 20 minutes from my home and the food is of good quality. I do have to buy in large quantities—but that's okay. I'm able to buy boneless chicken breasts in bulk from them for $2 a pound cheaper than from the best deal I've ever had at a grocery. And that is a better price than buying chicken breasts with the bone and doing the work myself. They also carry fresh produce and it saves me the five-hour round-trip to the state's farmer market. How do you find these places? Just look in the advertising section of your phone book under the headings "Food-Wholesale" or "Grocers-Wholesale." Call first. Of course, you'll have to drive through the industrial part of town, but when you can save 50-75% off your grocer bill, you can deal with it. I just pull my van up next to the semi-trucks to load.

There are times when I can become the middleman myself. I do this with herbs, vitamins, nutraceuticals, and other dietary supplements. I also did this when I managed a produce co-op. I know several families who have part-time, and some full-time businesses, acting as middlemen for lines of products they like. It makes sense. I can buy at wholesale and then get residual income for referrals to others. For example, by just passing the word along about what supplements we're giving our beloved son Trent, the referral income helped pay for his monthly supply. I like that.

When it is impossible or impractical to avoid the middleman, to work directly with a middleman, or to become a middleman myself, I negotiate with the local grocer.

RETAIL GROCERY SHOPPING

Don't get me wrong. I'm not saying to stop visiting your local grocer. It can be the smart shop. I am saying: Plan your attack and be wise to their methods. Consider them your allies.

Something that we, as Americans, do every week, but don't really think much about, is grocery shopping. We've worked hard all day. We're hungry. We know we have nothing at home worth eating or cooking. We drop by the local grocery store. We start through their carefully designed maze. Some of our shopping is so routine that the food knows us. We walk down the aisles and the food jumps in. "Ah, here's Mr. Smith again, he'll want three cans of chili . . . jump boys . . . now on to the fruity-frosty-gleemo-pops . . ." It's a no-brainer. It's easy. It's familiar.

I'm asking you to take a little more time. Within a few weeks, you can again shop quickly, but you'll be shopping wiser, spending less and bringing home more healthy food.

Key: DON'T EVER SHOP HUNGRY OR TIRED. OR WORSE—DON'T EVER SHOP WITH TIRED OR HUNGRY CHILDREN.

Perimeter Shopping: Have you ever thought about how grocery stores are designed? They are designed to encourage shopping. Rarely have I ever seen one designed for us, the shoppers. But one feature that I like very much and I've seen in most of the stores I've toured—they stock the whole food around the walls of the store. Think about it. I call it perimeter shopping. Almost all the time I shop, we just skirt the perimeter of the store. That's where the fresh food is. It has to be kept chilled. It's the stuff up and down the aisles that doesn't have to be chilled that is loaded with additives for that very purpose. I know that food goes bad. If it doesn't go bad, what of it is "food?" On my regular trips to the grocer, when I'm picking up weekly needs (95% of our food was purchased months before during a mega-session), we shop the perimeter. Milk, butter, eggs, apples, bananas, Trent's cucumbers, and a few other items—and we're out of there. Sometimes you'll find me up and down the aisles, but that is for a rare project or part of Trent's therapy.

I realize there are exceptions. There are reasons to go up and down the aisles, but hold those jaunts to a minimum. That is where the pre-packaged, heavily processed foods are. You can make your own convenience foods for much less money and for very little investment in time.

Evaluate carefully, before you reach and stretch for boxes, whether you couldn't make a healthier version yourself.

Deliberate Design: Grocery stocking is a real science. But be your own person. Don't run through the maze like a well-trained white rat. Be decisive and in control.

- ***Eye-Level:*** Speaking of reaching and stretching, have you noticed the high priced, name-brand items are at eye-level? The el-cheapo brand is on the bottom shelf—intentionally. And watch out—some stores stock the high-priced cereal and candy at the eye-level of your children! Skip your aerobic class that day and do your bending at the grocery store.
- ***Use of Color:*** We discussed marketing surveys about which color of green to use. Well, there are elaborate studies done to see how colors affect us. Not only colors, but color combinations.
- ***End-of-Aisle Displays:*** Check the expiration date. We're supposed to think those items at the end of the aisle are specially priced. It could be that they are about to expire and the store wants to move them *now.*

Impulse Buying: That's when we buy something not on our list. When you're shopping as a mega-cook, you should triple-check before you allow anything into your cart that's not on the list. You are going to have your hands full managing the ingredients you need. You don't need to waste time or money on "frills." Once in a while I'll add something to my list, but it has to be the bargain of the century.

Where is the milk in your store? I ask because it's important. This fits into the "store design" aspect because the store is designed to encourage impulse buying. Once I had to run in my mother's local grocer for a gallon of milk. She had warned me. The milk was in the back, far reaches of the grocer galaxy. I went around all the produce, past the meat, back, back, into the recesses of the store. Finally, after turning a few more corners and wondering if I'd run a marathon, or feeling I was in Death Valley stepping over tumble-weeds, there was the milk. Then I had to run the hurdles of cut flowers, cards, fresh baked bread, and apple pies before I made it to the register. My nose was sending all kinds of signals to my stomach who was pleading with my hands to reach out and grab. But I quieted all my body parts into submission. I felt like I had conquered Mt. Everest—I checked out with one gallon of milk!

I haven't always been that good. My dear husband used to fall for the chocolate donuts that one store had next to the milk display. He's doing much better now that we live three states away from that store.

If the stores really wanted to provide a service to us, they'd have a bin of fresh milk right at the express lane. We'd be in and out in 3 minutes flat. But no. Their goal in life is to sell us things. So, we run the maze.

There are some advantages. I do like the fresh flowers option near the checkout. Alan often has just picked up a bouquet to give me a smile. They cost little compared to ordering from a florist, and it is worth every penny for our marriage.

Not all impulse buying is evil. Sometimes it is quite beneficial. I just recommend that you try to limit those great buys to non-mega-sessions. And be sure you know what you are doing. Let your head think, not your stomach.

- ***Store Brands:*** I wonder how many hours the creative people labored over naming the soap I use in the washing machine. It is so clever and gets right to the point.

By the way, "green" is a big color now. It used to be avoided because it was thought to represent spoilage. Now with all the health and earthy emphasis, it is once again a "good color" and popular. You're supposed to think of health, vitality, and growing things. I wonder what color will be "in" next?

It says it all and communicates real meaning. It is called: Laundry Detergent. I knew you'd be impressed, too.

I'm a big fan of store brands. I like the fact that thousands of dollars didn't go into packaging and naming. I like the quality. And I especially like the prices.

Not all store brands are equal. Some are worse than the name brand and some are much better. Test them first. Buy a "normal" sized package. If you like it, stock up.

In some cases the store is packaging the same ingredients as the brand name, but because their marketing plan is different and they have built-in distribution, they charge less. They are cutting out middlemen, and doing it themselves.

With rare exceptions, I buy the store brand. One exception was that until we moved back to Florida, I had not found any store brand freezer bags that compared with the name brands in quality. Our local chain, Publix, makes a great freezer bag that holds up even under mega-stress. But they don't carry all the sizes I need. So I buy some Publix store-brand bags, and then use the brand name ones for the other sizes.

Sales Incentives

If a manufacturer doesn't get their product in your cart by clever names, they will use the word "new" on the label, or offer free samples (who needs to eat lunch anymore—go shopping and "sample" your way through lunch), or try to win you with coupons, rebates, and logo products.

COUPONS

I know. I've also heard the stories—people who buy hundreds of dollars worth of groceries, then whip out their coupons and only have to write a check for a few dollars. I've watched them in line. I've looked at what they buy. And with rare exceptions, I wouldn't let what they buy into my children. Maybe it's just the coupons that come through our mail, but rarely do I ever see a coupon for food I buy. It's for pre-fab food that is loaded with additives, sugar, salt, or fat. Yes, I might save 50¢ off a jar of commercially-made white sauce, which brings the price to only $1.22. But I can make that same amount of white sauce (see Beige Sauce, on page 362) with fresh whole-wheat flour, real butter, and fresh milk for about a dime (when it's part of a mega-batch). So why would I pay an extra $1.12 for the "convenience" of feeding my family chemicals and preservatives? It doesn't make sense to me.

When I see coupons for raw food, I'll use them. Also, many of the places I shop don't honor coupons. And I haven't yet seen a coupon for an 80-pound box of chicken quarters, redeemable at the wholesale grocers. Or, one for a 45-pound drum of wheat berries good through my flour mill contact.

I'm not against using coupons, but please be wise. Don't spend money on something you wouldn't buy, just to save 75¢. I have used a few coupons, but it was on items I was going to buy anyway, and doing the math, it was a better price than buying in bulk or the store-brand equivalent.

It takes a good deal of time and energy to clip, sort, and organize coupons. I can spend that time making food from scratch using ingredients I bought in bulk at 25 to 50% the cost.

REBATES

Rebates can be helpful, just as coupons. But realize that the strategy of the marketing wizards is for you to buy the product figuring in the rebate offer, but then never taking the time to send for it. And they're right. Less than 6% of shoppers redeem mail-in or rebate offers.

The rebate has to be substantial before I'm interested. Redeeming can be work.

1. Of course, check the requirements and make certain your purchase will qualify. Some stores keep "rebate offer" stickers on products after rebate time has elapsed. Check it out. Check for limits. Some offer only one rebate per household. Some refuse to rebate to post office boxes. If you live in a small community that doesn't have home delivery—you're out of it.
2. Before you buy, calculate what the "net" savings will be. Remember the cost of a first-class stamp to mail in the offer, including any copying fees and the cost of an envelope. Figure any check cashing fees your bank charges. Some banks allow only so many "free" deposits a month, and then charge. Some rebate offers insist you use a 3 x 5 card, so add that cost.
3. Always have the rebate-able item rung up separately. Pay for it separately. In every rebate offer I've seen, I have to mail in the original receipt. I don't want to give my only proof of purchase for the other items I buy. (Though they like to see a full receipt because they can gather all sorts of spending data from those sales tickets and form patterns about habits and interests of people who buy their products. For instance, if more than 54% of those who sent in rebates also buy diapers, they will spend their advertising dollars in parenting magazines. They can also generate some profits by selling this marketing data to other firms.) Calculate into the "deal" if writing another check or ringing up another credit card transaction costs you anything—even if it is just the cost of the printed check.

4. If after all this you'll realize only a 10¢ "net" savings, you probably have better things to do with your time. It does take some time to handle all the paperwork properly.
5. If you do buy the item, keep all the packaging. Mail in the rebate as soon as possible. Try to do it the day of purchase. Every rebate I have ever used had a time frame (e.g., must be postmarked within two weeks from date of purchase). Follow all their directions exactly. Circle what needs to be circled. They'll use any excuse not to pay.
6. Make copies of everything you send in. I lay the UPC, the receipt, and the offer on the copier to print. I then package all their requirements in the envelope, double-checking that I included everything.
7. I not only date and properly file the copy, I mark my calendar. You can do this on a wall calendar, but I use my computer calendar. If the offer states 6-8 weeks, I write on the 42nd day, "Start looking for "XYZ rebate," and look for it to arrive in the post until the 62nd day. My experience has been that 80% of the time, my rebate check arrives before or during those time frames. If I don't track rebate offers, I forget about them. This step only takes a few minutes, and pays.
8. If I haven't received the rebate within the specified time frame, I give the benefit of the doubt and wait about two more weeks, before acting. I send a photocopy of my records (my copy of the form, receipts, UPC sticker, etc.), reminding the company of their offer and politely ask them to honor it. I don't have to threaten any action. With 100% accuracy, the rebate check arrives after the first inquiry letter.

The statistic regarding the number of shoppers who redeem mail-in or rebate offers is from Phil Lempert's *Supermarket Shopping and Value Guide.* Copyright 1996 Phil Lempert, published by Contemporary Books, Inc.

Save on the cost of envelopes by reusing junk mail envelopes and writing in the rebate address over the "junk mail address." We get dozens of these window envelopes a month. And we save bill envelopes that we pay in person. For offers like this you don't need to use "nice" stationery envelopes—use freebies. Caution: be sure to mark completely through any auto-sorting coding on the envelope. I didn't realize this and a piece of mail was returned to me. The post office sent it to the coding address, not the one I had handwritten on the envelope. That was a wasted stamp, but a valuable lesson.

Some rebate offers are wonderful. The best ones we've used are for electronics or computer supplies. It's not uncommon to get $20 back in rebate money. Some offers are so good they pay for the product or close to it. I needed some 3.5-inch floppies. I could pay around $5 for a dozen, or pay $12 for 50 and get a $10 rebate back. It was simple; I bought the fifty and banked the $10 rebate!

Remember: Don't let the rebate offer entice you to buy unless you will claim it. Calculate the complete cost of claiming the rebate. If the "net" savings are worth the time involved, go for the rebate.

FREE WITH PURCHASE AND OTHER SPECIALS

As with any offer, carefully weigh the true costs. Some are worth it. Sometimes it's the only way to get a particular product. Though I prefer to make my own gelatin salads from my own fresh ingredients, I'll compromise once in a while and buy the name brand because the store offers a free mold if you buy one box. The mold is worth the cost. The children have fun and use the mold, not only for gelatin but for crafts and playtime. For instance, we got a mold of a map of the United States. We've used that for so many projects as a great learning tool. They've cut out each state from gelatin. Yes, Rhode Island was tricky and yes, everyone wanted the "Texas" piece. But it only cost me a box of packaged gelatin. That little bit of sugar isn't going to ruin them for life.

Be wary of gimmicks like collecting points for logo merchandise. If you'd buy the product anyway, then claim your "prize." I acquired a spare set of dishes this way by collecting stamps and then getting a free plate for each "full sheet of stamps." I've also found that some logo products are junk. Don't buy 20 cases of soda you don't like to get a shirt with their name on it. You could have bought 3 or 4 shirts for the same price. But if you buy that much of that brand of soda anyway, then you might as well wear the free clothing. Don't ever buy a product to enter a contest. Read the fine print. It should state that "purchase is not required." If it's that important to you, enter following those "without proof of purchase" alternative directions.

Don't rush in. Don't buy every offer. Use discernment. Realize there is no free lunch. Those "free" products are paid for by someone. If it's worth it, it's worth it.

When writing to inquire about rebates that I haven't received in the specified time frame, I don't have to pull the "I'm an author with thousands of readers and I'm sure they'd like to hear how your company didn't honor your offer." I write a polite note, and realizing that papers can be misfiled, etc., acknowledge that honest mistakes do happen. Why assume the worst? People are usually very nice and when treated with respect and courtesy they are wonderful.

BRAND LOYALTY

"Attention shoppers . . . Attention Shoppers . . . Squawk, Squeak . . . There is an ungrateful daughter on aisle seven. Yes, folks, we have a grown daughter who no longer loves her mother. That's her in the pink sweater . . . She has dared to buy a different brand of tomato sauce than the one her mother has used for forty years. What?— She doesn't trust her mother any more. I ask you. Please let's all go gawk at her . . .. By the way there's a car in the parking lot with its lights on, license . . .."

Either they'll publicly embarrass you or maybe a miniature guillotine will snap down and cut off your nails if you actually dare to buy a different brand than your regular one. It is called brand loyalty and companies vie for your loyalty. Once they have you sold on their product, they want to keep you. That's why you receive samples in the mail. Companies want you to break from your current brand and switch to theirs.

If you are using the best brand, then it makes sense to continue. But if you're buying a product because it is comfortable, then switch brands. At least try the other brand once. Give it a fair evaluation. If you find that you want to continue paying that additional 25% more for your old brand, then do so. But at least you tried to save some money. Who knows you might find, as I usually do, that the off-name is as good.

Your mother will get over it.

Attitude and Overview

Let's apply some of what we've learned about food and how it gets to your house, and incorporate it into our mega-cooking™.

BIDS

Start thinking like a professional. You no longer ask the price of an item. You collect bids.

Here's a walk-through:

You need 100 pounds of ground turkey on Friday. Start calling on Wednesday. Look in the phone book under meat and grocery stores. Call. Ask for the meat manager. Don't waste time talking to a clerk. They usually don't have the authority to change prices. With the manager you can state, "I'll be purchasing 100 pounds of ground turkey on Friday and I was wondering if you'd like to make a bid on that purchase." If you hear a calculator in the background, you've got a live one. If they immediately say, "Lady, it sells for $1.89 a pound and is in the bin," scratch them off your list and call the next one. Once they have quoted you a price, always ask this: "If I get a lower bid, would you like me to call you back so you can make a counter bid?" If they say yes, you know they can go lower. Sometimes it pays to remind them why they can cut the price for you.

1. You'll accept it in the bulk logs—straight off the truck (usually in 10-pound logs) so they don't have to spend any funds on labor or packaging. I asked a local butcher how long it takes to repackage meat into one pound containers. They told me about 5 minutes. That would take 500 minutes to process that 100 pounds into individual packets (like everyone else likes). That's 8 hours and 20 minutes. If they paid that clerk minimum wage (which is unlikely), that means a cost savings of more than $43, or $.43 per pound. They also save by not using 100 little Styrofoam trays, lots of shrink-wrap, and more than 100 labels.
2. By increasing their order by 100 extra pounds, they could qualify for a higher discount from their distributor.

Continue through the other butchers. Narrow it to the three best prices. Call them back, quote the lowest price and see if they can beat it. Go with the best price for the best quality.

Note: be certain to compare apples with apples. Get quotes on all the same grade of meat, or whatever you call about.

We've used more than a dozen meat suppliers. One time this one will have the best price, the next time, someone else, so I always call the best ones each time and give them the opportunity to bid.

One time the manager of the state-of-the-art grocery store had ordered too much meat for an advertised special. He was stuck and didn't want to take a hit and throw any away. The meat was still good, but he knew with the special over, he couldn't sell that much meat that quickly. All his regular customers had stocked up during the sale. I happened to call at the right time. He sold me that meat at a full $1.00 a pound off the advertised special. Alan had to go to the back door and ask for "Clyde" as if he was some secret agent safe-guarding government secrets. Bond, Alan Bond, licensed to shop.

BULK BUYING

Buying bulk only makes sense if you'll use the items before they spoil. For my mother buying in bulk means buying the family-sized jar. (Since my father is in an assisted care facility after his stroke, Mom only cooks for herself.) For us, buying in bulk means buying dozens of pounds of items. But we use it wisely.

Be careful about buying in bulk. There is the temptation to over-use or over-eat. Since you have so much, why not have seconds or thirds. We don't have to concern ourselves, because we have divided our food into meal-sized amounts. So, unless we thaw four meat loaves, we won't be tempted to over-eat.

We do have to watch the #10 cans of fruit though. For our family, that is enough for two meals. If we don't divide it and store half right away, Trent will "raid" and eat dozens of pears or peaches. We are aware of Trent's "isms" and we make adjustments. You might not have a special needs child, but you might have a sweet tooth. Try dividing your bulk purchases immediately, so you can't eat 600 crackers at once.

Expand this concept of bulk buying beyond food. In the appendix, I've listed a company that sells other items in bulk—like boys' underwear and socks, hair ribbons, and toothbrushes. Yes, you have to buy a dozen pairs of socks at a time, but isn't that a basic amount of socks for a teenage boy to have?

Let's recap.

After I've made my ingredient lists for any recipe I'm mega-cooking™, I check out my pantry to see what I have on stock. I note those items with a check mark. I then plan my attack. I've learned from experience where I'll probably get the best deal on each of the other items.

Here is my usual order of preference for acquisition:

1. My own garden or a farm
2. The farmer's market or grocery supply house
3. Wholesale buying club or co-operative
4. Local grocery store

Remember, I call first when it's appropriate. I'll call the grocery supply house to check their supply of produce. What I think is a good deal, I'll order. If there is still a lot of produce I need, it is worth the round-trip to Tampa. It is just a few items, I buy at the local "roadside" markets (they've been over to Tampa and are adding in their percentages, but it is less than it would cost me to make the trip). We'll pick up our order from the grocery supply house, then the remaining items from the wholesale club and the local grocery store.
At home, we cut, pare, dice, and assemble the recipes (see Methods Section, page 000).
We do visit the local grocery store about once a week for milk, eggs, etc. When my flour mill was broken, we bought bread directly from the outlet for a quarter the price that the local grocer charges.

Depending on where you live, you might have direct access to food processing plants and can shop direct. In Florida, we get great produce, but have few food processing plants. Benefit from what is in your area. In Texas, beef was a staple. Here in Florida, we have real orange juice—we measure fresh in hours, not months. Also, I've made friends with a lady whose husband fishes. When he catches more than they need, they call me. And I get *fresh* fish at a price I can afford. If I had to pay the standard market prices, we'd rarely eat fish.

However, we think fish should be one of our major meat sources; but with the restrictions on fishermen, the prices have tripled. Filet Mignon is usually cheaper per pound than Orange Roughy or Mahi-mahi (dolphin fish, not the mammal). You might not live on an island like I do, so fish isn't as available; but where you live has its benefits.

We have heard from many families who successfully use game meat in my recipes. They hunt and stock their freezers with deer, elk, and moose meat. One lady has access to lots of mutton, so she uses ground mutton in the same recipes that I use ground turkey.

Spend some time thinking of creative ways to provide good food within your budget.

Now about our attitudes:

As I've already said, I view myself as a professional. I'm on the hunt for the best quality products for my beloved family. These aren't just products. It is food—stuff that is going into my precious children and beloved husband. My choices can influence their health, mental acuity, disposition, and demeanor. If I make bad choices I could increase their probability of getting cancer or heart disease. If I make bad choices I could weaken their immune system and make them more susceptible to autoimmune diseases. If I make bad choices, I can stymie their education and ability to learn. By not choosing wisely, I can give them ingredients that wrongly affect their moods, their weight, and their appearance. This isn't just a "feed them something so they'll stop complaining" issue. We're talking about setting up lifelong eating habits that affect them.

Not only am I affecting their physical bodies, I'm affecting all of us by how wisely I spend the money we have. Wrong choices here can also harm them. If, because I'm too lazy, can't be bothered, or simply won't try to improve, I overspend, it affects the whole budget. Too much on food and then there isn't enough for savings or family treats or debt reduction.

I take my job of providing good, healthy food within our means, as an important job. I want you to think so, too. I'm not saying that you aren't already. But I do know that even if you agree with me that it is one of the most important things you'll do this week, you won't get the praise and encouragement you deserve. You've done a great thing if you've provided wholesome food for your family with a smile. Of course, we're supposed to do it. It's our task—it's in our "job description." But it is good work.

Buying meat in bulk logs benefits you because that is one less time the meat is handled. They have to allow it to partially thaw to reshape it into one-pound amounts. You're getting meat fresher, and then can handle it any way you want. Also, don't be fooled by some stores who merely run the packaged meat through their grinder and pass it as "ground on the premises." Sometimes you'll find a butcher who is handling and grinding raw meat. But be wary unless you hear turkeys in the back yard or see full birds on the hooks.

I applaud you. I know how much love you put into the work you do. So change the attitude about this, one person at a time. Did you regularly thank your Mom and Dad for the work they did for you? Think of all those meals Mom fixed. Give her a call and thank her. Let your children hear you. Whoa! It could start a trend . . .

Chapter 5: Methods

WHAT ARE MY OPTIONS AND HOW DO WE DO THIS?

Have you ever thought how much you use those little gray cells in managing your family's diet for one week? No wonder some people avoid their kitchens and dread going in there. On the other side, cooking seems to come naturally to some people. It is almost akin to those who can play music by ear. They do it and wonder about us who can only carry a tune via a CD player. Although we are not all called to play at Carnegie Hall, we do all eat. Being tone deaf isn't life threatening, but going without food is. We don't have to compete with five-star chefs, but somehow we have to feed our loved ones everyday.

Before you underrate yourself, think for a minute. Some of the most complicated reasoning any of us do is in getting a wonderful meal to the table. When you think of the financial savvy, precise timing, juggling of appliances, management of ingredients, and handling of labor problems, it is quite a task. I wonder if launching a new product demands as much brainpower. Yet, many of us have been doing it automatically for years—sometimes when we're tired after working hard all day.

We are combining logic with art. Corporate America has professional-sounding words to describe and give importance to their work. We could use some of those same terms in the kitchen. While they negotiate procurement contracts, we wrangle over the price of produce. They maximize the cost effectiveness of economies of scale (see below)—we buy the big jar of dressing. They mediate intricate labor contracts—we encourage our spouse and children to give a helping hand. They formulate optimal production quotients—we use the right size dish.

By using industrial engineering techniques, we are working smart. Mega-cooking™ just expands on the talent you already have in the kitchen. Take your mental calculations one step further. The good news is that there is a learning curve for this process. The more you do this, the easier it becomes. You'll soon be running with it. I've heard from thousands of mega-cooks who have made it such a part of their lifestyle that they don't have to "think"

Economies of Scale is a term used to describe the concept that the more you buy of something, the less you pay per each item. A rental car company does not pay the same price for each mini-van in its fleet that you pay when you buy one. The supplier reasons they would rather have a bunch of nickels than one dime. We can do the same. (See section on Shopping, page 72).

through each step each time. Like any acquired skill, aspects of it become rote. Enjoy and pace yourself.

In this section, we detail the ways you can start mega-cooking™. Remember to check the Topics section for specifics about a particular ingredient or method. If you aren't certain what I mean by a particular term, turn to the Topics section for clarification.

Duplicating

You don't have to start even doubling recipes. You can begin by duplicating one step. Here are some examples:

- **Onions:** Chop two onions tonight. Use one for tonight. Package the other one for use tomorrow night. You'll find that duplicating a step doesn't double your effort. Much of our work is preparing ingredients and washing the equipment.
- **Ground Meat:** As long as you are sautéing a pound of ground meat, you can do a second pound with very little extra effort. Use one pound for tonight. Store the other pound in an airtight bag and have ready for pizza tomorrow night. I try to duplicate steps as much as possible.
- **Salad:** Even with a fresh salad, you can tear the lettuce and put half in the salad bowl for tonight, the other half in a plastic bowl, and make two salads for just about 25% more effort. It takes about as long to chop two stalks of celery as one. Chop them side-by-side. Don't add any "wet" ingredients (e.g., tomatoes) to the second salad. Seal the second salad. Then tomorrow, adding some tomatoes makes your salad.
- **Dry Ingredients:** If you're making a recipe for a cake, quick bread, or biscuits, work two bowls side-by-side and mix all the dry ingredients for the recipe into each bowl. Finish the recipe in one of the bowls by adding the wet ingredients, mix, and bake. Take the other bowl of the dry ingredients, bag it and label it. You've just made your own "cake mix"—all you need to do is add the egg and water, mix, and bake on another day when you're pressed for time.

Try to duplicate steps as much as possible. Even when I'm pulling out an entrée from the freezer, I'll duplicate my work with one of the side dishes or the dessert. Remember duplicating doesn't double work, it maximizes output.

Doubling

One easy method is to start slowly. Choose one day this week when you have some time to fix a nice dinner. When you buy groceries, buy double the amount for that night's menu.

When you cook it, cook double the about. Eat one meal and freeze the extra. That gives you one meal for another night when your schedule is tight. With this method you're getting twice the results, but for little extra work. You don't have to double an entire dinner, try doubling the entrée or the dessert. Then work your way to an entire meal. At this level, you don't need to be concerned with special equipment. Instead of using your 1-quart saucepan, you'll use your 2-quart. You might want to purchase a second casserole dish. Doubling usually doesn't necessitate buying large containers or pots.

Step-by-step:

1. Once you select your recipe, calculate twice the ingredients and add them to your shopping list.
2. Buy twice as many ingredients for your recipe—take advantage of any 2-for-1 special prices or "family package" discounts.
3. Prepare as much of the recipe as possible at the same time. Cut bell peppers at the same time. Heat two cans of sauce together in the same pot.
4. Depending on the recipe, you might want to finish baking one of the meal's worth and freeze the other in a ready-to-cook mode or, you might want to bake both, eat one and freeze the other to reheat another day. The recipes in this book spell out how to do each option. Be sure to label what goes into the freezer.
5. When you are facing one of those busy days, thaw out the frozen meal ahead of time and then cook or reheat for that night's dinner. Enjoy a hot, warm, home-cooked meal without the fuss.

You'll be hooked. Plan on doubling a recipe each week.

Example: If Thursday is your low-key day, plan to double that night's cooking each week, because you know every Tuesday is a jam-packed day. Once you get some meals stored up, you can stagger the dishes. In other words you don't have to eat on Tuesday the same dish you had had on Thursday. It could be the meal you had a month ago.

When you are comfortable with that level of mega-cooking™, you might consider moving to the next stage.

Multiple Batches

This is very similar to doubling, except you're jumping to hyper-drive and making 3, 4, 6, 10 times a recipe. Until you can afford large pots, pace yourself to use the dishes on hand. The more you do this, the more you'll realize that for very little extra effort, you can make 6 times a recipe instead of just 3—that's 3 more times you don't have to cook again! Also, as you start to buy in bulk and take advantage of mega-shopping™, you'll discover the wonderful idea that often 6 times a recipe doesn't cost any more than making 2 or 3. That's like getting 3 or 4 meals *free!*

With this option you can plan to mega-cook one recipe a week.

If you mega-cook one recipe a week and make 6 times the recipe, eat one that evening, and freeze the other 5—within two months you'll have a surplus of 40 meals in your freezer ready to heat. If you continue to cook at this pace, five nights out of a week you could pick and choose wonderful home-cooked meals from your freezer—all you have to do is reheat them. Then on the seventh night of each week you could cook a meal the old-fashioned way of one-meal-at-a-time, but even then testing new recipes to add to your mega-cooking™ repertoire. Or with the money you've been saving off your food budget, you could afford to eat out, have a picnic, or invite another family for dinner.

Step-by-step:

1. Test a recipe to see if your family likes it. You don't want to make 10 times a recipe to find out it's a dud.
2. Consider your equipment (pot sizes, freezer-space, etc.), to determine how many times you want to "double" a recipe. Calculate the amount of ingredients.
3. Since you will be buying more in bulk, call for best prices. (See Mega-shopping™ section for ideas). Purchase the ingredients.
4. Prepare the recipe using as many duplicating and streamlining techniques as possible.
5. Enjoy one meal that night. Freeze the others after proper labeling.
6. Enjoy the other meals the following weeks.

This method works well, especially for families who can't afford to do an all-at-once mega-session. By spending a little more each week on groceries (at the first), you can reap long term benefits.

What if your whole family made a commitment to mega-cook for one night per week and everyone helped with the multiple-batch recipe? Then everyone would benefit the rest of the week. No one would get stuck having to fix a dinner from scratch. It really saves on the budget, because you don't have to call out for pizza, go to a drive-thru, or catch a quick bite on the way to a meeting.

Of course, you can pace this method of mega-cooking™ nights and choose to mega-cook a few recipes each month by multiple batches—to stock your freezer for those rush-around days.

Suppose next week you made eight meals worth of Tuesday night's dinner (let's say spaghetti), ate one meal, and froze the other seven. Then the second week you did the same (this time, Count Stroganov Beef), but ate one of those meals from week one on Thursday night. Then on week three you made eight meals of a different recipe (perhaps Chicken for All Seasons), had the beef on thursday and the spaghetti on Friday. Within seven weeks, you'll only have to cook on Tuesday nights. And within two months you'll have such a variety of meals you can wait weeks before you have to repeat a recipe. Here's a chart to give you a plan of attack. After each meal I've noted the number of meals you have left after you serve that one. The last two columns indicate how many meals in that week you eat from mega-cooked meals and how many from your regular cooking methods.

	Sunday	Monday	Tuesday	Wednesday	Thursday	Friday	Saturday	Meals from Mega-cooking	Meals from regular cooking
week 1			Spaghetti (+7)					1	6
week 2			Count Strog-anov Beef (+7)		Spaghetti (6)			2	5
week 3			Chicken for All Seasons (+7)		Count Strog-anov Beef (6)	Spaghetti (5)		3	4
week 4		Count Strog-anov Beef (5)	Cinquo de Mayo (+7)	Chicken for All Seasons (6)			Spaghetti (6)	4	3
week 5		Cinquo de Mayo (6)	Fish (+7)		Spaghetti (3)	Chicken for All Seasons (5)	Count Strog-anov Beef (4)	5	2
week 6		Spaghetti (2)	Porkie Pines (+7)	Fish (6)	Cinquo de Mayo (3)	Count Strog-anov Beef (4)	Chicken for All Seasons (5)	6	1
week 7	Fish (5)	Chicken for All Seasons (4)	Roast (+7)	Cinquo de Mayo (4)	Count Strog-anov Beef (2)	Spaghetti (1)	Porkie Pines (6)	7	0
week 8	Roast (6)	Count Strog-anov Beef (1)	German Dinner (+7)	Spaghetti (0)	Fish (4)	Porkie Pines (5)	Cinquo de Mayo (3)	7	0
week 9	Porkie Pines (4)	Fish (1)	Meat Loaves (+7)	Cinquo de Mayo (2)	Count Strog-anov Beef (0)	German Dinner (6)	Roast (6)	7	0

In summary, if you simply set aside one night a week to make a mega-batch of the recipe you're already preparing for dinner, soon (within seven weeks) you'll have to cook from scratch one night a week and the remaining days you'll have delicious home-cooked, frozen dinner. Just think how fast the meals would accumulate and what a variety you'd have if you mega-batched twice a week.

When you feel comfortable working with large quantities of food, you might want to consider working up to the next level.

Don't think of your dinner meals. We multi-batch lunches and breakfasts. Some desserts do great, as well.

Mini-Mega and Medium-Mega Sessions

This level of mega-cooking™ is more complicated than multiple batches, but not as intense as a full mega-session. With mini-megas, you'll be multiple-batching several similar recipes. These sessions take more time than multiple-batching a single recipe and, of course, you have to consider the initial increase in your food budget, as well as your supplies and equipment.

The rewards are real. Within a few hours, you could have 20 to 50 recipes ready for storage for later use. You can do a mini-mega in an evening, but plan well. I think these sessions work best for days when you're home all day. I recommend you start slowly and work your way up.

Start with a mini-mega session (2 to 4 different recipes which you multiple batch) and work your way to a medium-mega session (5 to 10 different recipes which you multiple batch).

With mini-megas and medium-megas, you'll want to select recipes that either have similar ingredients or have similar processing needs.

Example: Make all your recipes using cooked ground meat on one day. Purchase 50 pounds of ground meat at bargain prices (I've saved a full $1.00 a pound by purchasing 80 pounds at a time.) Brown all the meat. Store in the refrigerator as you work through each of the recipes. You'll benefit from processing all the produce at one time. If five of your recipes call for chopped onions, you'll peel and process all those onions at one time. I think you'll be pleasantly surprised at how quickly you can process a whole bag of onions once you get a method. It only takes a few more minutes, especially if you have a food processor. After you handle all the ingredients as you did the onions, start assembling the recipes.

The beauty of this method is that you can definitely take advantage of big savings by buying ingredients in bulk and you save time by combining tasks and streamlining your effort. I estimate it only takes about 6 hours for a mini-mega to complete 50 meals. Compare that to the 50+ hours it would have taken you to make those same recipes the old one-meal-at-a-time method.

A soup mini-mega, making five different soups, would flow well with assembly line processing.

A raw meat mini-mega in which you make batches of hamburgers, meatballs, meat loaves, and Salisbury steaks, would maximize time and effort.

Grill dozens of chicken breasts for a variety of recipes (see Chicken for All Seasons, page 275), for a chicken mini-mega.

With poultry mini-mega, bake a few turkeys and use the meat for several recipes that call for de-boned chicken.

There are so many ways to plan a mini-mega—it's up to you.

Step-by-step:

1. Plan well. Select recipes that are similar. To save money, choose recipes that call for as many of the same ingredients as possible to hold the cost down. To

save time, choose recipes that have similar steps that can be overlapped and assembly-lined. Plan your cooking. The first few times, you might want to literally plan out the steps and work out a schedule. As you get more proficient, you'll be able to just keep the information in your head and refer to the recipes for amounts.

2. Make your Ingredients List using the method described on page 39.
3. Call for best prices. Buy your ingredients.
4. Follow your plan for processing the ingredients and assembling the meals.
5. Store the completed meals properly.
6. Enjoy and use the prepared foods wisely. (See Serving section, page 129 for ideas.)

Remember to pace yourself. You're learning more each time you do this. I've heard from families who took days to do their first medium-mega-session, but the next time they did the same plan, they cut their time in half. They had learned what they were doing and discovered more ways to combine steps to make their work easier.

Don't overwhelm yourself. Please! Don't invest in more ingredients than you can handle, then feel terrible because the eggplant is going bad and you still haven't finished processing the zucchini.

Make a reasonable plan. You know who is helping you and their ability. When I'm working on a schedule, I adjust for skill level. I figure that a job that would take me 15 minutes to complete will take Stuart thirty minutes, Bethany Kay about an hour and Alan 5 to 10 minutes. I know my family and even with allowances for differences in skill, I always add in "bonus" time—time for those unexpected phone calls, spills, and other complications.

Mega-session

This is the big one, friends. This level requires the most work, the largest funding, the most time. It also yields the best return for that investment. As I wrote earlier, quite a few mega-cooks started at this level. They read *Dinner's in the Freezer!* and went right out and cooked enough for months worth of food. They amaze me!

I started at the multiple-batch level when I was pregnant with our first child. Once he was born, it was wonderful—the freezer was stocked with food. We then started with mini-megas and moved to medium-megas. For several years we cooked 3-4 months worth of food over a three-day weekend. Then one time I decided to add a few new recipes and made x8 a recipe instead of x6. We made enough food for 6-months (dinners only) in the same time frame (a three-day weekend) and when we totaled all the receipts, we found we had not spent any more than the previous time we cooked for 4 months only. Able to take advantage of bigger discounts, we kept perfecting the processing. It was wonderful.

Case History: I know of a lovely lady in Indianapolis who mega-cooks once a year. She stocks two freezers and her family loves it. She works with her local grocer who is fascinated with her program. He looks at it as a challenge and a change in his routine. She talks over her menu plan with him weeks in advance and he starts hunting for deals and good buys. This program works wonderfully for her family because she has a special needs child. She can make all their food from scratch (according to his dietary needs) and then she has all that time to work with him through his therapies each day.

Planning and completing a mega-session is a commitment. Even for me. In the middle of it, you'll wonder why you're doing it and wish you'd never heard of the concept. When you look around and see hundreds of dollars of groceries and realize you're committed, encourage yourself with the benefits. That's why I took the space to point those out in the first chapter. But believe me, though it is *work* during the session, three weeks later you'll be so pleased. I've heard from thousands of families who love it—once it's done.

During the mega-session, I do all I can to make it run smoothly. We rent some movies and some books on tape. We make it an event. We don't allow any other activities into our lives that weekend. We schedule it on a three-day weekend, usually. Several years ago we tackled it during the Thanksgiving holidays when Alan was home for five days. He took a vacation day on the Wednesday before Thanksgiving for the mega-shopping. I know that sounds crazy because of all the last-minute shoppers hunting for turkeys, but we had a great time going out in the morning. Sales galore! Prices were terrific. I say all that to say this: dedicate most of your time for several days to this project. My mom prays for us during that weekend and then calls, "Are you all talking to each other still?"

In other words, don't invite your boss over for dinner during a mega-session. None of us needs that added pressure.

Step-by-step:

1. Plan well. Many of you will have quite a repertoire of recipes that you have prepared in multiple batches or mini-sessions. Select your recipes. Make your Ingredients Lists. Plan your attack. Schedule your time. Delegate tasks.
2. Mega-shop.
3. Prepare ingredients for assembly into recipes. (See Streamlining Techniques, following).
4. Assemble recipes.
5. Divide.

6. Store properly.
7. Use wisely.

It sounds simple. It basically is. The complication comes as you try to maximize your time and equipment. You're basically combining tasks and recipes of several mini or medium sessions and doing them all during the same time frame.

You'll be maximizing your finances, your equipment, your skills, and your patience. The rewards are well worth it. Remember that you're accomplishing in only 3 days what would have taken you 180+ hours to prepare.

Techniques

STREAMLINING

Similar to duplicating, streamlining is going a few steps further and trying to work smart. It's not that we're lazy, rather we have better things to do with our time than waste it doing repetitive tasks.

Think of all the things you do over and over to prepare meals. How many of those can be combined, simplified, automated, or ignored?

- **Combinations:** Are their any steps that you can combine? If three of your recipes call for white sauce, make one big pot of white sauce and then divide it for the different recipes. We boil three dozen eggs at the same time to go into several recipes. Slice some and chop some depending on what each recipe needs. We combine every possible step from several recipes so we don't ever have to duplicate our efforts.
- **Simplification:** We simplify recipes. We think through the logic of recipes and figure out easier ways to do them. For example, with recipes using cooked stew meat, we don't want the meat in the 3-inch pieces from the butcher. But it takes hours to hand cut all that meat into ½-inch cubes. We found that if we cook the meat thoroughly in the 3-inch pieces, allow them to cool, we can quickly cut those cooked pieces with a pair of kitchen shears. We save at least 2 hours in processing time doing meat this way.

  You'll find our ideas for simplification for particular recipes written with the recipe. We encourage you to be creative with your own recipes. Always look for ways to simplify the processing. Even saving a few minutes here and there adds up during the course of a mega-session.
- **Automation:** We talked about this in the equipment session, but if I can find a machine to saving me time, I use it. If I only had to slice one carrot, I wouldn't

use my food processor. It is much quicker to grab a knife and do it by hand. Whenever I consider using equipment, I calculate the whole time—including set-up, use, cleaning, and storage. That's the beauty of mega-cooking™—it pays to use the equipment. It is worth the time to set-up the DLX to handle 100 pounds of carrots. It makes the work a breeze. It doesn't make sense to set up your beater attachment for one egg, but it is worth the effort to beat several dozen eggs at one time. We try to automate as much of the preparation as possible.

- **Elimination:** Very closely linked to simplification is elimination. We totally skip steps in recipes. For example, if a recipe calls for sautéd vegetables, we don't. We've found that we don't need the extra fat, the fat doesn't freeze well (it weakens the molecular structure of the food), and it "cheapens" the naturally good taste of the produce.

  Another example of eliminating steps is with pasta. With many pasta dishes, we don't have to cook the pasta first. For recipes that are going directly to the freezer and have a moist sauce, we rinse the pasta and add it in dry. Lasagna for instance works great this way. Build your layers with uncooked pasta. Add about 25% more water to the recipe than you would have other wise. While it is in the freezer, the pasta absorbs that moisture. It finishes softening during the long cooking time.

  In my recipes, I've already eliminated many time wasters. As you rewrite your own recipes, you'll want to be on the look out for steps that you can skip. Always ask "why" and you'll find that some of the techniques of cooking have changed since your cookbook was written, or that those steps were written for the one-meal-at-a-time method.

ASSEMBLY-LINE PROCESSING

This is what makes it possible to build 80 recipes in six hours. We "pre-fabricate" the ingredients. We go ahead and have the meat cooked, the onions grated, the bell peppers chopped, and the beige sauce ready for customizing. We have all these ingredients stored in the refrigerator ready for use. All this pre-preparing was done the first day. *Note:* with some produce, you'll want to spray it with Brown Away (mix one cup of water and one tablespoon of lemon juice) to keep it from darkening.

When I start assembling a new recipe, I make certain that we have prepared all the ingredients ahead. I start with a big container and begin to assemble all the wet ingredients to make a "sauce." *Note:* This is a key to getting a good mix and a proper consistency. When you made a single recipe, you could mix the ingredients together and not have to pay close attention. But when you're working with this much food, you have to consider mixing. In almost every recipe, we combine all the liquid ingredients together to get an even distribution. Even if it is ketchup and tomato sauce, we mix it together. We also mix all the spices together and then add them to the "liquid sauce." We've learned from years of experience that it is difficult to get the spices evenly dispersed in a x10 batch of a recipe. By mixing all the spices together dry, they are evenly mixed and can be folded into the "sauce." We then mix together the dry ingredients carefully. Sometimes we do this by hand. We don't want to damage or crush the dry ingredients. Then we gently fold in the liquid "sauce," stirring just enough to get a good mix.

As much as I like to streamline steps and eliminate wastefulness, this added step is well worth the effort. It makes less work for you and more tasty food. An example: if you stirred your chili hard enough to get all the spices and liquids evenly distributed, you'd ruin the beans.

Step-by-step:
When you are working with many recipes, you'll want to

1. Mix together all of the wet ingredients to make a "sauce."
2. In a separate bowl, mix together all the herbs and spices, so they are well blended.
3. Mix these spices into the liquid "sauce" until they are evenly distributed.
4. Gently combine all the dry ingredients, being careful to get an even distribution.
5. Fold the wet "sauce" into the dry ingredients gently. You don't want to crush the dry ingredients.

For a "Goosh-form" recipe: Assembling a recipe is a simple thing. Usually the ingredients are cold (stored in the refrigerator—we'll explain more about the concept of "make cold" on page 115). We open cans, jars, or bottles and make the sauce adding the appropriate flavorings of spices and herbs. In another bowl, we measure the dry ingredients. Then combine the dry and wet. At this stage of a recipe, the actual "building" of the recipe takes 10 to 15 minutes. I pass the mix over to Alan and he divides, labels, and bags that mix, while I'm combining the ingredients for the next recipe.

For a Layer-form recipe: I'll set out each of the ingredients in open bowls on the table in order of their use. My children each take a bag or pan and walk around the table, stacking in the ingredients into their bag. They think this is fun. For example with Seven Layer dinner, the children each will take a lined mold pan and begin to stack ingredients in their pans. We vary this by one child doing all the potatoes and one child stacking in the carrots.

It goes very quickly. When the pan is full, we seal it, label it and put it into the freezer. Remember, these ingredients are cold so I don't worry about freezer burns. There is very little heat to remove so the food freezes quickly.

I think you're beginning to see how easy the actual assembly is. The roughest part of the mega-session is the pre-preparation stage. You'll work all the first day and not feel like you've accomplished much because you don't have very many meals to show for your work. But the next day, the meals fall together. You use all those ingredients you chopped, cooked, or mixed the day before. You'll be thrilled when the meals start stacking up.

Remember to figure in the freezing capacity of your equipment. A freezer can only "freeze" about one shelf's worth of food in a 24-hour period. We are very careful how we distribute our food, and we have very little heat to remove from the food we put in there. Our food is "freezing" in hours, not days.

While you are assembling these recipes, you'll want to refer to your recipes and the Ingredients List often. You'll be glad you took the time to plan. If you don't monitor the use of the ingredients you could be too generous in the early recipes and run short in the ones you do later that day. For example, if you are assembling five cooked ground meat recipes, you might look at the huge bin full of meat and add too much to the first recipe. Refer to the Ingredients List so you'll know which recipes need which ingredients and you won't run short.

SOME ASSEMBLY REQUIRED (SAR)

Don't feel that all your recipes have to be completely ready to heat and eat. We freeze several recipes in various stages of preparation. We freeze a dozen packets of cooked and crumbled ground meat for use in pizzas. We buy a 10-pound package of grated cheese (we can get it grated for no extra fee) and divide it into one-cup packages. We do make our own pizza sauce (see recipe on page 357) and divide it into one-pizza's worth sizes. We do the same thing with all the ingredients. We even make a whole bunch of pizza rounds, half-baked, and wrap and freeze them. When we want pizza, we simply grab a round, a few packets, and with a little effort we're ready to bake it. Delicious, and about 1/10th the price of delivery.

We do the same thing with fajitas. We cook fajita meat and divide it up into meal-sized portions. We buy tortillas in bulk for pennies each and freeze them in meal-sized amounts. When we want fajitas, we pull the appropriate bags, add some fresh lettuce and tomatoes, and we have a fun and delicious dinner.

We do the same thing for quiche. We keep packets of the quiche ingredients in the freezer in properly measured amounts. Then it is a quick assembly to be oven-ready. You'll notice other ideas and suggestions in the Recipe Section. Keep in mind that many recipes can be done in the SAR mode, still be considered convenience meals, and yet fit perfectly into your mega-cooking™ style.

MEGA-SHOPPING ONLY

Some families choose to mega-shop, though they might not mega-cook. They make all their meals the SAR way. They buy in bulk, divide the ingredients into meal-sized portions and then cook them in regular fashion. This saves hundreds of dollars a year, and is worth considering. More on mega-shopping on page 72.

Other specific steps or cooking techniques are detailed in the topics section. The recipes in this book already include ways and methods to incorporate these ideas. As you rewrite your recipes, you'll want to consider these time saving methods.

Examples

Here are two examples of how we process some ingredients and incorporate them into our mega-cooking™:

- **Onions:** We process a 50-pound bag of onions all at once. Alan peels them and quickly quarters them. We need that size reduction to fit into our food processor. One of our children will stand at the DLX and feed those onions through the grater and let the grated onion fall into a clean bucket. We then seal them into airtight containers and refrigerate for use in recipes. We don't sauté onions, no matter what the recipe says. We find we don't need the extra fat, plus fat doesn't freeze well. For any recipe that calls for sautéed onions, we simply add raw. We've also found that by not sautéing onions we don't lose as much flavor, and thus don't need as many onions per recipe. I usually half the amount required of a "normal" recipe, to avoid a recipe being overwhelmed. Also consider the "marinating" effect the onion will have as it freezes. Since 50 pounds is usually more than I need for a mega-session, we freeze some of the onions on flat trays and then bag them (Individual Freezing Method). We also dehydrate the rest for use in dozens of other recipes, for seasoning, and for salads.
- **Apples:** Let's consider apples. In the fall I buy apples for great prices from the farmer's market. We buy several cases (boxes) of a variety. We'll process them a variety of ways depending on what recipes I'll need them for. In the German recipe, Deutsche Brats (page 306), I use peeled, sliced apples (similar to what you'd use in a standard apple pie). We'll use our apple corer/slicer and assembly-line process 2 to 3 boxes worth in about an hour's time. We start immediately to dehydrate the peeling.

Note: As we process the apples, we spray them with Brown Away (see page 373) to keep them from darkening.

When the peeling is dry (overnight is plenty of time), we blend it into powder form using a blender/chopper. It takes only seconds. We then put this apple powder in jars and seal air tight. It makes a wonderful seasoning for muffins, cakes, and breads and a good "sprinkle" over ice cream or other desserts.

Depending on what recipes we're working on, we'll take the apple slices, freeze some (Individual Freezing Method), dehydrate others, and make "pie filling" with some. With the pie filling we fill a 9-inch pie pan, letting it freeze in that shape. Then when we want to bake a pie we take a pastry circle out of the freezer, add the already shaped frozen pie filling, top it with some Dutch crumble topping mixed with apple powder and bake it. Delicious and easy.

Dutch crumble topping is simple to make. In a medium bowl combine 2 cups of flour, 1 cup of sugar (or substitute), ½ cup of softened butter, 1 tablespoon of apple powder (optional), and 1 teaspoon of cinnamon. Mix together into a crumbling topping. Sprinkle over the pie. It bakes wonderfully. For an even better taste, add apple powder to the flour when you make the pastry. Then you'll have Triple Apple Pie.

Chapter 6: Storage

NOW THAT I'VE COOKED ALL OF THIS, HOW DO I KEEP IT FROM SPOILING?

Food goes bad. If it doesn't go bad, it isn't food. The fact that food will spoil is really a good thing. It means it has some nutritional value to our bodies. But part of our job has been to slow down that rate of decay. Mankind has been doing this for a very long time: some methods work well, some are too expensive for the average home cook, and some new methods are being developed.

Since this isn't a treatise on the history of food preservation, I'll stick with explaining the options available to most of us: freezing, dehydrating, canning, vacuum sealing, and a few other methods.

Freezing

Freezing is the most popular method of food preservation. It is my main option because it works so well. Freezers are wonderful investments that pay for themselves very quickly. But to get the most benefit out of your freezer, you need to know a little bit about what we are doing.

Has your food ever had freezer burn? Does the idea of eating previously frozen food sound horrible? Has your experience with frozen food been awful?

If you learn a few principles of freezing, you can completely eliminate any of those freezing problems and have food that is delicious, attractive, and nutritious.

HEAT REMOVAL

I'm about to tell you something that will really help some of you. It will change forever the way you store food. You will get it instantly. And go, Oh! I get it! Then there will be some dear ones of you who will say, "Huh?" But continue reading and then understand more as you read and cook and store. Then there will be some of you who have gifts in other areas who will meet me in Heaven and say, "I never did understand what you were talking about." But somehow, then I don't think it'll matter.

You Can't Freeze Food.

There is No Scientific Reaction That "Makes Cold."

> I present this same message in my cooking classes and almost without fail, one third of the audience grasps the concept immediately and runs with it. One third starts to understand and by the end of the day can apply the principles. And there's always one third who shake their heads and never quite understand what I'm saying. But for those two thirds that can use this concept, it makes all the difference in the way your food will "behave" during storage.

Though we say we are "freezing" food, what we really are doing is "removing heat."

What I'm talking about is more than just word play or semantics.

This is a fundamental concept of mega-cooking™. Again, if you don't understand the science behind the concept, use it anyway. How many of us understand the telephone or our computer, but we still can use them beneficially.

A freezer removes heat from our food.

The less heat in the food, the less heat to be removed, and the faster it "freezes."

When I put food in my freezer, 90% is about 40°F (refrigerator cold). The freezer can quickly remove that initial 8°F and then complete the process of taking the food down to 0°. It happens very quickly.

The quicker the food's heat is removed, the nicer the texture, the less ice formation, the less freezer burn.

So, as you work with your food keep that constantly in mind. Put a note on the freezer if you need a reminder. Ask yourself about any food you put in the freezer, "How much heat has to be removed?"

Most freezers can only remove about one shelf's worth of heat during a 24-hour period. So, how can I make 6-months worth of food during a long weekend? The reason it works and works so well, is that I'm working with ingredients from my refrigerator. I've already cooked the ground meat and it is cold in the refrigerator. I'm simply assembling cold ingredients, bagging them and then putting in the freezer. There isn't a lot of heat to remove. So, my food "freezes" quickly.

ALAN: As heat is removed from a compound, the molecules slow down. They also begin to rearrange their structure. When some food is heated their molecules move and dance. Scientists are discovering the benefits of deep freezing. They are rapidly removing heat from items to promote a more structured bonding pattern. They are finding it improves metals (and other elements) to freeze them. Musicians are paying to have their brass instruments frozen to improve their performance. Industrialists are learning that deep-freezing improves the durability and tensile strength of products. Even pantyhose which have been through the deep freeze will last much longer.

Imagine a bunch of children running around on a playground wherever they want in a totally random manner. That's what the molecules look like in a warm or hot substance.

> Now imagine that same group of children stopping their random play and starting to organize into lines or into a marching band. That's what happens to the molecules as heat is removed. The random structure begins to gain order and structure. That is what is happening with your food as you "freeze" it. (Scientists know there is more involved, but please allow me this basic explanation. This is, after all, a cookbook, not a science text. I know there are many variables and not all compounds behave identically; but for many foods this concept applies, and an understanding at a basic level can benefit some cooks.)

I am controlling that structure by controlling the time factor. I set my freezer at "Quick Freeze" to maximize its heat removing ability. I'm putting in cold food. But I'm also managing the food's placement in the freezer.

I'm not turning on an empty freezer, loading it all at once with six-month's worth of cooked food, then expecting it to remove heat immediately.

Weeks before a mega-session, I've stocked my freezer with plastic cartons filled with water. They are now ice. That ice will help the freezer with heat removal later.

As we assemble meals, we label and put them in the freezer, spacing them among already frozen items and the blocks of ice. This process works quickly. We then assemble another recipe and add it. During the period of three-to-four days we have frozen all the recipes.

For those of you who are going to cook using the multi-batching method you can easily remove the heat from the food headed to the freezer. Bake a batch, let it cool in the refrigerator, and then place it in the freezer. Or you can add one or two warm dishes directly into the freezer and place it next to ice. Be careful about ever adding hot items to the freezer next to already frozen items. You don't want your previously frozen foods to begin to absorb heat and thaw. For that reason, I don't put hot items in my freezer. (One help is to use the Bag-in-Box method (see page 117) because of the minor insulating effect of the cardboard.) In most circumstances, if you follow these recipes and guidelines, the heat removal of your foods should work well.

Summary: Revise how you think about freezing. Instead of thinking that you are making your food cold, think about it as removing heat. Then do what you can to minimize the amount of heat you have to remove from your food. Aid your freezer in removing heat by keeping it packed with ice and then add in cold food.

MASS AND VOLUME

In addition to monitoring the amount of heat I need to remove from my foods, I also pay careful attention to the mass and volume. I try to minimize the bulk and maximize the surface area.

Picture one gallon of water spread out in your bathtub. It is very shallow. If you froze that much water in that shape, its heat would be removed quickly—it would freeze fast! Now picture that same gallon of water in a tight drum or container. It is deep. It will take longer for a freezer to remove that heat. It freezes slower.

The same thing happens with your food. I'm freezing my food in cubic rectangles only an inch or two thick. The heat can be removed more quickly than if I formed that same volume of food in a cube that was 6 inches thick.

When you freeze the food in blocks, the food in the middle of the cube is still warm and that heat then passes through the outer layers and affects the structure. You get a change in taste and texture of your food. Instead try to shape your food in long, shallow shapes. Try to avoid deep, short shapes. Not only will this improve texture and flavor (we sped up the heat removal), but it will cut the thawing time in half.

If you like doing experiments, freeze one half gallon of water in a cube shape and freeze another half gallon of water in a jelly roll pan. Time how long it takes to freeze both. Then time how long it takes for both to completely thaw. You'll see what I'm talking about. Now for that same reason, I want my ice (that I'm using to help my freezer) to be in thick, deep cubes. Its job is to not thaw quickly. The outer edges of the ice are absorbing the heat from my food, but the inside is still ice.

Note: I also use those ice blocks to "extend" my refrigerator space. I'll place a dozen half-gallon cartons of frozen water in my bathtub with some fresh produce to keep it chilled until I can process it. For those of you up North, you can use your back porch as a backup refrigerator or as an adjunct to your freezer (depending on the outside temperature).

Summary: Maximize the surface area of what you are freezing to speed heat removal. Freeze your food in shallow, long, wide shapes, rather than thick, deep, shapes. The closer the center is to the surface, the faster heat transfers out.

MAKING IT AIRTIGHT

Why all the fuss about making the containers airtight? It is critical. Let me explain. The exposure to air affects the moisture content of the food. As the heat is being removed, so is the water vapor. Think of it as condensation in reverse. How we prevent that loss of moisture is by trapping that water vapor in with the use of airtight containers.

It's not the air getting in as much as water getting out.

If you've been trying to keep air out, you probably have some problems with freezer burn. What you should think about is locking moisture in.

That may seem like the same thing, but it's not. It does affect how you wrap and handle food.

Let me give you an example. If all I concern myself with is keeping air out, then I can use a container with 6 inches of headroom. I can use a gallon container for only a half-gallon amount of food. Then I can seal it and all is okay, right? No. When the water vapor rises, and condenses, and forms in that airspace, it leaves the food and changes its texture—the dreaded crystallization and dry look. You could reason that if the moisture hasn't left the container, (if you don't open), when it thaws the water will go back to the food. Yes, but sometimes it sits on top of the food. It doesn't necessarily go back to the same position in the structure of the food. We get food that separates, or runs—it can look and taste horrible.

Instead, minimize the headroom. Use the proper size container. Leave less than 10% headroom in a hard container for expansion. With plastic bags and wrap, form it tightly. Don't leave any air inside the container for the moisture to evaporate out of the food so that it stays where you want it—in the confines of the sauce, the meat, or the vegetables.

Summary: Make a package airtight to keep moisture in. Minimize the headroom of the container. Use appropriate-sized containers—a quart container for quart amounts.

Methods

There are several methods to help you maximize the removal of heat from your food, and make the food easier to use later.

Bag-in-Box Method: I use this technique more than any other method for freezing. I collect, save, and hoard cardboard boxes. In a cabinet above my hot water heater, I have a "collection" of cereal, pasta, cracker, and tea boxes (friends save them for me also) in a variety of shapes and sizes. When it is time to freeze something, I choose the approximate size box and a re-sealable freezer bag. I place the bag in the box, hanging the edges over the box rim. The box then holds up the sides of the bag for me as I fill the bag. Once all the ingredients are in the bag, we close the bag—forcing out any extra air. We then freeze the bag inside the box. The ingredients then freeze in the shape of the box—a nice neat cubic-rectangle. Once it is frozen solid (the heat is removed), we slide the bag from the box and pack the frozen "brick" in tightly with other frozen food bricks.

This method solves several problems:

1. *Your Third Hand:* Sometimes it is difficult to pour a liquid into a bag as you try to keep it from falling over. It seems you need three hands: one to hold the bag open, one to spoon the ingredients in, and one to tilt the pan. With the Bag-in-Box method, the box acts as a third hand.

2. *No More Shelf-grabbing Bags:* If you aren't careful with freezing bags, gravity works to complicate your life—the liquid in the bag "reaches down and grabs" the metal shelves. The only way to get that bag out of the freezer is to remove the shelf, let the item thaw, and then "pry" it off. By using the box, the liquid keeps in a regulated form—one you want.
3. *Good Use of Space:* Since you'll be forming squared bricks, you can pack your freezer tightly using every bit of available space. When freezing, you want airflow around the food. However, once the heat is removed and the item is frozen solid, you can pack the food as compactly as you want.
4. *Economy:* The boxes are free! And the bags, if properly handled and cleaned, can be used and reused several times. (If you are working through a mega-session and have a lot of heat to remove from your food, you can help somewhat by freezing the boxes and pulling them out when you need them. Cardboard can be used as insulation, though the effect is minor.)

Individual Freezing: Another method of freezing I use quite often is freezing items individually.

- *Dry Items:* I use trays or flat pans. I place pieces of food on these trays so they don't touch each other. I set the tray in the freezer. I keep one shelf set aside during a mega-cook for exactly this purpose. The heat is removed from each item quickly. When they are frozen, we dump them into a plastic bag. Within minutes, the bag of individually frozen items is back in the freezer. Then whenever I want to use one or a few of those items, I can reach in the bag and pull out one or a dozen. Leaving the bag in the freezer and resealing quickly, I don't harm the remaining food. I can then thaw or process the food however I want.

  This works wonderfully for many dry items like fruits, vegetables, and a few other items. For example, we buy flats of grapes. We wash and dry them. Then we spread them on several trays. We stack the trays level on the freezer shelf. Within hours the grapes are frozen. We can quickly slide them into a plastic freezer bag and put it right in the freezer. I can then open the bag and pull out one frozen grape or a dozen. Since they were frozen individually, they don't clump together.

  Another example I hear often pertains to blueberries. People wash them, put them in a bag, and freeze them. The berries will freeze as one big clump, and the only way to use them is to let them completely thaw, leaving a soggy mess. So they decide you can't freeze blueberries.

But if you take those same blueberries and freeze them individually, you can then pull a cup's worth of blueberries to put into muffins. They are intact and work wonderfully. Depending on the application, you usually can put them in a recipe frozen and they will thaw and become wonderful as the food bakes. This is especially effective in muffins and other bread-like products.

We do this individual technique with many of our vegetables, and almost all of our extra fruit that we freeze. Depending on what I'm freezing, I may not take the time to make the tray airtight. With most fruits, the tiny bit of moisture loss during the brief freezing doesn't affect the taste or texture. But if an item is larger in size and will take a longer than a few hours to freeze, I'll cover the tray with plastic wrap to seal in that moisture.

Try to make the sizes of the items as uniform as possible. The smaller the individual pieces the quicker they freeze. Blueberries should freeze in 1 to 2 hours, and grapes in 2 to 3 hours. I try not to ever use this method on items much larger than the size of a grape. If I want to freeze a big strawberry, I cut it into smaller pieces.

- ***Liquid Items:*** If you want to freeze items that are more liquid and won't hold their shape on a tray, then use molds. My favorite method is to use ice cube trays.

Get good ice cube trays. Have you ever noticed how the trays that came with your freezer last for years, but the ones you buy at the dollar sale last only a few months? It has to do with the quality of plastic used. I buy my freezer trays from an appliance store for a little more than the cheaper trays and they last for years. I also look for appliance-quality trays at garage sales and swap shops.

I freeze all sorts of items in the ice cube trays. When it is solid, we pop the cubes and bag them. I can then use one cube or a dozen depending on the application.

I know my ice cubes are 2 ounces so I can use them in recipes very easily. Not only do we freeze all sorts of juice, but we also freeze sauces, gravies, and other liquid ingredients.

It is important to keep the trays straight—it can get confusing to know what is in an ice tray. We have written a number on the end of each tray with a permanent marker. We then keep a piece of paper on the refrigerator noting what is in each tray. It may seem simple to remember or that you can identify the ingredient easily, but believe me, we've learned the hard way. One of my sons forgot to mark down what he had frozen. He bagged it and didn't label the bag either. He then made a gallon of peachade, instead of lemonade. Any time we have any leftover juice, sauce or gravy, we fill an ice tray, note on the piece of paper the tray number and what it is. Then when it is solid, we can pop it and add it to a bag already filled with those kind of frozen cubes, or start a new bag. And we try to label every bag. This works well with a roux for a gravy. If I don't need to make gravy or have more than I'll need, I'll freeze the roux in 2-ounce amounts. Then I can make a delicious gravy another day using one of those roux cubes.

When I'm working with something that I want a larger size than 2-ounces, I use muffin tins. We use this idea with several of the "custard" type recipes or with a meat loaf-type recipe. We'll fill the muffin tin with the batter, freeze, and then pop it out and place it in a bag. That way I have the shape I want, quantity I want, but I don't tie up my muffin tins in the freezer. I can use the muffin tins as I need them during the week. Then when it comes time to bake those muffin-shaped ingredients, I pull them out of their bag (as many as I need), put them back in the tin, and bake.

Molds: Similar to working and freezing individually is how I use my mold shapes. I don't have dozens of extra pans that I can keep in my freezer. I need those pans during the weeks for baking. So, when I'm working with a recipe that requires a definite form, I freeze it in the mold. Pop it out of the pan. Bag it or wrap it in plastic wrap and put it back in the freezer before it has a chance to thaw.

Because glass is so rigid, it is almost impossible to "pop" out frozen food from them. So, I either use metal that gives a little (and then I can pop out the frozen ingredients), or I use plastic. Often, I use molds made for gelatin. The food freezes in shape perfectly. When it is frozen, we repackage in a bag or with wrap. Then we thaw on a baking dish and it keeps its shape. This only works with a very thick recipe like meat loaf. If the recipe is at all pourable, then it will loose shape as it thaws.

Another option is to line the mold with plastic wrap or a Teflon® sheet. Then you can lift out the ingredients.

Concentrate: Whenever possible I freeze a concentrate version of a recipe. My freezer space is valuable. I want it packed with food, not extra water. I can add water (or other liquids) to ingredients when I reheat them. So whenever I make soup, I make a concentrate. I then add water when we heat it up. When I make spaghetti sauce, I make a concentrate. We add water when we use it in a recipe. You want to use your freezer space to its maximum capacity. Think as you work through your recipes how you can use this concentrate idea to give yourself more space.

AIR SPACE

As you freeze food, you'll want some airspace until it is completely frozen. Once food is frozen solid, you can pack it tightly, not wasting a square centimeter of room.

At first, you do want airflow around the container (NOT the food itself). That airflow is working overtime to remove the heat. So, as we work we place the new items on shelves by themselves so that they have plenty of airflow. As the freezer begins to fill up, we don't have as much space to use; we'll place the ice blocks next to the new items to aid in heat absorption.

Then as the food freezes, we move it down into a tightly-packed shelf, using every available space. That's why I like to freeze in rectangles—we don't waste space. If we froze in rounds, it would be good for the initial air flow we need for quick freezing, but then that same air flow would work against us in use of space and in maintaining that constant freezing temperature. So, it really isn't contradictory.

A packed freezer is more cost effective because it runs more efficiently.

As you use your food, replace items with cartons of ice. Keep it packed tightly. That same air space that allowed for heat removal is also making your freezer use more energy—wasting your money on energy bills.

MATERIALS

We are fortunate to have a wide variety of freezing containers available. It wasn't that long ago the options were waxed boxes and little else.

Plastic Forms: They have their purpose and I use them regularly. I caution you to use the right-sized container. Don't use one twice the size you need. That headroom will defeat all the work you've done to insure quality taste. The plastic bowls, tubs, and bins can work well for you. They are ideal for liquid ingredients. Just use square shapes, not round ones. Make certain you have the lids on properly and you've expelled any extra air (sort of like burping them). To label, you can use a grease pencil on the smooth surface. It then will wipe off for the next time. *Note:* this only works on a smooth surface; if the surface is textured, it will not wipe off.

Advantages:

1. Reusable—Buy it once and use the same piece hundreds of times.
2. Airtight—They have engineered perfect sealing.
3. Free—You can earn "free" plastic containers by hosting a party.
4. Lifetime Guarantee—If it breaks, you can have it replaced (check for limitations).
5. Shape Definer—Excellent for molds and yielding a particular shape.

Disadvantages:

1. Expensive—It can be costly to use for everything you freeze (unless you host a really big party).
2. Possibility of wasted space—both space inside the container and around it.
3. Brittle—The plastic becomes brittle and can break if dropped.

Freezer Bags: I use freezer bags more than any other material because I like the way they seal and can be shaped. See above for use with the Bag-in-Box method and with individual freezing.

Advantages:

1. Low in cost—Buy in bulk.
2. Reusable—Clean them well. Don't reuse any from a tomato-based recipe. Wash them immediately. Don't let the food residue have a chance to contaminate the bag. Dry well.
3. Freeform—You can shape them any way you want to maximize your available freezer space
4. No headroom—You can remove any extra air in the bag. (One lady at one of our workshops told me she closed up the bag with a ¼-inch opening on one side, sucked the air out with a straw, and then quickly sealed it back. I use my PUMP-N-SEAL™ for the same effect.)
5. Easy labeling—Most brands now give you a place to write down the date and ingredients.

Disadvantages

1. Limited reusability—Yes, you can reuse them, but maybe only once or twice. So, you do have to buy new bags regularly.
2. Puncture—If you aren't careful, you can easily puncture a bag. To avoid this watch placement of the bag in the freezer and handle carefully.

3. Splitting bags—If you use a quality bag and don't over stuff it, this should happen rarely.

Foil: I do use foil for some applications. It works great with any food that I'll want to take directly from the freezer to the oven or the grill.

Advantages:

1. Low in cost—Buy in bulk.
2. Freeform—You can shape it into anything you want.
3. Temperature resistant—It goes great from freezer to oven and back.
4. Packet cooking—Use those wonderful "foil envelopes" to create easy-to-bake meals.

Disadvantages:

1. Health concerns—Be careful of aluminum getting into your food.
2. Acid—Avoid using with any acidic foods. The acid will react with the foil. The foil may flake or pit.
3. Airtight—You can work with aluminum to make an airtight seal, but it isn't as easy to do as with a bag or container. It takes a little more time. To play it safe, double wrap your food.
4. Labeling—It is difficult to label the food. Plus all foil-wrapped containers look alike. Write on freezer tape and then stick it to package.

Plastic Wrap: The second most frequent method I use to seal my food for the freezer is plastic film. I'm talking about commercial-grade plastic. I use Reynolds 914 Film. It works wonderfully. I don't even bother with the standard grocery-store shelf stuff. I work too hard and have spent too much to use cheap imitations. And one container of 914 Film will last for years. We discovered it when we needed shrink wrapping for an earlier edition of one of my books. We bought the 914 for use in production of book packets. We learned it was food-grade safe. So, I've been using it on our food ever since.

Advantages:

1. Low cost—Though the initial purchase is high, you are buying enough for years—the per recipe cost is low.
2. Freeform—You can shape it into any form you want.

3. Airtight—With a little work, you can get airtight seals. I still recommend double or triple wrapping all your food.

Disadvantages:

1. Freeform—You can't use it for the initial freezing of a liquid very easily. You have to freeze the liquid in a form, then wrap it in film.
2. Labeling—Labeling can be a problem. Here's a method that works: you can wrap item completely once. Then lay down a piece of paper on the wrap describing the contents. Then wrap the whole package a second time. You can then read the label through the second wrapping.
3. If you don't handle it well, the wrap can puncture. Even if you are careful, an edge can be damaged from movement of other frozen items around it. Solve this by educating your family about the potential for tears.

STOCKING THE FREEZER

There are many options for arranging and stocking your freezer. Choose a method that works best for you. We'll cover this in more detail in the next chapter about "Using the Food" because how you use your food will dictate how you should arrange it on the shelves.

Dehydration

Another excellent way to preserve your food is to dehydrate it. We already discussed the "science" of what happens in dehydrating. Here's how I apply it.

With some of my extra produce, we dehydrate it. We cut the produce into small uniform sizes. We line the trays and let the dehydrator do most of the work. We fill all ten trays with food and let it dry overnight. The next morning we place the dry ingredients in jars and then seal them with our vacuum sealer (see page 125). Some of the ingredients we'll jar in "chunk" sizes to use in granola, salads, soups, or muffins. Some of the ingredients we'll run through a food processor or blender and turn it into a powder. We then use the powder for seasoning. This powder is concentrated and rich in taste. We make our own vegetable powder for use in soups. We have apple powder made from dehydrated apple peel that is wonderful in muffins and other baked goods.

> Potatoes are one of the few items that I pretreat by dipping in Brown Away (see recipe on page 373) and then steaming them until translucent. Once they are pre-treated, I dehydrate them. By using fresh potatoes, the results are very good. They won't look as crisp and white as those done in commercially available mixes, but they will be healthy and delicious.

As your budget allows, I recommend buying or building your own dehydrator. Of course, you can make your own fruit leather snacks and jerky, but I use it to get the most out of my vegetables. It is a wonderful use for leftovers and parts of vegetables you'd normally throw away. For instance, if you scrub your carrots really well, you can dehydrate the peel and make a carrot powder, as we did with the apples. You could dehydrate potatoes and make your own "packaged mixes" like the commercial varieties. You could dehydrate clean potato peeling, powder it and then use it as a thickener in soups and sauces (See Topics section for more Powder ideas). There are so many applications that I suggest you look into the subject. Now that I have a dehydrator, I don't know how I cooked so long without it. By using it, we are controlling more and more of the quality of the food we are eating.

Here is one method that I use when I've been extremely successful at gleaning, harvesting, or bargaining. In other words, I have more produce than I can use in mega-cooking or that I can dehydrate immediately. As I work through the produce, I store the other filled crates, boxes, and gas in a bathtub surrounded by blocks of ice (gallon milk jugs filled with water and frozen). This will give me some time to wash and chop most of it before it goes bad. We use the individual freezing method to get as much of the produce frozen as possible. It is a round robin operation—some of us cleaning and cutting vegetables, while one child is laying the pieces onto trays for freezing, another child is bagging frozen pieces for refreezing, freeing a tray for the new produce to go into the freezer for individual freezing. (Of course, it helps to have as many hands as possible, but it can be done by one person, it will just take longer.) It may sound a little complicated, but it isn't. We just wait a couple of hours for items to freeze, then refill with a new batch. I fill my dehydrator trays and have it going, but that cycle will take overnight. So, we continue with the freezing and bagging until we handle all of the produce. Each time the dehydrating food is done, we place the dried food in jars and vacuum-seal them. Then we take a bag of individual frozen ingredients from the freezer and spread them on the dehydrating trays and turn it on. We'll have all the produce processed (cleaned and cut into small pieces) in one or two days and frozen in dozens of bags. It may take weeks to get it all dehydrated. This method works very well. There is no need to thaw the food before dehydrating. During these harvest times, my dehydrator is going 23.5 hours a day. We stop it only long enough to switch ingredients.

Vacuum Sealing

I don't use my electric vacuum sealer for plastic bags. I don't like the expense of the bags or the way it flattens my food. In contrast, I do appreciate the way my PUMP-N-SEAL™ seals my jars (for short and long term storage) and off-the-shelf bags (for short-term only). It only takes seconds and the jars are airtight. My food can sit on the shelf for months until I use it. I can measure out a few tablespoons of vegetable powder and then reseal it. It works great for keeping so many of my dry goods fresh.

For those of you with bug problems, it is ideal.

So, in addition to sealing my dehydrated foods, I use it to seal my dry goods, and with my do-it-yourself mixes. (See Many Muffins Mix, page 249; and Mega-Mix, page 256)

Because I am removing all the extra air and sealing it, I've "preserved" the dry contents. *Note:* This is not a method for "wet" canning.

For long term storage of our large bulk items, we nitrogen-pack those in food-grade 3½- and 6-gallon pails. Once I break the seal on those pail, I either reseal them with a Gamma Seal™ or repackage the ingredients into glass jars and vacuum seal them. I determine which process I'll use by estimating how quickly I will use the ingredients. Since we go through our wheat very quickly, I use the Gamma Seal™ for quick and easy access. A Gamma Seal™ is a wonderful product that replaces the standard lid on the pail with a ring and a screw-type lid. For easy recognition, we color-code our pails: white Gamma Seal™ for my hard white wheat, a red one for my hard red white, etc. If it will take me more than a few months to use all the contents of a pail (example: dehyrated milk, butter, etc.), I pour those ingredients into clean mason jars and vacuum seal them. That way the ingredients stay fresh until I use them.

Canning

Another method of preserving food is traditional canning. I've done a little canning, but for my time and energy, I prefer freezing and dehydrating. Canning still is wonderful for those who have their own gardens. To learn canning, I suggest you do some research—there are books dedicated to the subject. To give you an idea though of the differences, it takes me about one tenth the amount of jars to store my dehydrated produce as it would if I did the traditional canning. Also, canning takes many hours of pure labor. My experience is that preparing food for deyhdration and my actual physical labor is 10 to 15% as it would be for canning. Another key factor to me is that I can make the slightest mistake with traditional canning and ruin 30 to 40 jars of food. I have yet to mess-up any food trying to dehydrate it—plus I haven't had to throw any dehydrated food away.

In addition to traditional canning (Grandma with her large water bath and pressure cookers), some cooks looking for long-term storage are turning to home-canning with metal

We've been experimenting with long-term storage. Some of my dehydrated food still has great color, taste, and texture after four years of storage in vacuum-packed glass jars. I've tested some other carrots that we dehydrated at the same time, but we bagged them instead. They are pale and have very little taste. Those bagged carrots are still safe to eat, so we're using them as filler in soups and meat loaves.

cans. Some companies offer "canning services" where you can either rent, buy, or use their personal canning machines. You would then put your ingredients in cans, seal, and label them. Using these one-can-at-a-time machines is very do-able for the home cook.

Other Methods

There are other methods of preserving food. Some of these are quite impractical for many of us, but a viable alternative for some.

- **Smoking (Old smokehouse):** Not as popular as it once was, most smoking is done by the professionals.
- **Chemical preservation (natural solutions):** While we lived in the Republic of Panama we ate fish that was "cooked" by the use of marinating. It never was heated, but the citric acids did the work. There are natural alternatives to food preservation. If you are interested, research the subject.
- **Chemical preservation (additives and preservatives):** This is a very popular choice of many of today's food manufacturers. They add chemicals to stop the decaying process; the only problem is we then are introducing these chemicals into our bodies. Being a parent of a special needs child and having counseled thousands of other families, my advice is to minimize exposure to chemicals. Read about the subject. Before you feed chemicals to your children, learn what they do to their bodies. Yes, of course, the FDA approves them. But my standards are higher than the FDA's. I'm asking you to be careful and use them only because you don't have an alternative.
- **Decomposition, by choice:** There are some cultures who want "spoiled" food. For example, I've heard many a story from U.S. servicemen who were introduced to Korean Kimchee. They are amazed to watch the jar being dug out of the ground and then the contents eaten. But for some Koreans, that is a staple of their diet. They don't, for one minute, consider it spoiled. They consider it nutritious. And if you really look at what alcohol beverages are made of, it is "spoiled" juices and grains. So, there are some who choose to encourage bacterial growth in their food and drinks.

Summary

Once you've done all the work to prepare wonderful, wholesome food for your family, you want to invest the time to properly care for it. It doesn't make sense to let a roast go bad because I didn't invest an extra nickel in plastic wrap to triple wrap it. By the time I get to the freezing stage, not only have I invested a good sum of money, but a good deal of effort. And all that can be a complete waste if I don't store the food properly. So, please heed the advice in this chapter and invest the time and money into good storage materials and methods. And keep in mind that when freezing you're removing heat, not making cold. And if that doesn't make sense to you, don't worry about it. It will "click" one day.

Chapter 7: Serving

NOW THAT I HAVE ALL THESE WONDERFUL RECIPES PREPARED, HOW DO I USE THEM?

Ah, now most of the work is done and you can enjoy the fruits of your labor. In this chapter, we'll work through some options so that you use this prepared food to its best benefit.

Meal Planning

There are many ways you can utilize this food and plan your meals.

You'll want to consider what your day's schedule is like, how much thawing time you have, your "launch window," and other preparations or side dishes.

I currently plan an entire week's menu at one time. I take notice of meetings, field trips, orthodontist appointments, and my workload. I use my calendar and write in breakfasts, snacks, lunches, dinners and an occasional dessert. That way I have fewer surprises (though they still happen), and I can figure out thawing time and side dishes.

"Launch Window"

My husband worked with the Space Shuttle booster rocket program and so we all talk NASAese. One term that is day-to-day talk around here is the phrase "launch window." That is the time frame that NASA has to get a launch off so that the shuttle (orbiter) will "land" in the right orbit. For instance, for the orbiter to reach the correct coordinates they have to launch it between 10 and noon on a particular day. If the weather is bad, they have to scrub that launch and wait until the next day. Our family joke is "Let's do launch."

We have launch windows, too. That's the timeframe I have to get somewhere. "Okay, we have thirty minutes to get in the car and out of the driveway."

But I also have "lunch windows" and "dinner windows." That's the time I have available to fix dinner, get it on the table, eat, and clean up. Some days the dinner window is in hours, and some times it's minutes.

As I plan the menu for each day, I look at what is on the calendar.

BIG WINDOW DAYS

If I know it will be a peaceful, stay-at-home kind of a day, I'll schedule something like lasagna or another meal that can bake while we're home. Even though I'm physically home, it doesn't mean I have nothing better to do. I like spending my time with my family, not with their dishes. So, I still plan very little kitchen time and lots of time with them. Even if I've been home all day, I might not have stopped going—you know what I'm talking about. We don't lie on the sofa eating bonbons all day. I still would rather greet Alan when he comes home, sit down, review the day with him, relax, and have some prime family time. Then walk into the kitchen because dinner's practically ready. We have a "happy hour", instead of "Why don't you ever help me in here?" or "Do something with YOUR son!"

- **Preplanned Minute Meals:** When Alan and I both worked full time, we could drive home for lunch—but we didn't have a lot of time. Do you have "minute meals" sometimes, too? Well, you could use your crockpot and start a meal when you leave in the morning, and have it ready when you come in the door for lunch or dinner. There's a list on page 433 of meals that you can heat gently and slowly in your crockpot. Or have another lunch meal thawed and ready to microwave—spend your time eating and chewing rather than spreading and stirring.

  Now that I'm home full time, you might think I have time to fix dinner. That's true some days. But I do plan errand days—trying to get all of them done when I am out. So, I like having meals that I can plan ahead that are quick. I've thawed it out the day before and all I have to do is quickly heat it and eat it.
- **Spontaneous Minute Meals:** And then there are those days that just happen—you have meetings at night and they lost your order and the dog got sick and you can't find your keys and one of the children has stuffed a vitamin up his nose and the aquarium cracks and all the fish are going to die and the dining room will flood if you don't act fast and . . .

  So, even if I planned a wonderful, slow-cook, leisurely day, I'm elated that when I mega-cooked months ago, I prepared quite a few meals that can be grabbed from the freezer and served on the table in minutes.
- **Travel Meals:** On certain Thursday nights one year, Alan came home from work to pick up Stuart and they left immediately for Stuart's Civil Air Patrol meeting. I could feed Stuart early, but Alan needed to eat and there was no time. So, I planned a meal that Alan could eat while driving—like a pocket sandwich dinner, mini-pot pie, or other hand food. I make sure when I'm planning my menus to include "car food." With my hungry tribe, they can't hold off until we get to their grandmother's to eat, so we pack some car food. I think many of you have times like that, also. So, definitely plan on them.

We will drive the two hours to grandmother's house after church on Sundays, and they can't wait until 3 P.M. to eat. So I fed them a light lunch in the car on the drive over, then they still eat a full Sunday dinner with her.

COMPUTER PROGRAMS

I use my computer calendar and block out meal times using the "reoccurring" option. I can then go to each day and jot down the menu. The program I'm currently using, Microsoft Outlook, even has a feature that I can write in tasks. A reminder will come up on my computer (even with voice prompt) that will remind me to "thaw the meat loaf for tomorrow night's dinner" or "make gelatin salad for evening dinner." I can print out the menus for the week and post on the refrigerator. It helps the whole family to run smoothly.

I've also tried using a data file program on the computer and that worked well. I defined data files for each meal and then could quickly fill in my choices. By looking at the information in the table view, I could space the meals very quickly—spaghetti every other week, a chicken dish once a week, roasts one Sunday a month, etc. It took less than an hour to plan a whole month's worth of menus. And at a glance I could balance vegetables, meats, and side dishes for good variety.

I keep my menu list by me—the one that I used when I first planned my mega-cooking™ and then kept track of how many meals I actually yielded of each recipe. If I have four Puffed Stuff meals prepared, I'll space those 6 weeks apart on the calendar on days that are really busy since I'll only have to zap those for 10 minutes before we can eat them. I schedule the 32 meat loaf meals on days that appear to be calm. And then I continue working through the list. This is a roughed-in version and just a guideline. I've learned not to plan too far in advance because some things crop up unexpected around this house. How about at yours?

MANUAL METHODS

You don't have to have a computer to plan your meals. I used a regular wall calendar and index cards for years. You could simply use a sheet of notebook paper.

- **Wall Calendar:** Use different colored ink for each meal. Breakfast is yellow, lunch is green, dinner is black, and dessert is red. Write in the menus in the block. Or use a highlighter pen. Or make it so obvious that anyone could figure the pancakes are for breakfast, the soup is for lunch, and the roast is for dinner.
- **Index Cards:** Plan certain meals. Use color-coded cards for each meal—yellow for breakfast, pink for lunch, whatever. Then you can choose a certain meal and move them around in order for the week. Choose seven breakfasts, lunches, and dinners. Write in all the details for each meal. For instance, a dinner card may look like this:

Recipe	Location	Count	Need to buy	When to thaw	Prep time	Extras
Chicken Parmigiana	3rd shelf	5		Thaw in fridge day before	15 min.	Thaw out 1 pkg. pizza sauce, mozzarella cheese
Rice	Pantry	N/A			40 min.	
Steamed broccoli	2nd shelf	3			10 min.	
Carrot salad	Top shelf	7		Thaw pkg. of grated carrots 1 hour ahead of time		Thaw out 1 pkg. crushed pineapple, raisins in pantry
Dinner rolls	4th shelf	8		Thaw dough overnight in fridge	20 minutes	
Iced Tea	Pantry	N/A		Make in morning	5 minutes	
Milk		N/A	Buy milk			

- *Recipe:* That's what you want to serve. Abbreviate as much as possible. Use the supplied codes, if that helps, or your own tracking system.
- *Location:* That's so you find it quickly. You might not need to do this if you arrange your freezer well or don't have a lot of meals in there. We have to keep track or we'd stand for minutes with the freezer door open.
- *Count:* This is where you can keep track of your inventory. When you make a recipe, mark on the card how many you are putting in. Write this in pencil. Then as you use them, change the "6" to a "5," or whatever.
- *Need to buy:* This is where you pencil in any ingredients to buy that week to complete the menu. (e.g., lettuce for a tossed salad.)
- *When to thaw:* Jot down how long you plan to thaw the recipe. And then, if you need to, make yourself a reminder to thaw it. (e.g., note on Wednesday's date that you need to thaw Thursday's chicken breasts)
- *Prep time:* Put down how long you need from when you start working the recipe until it is ready for the table.
- *Extras:* Write down any other ingredients that you'll need to thaw or prepare to complete the recipe.

Punch a hole in the upper corner, place them in order of your use, and affix a ring to them. You can then take it to the store with you on your weekly quick trip. You'll have written what you still need to buy fresh to complete any of the recipes.

Keep a master file of the different meals you've prepared. Then each week sort through and make your choices. You can use the cards again and again.

For the information that changes, write in pencil.

For those of you who really are efficient, you could make cards for each number of the meals you had—easy if you have access to a copier or a computer. For example, If you made six meals worth of Count Stroganov Beef, then make six cards. You can then work your way through them, knowing what inventory you still have in the pantry. Use those cards instead of the "count" column.

On the back of the card you might want to list specific heating instructions. For example: "Option Four, page 295" and keep this book near by. Or specify where the recipe is (e.g., copper recipe box). Or staple or paper clip the recipe to the card. Or actually spell out the instructions: "Bake for 15 minutes at 350°F in 13 x 9-inch casserole dish."

(*Note:* I did work a card system for years, but I can now do all this on my computer, using the "copy" command to my heart's content and setting up "shortcuts" to the actual recipe.)

Plain Paper: You can take a plain piece of notebook paper and make four or five columns. Number the side 1 to 30 (or 31) and/or the days of a week. Head the columns with breakfast, lunch, dinner, snack, and dessert.

Then fill in the columns with your menus. Depending on how much detail you want to write, you can either use one sheet for a full month or for a week.

Keep this taped to your refrigerator and plan your weekly shopping list. Look at it each night to see if you need to thaw anything out for the next day.

WHAT AM I HUNGRY FOR? OR THE "WHY PLAN AT ALL METHOD?":
I know some of us get a brain-ache when we think of charts, graphs, and forms. I understand. There are those who love to organize and make lists—I'm married to one. I basically ran on a "What am I hungry for" planning mode for years. If I had my act together, the

I always know that no matter how well I plan, the schedule will change, so I don't lock myself in. I use it as a guideline. I really know first hand the proverb: Many are the plans in a man's heart, but it is the Lord's purpose that prevails.—Proverbs 19:21.

night before I'd take something from the freezer and stick in the refrigerator to thaw. Most of the time, around 4 P.M., I'd ask myself, "What am I hungry for?" Sometimes I'd consult the children or Alan. I'd grab an item out, zap it until thawed, and heat it up. Simple. It worked for me just fine, and I still rely on that method when I need to.

There was a time I only had four children 6 years of age and younger and nothing else to do with my time. Okay, stop laughing—or are you crying?—those of you who are in similar circumstances know I was grinning as I wrote that. The idea of planning more than an hour ahead seemed daunting.

If you are at that stage of life, enjoy it! Children grow so quickly—they go from drooling to dicing zucchini before you know it.

Feel like you accomplished something if there is anything edible (paste and playdough don't count) on the table at all. Leave the color coordinating to the coloring book, and relax.

AUTO-PILOT

Now I'm at a different stage of my life. My children are big helpers and I am "working" full time homeschooling and writing. So, now I can invest an hour a week in planning and they can run the kitchen easily. To test it, I planned a full week's meals and snacks. I gave them the menus and copies of the recipes with detailed heating instructions. I walked them through the plan verbally. They ran with it. They did 100% of the food preparation and clean up. I didn't set foot in the kitchen all week. Now I don't opt for that often, because I like to be with them and we have fun in the kitchen together (bubble-fights are enjoyable). But I wanted to prove it could be done.

There are meals they completely handle from start to finish so I can work with Trent on his therapy, or answer my e-mail. It is a blessing. The years of training have paid off not only today, but their future spouses will love it.

Don't you have times when you would like to come home to find your children have prepared a good home-cooked dinner and it's ready for you to sit down and eat? Or what if Mom feels bad, can Dad rustle up a decent dinner (without using the phone to call out)? It is worth the few minutes of planning and training to have several recipes that other members of the family can prepare from start to finish (with mega-cooking™ that means thawing, heating, and serving).

DO WHAT WORKS FOR YOU!

Please, whatever system you use, adjust it and make it work for you. No system is good if it takes more time than it is worth. Don't spend an hour on planning if that only saves you 10 minutes of work later. Now if planning an hour saves you 10 hours of work later, then it is time well spent.

The beauty of so much of the planning that I do is that I can do it once and then reuse it dozens of times. If I plan out a meal, I can cut and paste that plan for use many other times.

Obviously, I don't want to spend any time doing work that isn't necessary. I abbreviate as much as possible and only write in things that I know I might forget. I use all the built-in features of my computer programs. I especially appreciate the little messages that come up on my screen to remind me of what I had planned days ago.

Freezer Arrangement

In the storage chapter, I explained how we freeze our food, using a clear shelf for the quick freezing, and then packing the food in tightly once it's frozen.

We usually leave it like that for a few days while we rest and regroup.

But then we take some time and organize the freezer. We don't want to waste time or energy standing in front of the freezer digging for an item. That's not good for the electric bill or for the frozen food.

METHODS

You can organize however you want to. Here are some ideas:

- **By Week:** Plan out your menus. Stock each shelf (or section of your freezer) with all the recipes for a week. Then you can work your way through the shelf. Easy! Advantages: all the planning is done and it only takes seconds to remove a meal for thawing.
- **By Recipe:** Keep all the multiple packets of the same recipe together. You then can see easily how many you have left. You know where in the freezer each "recipe" is and can pull out as needed. The one drawback is if you pack one recipe behind another and forget about it. Then the last week, you'll have the same thing every night because that's what you have left. Good planning will prevent that. Don't be tempted to always eat what is on top, if you group by recipe. Dig down at least once a week and get a dish from the bottom of the stack.
- **By Groups:** With this method you store all your vegetables on one shelf, meat dishes on the next, breads on the third, etc. You can then just grab something from each shelf and your meal is done. Again, don't always use what is in front or on top, dig deep for variety or stick to your menu plans.

OUR CURRENT SYSTEM

Now don't go glassy-eyed on me, but I'll tell you how we have our food arranged. This isn't to be a model for you, just as an idea generator. Right up front, I know that we are unique. We're a "test kitchen." Few other families will have the equipment we have and need. We currently have two full freezers (one chest and one upright), and three small freezers that are part of refrigerator units. In addition to our testing requirements, we have Trent's and Stuart's special needs to consider. Trent, who is currently autistic, doesn't understand my meal plans. If we don't manage him well, he will eat what he wants when he wants. So, we have to keep some food under lock and key. Stuart's needs are a little different. He has Type 1 diabetes. We have to keep his snacks, emergency food, and insulin close at hand. So we've even put a small refrigerator in his room. This system is designed for our needs, but you may be able to glean it for some ideas. Where we can dedicate an entire freezer or shelf to one category, you can dedicate a section or corner of yours. Again, this is for ideas.

- **Side-by-side freezer unit (kitchen):** We store all our sauces, juices, frozen fruits, desserts, and breakfast items. I typed up labels and put them on the shelves, so the children can find and put away things easily. One shelf holds all our frozen juices and fruit for use in recipes and for blender drinks. The next shelf holds all our dessert items or ingredients. Then we keep sauces that we'll use with some of the frozen entrées. The next basket holds breakfasts (pancakes, waffles, etc.) In the small bins in the door, we keep condiment-type stuff. The top shelf is open for whatever we need it for. Then comes a bin for spices (I keep all my grated lemon and orange rind and some herbs there). The next door shelf is for cheeses, then syrups, and snacks.
- **The regular unit with top freezer (kitchen):** This is a small freezer so we use it for making ice. We make our water ice cubes for drinks. We keep squeeze bottles with a few inches of water in them. We add water and have cool drinks to take on errands, etc. We use this freezer to make our special cubes of other ingredients. (See page 119 for details.) And this is my "staging area" for that week's menus. On Monday morning, I pull most of the frozen packages we need for that week and place them in that freezer. It only takes me a few minutes and then they are right there ready to thaw and use—all in one place. I can also, at that time, make any adjustments to my shopping list. You don't need a separate freezer for a "staging area," just designate a section of your freezer for that purpose.
- **The Upright Freezer (locked up):** In this freezer, we keep all the rest of the side dishes. Three shelves are dedicated to vegetables and starches. The bottom bin has all the bread dough and related items. The extra shelf is for any fruit or other

items that wouldn't fit in the side-by-side. The food is organized together by ingredient. The carrots are all together (grated, sliced, and chopped packets). The broccoli packets are all together. The squashes are all together. So, it is easy to get at what I want and to see when I'm running low of a vegetable. The reason I only need one shelf for bread items is because we do eat a lot of bread and I know I'll be making more dough every other week (or so).

- **The Chest Freezer (locked up):** The entrées are in the chest freezer, packed according to recipe. All the meat loaves are together, all the Instant Thanksgiving packets are together, etc. We know in our head where the items are and can easily get to them by moving a basket around. For those entrees that are SAR (some assembly required), we pack them in the removable baskets. We group all the ingredients for pizza together so we don't have to hunt for that recipe. In one basket we line up a packet of sauce, then one of meat, cheese, vegetables, etc. Then we'll repeat it. So, it is very easy to get at those ingredients—they are all together in one place.
- **Small Freezer-Top Model (locked up):** This is Alan's freezer. We stock his lunches in there, and any left-overs for when we have "CORD" (Clean Out Refrigerator/Freezer Day). Usually, when we have one helping left of a recipe, we make Alan a lunch. In this freezer, we store all the little bits of this and that. I'll use up those packets by making a quiche, or Green Eggs and . . . or something like that. I hate to waste those little bits, so, by keeping them all together in one place, we don't lose them to the deep recesses of the freezer. You could set aside a bin or shelf area for "leftovers" and use them for lunches or for special recipes.

Again, I don't expect anyone to organize their freezer(s) like we do, but you'll see that we organize the food for how we use it. I'd rather take an hour today to know where my food is, than waste hours later (here and there) hunting for items on other days. I group the food according to use. I want my sauces in the kitchen within easy reach. I can move the entrees to the "staging area" all at one time. That keeps down the times we have that door open.

Please note that when we organize we don't do it all at once. That would be major and we don't want any of the food even thinking about thawing. I organize one shelf in the morning. Let my hands warm up and then spend another 15 minutes in the afternoon organizing another shelf. Within one week, my freezers are works of art that we can really use well. (Also, I know how I'm going to organize—we've been doing this for years so we figure that in when we are doing the initial freezing.)

Before You Heat

THAWING

Most of our food has to be thawed before we can work with it. Don't let it thaw on the counter for health reasons. Thaw in the refrigerator or microwave, use a thawing tray or steamer, or don't thaw it at all.

- **Overnight in Refrigerator:** This to me is the best method—if you can remember to do it. Some items need to thaw at least 2 days ahead because of the mass of the frozen item (e.g., a five-pound roast). We take the item out of the "staging area" or from the freezer and thaw it on a plate or in a dish in the refrigerator.

  There are some ingredients that need to be unwrapped, placed back in their mold (prepare mold first by spraying with a non-stick coating, using a Teflon® sheet, or other method according to recipe instructions). I cover the mold with either its airtight lid or with plastic film.

  For the recipes in "goosh" or liquid form, I always set the bag or wrapped item in a bowl to thaw so that as it "melts" no liquids drip down into my refrigerator. The bowl serves to give the "liquid" form.
- **Via Microwave:** My microwave has saved me from many a mis-planned day. I'm thankful for mine with that wonderful defrost button. If I forget to thaw out a dish, I simply grab it out of the freezer, place it in an appropriate microwaveable container and defrost. (Usually I can't remove it from the bag at first, so I'll place the bag in the microwave dish and defrost for 10-15 minutes. Then I can remove the ingredients from the bag and pour directly into the microwave dish. Most of my recipes are then completely defrosted within the next 15 minutes.) I can either heat in the microwave or process it as I would have if I had thawed it overnight. Microwaves differ—please make adjustments considering the wattage of your oven and the quantity of your ingredients.
- **Thawing Trays:** I've seen the ads for those amazing thawing trays. I'll be honest—I don't know how well they work. I've had such success with my microwave and steamer, I haven't needed an alternative. If you have one and are experimenting with it, I'd like to hear your results.
- **Steamer:** My steamer works great as a defroster. I don't use it on items that the added moisture would ruin. It is perfect for rice and some entrees. For the more "liquid" items, I place them in the steamer dish and let the steam thaw it out. It works great. As for the rice, I keep the rice in and let it completely heat also.
- **Crock Pot:** One simple method to "thaw" and then heat seamlessly is to use your crockpot. Keep the dimensions of your crock pot in mind when you freeze meals that you will thaw and heat this way. In other words, you can't place a 13 x 9-

inch rectangle into a 6-inch diameter cylinder. Plan ahead and I think you'll really enjoy coming home to dinner already done.

NOT THAWING

One other option is to not thaw the food at all. Quite a few of my recipes can be heated directly from the freezer. I remove any wrappings that aren't ovenproof, return the ingredients to the dish they were frozen in or an appropriate shaped dish, then bake it according to the recipe instructions for baking from frozen state. As a general rule of thumb for recipes, I can reduce the specified temperature (for normal baking) by 50 to 100°F. I cover the pan (even if I normally would bake it uncovered). I bake for the normal time and check. This is usually the halfway point. I prod the recipe with a fork and get a feel for how well it is doing. I then adjust the baking time.

Example: If a recipe which had been thawed would normally bake at 375°F for 30 minutes, I bake it covered at 300°F for 30 minutes, check it, then bake another 30 minutes (plus or minus depending on how well it was doing at the 30-minute mark). If the recipe is better with a "crispy" top, I'll remove the cover at the halfway point.

Heating and Reheating

For many of the recipes in this book, I presented you with several options. Some of the recipes are completely cooked and all you have to do is reheat them, but some are "raw" and have to be cooked. If you think you'll forget which option you froze, mark it on your cards, on the packet, or in this book. You don't want to only reheat when you really needed to cook, and vice versa, you don't want to cook when all you need to do is reheat. Don't assume you'll be able to tell or recognize the difference. I've been mega-cooking™ for more than 17 years and I'm constantly reminded at how alike different recipes look when they are frozen.

Follow the directions on the recipe for heating and reheating.

STOVETOP

Some sauces and more liquid mixes work great reheating on the stovetop. Watch your pans. Quality of pans does make a difference. You might have to add some liquid, so stir to check for consistency.

MICROWAVE

I did not include microwave-cooking times, since I have no idea what quantity-sizes you prepared and the quality of your microwave. I do recommend that you go slowly. You can always microwave for another minute. You can't undo over-zapping. Remember that heat continues to cook the food after the oven is off. So, I always under-zap just a little.

STEAMER

We mentioned the steamer above when talking about thawing options. I use my steamer more and more, as I find it a perfect appliance for heating many of my foods. I use it almost exclusively for all my vegetables, many of my starches, and some of my entrees. If you don't have a steamer, you can rig one in your microwave or on your stovetop.

OVEN

I use my oven quite a bit. I can take a couple of minutes and place an entrée in the oven to bake. Then go on to something else. During the summer, I don't use it as much because it heats the kitchen—then I use the microwave and steamer more.

CROCKPOT

Quite a few of these recipes can be taken directly from the freezer, placed in the crockpot, and slowly thawed and warmed all day long. See page 437 for a list of potential recipes that you can do this. It is a great method of heating when your "lunch window" is small. When you walk in the door, the food is ready to eat—grab your plate and dish it up.

FUTURE LOOKS BRIGHT

My sons like watching the educational channels and shows like *Beyond 2000, Next Step,* and *Popular Mechanics.* They are quick to tell me about developments and new inventions that are coming. One that some restaurants are using is the Flash Oven. I'm looking out for that one. There are new appliances and inventions coming out all the time. There is one infomercial after another about different ones. If you are a trailblazer and already have some of these nifty new gadgets, use them. Figure out how to get the most out of your recipes. They should have sent you adequate instructions on how to adapt "old-fashioned" recipes to the new method.

Presentation

Don't worry, I'm not going to intimidate you with images of watermelons in the shape of lighthouses, cucumber poodles, and hand-laced napkin rings. But I do want to encourage you to take a few minutes to dress up the food. Since I invested the hours months ago on food preparation, we have a few minutes to set a nice table and add a garnish to the dish.

DINING ROOM

Some of us have no choice about the dining room, or so we think. You'd be surprised how you can transform a room with little effort. I like as plain a dining room as I can get. And I mean plain. Some dining rooms are so pre-decorated that you can't do anything creative with them. If you want to turn you room into an open-air fiesta—you can't because the Mexican serape will clash with the English Tea Garden print drapes. You're stuck so that every meal has to look like an English Tea Garden. I like a dining room with very little "permanent" personality. I dress it up or down with table clothes, napkins, centerpieces, and quick wall hangings. Also, I think every dining room should have some kind of a sound system. We use music to set the mood with many of our meals. We've purchased CDs that feature music from other countries. The Russian folk music just adds the perfect touch to a dinner of Count Stroganov Beef.

TABLE

I have a few solid-colored tablecloths. I have a collection of fabric squares. We take a printed fabric square, lay it over the tablecloth and it's a whole new look. I have remnants of all kinds of fabric. We can take our red tablecloth through most of the holidays by changing out the center cloth. The green one can go from the look of a New Orleans restaurant to a picnic by the seashore to a Williamsburg-period feast—all by changing the center cloth and adding different center pieces. The navy cloth goes from Patriotic (with Stars and Stripes) to romantic (with mirrors and silver accessories) to comical with balloons and confetti. We bring in fresh flowers from the yard, or use toys, whatnots or pictures to create a mood. You might be thinking that we spend hours doing this, but we don't. Whenever I'm out, I look for sales on fabric or pick up stuff at garage sales—but mostly we're creative with what we already have in the house. Here are some examples of ways we decorate for a fish dinner.

For a fish dinner:

Cute: Sand, beach buckets, and toy shovel. This is a fun thing to do for breakfast—serve the cereal in a clean beach bucket and let them shovel it out. Use a beach-gear fabric cloth.

Sophisticated: Shells, coral, and driftwood. A seashore print.

Adventurous: Scuba gear for the centerpiece, with a deep ocean print.

Nautical: A sailing theme - model boat, or rope, captain's cap, etc, on a shipping cloth.

Fishy: Paper machè fish, or fish figurines on a print of tropical fish.

We make blue gelatin in a clean fish bowl with gummy fish inside. It looks great and the children love it. You can be as creative as you want to be.

If you like doing this sort of thing, check out your library for books filled with ideas. You don't have to spend a lot. I buy fabric or pick up remnants for 50¢ to $1 and then use pictures or objects we have around our house.

LIGHTING

We do like to play around with the lighting. We use candles or hurricane lamps. It is amazing how gentle music and a candle-light dinner can relax your nerves after a grueling day—even if you are eating tuna casserole.

DISH AND PLATE

If you don't want to dress up the table or dining room, you can add spice to the display dish or plate. Spend a few extra seconds and swirl the mashed potatoes or add a dash of paprika. Cut a sprig of herbs and lay beside the plate. Sprinkle the top of the casserole with cheese or lay down pepper rings. Dot the top with one teaspoon of butter or dust with powdered sugar. Think about how restaurants display food. You can go all out and carve fruit and vegetables, but you can also just add the simple, cute touches that say "I do care." It's like getting a hug and a kiss—tasty food that looks good, too.

Summary

The ideas in this chapter are to help you to use the food you've prepared the easiest way. Don't get bogged down in needless organization, planning, or primping. If the ideas help, use them. Otherwise, go on with your own style.

I want to close with encouraging you with this story. Alan and Reed were off on a scuba trip and I was rushing to get a project (on another book) that needed to be done overnight. I praise the Lord I don't have to live at that pace often. Stuart came to me while I was beating away at the keyboard and offered to make dinner so I could write. I mumbled something like, "Sure, honey. Whatever you want to do will be great." I once again got absorbed in my writing figuring he'd fix sandwiches or something.

About an hour later he called me. I walked into the dining room set for a banquet—table cloth, linen napkins, candle light, silver and china. He had grilled some chicken quarters, heated up some side dishes from the freezer and even baked dinner rolls.

Well, of course, I'm a mother, I cried. He, Trent, and Bethany Kay were so tickled. They had planned the whole thing and all worked together to pull it off.

It was just what my soul needed. It was a mental vacation in my "Tyranny of the Urgent" battle. I rested and dined like a queen.

I encourage you to invest in your family—every second is worth it. I've already been paid back in full for every sleepless night, whine and cry session, and thousands of other exhausting moments—and they aren't even half-grown yet.

If you haven't read *Tyranny of the Urgent* , it is a must for anyone who has demands on their life. *Tyranny of the Urgent,* Meridian Publishing Staff, 1995. ISBN: 1-56570-063-5.

Section Three

Topics

Let me explain how to use this section. It will serve as a combination glossary and index. When there is more detail within the narrative section of this book, I only give a brief explanation here with the symbol and a page number so you can read more on the topic. When this topic is not fully covered in another section, I give the details here. There is a food index in the back of the book to aid you in choosing recipes.

When a topic corresponds to other topics or is a "subtopic", we kept it in alphabetical order, but gave you the "main topic" under the heading "group":

- **Recipes:** these listings and their explanations are in context to writing and using recipes.
- **Labeling:** these listings and their explanations are in context to understanding current industry practices concerning labeling of products.
- **Ingredients:** these listings and their explanations are in context to ingredients or food and how we use them in cooking or meal preparation.
- **Techniques:** these listings and their explanations are in context to cooking techniques that apply to any cook, not just the mega-cook.
- **Mc:** these listings and their explanations are in context to and specific to mega-cooking™. Often they are terms I coined, so as to give the "process" some identification.
- **Safety:** these listings and their explanations are in context to safety or heath issues.
- **General:** these listings and their explanations either span several groups or are general in nature.

As you read a recipe or a section of the narrative and:

1. aren't sure what I mean by a term I use;
2. have an interest about a particular topic and want to learn more;
3. want to refresh your memory about how or what something means;

then please, read those topics. They are listed in alphabetical order for your convenience.

When you have the time, you might want to read them all. Some of the information presented here will equip you to be a more informed shopper and cook. It will aid you in getting the most from your mega-cooking™.

TERM	GROUP	EXPLANATION
Additional suggestions, tips or comments	Recipes	In that part of the recipe, I cover anything I think will prove helpful in preparing the recipe. I suggest you make notes on your recipes as to what side dishes you like with this, which option works best for your family and any particular brand of ingredients, flavor, or variation. I've also included suggestions and comments from the mega-testers.
Air Pressure	General	Air pressure affects cooking. It affects the boiling point of liquids and the elasticity of molecular bonding. See Boiling. Air pressure is important to a cook, especially with extremes in altitude or drastic changes in the weather.
Alliin and alliinase	General	Two elements in garlic that, when they interact, give garlic its flavor. Alliin is a chemical (pronounced "a-lean"). Alliinase is an enzyme (pronounced "a-lean-aze").
Anthocyanins	General	A natural dye in vegetables that gives them their red and blue coloring, as in beets, cabbage and berries (pronounced "an-tho-sigh-a-nins"). See Vegetables (Red).
Anthoxanthins	General	A natural dye in vegetables that gives them their white coloring, as in cauliflower, and onions. (pronounced "an-tho-zan-thins"). See Vegetables (White).
Assembling amounts	Recipes	Most of the amounts for the recipes are stated in shopping standards of measurement. Some ingredients though "change form" when you process them, and the shopping measurement doesn't help you as you try to figure out how much chopped onion to use in a recipe that calls for 4 onions. Chart your own results and use the chart on page 434 to benefit from what we've found to work for us.
Assembly-line	Mc	This technique makes you as efficient as some mechanized factories. You combine as many tasks that are similar, so you don't have to repeat them for each separate recipe. Think how a car rolls down the assembly line with parts ready to

be attached to the chasis. We're doing the same thing when we mega-cook. We are preparing the ingredients ahead, so we can quickly and easily assemble the recipes.

Automation — Mc — Some factories are so automated that they look like something out of Orwell's imagination. I like automation in the kitchen. I use appliances, and try to automate as many tasks as possible, so I can get the best results for my work. There is balance, though. Some steps have to be done by hand. Only automate your activities, and only use tools and gadgets, when they save your energy. That is another beauty of this system: it is worth the effort to pull out the food processor to grate fifty pounds of onions, whereas I don't know if I would go to all that trouble to chop one onion—I could do that quicker by hand. I calculate the total time—including setup, use, and clean-up. If automations takes less time than a manual method, I use it.

Background — Recipes — After the recipe title, I provide a little history about the recipe, some suggestions for preparation or serving, or some encouragement concerning the recipe. You might want to jot down some notes about how you created a recipe, who gave it to you, when you first served it, or any ideas you have as to how to make it more appealing to your family. I like when friends share recipes and personalize them.

Bag-in-Box — Mc — I use this technique more than any other method for freezing. I collect, save, and hoard cardboard boxes in which to freeze food. , page 117.

Bath Marie — Technique — This cooking technique is very effective for custards and custard-like recipes. You place the ingredients in ovenware dishes, and then place those dishes in a larger pan. Pour water into the larger pan to just below the top of the ovenware dishes (be careful, you don't want the water to get into the ingredients). Your ovenware dishes are then surrounded by water like islands and that controls the temperature. Since water cannot be heated beyond its boiling point, this

		Bath Marie technique gives custards the slow even baking they need. Be careful as you remove these pans so water doesn't enter the dishes.
Beans	Ingredient	Beans are a noble food too often ignored. They are loaded with protein and fiber, are very inexpensive, and can give delightful flavor and texture to many recipes. They are the brunt of jokes about poverty and "back when we couldn't afford anything else" stories. Too bad. I have a book on my shelf that goes into as much detail as anyone would need about beans (history, processing, methods, recipes): *Country Beans* by Carla Bingham. I use them in soups, as side dishes, for flour, and for filler. If you've had problems with beans never softening, the trick is to leave the salt out of the water. Don't allow any salt on the beans until they've softened. And remember that if you like to flavor with ham, the ham may be salty and therefore make your beans tough. Add the meat after the beans are cooked.
Beure Manié	Technique	Experienced cooks have known about this "trick" for years. This helps in making sauces and gravies. Have you ever worked on a sauce and added too much liquid? Well, at that stage you can't simply add more flour—the flour will clump. If you are making a "fat" based sauce or gravy, you can throw in some Beure Manié balls. To make these, suspend flour in soft butter by kneading it together. You can make these ahead and simply store in the refrigerator to use whenever you make a gravy or sauce that has a "fat" base. To thicken a water based sauce, dissolve flour or cornstarch in cold liquid first, then thicken in heat. (Pronounced "burr-may-yay.")
Blanching	Technique	Blanching is a method of boiling and then icing an ingredient to lock in its freshness. The boiling slows down the decaying process and then you stop the cooking process by taking the ingredients and submerging them into ice water. This is how I process many of my vegetables before freezing. It works wonderfully. Most vegetables only take a few

		minutes of boiling and then an equal amount of time in the ice water. Refer to blanching or canning manuals for specific timings and details.
Boiling	Technique	I know it would seem we all know what boiling is. But let's clarify what it really means. In "scientific terms" it means that heat excites the water until it can escape the liquid surface tension and internal pressure to remain a liquid, as well as the pressure on the liquid surface from the air. No liquid can be heated hotter than its boiling point. Why? When the bubbles pop, the moisture inside escapes taking the heat away in the form of steam. Turning the heat up will just make more bubbles and evaporate the liquid faster—boiling it away—but will not raise the temperature of the liquid. Chemists know that the only way to change the boiling point of an element is to change the air pressure. That is one reason that people living at higher altitudes have to adjust their cooking methods. Weather does affect our cooking. Is it starting to make sense now? Some recipes work great on normal days, but when a front comes in that changes the pressure even a few millibars, the recipe fails. (This same principle will affect cakes, egg whites, and other recipes that rely heavily on standard air pressure.) That is why pressure cookers work so well—by changing the boiling temperature, you can cook hotter.
Breadcrumbs and cubes	Ingredient	Save time and use your shears to cut up the bread. Depending on the recipe, you can include the crusts. If for appearance sake you don't want the crusts in a recipe, don't throw those away. Use them for breadcrumbs. Either store the breadcrumbs (completely dried) in vacuum-sealed jars on your pantry shelf or in bags in the freezer. If you don't make your own bread, then definitely check out a day-old bread store for bargain prices.
Bromelin	General	The enzyme in pineapple that tenderizes meat (pronounced "broam-meh-lin").

Term	Category	Description
Brown Away	Recipe	Mix one cup of water and one tablespoon of lemon juice. , page 373.
Burns	Safety	Deal with a burn as soon as possible. Every kitchen or garden should have a live aloe vera plant. Cut a section and squeeze onto the burn. Call your doctor or hospital emergency room to determine if it is severe enough for medical treatment.
Carotene	General	A natural dye in vegetables that gives their yellow or orange coloring, as in carrots, pumpkin, and corn (pronounced "care-ro-teen"). See Vegetables (Yellow).
Chlorophyll	General	A natural dye in vegetables that gives them green coloring, as in asparagus, broccoli, celery, and zucchini (pronounced - "chlor-row-fill"). It's when the chlorophyll dies in the fall that the carotene in some plants "shine through" for the beautiful changing of the leaves. See Vegetables (Green).
Cholesterol Free	Labeling	This one is really misleading. Food might not contain any cholesterol itself, but as soon as it starts interacting with your body, your body uses that food to make cholesterol. Also, according to the FDA a product can stipulate "Cholesterol Free" if it has less than 2 milligrams of cholesterol and fat per serving. That doesn't sound "free" to me.
Coding	Recipes	Cooks who do mega-sessions and are coordinating many recipes at one time will find it helpful to assign codes to the recipes. There is no need to write a title each time on Ingredients Lists. Use either a number code or a 3-letter designation to simplify your planning. This really isn't making more work for you, it is cutting out duplication of effort. Of course, you should use any method or system that makes sense to you. Abbreviate as you like.

Cornmeal	Ingredient	I like to make my own corn meal by grinding popcorn kernels in my flourmill. It works great and tastes delicious. Of course you can use store-bought varieties. For variation in muffin and other mixes, try adding in 10 to 25% corn meal as a substitute for white flour.
Crumble	Mc	Very similar to flaking when you cook ground meat. You'll want to break it into small pieces or crumbs. Since the consistency is different from fish, it isn't flaking. Wait until the meat is cool to the touch and then with your hands break the meat into bite-sized pieces. You also can break the meat apart with a spatula or wooden spoon as you cook it.
Dishes, rotating	Mc	I often freeze my recipe in the exact shape that I use for baking. I do this by freezing the recipe in the baking dish. Then once the recipe is frozen, I pop it out and either wrap in heavy-duty plastic or bag it in a freezer bag. I don't have a lot of pans that I can keep in the freezer, so I have to do this. I use the same pan for dozens of recipes. It is extremely difficult to pop a frozen meal out of a glass or ceramic dish. You can do it, but expect some effort. For a basic casserole that will be baked in a 13 x 9-inch pan, I freeze the recipe in an expensive metal pan that came with a plastic, airtight lid. The frozen meal pops out of it in a second. Then I can bake it in my nice glass casserole dish (the pan and dish are exactly the same size). *Note:* I pop and rewrap very quickly—the recipe is usually out of the freezer for less than a minute—I don't want it to thaw at all.
DitF!	Mc	*Dinner's in the Freezer!*™, my first book on the subject of mega-cooking™.
Doubling	Mc	When you buy groceries, buy double the amount for that night's menu. When you cook, cook double the amount. Eat one meal and freeze the extra. You will have one meal for another night when your schedule is tight. With this method you're getting twice the result, with little extra work. 🍳, page 100 for more details.

Duplicating	Mc	A technique in which you start to duplicate your cooking efforts. Whenever you chop up one bell pepper, do the second one at the same time and use the extra for the next night's salad. Think ahead, and reduce the set-up and clean-up time. It only takes another 30 seconds to cut up the second pepper, but you only bring out the cutting board and knife once, and only have to wash them once.
Eggs	Ingredient	Eggs are fascinating when you think of all the ways you can use them. In the recipes in this book, I have used "large" chicken eggs. Be careful. Always use the freshest eggs you can. When we mega-cook, we process the eggs the day we buy them. I have trained my children to always crack eggs individually into a separate dish. It does mean one more bowl to wash, but it has saved us many times from having to throw good eggs away. By cracking an egg by itself into an empty bowl, you don't ruin all the other eggs if that next egg is bad. If they drop the bad egg on top of the other already-cracked eggs, we'd have to throw them all out. Also if they miss a piece of shell, it is much easier to get out a piece from the volume of one egg than to hunt it down among half a dozen eggs. If you do get shell into eggs, use another piece of shell to get it out. The membranes will "attract" each other and make your work easier. The shell fragment tends to "run" from a metal spoon. And of course, we follow this same procedure of one egg at time into the "cracking bowl" when we separate eggs. (See Eggs, whites, below.)
Eggs	Safety	The Center for Disease Control and Prevention states, "Since foods of animal origin may be contaminated with Salmonella, people should not eat raw or undercooked eggs, poultry, or meat. "Raw eggs may be unrecognized in some foods such as homemade Hollandaise sauce, Caesar and other salad dressings, Tiramisu, homemade ice cream, homemade mayonnaise, cookie dough, and frostings." Please follow the safety directions about handling eggs in the recipes for Eggnog (page 203) and Mega-mayonnaise (page 381).

Eggs (extra)	Ingredient	When we have more than we need for the specific recipes, we go ahead and beat the raw eggs with a little milk and freeze it. Then when I know a busy morning is coming up, I can thaw a bag the night before in the refrigerator. I simply pour it into the skillet and cook a few minutes—scrambled egg breakfast almost instantly.
Eggs (boiled)	Ingredient	Because of the "air sack" that is between the two layers of membranes in an egg, you need to puncture an egg on the large end of the shell. You can use the neat "egg-puncturerers" in gourmet shops or just use a thumbtack. Be careful. The hole should be about 1⁄10th of an inch in diameter. This one step will help to keep the egg from cracking and give the egg a nice oval shape. (Instead of the flat-ended egg you get when you don't release the air from the sac.) Start cooking in cold, slightly salted water—enough water to cover the tops of the eggs. Heat until boiling. Then reduce the heat and let simmer. (The salt keeps the white from making streamers if an egg should crack). Try to have the eggs at room temperature before cooking—this prevents "thermal shock" where the materials in the egg expand too quickly and shatter—not as tasty or attractive. For soft-cooked eggs: allow simmering for 2 to 3 minutes. For hard cooked (boiled eggs): allow to simmer for 10 to 12 minutes. When mega-cooking™, I boil 2 to 3 dozen eggs in a large Dutch oven. It works great. Immediately after the simmer, give the eggs a cold water bath. Place the pan in the sink and start running in cold water until the eggs are cool enough to handle. This not only prevents overcooking (the hot water would continue to cook the eggs if you let them sit it in and cool naturally), but you force the hydrogen sulfide gas to collect near the shell and away from the yolk. (This sulfur reaction is what sometimes gives you the "green" look to your eggs—most unappealing).
Eggs (health issue)	Ingredient	Eggs get a bum rap. Eggs are good food and can be a very economical part of your diet. Like with anything, don't go to extremes. We have an "egg breakfast" once a week. We

don't do it everyday—that would be boring. Egg whites are a wonderful, healthy option. (See Eggs, whites). Be careful with eggs. Since they are a poultry product, you need to be aware of possible food poisoning. Treat a raw egg and all that touches it with the same respect as you would raw chicken meat. If you have any doubt to the safety of your eggs do not eat raw eggs in any form. *Note:* The Eggnog recipe in this book must be made with sound, good eggs (eggs free from any bacterial strains that cause food poisoning). To be certain, use a pasteurized egg product, or buy commercial eggnog and use it for the other eggnog recipes.

Eggs (whites) | Ingredient | Have you ever wondered how egg whites can turn into meringue, soufflé, or "angel" cake? When you beat the white, you are in a way "cooking" the protein in the white. Without getting too technical, the beating pulls the protein molecules (sort of like stringing taffy) out into an elongated shape that, as it starts to form a structure, traps air. Voila—foam. This foam is one of the best leavening agents, and is a very healthy alternative because it is low in calories and low in cholesterol. To improve your chances of your egg whites working into a proper foam:

1. Don't use a plastic bowl or spoon or beater (copper works the best, but glass or enamel will do—don't use aluminum because it could give the whites a grayish tinge).
2. Make certain the tools you use are completely clean, dry, and free from any fat. I like to wipe all the surfaces of the bowl and beaters with a clean, dry paper towel.
3. Make sure you are using 100% egg whites only (even a drop of egg yolk will ruin the whole process).
4. Add a weak acidic ingredient (I recommend cream of tartar). That little bit of acid will neutralize the weakly alkaline egg white, breaking the protective water sheath in the whites because of the change in the electric charge of the molecules.
5. Room temperature eggs work best. The temperature changes the surface tension of the eggs. Since we want to

increase that tension (so the molecules will hold more air) we don't want cold eggs.

6. Don't overbeat. When it looks right, stop! Don't continue or you'll ruin the whole batch.
7. Always treat the foam with respect and fold any other ingredients in very gently. Very gently.

Egg whites also are called "albumen" (pronounced "al–BU-men").

Elimination	Mc	As I research recipes, I try to cut out as many superfluous steps as possible. I don't need to waste my time doing a step that was important years ago, or that serves no culinary function. In other words, I try to cut the steps and processing procedures of my recipe. I'm always looking for ways to be more efficient. I don't want to waste effort, so I recommend you look for ways to cut out steps (For example: sautéing in butter: there rarely is a need for this step. It takes time and energy, adds calories, and robs the vegetables of some of their nutrients.)
Equipment	Mc	Under this section of each recipe, we list any special equipment needed to make the recipe easier to prepare. Of course, we need measuring spoons and cups, mixing bowls, etc. (standard kitchen equipment) for every recipe, so I don't mention those. I only add equipment that I consider specialized, or something that isn't basic to common recipe preparation. It is only a suggestion of how to make the best use of your time. For those who have not started collecting extra kitchen equipment, you can do these recipes by hand and each recipe features alternatives. , for a whole chapter on Equipment, page 51.
Ficin	General	The enzyme in figs that tenderizes meat (pronounced "fissin"). Figs have a rich culinary history, including many mentions in the Holy Bible.
Fish	Ingredient	I don't think Americans eat enough fish. I'm amazed at how rarely many families eat it at all. It is a wonderful food. Is it

the fishy smell that bothers you? Then cook the fish using some kind of an acid to get rid of the smell. Use vinegar or lemon, or an acidic liquid of your choice. That fishy smell is caused by amines (pronounced "a-means") which only make up 0.0001 percent of the fish's weight—pretty potent, huh! The action is very simple. By using an acid, we change the electrical charge of the amine. It is now water-soluble. There goes the smell. So, now you know why so many good restaurants serve lemon wedges with fish. It is so you can neutralize any offending amines. Tips:

1. If you are cooking a thick fish in a bouillon, always start with a cold bouillon—or else you'll have the outer surface cooked before the inner temperatures are safe. So to get the inner temperatures correct, the outer surfaces have to be overcooked.
2. If you are cooking a thin fish in a bouillon, always start with a hot bouillon—it will seal the surface, so the fish will retain its shape better. Since it is thin, the whole piece will cook evenly in about the same time.
3. Fish freeze wonderfully. Freeze as fresh as you can. My fish is usually in the freezer within hours of being caught.
4. Don't ever boil fish. It breaks the fish's tender texture. Steaming works great, though.
5. I don't recommend frying fish. That's my personal preference.

Like all the recipes in this book, the fish recipes were tested, and "passed" the quality standards. The recipes are more complicated than just baking fish. I figured you could do that without a recipe. Some of them call for more economical cuts of fish, or surplus fish. When we get a beautiful Mahi-mahi steak, we just grill it or bake it with a little lemon juice. Then with what's left, make other recipes. One dish we loved when we were in Panama was Ceviche (Si-vich-A)—non-heat-cooked fish. The citric acids "cooked" the fish as it marinated. I haven't perfected the recipe enough to publish it yet. But I'm working on it.

Flake	Mc	When working with fish and some other ingredients you'll want to "flake" the meat apart. Separate the meat into small pieces with a fork or with your hands.
Flour	Ingredient	I use freshly milled whole-wheat flour for almost every recipe. Because I'm making recipes for many different families, I have tested using white flour. The recipes work, I just don't think they taste as good. I have compromised with pastry. It is one of our few indulgences—I use white flour or fresh ground from soft white wheat. The hard whole-wheat pastry just isn't as smooth. I've experimented with quinoa, spelt, oat, corn, kamut and a variety of other grains. Some Alan would allow me to use again, some I had to promise never to bring back into the house. I've gotten a great deal of help and good information from mill dealers and in particular, Donna Spann. She has written a fascinating book, *Grains of Truth,* in which she goes into detail about grains, giving us history, uses, sources, and recipes. , see "Wheat:" on page 194.
Fluff	Mc	Sifting is very difficult and time consuming when you are working with such large quantities. Instead of sifting, I "fluff." Place dry ingredients in a large bowl and whip the ingredients together with a wire whisk. That will give the volume sifting does, as well as an even distribution.
Freezer	Equipment	Freezers are worth their price in the return of quality food and time savings. Remember freezers do not make cold. Freezers remove heat from your food. , see whole chapter on Equipment, page 51.
Freezing, individually	Mc	Another method of freezing I use often is freezing items individually. , page 118, for a full explanation. Basically, I freeze each berry, meatball, or whatever separately on a tray. Once frozen solid, I then can bag the frozen items. I can pull out one or two needed items without having to thaw the whole lot.

Fresh	Labeling	The term "fresh" should only be used with foods that have never had heat added or removed (cooked or frozen). It should not contain preservatives of any kind. An apple is fresh if it is in the same "state" or form as when it left the tree. Unfortunately, the term "fresh" can be placed on foods that have been irradiated.
Fruits	Ingredient	Fresh fruit is a personal favorite, and one of our main food sources. I've also learned some interesting things about certain fruits (see specific fruits in topics). Here are some tips: 1. Buy organic, ripened on the tree or vine, if you can afford it or have that option. 2. Cut and store fruit using glass, ceramic, or plastic. Try to avoid metal as much as possible. I only use a stainless-steel knife to cut really hard fruit open (e.g., pineapple). Use a plastic knife whenever you can. This will make a substantial difference in the discoloration process. 3. If you use canned fruit, remove the fruit from the can immediately upon opening. Some juices are so acidic they dissolve metal. Test this: open a can of pineapple, remove the pineapple and allow the can to sit with the juice over night. You'll be amazed at the gray-sludge the next morning. 4. Browning of some fruit occurs because the "meat" of the fruit is exposed to oxygen (another enzyme reaction). Without getting too complicated, the compound phenol (also known as carbolic acid) forms a brown polymer on the surface of the fruit. So, you can either shield the fruit from the oxygen (e.g., guacamole dip or Waldorf salad), or render the enzyme ineffective (use Brown Away or a similar acidic deterrent—apple juice, vinegar, vinegar-based dressings, citrus juice). Also realize that by changing its temperature, you can stop the browning process. Cooking prevents it altogether; freezing gives it a temporary hold. Even when we're freezing fruit, we spray on Brown Away to keep the enzyme reaction down while we work. 5. When using fruit in a recipe, always allow for their high

water content. When I cook with fruit, I plan on that moisture to do the work that additional liquid would do (e.g., Deutsche Brats).

6. Adjust cooking times for fruit. Since some fruit does leave off juice or soften early, I won't add the fruit until the last few minutes (e.g., Harvest Bird).
7. Remember the high sugar content of some fruit. Let it do the sweetening for you. Rarely do you need to add extra sugar to fruit. If you are in the habit of doing that, start using less added sugar. Wean your family to enjoy the natural sweetness.

Frying	Technique	I rarely fry. Once in a while I'll fry some vegetables as in a stir-fry with very little oil. When I do deep-fat fry, I use the healthiest oil I can afford.
Frying (deep-fat)	Technique	Once in while, we'll use the deep-fat fryer as it was designed. We'll make "dough-knots" or fritters. But when we do we are very careful. Hot oil is not something to take lightly. Hot oil is very flammable. Oil and water don't mix, so make sure ingredients are as "dry" as possible. This can be done by blotting and/or by using a breading. Never attempt to put out an oil fire with water—it will make it worst. Keep a properly-charged Class B (or Class B/C) fire extinguisher in your kitchen and train your loved ones how and when to use it. Class A fire extinguishers are designed for use on wood and paper fires (and usually use water or soda water). Class B fire extinguishers are designed for fuel fires (and often use carbon dioxide). Class C fire extinguishers are designed for electrical fires (use similar materials as Class B extinguishers). Class D fire extinguishers are rare and are designed to fight burning metal fires like magnesium (used in flares).
Garlic	Ingredient	Garlic is amazing. Not only does it have a vibrant history and flavor, it has some medicinal benefits. What makes the "garlic" flavor is when the chemical allin and the enzyme allinase interact. In its natural form, a membrane separates

		these two. So by controlling the membrane, you can control the amount of flavor. (FYI: in reality the allinase destroys the allin.) There is also a sulfur compound that adds to the garlic flavor. So by cutting or crushing the membranes you determine how "garlicky" your food is. Heating does release some of the reaction, but it takes time. So when I'm mega-cooking™, I use whole, un-crushed cloves, knowing that they will slowly release flavor through the assembly process and the heating process. I can then take the cloves easily (they are large enough to spot) off my children's helpings (they aren't wild about garlic and with this method of cooking they get a little flavoring in their food), add the garlic to my plate, smash it with my spoon, and eat as much as I want. (It's a "garlic" version of the idea of salting at the table.)
Gelatin	Ingredient	Gelatin can be a wonderful addition to your diet. I schedule at least one gelatin salad each week. Know that it is made from mammalian bones and hide. I know it sounds gross, but it is basically purified glue. But don't let that stop you. The molecules unhook and bond during temperature changes. I like to use plain gelatin (e.g. Knox brand) and add my own flavorings and sweeteners. That way I don't have to choose the sugar or aspartame option. It is quite easy—follow the package directions. Also realize that the longer the gelatin molecules have to bond, the more stable those bonds will be. If you're making a mold that has to sit on a buffet table for very long, make it about 2 days ahead. It will keep its shape longer than one made a few hours ahead.
Goosh	Mc	Children know how to do this well. Some adults have to remember. Gooshing is a highly technical term (smile) for kneading ingredients together by hand. Not only is it gooshy, but makes a gooshing sound. Squeeze, push, and knead the ingredients together. This is what we do when we make meat loaf—getting the meat, eggs, and other ingredients up to our wrists.

Grapes	Ingredient	We buy grapes in bulk and freeze them individually. Frozen grapes are about my favorite snack—so much better than a candy bar.
Green Harvesting	General	A term used to describe the practice of picking fruits and vegetables when they are still "green" and either giving the appearance of ripeness by spraying them or allowing them to mature in route on a truck away from the soil and sun. For example, some agribusinessmen spray ethylene gas on green tomatoes so they look red like ripe ones. Ethylene ($CH_2{=}CH_2$) is a chemical that fruits produce during the ripening process, but can be manufactured and then artificially added (gassing) to give the appearance of ripening. Of course, those gassed tomatoes don't have the flavor and nutritional value of tomatoes that ripen on the vine. I'm allergic to raw tomatoes, and sometimes break out in a rash. But when we grew our own and picked them perfectly ripe, I never once had a rash. Makes you think.
Grilling	Technique	Grilling is such a wonderful way to cook because it is a truly "dry" method; none of the steam can recondense on the food affecting the texture and flavor. We grill quite a bit of our meat and some of our vegetables. We then freeze them and reheat. As long as we have the grill fired up, we maximize the heat and grill quite a bit of food. Delicious!
Healthy	Labeling	That is such a great word. Healthy. Don't we all want to eat healthy food so we can be healthy? But what does it mean? As companies started making "healthy" part of their brand name, the issue became even more confusing. The government has banned any new products from using "healthy" as part of their name. But those companies already doing it were "grandfathered" in and are allowed to continue using the term. Technically the word "healthy" can only be used on a food label if the food has less than 480 milligrams of sodium and less than 60 milligrams of cholesterol per serving. It must also be low in fat. That is what the government

		defines as "healthy." It could still be loaded with all sorts of preservatives, additives, dyes, and other non-foods and still be called "healthy."
Herbs	Ingredient	Though I'm learning more and more about herbs and am starting to grow my own, I realize that many women don't have access to fresh herbs. ALL the test recipes are for dried herbs—the ones you can buy in bottles at the grocery store. The few exceptions are noted. If you do have access to fresh herbs, here is how to convert: Use 3 times as much fresh as dried. (The dried is more concentrated, so you only need one-third as much as if you were using fresh.) If your herbs are a little old, just use ½ times in a recipe to get the same flavor. To make more of an impact with dried herbs, mix all the herbs together and spray on some water to assist them in rehydrating—they'll mix better into the rest of the ingredients. Again, I prefer to cook with fresh as much as possible, but sometimes I can't get fresh and I use the dehydrated. I also like to make my own dehydrated versions. One herb I have had great success with that might be new to you is kelp. Kelp is loaded with good nutrition. I buy it dehydrated and ground. It spices just like nutmeg does.
High and Low, More and Reduced or Less	Labeling	Even the terms "high" and "low" have quantifiable measurements before a company can use them. Always check the ingredients list and nutrition facts. Some of these terms, though they have one definite meaning, can confuse us. Here's the chart:

	More (used in comparisons	**High**	**Less or reduced (used in comparisons)**	**Low**		
Particular nutrient	=>10%	=>20%			Daily Value	
Calories		Not defined and cannot be used	=>25% (fewer than)	=<40	Calories per serving	
Cholesterol		No one wants to claim this	=>25% (less than)	=<20	Milligrams per serving	AND =<2 grams of saturated fat
Fat			=>25% (less than)	=<3	Fat per serving	
Saturated Fat				=<1	Grams of fat per serving	AND =<15% of calories from saturated fatty acids
Sugar				Not defined		

Hot dogs	Ingredient	I realize health purists would avoid hot dogs all together. I understand their concerns with nitrites used in some commercial hot dogs. Nitrite reacts with meat proteins to form nitrosamines, which are very effective carcinogens. Nitrite also leeches the body of Vitamin C. If you do want to serve your children hot dogs (or at a picnic where you have no choice), you have some options to reduce the health implications. One option is to make your own buns from fresh ground whole wheat. (This has two benefits, you've replaced sweet bread—some prepackaged buns are too "cake-like"—with health-bread and because the whole-wheat bread is so filling, children will fill up on one or two hotdogs in these buns, compared to the four-to-five with the cake-like buns. They are filling up on good bread and less nitrite-filled meat.) Another option, to replenish the body from the nitrite damage, is to load up on Vitamin C and phytochemicals before and after eating the hot dogs. You could purchase nitrite free hot dogs or health-food substitutes. Or at the very least, space your hot dog eating by months.
Ingredients	Recipes	I list the ingredients needed for the recipe and the amounts for different size batches. You'll need to make any adjustments for your family's size and taste preferences. This is one aspect that is critical to mega-cooking™: listing ingredients and their amounts in a useable format. The entire chapter on Ingredients and mega-cooking™ provides more information. In the Methods Section there are details of how to use the recipe. You might want to use the conversion chart, and also track your own results for assembling amounts.
Irradiation	General	Irradiation is a big controversy. Some people like it because it makes their food "safe." Others say it is more dangerous than what it is preventing. Basically, technicians x-ray the food to extend its shelf life. They bombard it with gamma radiation (different sources are used). I'm very cautious. My father was on the board of a medical corporation specializing in radiation equipment and supplies for years and served as a radiological technician in the military. He knows first

hand the dangers of excessive radiation. He is very adamant against such programs. Alan, my husband, who is level three certified in NDE radiography, explains: when radiation energy, in the form of x-rays or gamma rays, interact with tissue, some ionization occurs. Either the affected tissues are temporarily damaged, permanently damaged/mutated, or destroyed. It all depends on the kind of tissues (their susceptibility to ionizing energy), the energy intensity (in electron volts), and the amount of exposure. If a person ingests plant material while it is still actively ionized, their body has to deal with the residual energy as well. One problem that needs to be fixed now is the method and procedure of alerting the public to foods that have been irradiated. We should be able to make our own choice. I think we are very aware of the dangers of radiation to fetuses. I talked with a mother recently who suspects that a series of x-rays she had when her baby was 8 days into gestation could have caused his autism. Again, I recommend caution on this topic.

Juice	Ingredient	This is a debated issue with health enthusiasts.

1. Some say drinking good juice has "saved their lives." Since juice is easier to digest, your body can more readily benefit from the nutrients. It is quick fuel that the body can use.
2. Others claim that juice was made to be consumed with the fibers of the vegetable or fruit. It's the "throwing away" or the not consuming of the fiber that is a cause for colon cancers and colon problems. You are also, in the case of fruit juice, consuming much more sugar and calories drinking juice. If you drink a 12-ounce glass of orange juice, you'd have to eat 3 oranges to get that much juice. The argument is that you would have filled up after one or two oranges and not had all the extra calories and sugar of that third orange's juice.

It is an interesting argument and like so many of these discussions, it's the extremes that get us into trouble. If I only drank juice and stopped eating carrots, I would have bowel problems. But by sometimes drinking good juice along with whole vegetables and fruit, we're getting the benefits of both.

The kicker is good juice. You shouldn't be able to see through your apple juice. It should be thick and cloudy if it is really pure apple juice. Your orange juice should be loaded with healthful pulp and H_2O_2 (hydrogen peroxide). Your vegetable juice should be thick and a little hard to swallow. If it is water-like, then drink water. Don't be fooled by anything called "fruit drink." Either it's juice or it's not. If I can't find 100% juice with no added sugar, we drink water. My family doesn't need flavored sugar water.

Juice, Hot Squeezing	Technique	Growing up among citrus groves, I've learned some things about oranges, lemons, and grapefruits. One trick that still amazes me, is that heating citrus fruits before juicing will yield more juice. I zap my lemons in the microwave for about 30 seconds, then I squeeze them. They will yield about 1/3 more juice than if I had juiced them cold. If you don't have a microwave oven, soak in hot water for a few minutes. Doing this procedure with oranges leaves you to consider: do you want more juice or do you want less juice but more nutritious juice? I like pure orange juice and I don't want to destroy any of the H_2O_2 or phytochemicals by heating. The determining factor is if we are going to drink the juice right away. If we are, I don't heat the oranges. If we will heat the juice in a recipe or freeze it, then it doesn't matter and I want all the juice I can get. With lemons, I heat the juice anyway, so it doesn't matter if I pre-heat for juicing. I heat my lemon juice when I make lemonade so the sweetener completely dissolves—and it is good lemonade.
Labels, how to translate	Labeling	You'd think a word in English has a definite meaning. But when it comes to English words on labels, throw away your dictionary and pick up the FDA regulation handbook. Here in Topics, I've listed several "popular" label claims and translated their "labelese" into something more comprehendible. If you've wondered about a particular labeling

		term, some are here in alphabetical order with the word Labeling in the Group column. There are volumes of manuals on this topic and I barely list a fraction of the policies. If you have a particular sensitivity, go to your public library and research. I've researched MSG and I'm astounded by all the ways "MSG" can be listed on a label that wouldn't give the average person a clue that the term means MSG (e.g., natural flavorings). Also, these restrictions were current at the time I wrote this book. As with any government regulations, they are subject to change. So, please do some research yourself. Also, if you have family members who are sensitive, do what I try to do most of the time—buy food that is easily identified and doesn't have a chance to have any of the "factors" in it.
Lean, extra lean	Labeling	There is a definite criterion for evaluating the fat content of food. **Here's the formula for lean:** One serving must have less than 10 grams of fat *and* less than 4.5 grams of saturated fat *and* less than 95 milligrams of cholesterol. **Here's the formula for extra lean:** One serving must have less than 5 grams of fat *and* less than 2 grams of saturated fat *and* less than 95 milligrams of cholesterol. One other concern about labeling is the serving size. While one product may seem wonderful for having only 1 gram of sugar, you have to check the serving size. With my second son, having Type I diabetes (childhood onset), we have to really monitor his diet. I'm amazed at how very small standard servings are. Once I convert the amount to a Stuart-sized serving, the "health" of a packaged food is quite questionable. It convinces me every day to make more and more of our food from scratch.
Marketing terms	General	The four "textbook" concepts of marketing are Product, Place, Promotion, and Positioning. I also think we're paying for Pizzazz and Politics. , page 73.

Meat, Searing or Sealing	Technique	Beef and some other red meat contain enough sugar that you get a sugar-amine reaction when you cook meat at high temperature in very hot oil. It doesn't take much oil. If you don't use a hot enough temperature, the meat can turn gray. So, you want to work quickly and seal in the meat flavors. The sugars will brown and create a natural barrier for the juices. Process the meat according to the recipe. Always seal the meat first. Then, you can cook the vegetables. Also, monitor the amount (of oil) and temperature as you cook. Think about adding ice cubes to tap water. That is basically the same effect that cool meat has on the hot oil. So, pace yourself. *Note:* If you are making stock, don't pre-seal the meat—you want the juices and flavor to go to the liquid.
Medium-mega	Mc	Medium-mega sessions are a step more complicated than mini-megas—you'll now be working 5 to 10 different recipes which you multiple batch all at one time. You'll want to select recipes that either have similar ingredients or have similar processing needs. , page 103 for more details.
Mega-cooking™	Mc	The term I coined to describe how I combine cooking techniques and ingredients to produce more than one recipe-amount's worth. Mega-cooking™: A method of cooking in which you duplicate as many repetitive steps as possible, purchase food at the best prices, streamline preparation, and make multiple batches of recipes.
Mega-session	Mc	This is the big session of multi-batching more than 10 different recipes in the same time frame. , page 105.
Mega-shopping	Mc	This technique will manifest itself in mega-savings off your food budget. Part of an entire chapter is dedicated to explaining how to get the most for your effort. , page 72.
Milk, dehydrated	Ingredient	Don't forget the economical benefits of cooking with dehydrated milk. I try to always keep some on hand—it has saved me many a rush trip to the store when I run out of

fresh milk and am in the middle of a recipe. All dehydrated milk is not equal. We have found a source (a Quebec company) that makes such a quality product it is even good for drinking (unlike most of the others that are only good for cooking).

Milk, freezing	Ingredient	You can freeze milk for later use. We go through so much milk that I don't need to store it up. But I do like to have some bags of milk available in case I run out and need some quickly for a recipe. Freezing will change its consistency. Some people will not like the taste or texture of thawed milk. That's a personal preference. But for cooking, it works fine. Freeze some milk in one-cup amounts using the Bag-in-Box method. Then it is pre-measured for you to use when you need it. Thaw in refrigerator or if it is going directly into a recipe, thaw in the microwave.
Milk, health issues	Ingredient	Mention milk in some groups and you are in for quite a discussion. There are those who will not allow it in their homes, and some who use it and its by-products (butter, cheese, cream, etc.) regularly. Some people do have an intolerance to milk and then need to use substitutes like soymilk, rice milk, and such. Some who don't drink milk, do it for peculiar reasons and I question their intellectual integrity. Those that say milk is only for baby cows will then eat honey or seeds or grain or fruit. If food is only made for one purpose and all other uses of it are unnatural, then by that same logic almost everything we consider food would be off limits. Honey's first use is for the propagation of more bees. Seeds are for further harvests. Fruit is the natural "compost" and food source to nurture the seed as it starts a new plant. And the list goes on. My God is more competent than that. He gave things multiple purposes. I can eat honey and not feel any guilt about robbing some baby bee of its nursery. I can enjoy seeds, grains and fruit, knowing there is more than enough for us and for the propagation of more plants and a continued harvest. I can also drink milk not fretting that I have gone against nature by drinking

something that is only made for baby cows. Now, if you have taken a religious vow or are allergic to milk, of course, don't consume it. But do it for the right reasons, not for illogical ones. (And, of course, mother's milk is best for your baby.) There is a very legitimate concern about some dairies' practice of giving the cows hormones that end up entering our children's bodies and altering their delicate hormonal balances. If you have teenagers, you know that their normal hormones are enough to deal with. Our favorite solution is to obtain our milk directly from a farmer—pure, straight from the cow (a cow that was not being "supped up" with hormones, etc.)

Milk, safety	safety	When you buy milk, take the time to dig to the back and get the freshest milk; buy it last—right before you check out. Don't let it sit in your cart as you shop. That time away from the refrigerator will affect its storage time. Keep your milk in the refrigerator as much as possible. Don't let it sit out. Get in the habit of pouring what you'll need into a cup and immediately returning the sealed container to the refrigerator. If you do pour it into a pitcher for use at the table and have any left over—do not pour that into the main carton. Put it in a separate airtight container and use *first.* Even sitting out for only 30 minutes can affect the storage life of milk. Keep milk sealed, it absorbs odors easily. Light also affects milk, so keep the carton's exposure to light to a minimum. Some of you might want to move it to a "light-proof" airtight container.
Milk, scalding	Technique	Our grandparents had to scald milk to fight bacteria. We don't have to if we're buying pasteurized milk. The reason I scald the milk is that it is then warm when I add it to some sauces, shortening the time I have to spend stirring—it makes a sauce or pudding "work" quicker.
Milk, sour	Ingredient	To make sour milk (some recipes call for this ingredient) add 1 tablespoon lemon juice or white vinegar and enough

		milk to make 1 cup—let it stand for 5 minutes to "cure." You can substitute slightly sour milk for buttermilk in some recipes. If your milk starts to sour and you don't want to drink it, use it in recipes for baking. In most cases, it works fine. Use common sense—sour milk can still be salvaged in a baking recipe, but rotten/spoiled milk shouldn't be used in any recipe.
Milk, types and use	Ingredient	We mostly use whole milk. Not only do we prefer the flavor and texture, I want my children to have milk as close to its natural form as we can get it. But there are quite a few people who for health or budget reasons prefer other grades of milk. That's fine. Just realize that the sauce might not be as creamy if you do substitute milk. Whole milk has at least 3.25% fat content. Skim milk has most of the fat removed and should have less than 0.5 fat content. Low-fat milk runs from 0.5 to 2.0% fat content. Read the label! Evaporated milk has had 60% of the water removed, so you can add a can of water to a can of evaporated milk and end up with "normal milk"—a good mix for recipes. Sweetened condensed milk has half the water removed and lots of sugar added. Milk solids or powdered milk is what is left when the water and fat has been removed. Follow the directions for reconstituting. I do use milk solids in recipes as a thickener and flavor-enhancer. I buy it in bulk and keep it on the shelf for recipes and emergencies (when I run out of fresh milk.) Yogurt is cultured milk. But because it is cultured properly, it is delicious. (See other topics for specifics about grades and types of milk.)
Mini-mega	Mc	With mini-megas, you'll be multiple-batching several similar recipes. It is a good transition from doubling and multi-batching—2 to 4 different recipes that you multiple batch all at the same time.
MOL	Mc	In quite a few of my recipes, I use the term [mol]. It means "more or less." When you see [mol] that means you can vary the amount either by adding more or less of that ingredient

		according to your family's tastes without jeopardizing the recipe's consistency. I don't like really salty food, so I cook with the bare minimum to maintain the chemical balance. If you like salt and your blood pressure can handle it, add more to these recipes. For some of the recipes you can adjust the meat content according to your budget and taste for meat.
Molds, freezing in	Mc	I also freeze some of the "meat loaf "styled meals in molds. I use plastic molds that would normally be used for gelatin salads. Once the ingredients are frozen, I can pop them out of the plastic mold and bag or rewrap. This works great for recipes that will keep their own shape (very little moisture). I can place these frozen ingredients flat in a glass-baking dish. Then bake. They come out lovely. You can also do this with metal molds. If the ingredients are very liquid, I have to return the frozen ingredients to the metal mold and bake in it. *Note:* I pop and rewrap very quickly—the ingredients are usually out of the freezer for less than a minute—I don't want them to thaw at all.
MSG	Labeling	MSG or monosodium glutamate is a "hidden" flavoring in quite a few foods. Though a growing number of people are developing allergies to MSG, it is still being used in products. If you have a problem with MSG, (I do), I watch for words like "Natural Flavorings." How the "labeling powers that be" can consider adding MSG to be natural, I don't know. Makes you wonder. MSG reactions can include "Chinese Restaurant Syndrome," learning disabilities, severe allergic reactions, anaphylactic shock, and worse. I strive to make my food with my own ingredients and I don't use any MSG. Why do companies use MSG if it is so controversial? It means more profit. Or so they think. MSG is cheaper per pound than "real" ingredients. , please note the comments on Rosa's Con Pollo on page 350 about MSG in some packages of yellow rice.)

Multiple Batches, multi-batching	Mc	This is one concept that many mega-cooks use. Instead of just making one batch of a recipe, they make multiple batches. It doesn't take much more work to make three or four batches of a recipe—set-up and clean-up is about the same, the actual assembling takes a little bit more time, but the rewards are great. That means three times when you have the food ready to heat and you don't have to do all the work again., there is more detail about this concept through the book, but specifically see pages 101.
New and Improved	Labeling	The word "New" on a label is considered a major selling point. It doesn't make sense to me. When they say "New and Improved" does that mean the previous version was "Old and Inferior?" In six weeks are they coming out with another "New and Improved" version that makes this current bottle the "Old and Inferior" version? Yet, the statistics "prove" the premise. People like the word "new." The government limits the use of the word "new" to six months, and then it could be that all that was changed was a minor aspect of the product. Don't fall for it.
Nitrites	General	An additive used by some meat handlers to reduce the microbial degeneration. But that same effect also happens in humans. Nitrite reacts with meat proteins to form nitrosamines, which are very effective carcinogens. Try to avoid nitrites as much as you can. If you can't avoid eating them, try to counter their effects by adding extra Vitamin C, phytochemicals, and glycoproteins to your diet.
Oats	Ingredient	We really enjoy using raw oat groats for a variety of recipes. We can grind groats (the "berries") into flour or flakes (comparable to oatmeal). All of the recipes become more nutritious and more flavorful when we use groats and either grind or flake fresh. It may seem like a "way out there" concept, akin to spinning my own thread to sew on a button, but it really is easy. If you came to my kitchen and saw how quick and inexpensive it is, you'd be hooked. My oatmeal

costs less than 50¢ a pound. And in less time than it takes to boil water I can flake groats using an inexpensive hand-crank machine or an electric flaker. The health benefits are dramatic. , page 61.

Oil, safety

Safety

Never leave hot oil unattended. Watch the temperature. Know how to stop an oil fire. Train your whole family. Don't wait until you have to know— learn now. Don't rely just on what I tell you. Check with your fire station and ask for instructions.

1. Don't try to put an oil fire out with water—the water could spread the fire;
2. Have an ABC extinguisher in your kitchen because it is good for all kinds of home fires. Know how and when to use it;
3. If you can, deny the fire any oxygen—put the lid on the pot or cover the flames with baking soda (as it burns it releases carbon dioxide and acts as a mini-CO_2 fire extinguisher.
4. Don't panic. Get it under control. Don't take chances. Know when to leave a situation.
5. Again, consult your fire marshal for proper instructions and take the time to go through their community-training program.

Oils

Ingredient

This is an entire subject in itself. I recommend the healthiest oil you can afford. First of all, oil is not evil or bad. Too much of it isn't good. We need some oil. No one should go on a completely fat-free diet. That is unhealthy. But few Americans are in danger of 100% fat free. If you watch the fat content and stay reasonable, you'll be fine. Did you know that some oils, especially those from sea creatures—Omega-3 oils—are actually beneficial to coronary health? I like to use monounsaturated oils like olive and canola. They also are more perishable and should be refrigerated. (See specific oil for details.) Check your oil before you pour into a recipe. A little bad oil can ruin a perfectly good batter.

Olive Oil	Ingredient	Should be refrigerated because it is monounsaturated. *Note:* you'll find when you refrigerate olive oil it turns cloudy—to solve this, let it sit out for a few minutes and shake gently. Olive oil comes in grades: the finest is extra-virgin olive oil. Not only is the purest, but it is the most expensive. Then, in order, superfine, fine, virgin and pure. Tricky isn't it? You'd think "pure" would be better than "fine", but it is the least flavorful and least expensive. I like the flavor of olive oil, but it is distinctive. Test first before you make a mega-batch of something using olive oil instead of your regular brand. Some people consider it an "acquired taste."
Onions	Ingredient	First, please read the topic "Garlic" because the process that gives garlic its flavor is almost identical with onions. Except in onions, two different reactions are going on: one causes onion flavoring and the other causes the tearing. The tearing effect is a result of what we do to the onion. It is a chemical reaction that happens immediately when we break the separating membranes. This reaction is water-soluble. So you can cut your onions under running water, use an airtight chopper, or work quickly with a food processor. The flavor is affected by how we treat the membranes by chopping, dicing, grating, or cooking. I like to grate my onions and then use them "raw" in my recipes. That makes a tolerable flavor for all of us. People have different tastes, and you'll need to adjust the recipes in this book according to your family's tastes. If you like more of an onion flavor, add more onions, cook them ahead of time, or process them more. If you like less of an onion flavor, cook with big chunks of onion and then remove either at the table or during the cooking process, or simply add less to the recipe. And, of course, different onions have different flavors. I use the large white onions for the recipes in this book.
Opportunity Cost	Mc	Opportunity costs are the "prices" we pay that may seem invisible, but should be something we consider whenever we make a decision. When we choose to do option "A" the opportunity cost is all the other options we could have

done instead. For example, we buy a raw beef steak for $10. You could say that steak costs $10, but if you also consider the opportunity cost of that steak, you'd be acknowledging all the other things you could have purchased with that same $10. That steak cost you ten pounds of ground beef, two movie tickets, four bags of fruit, a newsletter subscription, or ... hundreds of other things you could have used that $10 for. Remember we can only spend that ten dollar bill one time. This idea applies to time also. Each time we choose to spend an hour doing an activity, the opportunity costs is all the other things we could have done for that same hour. When you start looking at your decisions from this viewpoint, it helps you set priorities straight. Don't make decisions as if they were mutally exclusive from the rest of your life. For example, if spending didn't affect your whole budget then you might think it's okay to order pizzas for $30. But do that too often and then you won't be able to pay your charge card bill in full when it comes in.

Options	Recipes	When a recipe can be prepared using different methods, I've supplied you with options. Many of these recipes can be prepared by doubling, multi-batching, or during a mega-session. Some can be frozen "raw" or frozen "cooked." You need to evaluate how you'll use the recipe, your freezer space, and how much time you'll have on the day of serving.
Organic	Labeling	Different states have different requirements for farmers to qualify as organic. At the time I wrote this, California had the strictest laws. For a food to qualify as organically grown, they should be pesticide and chemical-free. The food is better tasting and more nutritious. It also might not appear as "polished" as regular produce. There is a reason, much of what we "think" a tomato should look like is because we've trained ourselves to expect perfect looking specimens (that have been sprayed and chemically fertilized). Organic produce looks more like what home-gardeners produce or what our grandmothers bought. Don't let the less than symmetrical appearances deter you. They are more delicious than

		their sprayed and zapped counter-parts. The way to bring the price down is for the demand to go up. When farmers realize that more of us want organic produce, they'll find ways to produce it more cost effectively.
Oven Mitts	Equipment	I've had dozens of oven mitts in my married life and I've been disappointed by almost every one of them. They are cute, yes, look great on the hook, yes, but defend me against hot plates, rarely. Or they have a short lifespan—a few washings and they are useless. That is until I, gulp, paid full price for a set of professional mitts that I bought at a restaurant supply store. They are big and go up to my elbow—I like that. They really protect my children and me. I did have to pay almost twice as much for them as a pair I'd buy in a department store, but they are worth every penny. They wash well and really are insulated, not just quilted fabric.
Pan, rotating	Mc	When you are baking several batches of a recipe, you'll need to rotate the pans through the baking process. Switch shelves and forward to back. Few ovens generate the exact same amount of heat to every cubic centimeter of oven space. Even the effect of distance from the elements will cause uneven browning. This is something you might not have had to worry about when you baked one loaf of bread, but when you bake 8 loaves, you have to rotate the pans during the baking.
Papain	General	The enzyme in papaya that tenderizes meat (pronounced "pa-pa-yin"). Cortes discovered this tenderizer when he saw the Mayans tenderize their meat by wrapping it overnight in bruised papaya leaves.
Pasta	Ingredient	Depending on the recipe calling for pasta, I either fully cook, three-quarters cook, or leave the pasta dry (uncooked). 100%—The only time I fully cook pasta is if the pasta is going to be eaten at that time. If the pasta is going into a dish to be frozen I don't fully cook it. 75%—If it is a casserole in which the pasta makes up less than ⅓

		of the bulk, I cook the noodles only for 75% of the normal time (listed on the package instructions). The noodles will absorb some of the liquids of the casserole and will continue to soften as it freezes. 0%—If the pasta is going into a dish like lasagna or manicotti (a dish that will be baking for at least 45 minutes when it is heated), I don't cook the pasta at all.
Phytochemicals	General	The chemicals (good guys) we get from plants. The optimal method is to get these from mature plants organically grown. Unfortunately much of our American produce is picked "green." The vegetables finish "ripening" on route to the markets away from their sources of energy (sun, water, soil). Because we can't grow all the produce we consume, my family supplements with phytochemical products.
Pineapple	Ingredient	Pineapple is an amazing fruit. I cook with it often. There is quite a difference between canned and fresh pineapple. When shopping for fresh pineapple, pull out one of the center leaves. It should come out with a slight tug. If it comes out easily, the pineapple is too ripe. If it comes out after a hard pull, the pineapple is too raw. Pineapple has an enzyme called Bromelin. It is this active enzyme that breaks down meat protein. That is what makes it almost impossible to ever use fresh pineapple in gelatin. It is not the acid that fails the gelling process. *Note:* canning usually happens at such temperatures that the bromelin enzyme is destroyed. So, canned pineapple has a different effect in recipes. I try to buy fresh pineapples at the farmer's market and then dehydrate the extra. We plant the crowns (leaves [fronds] and top core) in pots which we can bring in the house when the temperature drops to freezing. I don't throw the fruit core away (the center section), instead we chop (it'll be very tough) and dehydrate it. Those core pieces make wonderful powder for use as seasoning and flavoring in salads, breads, meat dishes, and desserts. If you can't get fresh pineapple, but want to dehydrate some for long-term use or for snacks, then used canned. It won't be as good as fresh, but it still tastes wonderful.

Post Purchase Dissonance	General	That "yuck" feeling you get after you buy something—the regret. It could come from realizing you paid too much, didn't really need it, or can't pay the bill. Avoid PPD by buying wisely and don't let anyone talk you into something. Be your own person.
Potatoes	Ingredient	I think I've been asked more about potatoes than any other ingredient. Since potatoes are relatively inexpensive, everyone wants to use them. I've been experimenting and researching for more than ten years and I've learned a little, but I'm still open for more ideas. There are two types of potatoes: mealy and waxy. 1. Mealy ones work best when fried, baked, and mashed. Mealy ones also dehydrate better than waxy ones. Mealy ones are higher in starch and lower in sugar. Because they are lower in sugar, they don't brown as well. 2. Waxy ones work best when boiled, in salads, and for such dishes as scalloped potatoes—they are usually sweeter and have a more firm texture. These make lousy fries because the sugar browns too quickly. How can you tell? If it is that critical to you, you can make brine of one pound salt water to one gallon of water. Then test each potato. Mealy potatoes will sink; Waxy ones will float. Why the difference? It could do with soil, fertilizers, climate; I haven't found a good answer yet. Do your potatoes ever discolor? Try adding a little cream of tartar or some citrus juice to the water. That should neutralize the oxidation. Store you potatoes in complete darkness. It is exposure to light that causes the green spots (and accompanying bitter taste). If you get green spots, cut them out completely. **Some options:** Blanch the potatoes before using them in a casserole recipe. Cooks have tested the recipes in this book and the recipes "worked." Please heed the directions. Changing some of the ingredients will affect the way the potato comes out. Don't expect as high a taste or preferred texture with some of the options. It's the way we process the potato, store it, and surround it with certain ingredients that works.

Remember potatoes are cheap. With some recipes that call for potatoes, I do everything but the potato, and then add fresh potatoes to the recipe before baking. It isn't that much trouble.

One thing I hear from people who find they have some potatoes about to go bad is they want to "save them." They try freezing them and have a disaster. The only time I freeze potatoes is when the potatoes are fresh! Very fresh! If you have more potatoes than you need, try dehydrating them. You'll need to pre-treat. Here are two options: 1) blanch them in water with an acid added (cream of tartar or citrus juice to prevent discoloration), or 2) after you have peeled and sliced them, soak them in Brown Away then steam (I use my steamer appliance for about 2 minutes) them until they are translucent. Then dehydrate. We have experimented with several options and combinations of options. We then tested them for color, texture and taste. My family prefers method 2 above. Please note that if you are used to the processed potatoes from the boxed mixes, you'll have to adjust your eye-gate a little. Your home-made versions won't be as white and smooth. You can use them like you would a pre-packaged version. Rehydrate with boiling water, add in a white sauce, (and/or seasonings) and bake.

Poultry, care and handling Safety

Raw poultry is dangerous—if not handled properly you run the risk of food poisoning. Eggs are in effect raw poultry. People can get really sick if someone cuts up a raw chicken on a cutting board, then cuts up vegetables on the same board without sanitizing it first. The raw vegetables are then contaminated with salmonella from the raw chicken juices, which haven't been cooked. And since those juices have been sitting there at room temperature, the germs go wild. Those people that then eat the raw vegetables get ill. To avoid this, either have two sets of boards (one for vegetables and one for meat) and still clean them well or sanitize your cutting board after each use—even during the same meal preparation. *Never* use anything but a clean cutting board (and knives) when you are preparing anything that is going to be eaten raw—uncooked. Clean your boards in hot soapy water. If the cutting boards are dishwasher-safe, clean them on the hottest setting. One method for sanitizing that works well is to use an anti-bacterial cleaner. Or after you've washed them in hot-soapy water, rinse them with a water solution of 1 gallon of water to 1 tablespoon of bleach. Then rinse well. These procedures should be done for all meat, not just poultry.

Powder Mc

In addition to dehydrating produce in small pieces, I like to take the ultra-dry pieces and process them in my blender until they are pulverized into a powder. I then vacuum-seal these in glass jars. I use these powders for a variety of recipes. Here are some ideas:

Tomato powder:

- Reconstitute with a little water for a delicious paste.
- Reconstitute with a little olive oil and some spices for an easy and rich pizza sauce.
- Reconstitute with by adding more water for a tasteful tomato sauce.
- Reconstitute with milk for a tomato soup—for a five-star tomato soup, make a thin beige sauce and sprinkle in the dehydrated tomato powder with oregano to taste.

Apple powder:

- I make two different powders—coarse and fine. (To make it fine, just run the blender motor longer.)
- With the coarse powder, reconstitute with water or apple juice and some cinnamon, heat and you will have the most delicious apple sauce you've ever had.
- With the fine powder, blend with water for a hearty apple juice.
- With either the coarse or fine (personal preference), sprinkle the powder over bread dough rolled into a rectangle. Add raisins, sugar, and cinnamon. Roll up and either cut into slices for apple rolls, or fold and place in a bread pan—make two because it'll be in high demand.
- With either the coarse or fine, sprinkle the powder into your muffin mix (see Many Muffins Mix, page 249).

- Double Apple Pie—Alternate layers of dehydrated apple slices and cinnamon/sugar mixture. Sprinkle ½ to 1 cup of water over the apples (depends on how "deep-dish" you make it). Top with Apple Crumble: 1 cup Better Butter, 1 cup brown sugar, 1 cup fresh flour, ½ cup apple powder. Bake at 350° for about 40 minutes. There really is no need to add the extra work and calories of a bottom crust—unless you want to. If so, add apple powder to the flour in the pastry for a Triple Apple Pie.
- Use as a topping—sprinkle it over ice cream, or in homemade ice cream recipes.

Other Fruit Powders:

- These same ideas work with pineapple, banana, peach and other fruit powders.
- Before we peel a lemon or orange, we wash it very well. Then we dehydrate the peeling and then pulverize it into a potent citrus powder that is great for seasoning and cooking.
- I don't throw away pineapple cores. I dehydrate those, making a very flavorful powder.

Vegetable Powders:

- Use as seasoning in side-dishes, as a replacement for salt and in salads.
- You can make your own onion powder, etc., and use in many recipes.
- Sprinkle over pizza for added nutrition and flavor. Since it is a powder, you might be able to get past the "yuckie" threshold of children.
- Make a "combined powder" by mixing the dehydrated powder from many vegetables for extra flavor and variety.
- Use powder (especially zucchini and carrot) in cakes and muffins.
- Sprinkle powder into Thin Beige Sauce for "Cream of ____ Soup." (See page 364)
- And of course, you can reconstitute it into baby food.

These are just a few ideas for use of these powders, we are finding new ways to use them all the time. Because we made them ourselves from dehydrated food, the smell and flavor

		is so intense. It is so much more rich than any commercial spices I have purchased. Enjoy.
Pressure Cookers	Equipment	To understand how your pressure cooker works, read the topic Boiling. Pressure cookers are wonderful tools for reducing cooking time. It takes 1⁄10 the time to cook in a pressure cooker what it would take using a regular method like boiling.
Pre-steps	Recipes	In this part of a recipe, I draw attention to those aspects of the recipe that I can either do ahead of time, do to save money, or incorporate with other recipes. These lists are not conclusive. Depending on what methods and other recipes you prepare during the same session, you might be able to combine more steps to streamline your work. These are steps with which you may want to do ahead or "assembly-line"—combine with steps from other recipes. By doing these steps "assembly-line" style, you'll really save time during your mega-cooking™.
Ratings	Recipes	I like to know what I'm getting into before I start a recipe. Here is where you read how difficult a recipe is to make, how time consuming, how expensive, etc. For the recipes in this book, these ratings are a result of years of mega-testing and responses from other cooks. Your actual results will vary. Use these figures for comparing recipes with each other. Rating recipes is a good discipline. My cookbooks are marked up with my notes and comments.
Refrigerator	Equipment	I use every bit of space in my refrigerators when I mega-cook because I don't want my ingredients to be out at room temperature, and also because I want the "headstart" that the refrigerator does in removing heat from my ingredients.
Rice	Ingredient	I have to consider health, budget, and availability of ingredients whenever I cook. We have compromised and come up with our choice for rice. I buy a 50-pound bag of white rice, 20 pounds of natural rice (brands vary), 20 pounds of

Basmati (our favorite and if we could afford it, we'd eat Basmati exclusively), and 10 pounds of converted rice. Alan mixes these four types together to get an even distribution. This rice blend (50% white, 50% whole) works for us. I know it isn't the best health-wise, but it is better than 100% white rice. Always rinse rice before cooking. Put your rice in a bowl and cover with water. Run your fingers through the rice to loosen any dirt or debris. Drain the water. Repeat the rinse process. On the third rinse, rinse handfuls of rice under running water. Let the rice drain in the colander. It should be clean after three rinses. If you haven't been taught to rinse your rice, you'll be in for a surprise when you do. I have not come across a single brand of rice that doesn't need rinsing. I interviewed a rice farmer and learned quite a bit about rice production. It didn't make any sense that white rice costs less than whole-grain. Whole-grain takes less processing so should cost less, but because of supply and demand, the white is cheaper. So, with that in mind, talk all your friends into eating more whole-grain rice and let's bring the price down together. I also like to make up some rice blends (instead of Uncle Ben's, it is Aunt Jill's). It is easy to use when I need it and costs a lot less.

Rice, steaming	Technique	I cook rice in a steamer. I've found many rice packages give lousy instructions. They use too much water in cooking. Rice is best when steamed. I make my rice with the ratio of 2:3, not the 1:2 that most recipes call for—in my steamer. (That's two cups rice to three cups water.)
Roux	Technique	The technique that produces a "roux" is a way to make a wonderful sauce. You start by dispersing the thickening agent (flour or cornstarch) into melted fat or oil. The melted fat, butter, or oil makes a good base leading to a creamy sauce or gravy. The trick is to evenly mix the thickener into the melted fat, then as you heat it, the liquid will thicken. Roux is the term cooks use to describe both the technique and the flour/melted fat base. When making gravy, I'll make a roux of the meat drippings, flour, and some oil.

Safety

Safety

Learn about food safety. Food poisoning is not funny. I spent three days in the hospital because a clerk at the commissary didn't understand proper handling of seafood. It was nearly fatal. The food didn't taste or smell bad—or I wouldn't have eaten it. The clerk had found a freezer unit off and simply turned it back on. The shrimp had completely thawed and then it was refrozen. Alan and I were some of the first on the base to eat the bad shrimp. There was a total recall and retraining. So, I take food safety very seriously. I follow directions. I wash and wash and wash. One thing that we are very careful about since we are handling so many ingredients simultaneously is washing our hands. I've trained my children to go to the sink and wash whenever they switch stations or ingredients. For example, Stuart was bouncing back and forth between the task of browning meat in a skillet and the task of cutting bread into cubes. Since the skillet didn't need his constant attention, he would cut cubes for a few minutes than stir the beef then cut cubes . . . It was good use of the 4 to 5 minutes of "down-time" between times when the beef needed his attention. He washed his hands with an anti-bacterial soap (a few seconds labor) each time he moved from handling the beef and then handling the bread. We'd rather overkill the germs than leave them on our hands to contaminate other foods. Please be careful. Another point, I rarely have any food out at room temperature. We process it quickly and then return it to either cooling or heating. If we are working with a large quantity, we keep most of it in the refrigerator until we need it. Please learn about food safety. Heed the precautions in this book *and* do your own research. I don't know everything about food safety and I didn't include everything on the subject in this book. You need to take charge of this aspect of your life. Our local news program ran a series of stories about the sub-standard conditions in some area restaurants—some of the footage was disgusting! It really brought home to me the importance of what we're doing in our home and that we have to check things for ourselves. We can't just assume that an over-worked inspector hap-

		pened to be investigating the processing plant or restaurant or store when a violation occurred. So, we go by this rule: When in doubt—throw it out. Our health is far more valuable than the few dollars that the ingredients cost us.
Salt	Ingredient	All salt is not the same. I've tried many different brands from the local grocery and from health food outlets, but hands down my favorite is a product called Real Salt®. Produced by Redmond Minerals of Redmond, Utah, this salt is a natural, pure sodium chloride with valuable minerals. Not only does it taste wonderful, but it cooks great. It is so flavorful that I reduce by at least half the amount of salt I add to any recipe. The recipes in this book reflect the amount for ordinary salt, and should be cut in half if you use Real Salt. You can reach Redmond Minerals at 1-800-367-7258, through several websites, or ask your local grocer or health food store to carry it.
Sausage	Ingredient	Some commercial sausage contain nitrites. Nitrites react with meat proteins to form nitrosamines, which are very effective carcinogens. Nitrites also leech the body of Vitamin C. The nitrite acts to kill off microbes that could cause the food to go bad. You can avoid this by being very selective with your purchases. Buy directly from a butcher (check his recipes). Make your own sausage. Buy health-food substitutes. There are even some vegetarian varieties available. Counter the negative effects of nitrites by dosing with Vitamin C and phytochemicals.
Shear Delight	Technique	I use kitchen shears quite a bit. I've found they save me time, and when I'm mega-cooking™, I like time-savers. When a recipe calls for bread cubes, cut the crust away with shears, cut the bread into three strips, then cut the strips into 3 to 4 pieces. It will take less than half the time to do it with shears than it would with knives. When a recipe calls for small pieces of meat, I cook the meat first, then cut it into smaller pieces with shears—much easier than trying to cut raw meat with a knife.

Simmer	Technique	Some stovetops dials have a "simmer" setting while some just display numbers or "low." When instructions in a recipe say, "simmer" you should turn the dial to the lowest setting and either cover the pot or leave it uncovered according to the recipe directions.
Simplification	Mc	I don't need my life to be any more complex. I like simple. Simple and I are close friends. Throughout my home, I try to make tasks simple. Throughout this book, I have tried to simplify complex issues and tasks to make them easy to do and to understand. One thing I do is to label everything. I tape recipes to the inside of my cabinets so they are handy and within reach. I copy (or cut off) the "finishing" instructions to recipes or mixes and keep those handy (in the bag or jar or as close to where I'll be finishing the recipe as possible). The fewer steps I have to take, the less time I spend doing needless work. The less time I have to spend hunting for tools and ingredients, the more time I have for hugging and reading with my children. My home is organized for use and comfort not for show or for impressing others.
Some Assembly Required (SAR)	Mc	I schedule several recipes in my meal planning that are SARs. I'll need to do a little bit of assembling of the ingredients before heating or serving. For instance, for Fajitas—I'll need to thaw bags of torillas, grilled chicken breasts, and cheese. From the refrigerator, I'll grab the lettuce, sour cream, and salsa. Easy! There are recipes that don't do as well pre-assembled as they do when you freeze the ingredients separately. In other words, not all the recipes are ready to heat and serve. But even with the SARs, I try to simplify the serving steps as much as possible.
Soups	Ingredient	I like to make soups. They are a wonderful addition to most meals. We can often have a soup on the table in the matter of minutes, and while we are eating the soup, the rest of the dinner is heating. So that way we're spending our time at the table over a pleasant dinner. The Campbell soup commercials are correct when they proclaim soup is good food. The

		body loves them. There are several soup recipes in this book. When you are making your own soup, make concentrate. Then when you heat it for serving, add the milk, water, or additional broth. Don't waste precious freezer space on bonus liquids.
Steamer	Equipment	I like my steamer more than my microwave. It works as a distiller, so it is a purification unit. The volatile acid or alkali elements in the water (or food) are left as the steamer works. When the water condenses on the food, it is in a pure form. It is quick and healthful. We reheat many of our frozen recipes this way, especially vegetables and starch dishes. Bread will soften up nicely. Pasta will be moist and smooth. In my opinion it is one appliance you should invest in. With the stackable option of some steamers (there are electric models, wooden models that fit over your pan of water, microwaveable steamer towers, and home-made versions) you can cook your whole dinner at one time over one burner or using one appliance. If I had to give up my microwave or my steamer, there would be no question, the microwave would leave. Before steamers came down to a reasonable price, I made my own using a metal colander and my Dutch oven. I'd boil water in the bottom of the Dutch oven, place the ingredients in the colander, and put the Dutch oven lid over the ingredients. It didn't make a perfect seal, but it was better than boiling out my food.
Steps	Recipes	On each recipe, I spell out the steps you need to go through to complete this recipe. One of our goals is to incorporate as many steps as we can with other recipes, so we aren't duplicating our effort. For instance in all the recipes that call for a beige sauce, I'll make one large batch and then use it for all those recipes. You'll notice on most of the recipes I start with those common steps that can be completed no matter what your mega-cooking™ style. Then I offer options depending upon if you are doing a mega-session, duplicating, or multi-batching. When you write your own recipes, you can get as detailed as you want. You can make

as many separate steps to your recipes as you need. Some ladies want to separate the steps of washing their produce from the steps for peeling or chopping. That is your choice. In the recipes, I choose a medium level of step differentiation—I combined several related steps into one numbered row, such as divide, label, and freeze.

Stew	Ingredient	Since you'll be using lots of water, you don't want to lose the flavor into the water. Seal the meat first. Brown it at a high temperature. There should be enough sugar content in most red meat to make a brown seal. Then you can simmer it for hours with appropriate flavorings and vegetables. There are several options to combine steps for mega-cooking™: 1. After browning, you can bag the meat, raw vegetables and about one-fourth the water you would normally use for cooking and freeze. One-to-two days before you plan on eating the stew, thaw in the refrigerator. Either pour into a crock-pot and let it simmer all day, or cook at low for about 3 hours in either a Dutch oven or a roaster. 2. Combine the sealed meat, spices and vegetables, cook for 2 hours and 30 minutes on low. Bag. Then when you're ready to eat it, thaw, heat in microwave, oven, or stovetop.
Stock	Technique	To make a good stock, do not seal in the flavor into the meat. You want that flavor to go into the stock. In other words, do not brown the meat first. Use lots of bones. You want that collagen to transform with slow cooking into gelatin. That's what makes it "stock" and not just colored water. Try to always give yourself enough time so the stock can set overnight in the refrigerator. Skim off the fat. The collagen from the meat and bones should have set and the stock is ready to use. Save that meat for use in other recipes (e.g., turning stock to soup or a hash). For mega-cooking™, you can freeze the stock (after removing the fat) for use in other recipes on other days, or incorporate it directly into the mega-cooking™ recipes.

Streamlining	Mc	Preparing ingredients for the recipe you are currently making and then saving some of it for other recipes. You might go ahead and peel, chop, and bag extra onions so you can use them in another recipe later.
Stuart Technique, The	Mc	When I would whip large ingredients together, my shoulders and arms would begin to ache. I was using the big arm circles method of beating. I'd pass the job to Stuart, my son. He is a fixer. Seeing the problem, he used his brain and came up with a much simpler method. I wondered why I had never seen any one do it. In his honor, we call it the Stuart technique. He takes the professional wire whisk and rolls it in his palms. You might have seen this same approach used for fire starting. It works better for the mixing, and he can do it for hours without straining anything. Sometimes you'll want to spin the bowl for more even distribution.
Sugar	Ingredient	A term broadly used to mean a class of carbohydrate, but specifically the term for sucrose (cane sugar). Sucrose, like dextrose, maltose, fructose, glucose and others, are called simple carbohydrates, as compared to the complex carbohydrates that make up the starches of potatoes, rice and wheat. Simple carbohydrates are easily and rapidly broken down in the body and transformed into energy for the body to run on. They have a place, and are found in a number of natural ingredients. But too many at once is like putting too much coal in the furnace—the body will over heat. To regulate the excess energy, the body puts out insulin to "insulate" the digested sugars in the blood stream. When insulin floods the bloodstream, another regulator, glucagon, ceases in its job of converting fat into simple carbohydrates. (That's the purpose of fat: long-term energy storage from times of plenty to survive those long, hungry winters. Unfortunately, we Americans tend to pack away a bit too much "plenty" for a tad too many winters.) The result is twofold: first is the burst of high energy followed by the crash as insulin isolates any and all sugars out of the blood and tissues (tak-

ing it to the liver to deal with) and the slow, steady glucagon/fat-burning mechanism is shut down. Secondly, the liver converts the mass of dumped simple carbohydrates into complex forms, to include fat, and sends it to central storage—those hips, thighs, stomach! Once the insulin levels drop to normal, the glucagon level returns to normal and the crash victim returns to a more normal pace.

Sugar	Ingredient	We literally went for years without any white sugar in our home. It has only been recently that I've been using it to test these recipes. About ten years ago I was diagnosed as hypoglycemic, so I had to learn about sugar and what it was doing in my body. I experimented with many substitutes and found some that my body could handle. With years of work and proper eating, the levels in my blood are more normalized and I don't have to be as strict. Still in recipes I try to reduce the amount of sugar and/or use substitutes. I also realize that not everyone is as concerned with sugar intake as I am, so some of the recipes in this book are written using white table sugar. I usually substitute sugar with granulated fructose (I can use about half of the amount called for white sugar), raw cane sugar, sucanat, honey, or concentrated fruit juice. When I substitute with honey or fruit juice, I have to reduce the liquids in the recipe and sometimes increase the solids to get a proper balance. I've been using good concentrated white grape juice more and more, and it cooks up wonderfully. (I buy it in a case lot for much less than retail.) There are several recipes like Love Sweet Syrup that offer a delicious alternative to super-sweet syrups. If you are using a commercial brand syrup, investigate the ingredients for yourself. Some of the "syrups" are mostly sugared water with added flavorings.
Sugar	Labeling	If you are trying to cut back on sugar, don't let the absence of the word "sugar" from a label give you a false impression. "Sugar" can also be named: sucrose, dextrose, maltose, fructose, glucose, lactose, or any other ingredients ending in "ose."

Sugar, no added	labeling	For a company to legally use this term, they can not have added any sugar during the processing or packing. Now if the product already contained sugar, it still has it. Don't think that "no sugar added" means sugar free. It doesn't. It means "they" didn't add any *more* sugars.
Sugar-free	labeling	This is a real kicker for me. When I was battling with hypoglycemia I had to watch out for any sugar. Even small amounts would imbalance my blood sugar level causing me to get the shakes or become dizzy. I learned to make food myself because even "sugar-free" did not mean free of sugar. A company can claim "sugar free" on the label if the food has less than 0.5 grams of sugar per serving. If you are sensitive as I was, that is too much. I needed free of sugar, not sugar-free.
Supplementation	General	We augment the nutrients in our food with food-form dietary supplements. As much as I'd prefer to get all the vitamins, minerals, and glycoprotiens from our foodstuffs, I'm not that naïve or ignorant of current farming and the state of our environment. We supplement not as an excuse for improper eating—that idea that I can eat anything I want as long as I swallow a multi-vitamin—but to fill in the gaps that even careful meal preparation can't meet. All that our bodies need isn't in the food chain anymore.
Tenderizers	General	Some of the best tenderizers for meat are 100% natural: fresh pineapple, papaya and figs. They have enzymes (bromelin, papain, and ficin respectively) that tenderize meat. Some commercial tenderizers have these enzymes as the active ingredient. Tenderizers can not make a bad piece of meat good. And it can only affect the surface layers of the meat. You can maximize the process by cutting your meat into smaller pieces and/or increasing the amount or time of marinating. Be careful not to over tenderize the meat to avoid a mushy texture. Freezing meat in pure pineapple juice can add flavor and make a tough piece of meat more palatable. Aging (allowing a coating of mold to

		grow on the meat as it turns "gamey") is also another method for tenderizing meat, but I would not recommend any home cook attempt it.
Title, naming a recipe	Recipes	I see no point in giving my recipes boring titles. I market my recipes to my family. For instance, who can get excited about "Lima Bean Casserole"? I changed that recipe around and then renamed it "Chuckwagon."
Vegetables	Ingredient	One quick way to know how to properly cook and treat a vegetable is by its color. The different dyes affect the way it reacts to different processes (see anthocyanins, anthoxanthins, carotene, and chlorophyll). For more information about specific colors, see below.
Vegetables (Green)	Ingredient	Green vegetables are green because of the chlorophyll in them—a wonderful dye that works hand and hand with photosynthesis. However, chlorophyll is very sensitive and will fade or change to an unappetizing brownish green under certain conditions. Both alkalis and acids can destroy chlorophyll. This happens in some cooking processes. To help eliminate this problem, cook as little as possible. When you do cook, steam. Reduce the cooking time by cutting up the vegetable into smaller pieces. When mega-cooking™, I'll blanch my vegetables before freezing (if I'm working with vegetables by themselves). If the vegetables are going to be a component of a recipe, I usually put them in raw. Also, using a pressure cooker, since the vegetables cook for such a short time, is wonderful for retaining the color and nutrients. Another option to retain color and flavor of green vegetables is to dry cook (baking, frying, or using water-less cookware).
Vegetables (Red)	Ingredient	Vegetables with a red/blue pigment are very acid/alkali-dependent and therefore are soluble in water. That is why when you cook with beets it turns everything red. That's the attraction of borscht—even the white potatoes come out reddish. Plan on it and make the most of the dye. If you

		want the vegetables to retain their color—do this—cook them whole, so their skins help retain the pigment. Then remove them from the water and slice and peel. They will not only taste better, but it will be much more attractive on your plate. Also, try cooking these red vegetables with an acid (e.g., lemon juice, vinegar, sour cream, citrus juices, or honey). As when cooking white vegetables, don't use iron cookware—it will cause discoloration.
Vegetables (White)	Ingredient	These vegetables are similar to the red vegetables in that they do better if cooked with acidic ingredients. Be careful because white vegetables can react funny to iron or aluminum cookware—causing discoloration. Even an aluminum spoon can affect discoloration. It has to do with the tannin content. Alkali substances can cause them to yellow if they are exposed for too long. Again, steaming is a wonderful option for vegetable, or use them raw in a recipe you'll bake later.
Vegetables (Yellow)	Ingredient	These beauties don't need the special treatment of other colored vegetables and you don't have to be as delicate with them.
Vitamins	General	So many things affect the vitamin content of foods. Just realize that the closer the food is to its source, the more it is like its natural form, the more vitamins will be intact. The sooner produce is separated from its plant before being ripe, the fewer vitamins it will have. Exposure to water and oxygen will reduce vitamin content. The B and C vitamins are water-soluble. The A and D vitamins are soluble in fat and more resistant to cooking processes. Some vitamins are destroyed with contact with oxygen, for example Vitamin C. As you mash a potato and expose it to air, you can destroy 50% of the Vitamin C. Don't get depressed. Just treat your produce with respect. Try to eat at least one helping of raw vegetables each day (more helpings would be better). Those you do cook and process, be sure to follow directions and minimize the draining effects of overcooking.

Weaning	Technique	I've learned that with my family, it is usually best to wean them into healthier eating. Here's how I got Alan off white rice: I starting by making a mix that was 95% white, 5% brown. When he was okay with that, I made a mix that was 90% white, and 10% brown. And continued until he liked 100% brown—now I can make any combination and he likes it. I've been doing the same with sugar—gradually reducing the sugar in their diets and letting their taste buds normalize. Some people's taste buds are so out-of-whack that they can't "taste" much of the natural flavors in food. One lady I counseled found out she was hypoglycemic also. She instantly removed 100% of the sugar from her diet. Her taste buds healed. Within a few weeks, she remarked to me about how sweet carrots are. She had not been able to taste the natural sweetness of carrots because her tongue had been so addicted to artificial sweeteners. In fact carrots are so naturally sweet that they are "off-limits" to those on a "Candida-Attacking" diet. Taste buds are very teachable and the weaning method works well to do that. It doesn't "shock" them, but gently gets them off "wanting strong tastes" into sensing more subtle and delicious natural flavorings. We're learning more about this as we work with Trent's hypo- and hyper-senses.
Wheat	Ingredient	Wheat is so versatile, we use it for many recipes. Here is a quick primer on wheat. I use three types: hard red, hard white, and soft white. How do you know which one to use in which recipe? Think North/South. The hard wheats grow in the North and the soft in the South. Picture good'ol Southern biscuits and you'll be able to remember the key distinction. Hard wheat is wonderful with recipes that include yeast—the chemicals react quite well and you'll get the wonderful gluten and yeast reaction that yields delectable yeast breast. But if I'm making a recipe that doesn't call for yeast, I'll use my soft wheat. It doesn't work well with yeast, but performs wonderfully with baking soda and baking powder. So, hard wheat for yeast; soft wheat for non-yeast recipes. But which hard wheat to use, red or white?

That is merely a matter of taste. The red wheat has a hearty flavor and is our favorite for loaf bread. The white wheat is more bland in flavor and I choose it for recipes that have other ingredients that I want to taste more than the taste of the wheat. For instance, if I'm making apple bread, cinnamon rolls or pizza, I want the taste to come from the added ingredients, so I'll use white wheat. But again, this is just a personal matter of taste. Red and white hard wheats perform equally well in baking. The most versatile of the three is hard white—I have used it in non-yeast recipes and it will do a good job. The hard white is a good transitional grain for those who aren't used to whole-grains. It bakes up paler—not as dark as the red does.

Be careful about your wheat. I once bought bad wheat and had a time trying to get it to work. It was best just to trash the whole lot. If you want a good gluten reaction and a perfect bread, get 14% protein or better. Anything less than 14% and you'll have problems and will have to add gluten and still your bread may never rise well.

As your bread making skills improve, you'll want to mix grains and experiment with rye, oat, bean and other flours. Whenever I include non-high-quality wheat flour in my recipes, I definitely add either gluten or dough enhancer to make up for the lack of wheat gluten. About 2 tablespoons to ¼ cup added for each cup of non-wheat flour should be more than adequate.

Section Four

If you've never mega-cooked before, please take some time and familiarize yourself with this cooking method. These recipes are not like those in most other cookbooks. If you don't know what I mean by a particular term, use the Topics section for an explanation. It would be a waste of space to re-explain every technique and proper handling of each ingredient on each recipe. So, please review. The techniques aren't complicated. There just might be some methods and handling that you're not used to. That's fine. That's what I'm here for—to teach you so you can save time and money to give your family healthy meals.

Mega-testing

We are truly blessed to have volunteer mega-testers who experiment with my recipes. They are a diverse group living throughout the United States. The family-size varied from 1 (those who live alone) to 10 (those with many children). Some of them were young couples just starting out. Some were grandparents. They have a wide range of socio-economic backgrounds and lifestyles. Some of the testers work outside of the home, some do not. Some eat more vegetarian diets than others. Some grew most of their food or were ranchers. Some lived in metropolitan areas and some out in the country. We sought a diverse group so that we could really run the recipes through the paces. The testers evaluated the recipes on a 1-10 scale on 21 items in addition to informing us on some demographics about themselves and specifics about how they used the recipe. We could then glean the answers to questions like:

- Were ingredients readily available in all parts of the country?
- How did climate affect recipes?
- What about taste and texture?
- Did it affect your overall budget?
- Did your children like the taste?
- Would it be good for company or ministry?

We've included a sample evaluation form in the appendices for your information.

Not only did we work with a recipe several times over the span of years here in the "Bond Test Kitchen," but other families tested each of these recipes. When we received their results we choose 60% of those recipes to appear in this book. I then made any changes to the recipes making them easier to understand and prepare. Some of their comments and suggestions were so helpful, we added them for you.

Key Recipes and Variations

Key recipes are the main or first recipe among variations. Following a key recipe, when appropriate, is a listing of variations to that main recipe, or similar recipes. The recipes are organized in alphabetical order according to the key recipe within their proper section. The index will aid you in finding a specific recipe.

Explaining coding and ratings

Please note that we not only considered our own experience in ranking the recipes, but calculated information provided by our mega-testers.

$

With each key recipe, I've indicated what a serving costs when I mega-cook during a mega-session and have purchased and cooked using all the cost-saving measures in the book. Your actual cost will vary according to availability of ingredients, how much you're able to buy in bulk or grow your own food, and what variations you choose. This figure is for comparison only. Please don't budget your shopping dollars according to my figures. You might be able to get better prices or not as good.

EASE

This indicates on a scale of 1 to 10 how easy this recipe is to prepare. A 10 rating would be a very simple recipe that a beginning mega-cook could accomplish easily. A 1 rating would be a more complicated rating—more toward the gourmet side of the spectrum.

PREP-TIME

The prep-time rating indicates how much time it takes to assemble or prepare that recipe. Since many recipes have variations, we've given you an average. When there is a mega-session variation, that is the one I used for this rating—actually assembling the recipe—not including all the pre-preparation of ingredients on the first day. Of course it will take you more or less time than it does us. So much depends on your experience and equipment. We stated how long it takes our family and you can use these figures for comparing one recipe to another. *Please* do not compare your time with ours. Don't feel at all defeated if it takes you an hour to assemble a recipe that I do in 15 minutes. Remember, I've been doing this for more than 17 years and have five helpers. You're working with different equipment and different helpers. Pace yourself. (Note: also when I say a recipe takes me 30 minutes, I rarely am working only one recipe. During that same 30 minutes, I'll be juggling 2 or 3 others.)

HEATING TIME

This indicates how much time it will take to heat this recipe on the day of serving. In most cases this time will reflect heating or reheating ingredients that have already been thawed. Thawing time is not added in. For example, if it states 15 minutes, that's how long it takes to reheat a thawed serving. It doesn't include the few minutes that it would take you to place the ingredients in a dish—just the actual baking, steaming, or microwaving time. You'll need to make adjustments in this figure if you heat different amounts, use a different type or size pan, or use a different method of heating.

MEGA-SESSION

This indicates how well this recipe will fit into a mega-session. Admittedly some recipes are so time consuming that it would be better to do them at another time all by themselves. Some recipes work great assembled along with other recipes. On a scale of 1 to 10, a 10 means the recipe fits perfectly into a mega-session and a 1 indicates a recipe that you will want to seriously consider making a multi-batch in a separate time frame.

EQUIPMENT

With this rating, we wanted to give you some idea of what equipment is most helpful in preparing this recipe. These are just suggestions. For instance, with some of the recipes I recommend a food processor—it will cut your work time by 90%—but if you don't have a food processor, you can still prepare the recipe using a knife and cutting board. Since most recipes need the basic equipment (bowls, spoons, measuring spoons and cups, basic pots and pans) we don't mention them. I'm only flagging equipment that might not be considered "basic" or equipment that you wouldn't need if you weren't mega-cooking.

WHAT'S MISSING?

One rating I wanted to give the recipes was a nutritional rating. But as we worked on this rating, we realized that was impossible. There are so many variables to these recipes—how you prepare them and what ingredients you use—that any rating would be useless. For instance, with the fajita recipe (Chicken for All Seasons, page 275), are you using fresh tomatoes just picked from your garden or some that were harvested green and sprayed with phenol to look red? Options like that could vary the nutritional quality of these recipes by a factor of ten or more. When a recipe is obviously a "treat" or a break from a really healthy diet, I'll mention it on the recipe. Most of my recipes are low in fat, salt, and sugar—or (when applicable) we give you some alternatives or ideas to adjust the recipe.

SUMMARY

Again, if you have never mega-cooked before, don't let the different format throw you. The recipes make sense as you work through them. Please read an entire recipe before you start cooking it or even buy the ingredients. All the suggestions are there for a reason—to either increase your options or to clarify why a step is done a certain way. Whenever you are unsure of a term or technique, read more in the narrative part of this book or the Topics section.

Eggnog

(NOGK-NOGK)

When Bethany Kay was a toddler, she really liked eggnog. But when she asked for it, it sounded like "nogk-nogk." Well, the name stuck. As some of my readers know, I'd been hunting for years for a good eggnog recipe. I mentioned it at most of my speaking engagements. Then, a beautiful lady in Blairsville, Georgia, gave this to me and it is not only easy and delicious, but you can make it in mega-batches (2, 3, 4 times the recipes). Thank you, Beth Daniels! The recipes following can be made using Nogk-Nogk or commercial eggnog.

Do Ahead:

- Purchase as many ingredients in bulk as possible for best prices.
- Make mega-batches and freeze for drinking and use in recipes.

X1	X2	X4	
4 SERVINGS	8 SERVINGS	16 SERVINGS	1 CUP (8 OUNCES) PER SERVING
6	12	24	Eggs (pasteurized egg product equivalent)
½ cup	1 cup	2 cups	Sugar (or one-fourth of that of fructose)
2 cups	4 cups	8 cups	Half and half
2 cups	4 cups	8 cups	Milk
Dashes	Dashes	Dashes	Nutmeg (fresh ground is wonderful)

Steps:

1. Separate the eggs. Leave whites out to become room temperature (Please read about egg safety below and in Topics section.)
2. In a large bowl beat the egg yolks.
3. Add the sugar. Mix well.
4. In a separate bowl beat the egg whites until stiff.
5. Fold the egg whites into the sugared egg yolks.
6. Slowly add the half and half and milk. Fold gently.
7. Chill until very cold. (Best if chilled at least 12 hours before serving.)
8. Sprinkle with nutmeg.
9. Freeze any extra. I like to use waxed milk cartons for freezing eggnog blocks. You can also freeze some of it in ice cubes for a delicious snack.

Variations:

Eggnog French Toast: Use this eggnog just as you would egg/milk mixture in making French toast—delicious.

Eggnog Bavarian Pie: Allow a dozen 2-ounce eggnog cubes (that's 24 ounces of eggnog) to partially freeze. Crush in a blender until consistency of a slushy drink. Fold into cold whipped topping. Pour into a baked pie shell. Serve cold.

Eggnog Sundae Desserts: Make a cookie crumble by crunching 1 4¾-ounce package of vanilla wafers. Toss with ¼ teaspoon of nutmeg and ⅓ cup of melted butter. Set aside. Make the eggnog filling: sprinkle 2 packages of unflavored gelatin over 1 cup of eggnog. Let it stand 5 minutes to soften. Heat the gelatin eggnog mixture until the gelatin is completely dissolved. I recommend using a double boiler. Remove from the heat and add 1 more cup of eggnog. Stir until mixed. Refrigerate until the mixture is thick and syrupy like unbeaten egg whites—about 40 minutes. Beat the mixture until frothy. Stir in 2 cups of whipped cream. In sundae glasses spoon some cookie crumble, then some eggnog cream. Alternate layers until you reach the top. Refrigerate until firm. Serve with a dollop of whipped topping.

"Very good recipe."—Debbie China

"The Eggnog French Toast is incredible! Perfect for a festive Christmas morning breakfast!"—Judy Clark

Additional Helps and Suggestions

- Judy Clark suggests adding 1 teaspoon of imitation rum extract (for flavor that mimics store-brands).
- Karen B. Collins asked about the safety of drinking raw eggs. We had several families write us about this. They have a very legitimate concern. Raw poultry is dangerous—if not handled properly you run the risk of food poisoning. Eggs are in effect raw poultry. It is dangerous to cut up a raw chicken on a cutting board and then cut vegetables on the same cutting board without sanitizing it first. The raw vegetables can be contaminated with salmonella from the raw chicken juices. And since those juices have been sitting there at room temperature, the germs go wild. If eaten raw, the vegetables will carry the salmonella germs. To avoid this, either have two sets of boards (one for vegetables and one for meat) and still clean them well or sanitize your cutting board and knives after each use—even during the same meal preparation. Never use anything but a clean cutting board and knives when you are preparing anything that is going to be eaten uncooked. Please read about food safety in the Topics Section. As to the use of raw eggs in this recipe, be careful. Get your eggs from a trusted source. We keep our eggs in the refrigerator. The yolks are not to be left out at room temperature at all. We only do this with the whites for about 30 minutes to aid the "foaming" effect. If you have any concerns about the quality of your eggs, whip them immediately after removing them from the refrigerator. They won't foam as well and you'll have to work a little harder, but if it insures safety, do it. Still to play it perfectly safe you can use a pasteurized egg product. Or if you still are concerned and can't monitor the "temperature" of the nog (for example, a party situation where people leave their cup sitting for a few hours and then pick it up to drink) use commercial eggnog. Of course, you don't need to worry at all when you use the eggnog for French toast because you're cooking the eggs. Again, we're taking our eggs from the refrigerator,

working with them, then putting them right back in the refrigerator, and drinking the eggnog immediately after pouring it up from a pitcher we keep chilled. When it comes to food poisoning—don't take chances. It's better to be over cautious than filled with regret later.

- The Center for Disease Control and Prevention states "Since foods of animal origin may be contaminated with salmonella, people should not eat raw or undercooked eggs, poultry, or meat. Raw eggs may be unrecognized in some foods such as homemade Hollandaise sauce, Caesar and other salad dressings, tiramisu, homemade ice cream, homemade mayonnaise, cookie dough, and frostings." (From "Questions and Answers about Salmonellosis." CDC, 1600 Clifton Road, MS D-25, Atlanta, GA 30333.
- Again, to play it safe, use a pasteurized egg product, or use the eggnog in a recipe that you will cook. Or purchase commercial eggnog.

Ratings

$ = 10¢
Ease = 9
Prep-time = 15 minutes
Heating = none
Mega-Session = 8
Equipment = quality mixer to beat egg whites or wire whisk, copper bowl

Liquid Sunshine

AND FROZEN SUNSHINE POPS

Yes, I'm spoiled about my citrus. I grew up in the middle of citrus groves and my siblings still own groves. Here in Central Florida we evaluate "fresh" in hours, not days or months. I guess those in Georgia are as picky about their peaches, and in Washington about their apples. We must have at least a hundred citrus recipes. This is one of the most popular. Of course, real orange juice doesn't need any help and is most delicious just as it is, but if you can't get real orange juice or want a change of pace, try this recipe. A similar drink used to be available in mall stores. The Frozen Sunshine Pops are a big hit with kids and adults.

Do Ahead

- Buy oranges in bulk and squeeze juice. Juice does freeze well.
- Buy as many ingredients in bulk as possible for the best prices.
- Round robin this recipe, using a blender.

X1	**X2**	**X3**	
4 SERVINGS	8 SERVINGS	12 SERVINGS	10 OUNCES PER SERVING
¾ cup	1½ cups	2¼ cups	Orange juice (as fresh as you can afford)
½ cup	1 cup	1½ cups	Sugar (or half that amount in fructose)
1 cup	2 cups	3 cups	Milk
8	16	24	Ice cubes (standard, 2-ounce-sized cube)
1 cup	2 cups	3 cups	Water
1 teaspoon	2 teaspoons	1 tablespoon	Vanilla extract
			Fresh orange slices for garnish

Steps:

OPTION 1: MAKE A SINGLE BATCH TO DRINK RIGHT AWAY

1. In a blender combine all of the ingredients.
2. Whip until foamy.
3. Pour into glasses. Serve immediately. Garnish with fresh orange slices.

OPTION 2: MAKE ROUND-ROBIN BATCHES FOR LARGER QUANTITY

1. Have the ingredients for as many batches as you want on hand.
2. Determine the blender pitcher capacity. Don't exceed it or you'll have a mess. For example, my blender is a 6-cup blender and x1 works perfectly—plenty of blending room.
3. Blend as large a batch as you can. Then repeat the process as many times as necessary.
4. Pour into glasses. Serve immediately. Garnish with fresh orange slices.

OPTION 3: MAKE ROUND-ROBIN BATCHES AND USE EXTRA FOR HOMEMADE FROZEN SUNSHINE POPS

1. Follow steps 2 through 4 in Option 2.
2. Pour into plastic molds or paper cups. (Insert a stick as a handle once it is partially frozen, that way the stick will stay in the center and not fall to one side). Freeze. (Note: The liquid "separates" into 3 layers and comes out looking so fancy. They are delicious.)

OPTION 4: MAKE UP "MIX" AHEAD AND THEN BLEND WHEN NEEDED

(I use this option when we're having guests over. I don't want to spend my time measuring out ingredients. I'll make the "mix" ahead, and have it ready in the refrigerator. Then all I have to do is blend it when my guests arrive.)

1. In a large pitcher mix together all of the ingredients except the ice cubes.
2. Store in an airtight container in the refrigerator until needed later that same day.
3. Pour the mixture into the blender no further than halfway up the pitcher. Add the ice cubes. Blend.
4. Pour into glasses. Serve immediately. Garnish with fresh orange slices.

OPTION 5: MAKE UP "MIX" AHEAD AND FREEZE FOR USE ANOTHER DAY

5. Follow the directions for Option 4 except freeze the mix.
6. Thaw in the refrigerator.
7. Follow steps 4 through 5 in Option 4.

"Yummy! My 10 year-old can do it."—Michelle Manson
"They loved it!"—Gina Pearcy

Additional Helps and Suggestions

- Michelle Manson made a good point: "Lots of sugar, but healthier than soda or powdered drink mixes."
- Lauri Swanbeck experimented with the recipe and options and shared her findings: The first time they prepared it just as the recipe here, but the next time she made it, she used VitaSoy Milk in place of the milk in the recipe. She said, "No one noticed the difference, and it is a bit healthier for us!"
- Becky Valentine also experimented and here are her results: She and her son preferred the recipe as it is. Her husband preferred water replaced with additional orange juice. She also tried varying the number of ice cubes and found 8 to be the perfect number. Additional cubes tended to make it more slushy, not creamy.
- Gina Pearcy pointed out that it is important to blend long enough or the ice won't breakdown into small enough bits.
- Mary Lu Kusk cut the sugar in half and liked it much better. That's wonderful to know for those trying to reduce or eliminate the sugar from their children's diets.
- One other option for a buffet or a special function is to pour this mix into ice cube trays. Each

piece of ice will have a slight variation of color. Then use those to serve more orange juice, iced tea, or a clear soda. Try it first to see if you like it before serving to a houseful of guests!

- This was a very popular recipe among the mega-testers. One point that several of them made was that they thoroughly enjoyed it but would save it for special occasions. Depending on your location, it could be expensive. Those in the citrus states said things like, "I had everything I needed on hand." While those in colder climates said they'd save it for a special treat.
- Though my siblings all own orange groves, they are two hours away, so I get my fresh juice (squeezed within hours from fresh picked fruit) from a shop in town. We're addicted to it and go in regularly for our OJ "fix." We did shop around and found the best price for the highest quality. It is just a few cents more than the "off-the-shelf" processed stuff on the grocer's shelf. There is a major nutritional difference between fresh-squeezed and pasteurized or processed. But even the processed juices are much better than about any other "commercial" drink. If we aren't drinking water, it is usually juice. Ask you grocer to stock fresh squeezed. They may be eager to please. *Note:* if I'm going to "cook" the juice, I use the cheapest I can find because the cooking would negate any additional nutrient value and isn't as cost effective.
- Experiment with other juices. This works great with orange juice, but the idea holds for some other applications. (If you like this recipe, try the one for Smoothie Frothies, next page.)
- You can substitute honey for the sugar. Reduce the water by half. If you use honey, for options 4 and 5 you should wait to add the honey until you add the ice or it will sink to the bottom.

Ratings

$ = 50¢ (depends on what you have to pay for oranges or OJ)
Ease = 10
Prep-time = 5 minutes for the drink (hours for the pops)
Heating = 0
Mega-Session = 4—You can buy your oranges in bulk, but I prefer to make this up fresh or as pops
Equipment = A blender or juicer is necessary for making the orange juice (if applicable).

Smoothie Frothies

On one of our visits to a health food store, I ordered their $6.00 Brain Booster drink. They basically made the same smoothie frothy we had been making for years but added bee pollen and lecithin. So, if you really want a brain boost, add those ingredients. We have made dozens of varieties of this depending on what fruit and juice we have on hand. You can omit the yogurt, use frozen grapes and fruit juice, double the ice and it'll be a wonderful alternative to sherbet—and low in calories, no fat, and no added sugar. As an alternative to ice cream, use the frozen banana, milk, and yogurt options.

For one blender full

MAKES 5 SERVINGS (1 CUP EACH)

1	Frozen banana (peel before freezing!)
1 cup	Fresh, canned, or frozen fruit
1 cup	Milk or fruit juice
1 cup	Yogurt (plain or frozen) (optional)
1 cup	Ice [mol] depending how "slushy" you like it
¼ cup to ½ cup	Honey, natural sweetener, or sugar (to taste) optional and depending on the fruit, you might not need this extra sweetness at all

Additional ingredients to make it a health-drink

1 teaspoon	Bee pollen
1 teaspoon	Liquid or powdered lecithin
¼ cup	Local honey (to normalize any allergies)

Note: This works in a 6-cup blender. If the pitcher on your blender is smaller, cut the ingredient amounts in half.

1. Blend all the ingredients in the blender until smooth. Add more ice or more juice until you reach the consistency you need.
2. Serve immediately.

Note: If you have any problems blending the bee pollen, then break it first with the juice or milk on high until it is completely dissolved, then add the other ingredients. If you've never had bee pollen, make a small amount first and taste it. It does have a distinct flavor that some people do not like. It may seem expensive, but a jar will last for months and months if you store it in the refrigerator.

These are delicious! And so easy. We have them 2 or 3 mornings a week as our mid-morning snack. The kids really enjoy them and they are good for them. Much better than about any other "regular" snack I know.

"Overall rating '10'"—Janice Miller

Additional Helps and Suggestions

- Michele Nielsen tried this variation: using apple juice instead of grape. She also added a frozen banana and a dash of cinnamon. With some of the leftover frozen yogurt they put it in the blender with some milk to make a "shake."

Ratings

$ = 30¢
Ease = 8
Prep-time = 5 minutes (not including time required to freeze fruit)
Mega-Session = 1 (best to try this another day)
Equipment = blender

And A Berry Good Morning to You

(SCALLOPED BERRIES)

You have to try this recipe. It is not a dish you want to have every breakfast. Your taste buds would be thrilled, but your waistline would beg for extra sit-ups. But once in a while, we can all afford to indulge. This works great to make ahead, freeze, and then heat for one of those special mornings when you have time to eat a nice breakfast. Some mornings I have time to either cook or set a nice table. With this recipe I can make a lovely table arrangement while it heats. Note: This dish must refrigerate for several hours before baking, so assemble it at the very least the night before you want to serve it.

Do Ahead

- Buy berries in bulk or directly from the farmer for freshness and best price.
- Purchase as many of the ingredients as you can in your area in bulk.
- Buy bread from the day-old bread store. Or make your own healthy version.
- Make several of these at the same time and freeze them for other mornings.

X1	**X2**	**X4**	
12 SERVINGS	24 SERVINGS	48 SERVINGS	APPROXIMATELY 1 3-INCH SQUARE PER SERVING
1 loaf	2 loaves	4 loaves	White bread (standard 16 slice-loaf)
16 ounces	32 ounces	64 ounces	Cream cheese (mol or none at all)
1 cup	2 cups	4 cups	Blueberries
1 cup	2 cups	4 cups	Strawberries or cranberries depending on season
1 cup	2 cups	4 cups	Raspberries or blackberries or your choice of berry
12	24	48	Eggs
2 cups	4 cups	8 cups	Milk
⅓ cup	⅔ cup	1⅓ cups	Honey
1 cup	2 cups	4 cups	Love Sweet Syrup, optional (see page 378)

Steps:

At least 12 hours before serving:

1. Trim the crusts or edges from the bread. Cut each slice into 3 strips and then again in the other direction. (*Note:* this works for a standard slice.)
2. Cut the cream cheese into ½-inch cubes. (Aim for pieces about ½ inch in diameter for even baking.)
3. Spray 13 x 9-inch baking pans with nonstick spray or line with Teflon® sheets. (Since I make

one for eating and freeze the rest, I use 1 glass 13 x 9-inch dish and 3 metal ones with sealable lids, based on the "x4" recipe.)

4. Arrange half of the bread cubes in the bottom of the pans. (*Note:* You don't want smooth layers. It is better if the bread and cheese are somewhat co-mingled.)
5. Arrange half of the cream cheese over the bread layer in the pans.
6. Mix the berries all together and place over the cream cheese.
7. Arrange the rest of the cream cheese over the berries.
8. Arrange the rest of the bread over the cream cheese.
9. In a large bowl beat together the eggs, milk, and honey.
10. Pour the egg mixture over the bread cubes in the dish.

OPTION 1: BAKE ONE AND FREEZE THE REST FOR BAKING ANOTHER TIME

11. Place the glass pan in the refrigerator to "marinate" overnight.
12. Cover the other pans and freeze. As soon as they are frozen solid, you can pop them out and either bag them or wrap them in heavy-duty plastic. Be sure to label. Return them to the freezer.
13. The next morning, remove the dish from the refrigerator, cover, and bake at 350°F for 30 minutes. Remove the cover and bake for another 30 minutes. Serve. This is wonderful with Love-Sweet Syrup (see page 378).
14. To cook those that were frozen raw, thaw in the refrigerator for at least 12 hours, then bake as in step 13 above.

OPTION 2: HALF-BAKE THEM AND FREEZE FOR ANOTHER TIME

11. Cover all the pans with their lids or plastic wrap and refrigerate overnight.
12. Next morning, remove the pans from the refrigerator, cover, and bake at 350°F for 30 minutes.
13. Place the pans in the refrigerator to cool.
14. Once they are cool, place them in the freezer.
15. As soon as they are frozen solid, you can pop them out and either bag them or wrap them in heavy-duty plastic. Be sure to label. Return them to the freezer.
16. The day before you need one, allow it to thaw in the refrigerator.
17. Bake at 350°F for 30 minutes. Serve with Love-Sweet Syrup (see page 378) if desired.

OPTION 3: FULLY BAKE THEM, FREEZE, AND SIMPLY REHEAT

11. Follow the directions above for Option 2, but instead of freezing after 30 minutes of baking, remove the cover and bake for another 30 minutes.
12. Place the pans in the refrigerator to cool. Then proceed with steps 14, 15, and 16 of Option 2.
13. To reheat, cover with an ovenproof lid and bake at 350°F for 30 minutes. Serve with Love-Sweet Syrup (see page 378) if desired.

Note: I use this recipe for Sunday mornings. My preference is Option 1—it gives me a whole hour to do other things. On Saturday, I simply pull one of these out of the freezer and place it in my fridge. Then on Sunday morning, I bake it, setting a timer for 30 minutes. That gives me time to supervise my children's dressing and to fix Bethany's hair. When the timer goes off, I take off the lid and finish baking it for another 30 minutes. I have time to set a lovely breakfast table or finish dressing myself. We can then have a wonderful start to worship instead of dashing out the door screaming at each other to hurry.

"Absolutely delicious! Will use this recipe again and again."—Sheryl Hartzell
"Wonderful recipe!"—Bretta Ogburn

Additional Helps and Suggestions

- Jill adds: Since my children aren't wild about cream cheese, I don't put any cream cheese in about two-thirds of the casserole. Only a few servings on one end will have cream cheese. So, the amount of cream cheese this recipe calls for is reduced by 75%. I use only 16 ounces of cream cheese for a "x4" recipe. The recipe works without the cream cheese—it has a different personality. By reducing the cheese, you lower the fat, calories, and cost. Judge for yourself.
- Devin Vaughn suggested adding a little cinnamon for extra flavor, and thought this would be good for a ladies' brunch.
- Paula Farris says it is very easy and is better when fresh berries are available. She needed to bake hers for 15 minutes longer, so check it.
- Sheryl Hartzell recommended multi-grain bread to increase the nutritional value of the recipe.
- Jill adds: To reduce preparation time, use kitchen shears to cut the bread. We set up two of the children and let them watch a good video. One cuts off the crusts, and then cuts those crusts into cubes. The other takes the whole slice, cuts them into 3 to 4 strips, then into cubes. They can do about 4 loaves during a 30-minute video. We use the crusts for a variety of recipes including this one. We even make a "for our mouths only" version of this recipe with crusts. Then we'll make a "hospitality" version with only the more attractive white cubes. That way we don't waste anything. We use the bread bags themselves to hold the cubes as we work using a "bread buddy" to hold the bags open. (A "bread buddy" is a plastic container that is a little larger than a standard loaf of bread with a lid at one end. If you don't have one, then rig a cardboard box to hold the sides of the bag.)
- Alan points out: The differences in milk fats and proteins influences how the milk will perform in cooking. The more fat, the creamier the dish (the fat works as an emulsifier); the less fat, the more crystallized and watery.

Ratings for "Scalloped Berries"

$ = 55¢ a serving when we make it using only one fourth of the cream cheese, getting our berries from the farmer, and buying the bread from the day-old store or making my own with hard white wheat. If you use all the cream cheese, the cost will be more per serving.
Ease = 9—the only time-consuming part is cutting the bread. See the suggestion above for how to do that step more quickly.
Prep-time = 30 minutes—while my children are doing the breadcrumbs, I prepare the berries, batter and pans.

Heating = 1 hour (approximately, check it)
Mega-Session = 10, we make this at the same time we do some of the scalloped recipes and it goes very smoothly.
Equipment = kitchen shears, electric mixer to blend batter, bread buddy works great.

Bethany Kay's Granola

My little girl would munch on my granola all day if I let her. It's never a mystery if we ask her what she wants for breakfast, she'll always answer, "Your Granola, Mommy." Though I make it several different ways, she still loves it. We found that it is so nourishing that my children don't need to eat three full bowls like they do of the popular mass-produced cereals. One bowl and they feel full for the morning. They can eat three full bowls of the boxed stuff and still feel hungry because mostly what they have eaten are empty sugar calories. When I serve this I make the basic granola, and then serve a "buffet" of goodies so that each person can add their favorites. When we use this as "trail mix," I'll add the goodies to each person's bag according to their tastes. We also eat it to ward off the "munchies." While I was working on this book, I'd keep a bowl beside me and munch—it was a very healthy alternative to chips or candy. Note: *I use this granola in other recipes.*

Do Ahead:

- Purchase oatmeal in bulk for the best price or buy oat grouts and flake your own.
- Buy a case of juice concentrate to really save $$$.
- Make or buy the added goodies at bulk prices.

x1	**x2**	**x5 (baseline)**	
6 SERVINGS	12 SERVINGS	30 SERVINGS	1 CUP PER SERVING
BASIC GRANOLA			
½ cup	1 cup	2½ cups	Cooking oil (use the healthiest you can afford)
½ cup	1 cup	2½ cups	Honey (optional)
5 cups (1 lb.)	10 cups (2 lbs.)	25 cups (5 lbs.)	Old-fashioned oats (pound amount in parenthesis is for groats)
½ cup	1 cup	2½ cups	Milk solids (powdered milk) or substitute
6 ounces	12 ounces	32 ounces	Concentrated juice (see details below)

GOODIES (Any combinations of the following; adjust measurements to personal tastes)

x1	**x2**	**x5 (baseline)**	
½ cup	1 cup	2½ cups	*Seeds (variety from sesame, pumpkin, sunflower)
½ cup	1 cup	2½ cups	*Raisins
½ cup	1 cup	2½ cups	Dehydrated fruit
½ cup	1 cup	2½ cups	Fresh fruit (add only at time of serving)
½ cup	1 cup	2½ cups	*Nuts (variety from walnuts, pecans, almonds)
½ cup	1 cup	2½ cups	*Flaked coconut

Steps:

1. Prepare pans. Line 1 (or 2 for the larger quantity) jellyroll pan(s) with waxed paper or use Teflon® liners.

2. In a large enough measuring cup measure the oil, then pour the honey into the oil until it measures the combined total. (The honey will pour out wonderfully and you won't waste any.)
3. In a large bowl toss the oats and milk solids together.
4. In a saucepan heat the oil, honey, and juice until warm and well blended. (Don't boil, just warm.)
5. Pour the liquids over the oats, stirring as you pour. (Though you can stir this all with a spoon, I found it much easier to reach in with clean hands and goosh the ingredients together. It will be very clumpy.)
6. Spread the granola mixture across the bottom of the prepared pans.
7. Bake at 250°F for 1 hour.
8. Rotate the pans if using more than one.
9. Bake for another hour. Rotate the pans. If desired, add some goodies at this point for that baked flavor. See the following list. Those that can be baked ahead are marked with an "*." Be careful when baking items like raisins or other fruit, because they will become dryer during baking. To avoid this, soak the dried fruit in water or juice before baking. (We don't like the goodies baked; we like to add all our goodies at the serving table.)
10. Bake 30 minutes longer or until golden brown and no moisture is visible.
11. Divide, store, and freeze any that you will not be eating within 1 week.

Variations:

Note: The kind of juice you use will change the whole flavor and look of this granola.

Harvest Granola: Use concentrated apple juice. Serve with dehydrated apple pieces, raisins, nuts, and sprinkle with cinnamon sugar. (I sometimes add cinnamon and nutmeg to the oatmeal at step 2.)

Blueberry Morning Granola: Use concentrated white grape juice. Serve with dehydrated blueberries.

Tropical Island Granola: Use concentrated pineapple juice. Serve with dehydrated pineapple, papaya, banana pieces, and coconut.

From the Bog Granola: Use concentrated cranberry juice. Serve with cranberry-raisins.

Rock Climbing Granola: Use any concentrate of your favorite juice and mix with seeds, nuts, coconut, raisins, and several types of dehydrated fruit.

"This is the best granola I have ever made. We love it! It's great in trail mix or as a breakfast cereal/or snack."—Marcille Lytle
"This was very easy!"—Leslie Gipson

Additional Helps and Suggestions

- Kathy Morse only had to cook her granola for 2 hours and it was golden brown. Check your ovens and monitor the baking. She also added wheat germ to give it a nice nutty flavor.
- Cindi Sheahan heated the honey and oil and juice concentrate in a glass measuring cup in the microwave on high for about 2 minutes until warm (not boiling). It saved having to clean both measuring cup and pan. She is on a low-fat diet, so she reduced the oil by one-half—granola still tasted great! She's going to make batches to give as Christmas gifts in a food basket.
- Jill adds: I know I mention the Teflon® liners several times, but they are wonderful for this recipe. It makes the granola so simple to bake and clean up is a breeze.
- Oat groats almost double their volume when flaked, but the mass stays the same. In other words, five pounds of oat groats will flake into five pounds of oat flakes, but their volume will double. Keep this in mind when estimating the amount of groats to flake for this or any recipe. With my electric flaker, one cup of groats yields about 1⅞ cups, just shy of 2 cups.

Ratings

$ = 10¢ per serving for the basic granola. Depending on what fruit you add, the price will vary 15¢ to 25¢ per serving
Ease = 10
Prep-time = 5 to 10 minutes
Heating = 2 to 2½ hours
Mega-Session = 10
Equipment = Teflon® liners are a big plus, large mixing bowl or container

Breakfast Lasagna

My friend Sue Chandler brought this dish to a Sunday school brunch and it was a hit. Of course, I asked her for the recipe and experimented with it so it would fit with mega-cooking™. Delicious. Simple. And "do-ahead-able." I like to make four batches, cook and eat one on the day of preparation, and then freeze the other three for future breakfasts.

Do Ahead:

- Make your own frozen French toast. Whenever I'm making regular French toast, I cook triple batches and freeze the extra. Then use some of them in this recipe.
- Make your own apple pie filling. Freeze or can it for a multitude of uses.
- Buy any of the other ingredients in bulk to bring down the cost.
- Make your own granola. (See recipe on page 215.)

X1	X2	X4	
6 SERVINGS	12 SERVINGS	24 SERVINGS	1 4-INCH SQUARE PER SERVING
12 slices	24 slices	48 slices [mol]	Frozen French toast (I make my own, but you could use store-bought)
½ pound	1 pound	2 pounds	Sliced ham (or ham substitute)
2 cups	4 cups	8 cups	Grated cheeses (blend 3 or more different cheeses, Cheddars are especially good)
2 cups	4 cups	8 cups	Apple pie filling (I made my own)
1 cup	2 cups	4 cups	Granola with raisins (see page 215)

Day One:

1. Spray 13 x 9-inch baking dishes (freeze-able) with nonstick coating or line with a Teflon® sheet.
2. Place a layer of toast (approximately 6 per pan) on the bottom of the dish. You may have to trim some of the edges of the slices to fit. (If you plan it well, you can make the fourth batch with the leftover pieces from the other three, depending on the size of the bread.)
3. Make a layer of the ham slices.
4. Layer 1½ cups of the cheese over the ham.
5. Top with the remaining 6 slices of French toast.
6. Spread the top layer of toast with the apple filling and sprinkle on the granola. (See Bethany Kay's Granola on page 215.)
7. Bake one at 350°F for 25 minutes. Enjoy. (Of course, if you opt to freeze them all, then go directly to step 8.)
8. While the first one is baking, cover the others with heavy-duty plastic film. Freeze.
9. Top with the remaining cheese and bake 5 more minutes until cheese is melted.
10. Serve with either Love-Sweet Syrup (see page 378) or Special Topping (see below).

11. Once the breakfast lasagnas are frozen solid, pop them from their baking pans. Wrap completely in film. Return them to the freezer.

Day of second serving and subsequent servings:

OPTION 1: THAW AND HEAT

12. Remove the Breakfast Lasagna from the freezer, and carefully remove the plastic film.
13. Spray the dish it was originally frozen in with nonstick spray or line with a Teflon® sheet. Place the lasagna in the prepared pan.
14. Thaw overnight in the refrigerator.
15. Bake at 350°F for 25 minutes.
16. Top with the remaining cheese and bake 5 more minutes until the cheese is melted.
17. Serve with either Love-Sweet Syrup (page 378) or Special Topping (see below).

OPTION 2: HEAT WITHOUT PRE-THAWING

12. Remove the Breakfast Lasagna from the freezer, and carefully remove the plastic film.
13. Spray the dish it was originally frozen in with nonstick spray or line with a Teflon® sheet. Place the lasagna in the prepared pan.
14. Bake at 300°F for 50 minutes. (Check your oven and test half way through, and adjust the time accordingly.)
15. Top with the remaining cheese and bake 5 more minutes until the cheese is melted.
16. Serve with either Love-Sweet Syrup (page 378) or Special Topping (see below).

Special Topping (Optional)

X1	X2	X4	
1 cup	2 cups	4 cups	Sour cream (or plain yogurt)
⅓ cup	⅔ cup	1⅓ cups	Firmly packed brown sugar

In a mixing bowl blend the sour cream and brown sugar. Chill until needed. *Suggestion:* Prepare only x1 on day of use. Don't try to store the topping.

"This recipe was wonderfully quick, easy, and very little mess!"—Leslie Gipson

Additional Helps and Suggestions

- Terri Houchin thought that 1 cup of granola wasn't enough. They didn't think it needed syrup or topping, and liked it with shredded Cheddar. She used twice the granola and skipped the topping.
- Leslie Gipson suggested using low fat ham and cheese to increase the nutritional value. She also recommended that smaller families use two 9-inch square pans instead of the 13 x 9-inch dish.
- Cindi Sheahan served this when company came (10 mouths to feed). She said the power went off 20 minutes into the baking time but it still came out fine! She reported a 50/50 reaction to the

taste—half liked the combination of flavors (salty-ham, sweet-apples) and the other half didn't care for it. So, please take that into consideration.

- Jaqueline Howe had ideas for two variations: skip the apple filling and make it hearty with cheese and meat, or skip the cheese and meat and make it fruity—the eggs give it enough protein.

Ratings

$ = 75¢ depending on how much you make ahead yourself and how many of the ingredients you buy pre-made or processed.
Ease = 10
Prep-time = 20 to 30 minutes (not including making the granola or French Toast ahead of time)
Heating = 25 minutes
Mega-Session = 10
Equipment = meat slicer for cutting ham meat

Breakfast Pizza

I get ideas from the freezer section of my local grocery store. One item that my husband and children found interesting was pizza for breakfast, and not just the leftover slice from the delivery-boy version the night before. I set out to "conquer" that challenge. We have tried various methods and types. Here is our favorite method, not only because it is the tastiest, but also because it is the most do-able. Note: *You can vary the size of these pizzas according to family's needs: smaller circles or larger. We make custom pizzas for each of our children, since they each have their own "yucky list." We line up all the possible toppings and they make their own pizzas. We label the trays and then are careful to keep track—label, label, label.*

Do Ahead:

- Purchase as many of the ingredients in bulk as possible for best price.
- Grind your own wheat or buy the freshest you can afford.
- Make your own bread dough.

X1	X2	X8	
8 SMALL PIZZAS	16 SMALL PIZZAS	64 SMALL PIZZAS	1 5-INCH PIZZA PER SERVING
1 batch	2 batches	8 batches	Bread dough to make "x" number of loaves (see recipe on page 240 or use biscuit dough for a different texture)

Steps:

1. After following all instructions for your bread dough through dividing and shaping into loaves, divide each loaf portion into 8 equal circles.
2. Roll each circle out into a 3-inch diameter circle—the dough should be ½ inch thick before rising.
3. Spray cookie sheets with nonstick spray. Place the circles on the cookie sheets to rise. Leave about 3 inches between circles. Shape with a slight "lip" on the edge to hold the toppings in place. You can do this easily with your fingers.
4. Let rise for about 1 hour (this will vary depending on which bread dough recipe you used) until circles are approximately 5 inches in diameter and 1 inch thick.
5. Bake at 350°F for 15 to 20 minutes (or less for smaller circles). They will finish baking when you add the toppings. Be certain to adjust the baking time for your bread dough. Check after 8 minutes.

OPTION 1: FROZEN PIZZA DISKS, ADDING TOPPING FRESH ON THE DAY YOU'LL EAT THEM

6. Gently cover the pizza disks on baking pans and freeze flat.
7. Once the pizza disks are completely frozen, you have a choice for storage: a) rewrap individually in plastic wrap; b) rewrap several together; c) seal individually in freezer-quality bags; or d) seal several in each freezer-quality bag. Since they were frozen individually, you will be able to reach into a bag and pull out one or several from a bag—as many as you need at that time.

8. Thaw as many disks as you need for that meal. (This doesn't take long and can be done in a steamer, microwave, or in the refrigerator.
9. Top with your favorite toppings (see Topping List).
10. Bake at 350°F for 5 to 10 minutes until hot and the cheese is melted.

OPTION 2: FROZEN TOPPED PIZZAS READY TO HEAT AND EAT

6. Top each pizza with your favorite toppings (see Topping List).
7. Gently cover the topped pizza disks on a baking pan and freeze flat.
8. Once the pizza disks are completely frozen, I recommend wrapping them individually in plastic wrap; if you try to mix them, some times the toppings fall off. I make an effort to store these pizzas flat in the freezer.
9. Thaw in the refrigerator. Bake at 350°F for 3 to 5 minutes until hot and the cheese is melted.

    Or microwave from the frozen state on medium for 3 minutes. (Check your oven and test one first. Microwaves vary in power.)

    Or bake from the frozen state at 300°F for 20 minutes until hot and the cheese is melted. (Double-check this because, depending on how large you made your disks and your bread recipes, this time might need to vary. This works for the recipe as described here, using my bread dough and sized disks. Check it after 10 minutes and make adjustments. You can always bake them more; you can't "unbake" them if they cooked too long.)

Personal Pizzas

In addition to storing these pizza-dough disks for future use for breakfast pizza, if you store them without topping, you can use them for snack, lunch, or dinner pizzas.

Or for the "already topped" version, simply add breakfast toppings to some and dinner or snack-time toppings to the rest.

Be careful to label. These all look alike once they are frozen.

TOPPINGS

(I recommend at least using sauce and cheese, the rest are optional.) These are listed in order of how we layer them, with the exception that we add the cheese at several layers as we build. All these amounts are [mol]. Vary them according to your tastes.

Per Pizza	x1	x2	x8	
¼ cup	2 cups	4 cups	16 cups	Sauce (see note)
¼ cup	2 cups	4 cups	16 cups	Scrambled eggs (crumbled into small pieces) or "omelet" (see note)
½ teaspoon	4 teaspoons	3 tablespoons	¾ cup	Chopped green onions
½ teaspoon	4 teaspoons	3 tablespoons	¾ cup	Chopped white or yellow onions

½ teaspoon	4 teaspoons	3 tablespoons	¾ cup	Chopped bell peppers
½ teaspoon	4 teaspoons	3 tablespoons	¾ cup	Salsa
½ teaspoon	4 teaspoons	3 tablespoons	¾ cup	Mushrooms
2 tablespoons	1 cup	2 cups	8 cups	Cooked and crumbled bacon
2 tablespoons	1 cup	2 cups	8 cups	Cooked and crumbled sausage
2 tablespoons	1 cup	2 cups	8 cups	Ham cubes
2 tablespoons	1 cup	2 cups	8 cups	Chopped tomatoes (dried or fresh)
2 tablespoons	1 cup	2 cups	8 cups	Fruit chunks (some of kids like it on their breakfast pizza, especially pineapple bits)
Dash	1 tablespoon	2 tablespoons	½ cup	Spices and herbs, such as salt, pepper, oregano, cilantro, basil, dill, etc.
2 tablespoons	1 cup	2 cups	8 cups	Grated mozzarella cheese
2 tablespoons	1 cup	2 cups	8 cups	Grated Cheddar cheese
2 tablespoons	1 cup	2 cups	8 cups	Grated Monterey Jack cheese

Note: About the sauces: Alan and I like to use Holidays Sauce (page 375) or one of the flavored beige sauces for our breakfast pizza. Since the children already like catsup with their eggs, they prefer regular pizza sauce (tomato base) for breakfast pizzas. We use homemade Spaghetti Sauce (before the meat is added) as pizza sauce (page 357).

Note: About the eggs: If you prefer, you can add the toppings you like to the eggs as you cook them, for an "omelet" as the egg layer.

Ready-to-use Toppings

We batch prepare the toppings and sauces, then divide them into small bags for future use. For instance, we'll buy 10 pounds of cheese (either grated or not, depending on the best price) and measure the grated cheese into 1-cup amounts, bag and freeze. That way we can thaw out just enough to top our pizzas or use in dozens of other recipes. We do the same for chopped bell peppers, onions, ground meat, etc. There is a longer explanation of this money and timesaving method on page 110.

Fast and User-friendly Pizzas

Instead of using homemade bread dough, build pizzas on English muffins. *Dinner's in the Freezer!*™ has a recipe for making English muffins.

Additional Helps and Suggestions

- Pam Geyer didn't like the lemon flavor of the Holidays Sauce (similar to a Hollandaise sauce), so she'll make a different sauce.
- Jill adds: If you like Eggs Benedict (that recipe uses a Hollandaise sauce) you'll like the Holidays Sauce with your eggs. If you, like Pam and others, don't like the lemony flavor of that sauce, try a flavored white sauce.
- Varying the type of bread dough you use will give you slightly different flavors. When we use biscuit dough, we use extra sauce because biscuits are so "thirsty." English muffins will give you a crunchier crust. By using bread dough, you can adjust the time and whether you want "thin and crispy" or "thick and chewy." For thin and crispy, roll the dough out into larger, thinner circles. For "thick and chewy," form your circles thick with more of a squatty shape. Adjust your baking time accordingly. Again, remember to check them at the halfway point so you can get them the way your family likes them. For instance, some of us like soft, chewy crusts, so I make some that way. Trent likes almost cracker-like crusts, so I make some especially for him.
- We have had success using pork substitutes: turkey bacon, and a wonderful product from Frontier Natural Products co-op called Bac 'Uns. If your local grocer doesn't carry them, your health food store should or you can check for a co-op in your area with buying privileges.

Ratings

$ = 15¢ (this will vary as to what toppings you choose)
Ease = 5 to 8 (depending on if you bake fresh bread and make homemade sauces or use already packaged products)
Prep-time = 30 minutes (to make bread, less time with purchased bread or bread dough)
Heating = 10 to 20 minutes (depending on type of bread used and size of rounds) plus approximately 3 minutes for reheating.
Mega-Session = 8
Equipment = If baking your own bread, it is wonderful to have a mill and heavy-duty mixer/kneader.

Breakfast Sundae

This is a delicious breakfast that looks great. We have some family members who don't like yogurt, so I substitute whipped gelatin.

Do Ahead:

- Make mega-batches of homemade granola (see page 215).
- Buy fruit in bulk and process (dehydrate, can, or freeze).
- Make your own yogurt or gelatin.

X1	X2	X6	
1 SERVING	2 SERVINGS	6 SERVINGS	APPROXIMATELY 2 CUPS PER SERVING
½ cup	1 cup	3 cups	Homemade granola (see Bethany Kay's Granola, page 215)
½ cup	1 cup	3 cups	Yogurt or whipped gelatin
1 cup	2 cups	6 cups	Fruit (fresh is best, but use what you have available in canned, re-hydrated, or frozen)

Steps:

THE NIGHT BEFORE:

1. If you haven't already made the granola, make it.
2. Make your own yogurt or use a commercial brand. (Or make a batch of gelatin and chill for 1 hour. Whip with a rotary mixer until frothy like whipped topping. Refrigerate until assembly.)
3. Cut the fruit into bite-sized pieces and treat with Brown Away. Or rehydrate any dried fruit. Thaw (when appropriate) any frozen fruit. (*Note,* if you have time in the morning, you might want to cut any fresh fruit then.)

MORNING:

4. Set out as many sundae glasses as needed. (If you don't have sundae glasses, use goblets or bowls.)
5. Place one fourth of the fruit in the bottom of each glass.
6. Spoon in either one fourth of the yogurt or one fourth of the whipped gelatin.
7. Sprinkle in one third of the granola. (Make only 3 layers of granola.)
8. Repeat steps 6 through 8 until you have reached the top of the glass. End with a yogurt layer, and garnish with a piece of fruit.
9. Serve to the "ohhhs" and "ahhhs".

Note: Depending on what fruit is in season or I have available, this sundae can appear and taste quite different. I try to coordinate the dish. You can have fun and make up several varieties. Here are some suggestions:

All-the-Way Sundae: Use mixed fruits with the Rock Climbing Granola (see page 216) and a mixed berry or punch-based yogurt or gelatin.

Blueberry Morning Sundae: Use blueberries with Blueberry Morning Granola (see page 216) and white grape juice-based gelatin or blueberry flavored yogurt.

Cranberry Sundae: Use cranberries (softened) or whole berry sauce with From the Bog Granola (see page 216) and cranberry juice-based gelatin or a mixed berry yogurt.

Georgia Morning Sundae: Use peaches with Bethany Kay's Granola (see page 215) and peach-based gelatin or peach flavored yogurt.

Harvest Breakfast Sundae: Use apples and raisins with Harvest Granola (see page 216) and apple juice-based gelatin or yogurt.

Mocking Bird Sundae: Use seedless grapes with Blueberry Morning Granola without the blueberries (see page 216). Make gelatin with half ginger ale and half white grape juice, or use a lime or lemon flavored yogurt.

Tropical Island Granola Sundae: Use pineapple, banana, papaya, and/or mango chunks; sprinkle with coconut. Use Tropical Island Granola (see page 216; remember you can't use fresh pineapple in gelatin), and pineapple flavored yogurt.

Florida Sunrise Sundae: Use fresh citrus wedges with Tropical Island Granola (see page 216) and a lemon-lime based gelatin or yogurt.

"I made this with chopped peaches, vanilla yogurt and my own Coconut-Almond Granola. It was wonderful! I thought it was good and I can't stand yogurt!"—Terri Houchin
"We love this stuff!"—Cindi Sheahan

Additional Helps and Suggestions

- Cindi Sheahan says that these look very pretty in parfait glasses, but taste just as good in a cereal bowl! Her family has enjoyed this for many years. She usually purchases large containers of honey-sweetened vanilla yogurt through her food co-op, but has used flavored yogurts, too.
- Our family has fun with this basic recipe and tries different kinds of combinations. You can get ideas from different flavored yogurts like key lime pie and cheesecake and mixed berry. Likewise, you can browse the gelatin aisle at your favorite store to come up with ideas. When you make your own gelatin there are no limits to flavors and combinations.
- Our children like a drink we affectionately call Mocking Bird: half ginger ale (or lemon/lime soda) and white grape juice. We use it for special occasions. It really is a "mock champagne" but we

learned to call it something else when one Christmas morning one of our toddlers proudly announced at our Baptist church that we all had champagne at breakfast. He had forgotten the "mock" part. That took too much explaining, so we changed the name.

Ratings

$ = 50¢ to $1.00 depending on the fresh fruit you use (By gleaning or growing your own, making your own granola, and buying the yogurt in bulk, you can hold the cost to about 30¢ a serving.)
Ease = 10
Prep-time = 5 minutes (not including making the granola, yogurt, or whipped gelatin)
Heating = none
Mega-Session = 8—You can make the granola ahead, but assemble these right before serving
Equipment = Sundae or parfait glasses are nice, but not necessary.

Dutch Baby Pancake Puff

I originally got the recipe for this from a pancake mix box. Of course, I customized it, mega-cooked it, and made it my own. This is a wonderful Sunday morning breakfast. Remember to only make as many as you have pans to bake them in. It always comes out good. Also, I can certainly tell how my family is growing. When I first made this recipe, one puff was all we needed for a breakfast. Now we're up to four puffs a meal. And the boys are still growing . . . I make the "x8" recipe so we can eat four and freeze the other four for another breakfast or snack.

Do Ahead:

- Make your own "pie filling."
- Buy pancake mix in bulk, or make your own.
- Buy eggs in bulk at a good price.

X1	X2	X8	
2 SERVINGS	4 SERVINGS	16 SERVINGS	½ PUFF PER SERVING
½ cup	1 cup	4 cups	Water
¼ cup	½ cup	2 cups	Butter (margarine doesn't work in this recipe, but Better Butter does. It isn't as good, but sometimes you sacrifice flavor for a healthier lifestyle)
½ cup	1 cup	4 cups	Pancake mix (See Mega-Mix, page 256)
2	4	16	Eggs

FOR SMALL BATCHES (X1 OR X2)

Steps: *(You can do all these steps by hand easily or use a mini-mixer.)*

1. Preheat the oven to 400°F. Spray 1 or 2 8- or 9-inch pie or quiche pans with nonstick spray.
2. In a large pan bring the water and butter to a steady boil.
3. Quickly stir in the pancake mix. The mixture will form a ball and leave the sides of the pan.
4. Remove the pan from the heat.
5. Add the eggs one at a time, beating well after each addition. Beat the egg in quickly—you don't want it to cook in lumps when it hits the hot batter.
6. Spread the batter evenly into the pans.
7. Bake at 400°F for 15 minutes.
8. Reduce the oven temperature to 300°F and bake an additional 10 minutes or until golden brown.
9. Serve with pie filling as topping or simply sprinkle with confectioners' sugar.

FOR MEGA-BATCH (X8)

Steps: *(Because I'm working with so much batter and I want to work quickly, I use an electric mixer.)*

1. Preheat the oven to 400°F. Spray 8 8-or 9-inch pie or quiche pans with nonstick spray.
2. In a Dutch oven bring the water and butter to a steady boil.
3. Quickly stir in the pancake mix. The mixture will form a ball and leave the sides of the pan.
4. Remove the pan from the heat. Transfer to the bowl of an electric mixer (or a handheld unit).
5. Add the eggs one at a time, beating well. Be careful to beat the egg in quickly so it won't cook in lumps when it hits the hot batter.
6. Spread the batter evenly into the prepared pans. (Since I don't have 8 pie pans, I use my quiche dishes, also. See the note below for a way to re-use the pans you have.)
7. Bake at 400°F for 15 minutes. (Manage your ovens. Since we need 4 for breakfast, I cook 2 on the top shelf and 2 on the bottom shelf.)
8. Reduce the oven temperature to 300°F. (Switch shelves for more even baking if your oven isn't perfect.) Bake an additional 10 minutes or until a golden brown color.
9. Serve with pie filling as topping or simply sprinkle with confectioners' sugar. (I bake the other four while we eat the breakfast.)
10. Bag. Label. Freeze.
11. Thaw.
12. Reheat in the microwave for 2 minutes or in the oven for 5 to 10 minutes.

Note: For even larger batches, judge your time, mixers, and oven capacity. "Store" the batter in the refrigerator as you cook a batch. Wash and reuse your plates. Repeat the baking process.

"Easy!"—Joy McKelvey

Additional Helps and Suggestions

- Sherry Sartain liked that it has ingredients she would often have around the house most of the time. They liked it best with peach pie filling, but thought it was good with pancake syrup, too—then it tasted like French toast.
- Michele Nielsen commented: "I wouldn't count 1 pie as a meal's worth. I made 2 and we probably could have eaten 4!" She suggests that a bit of cinnamon or vanilla would be a nice addition. Jill agrees: As my sons grow (and grow and grow) they could each eat one of these and still one more!
- Joy McKelvey says, "You can use syrup. My kids and husband like syrup. For guests I'll probably offer a variety of tops." You could use doilies (paper or lace) as a template for the sugar. Just lay the doily on the pancake, sprinkle on the sugar, and carefully lift off the doily. The sugar will have made a beautiful pattern through the holes of the doily. She also had the idea of combining this recipe with the one for "Clouds" to make a formal dessert—a pancake filled with clouds mixture and fruit.

Ratings
$ = 20¢
Ease = 8
Prep-time = 10 to 15
Heating = 25 minutes
Mega-Session = 8 (I usually make these in a separate multi-batch session)
Equipment = glass pie plates or quiche pans

Elsewhere Eggs

(SHIRRED OR BAKED EGGS)

I like breakfasts that don't need my constant attention. This is one of those. I can fix up these dishes the night before and store them in the refrigerator. Then in the morning, I can pop them in the oven and then go take a shower. By the time I'm done, breakfast is ready. I almost always make a double batch so that I have them available for my dear husband, Alan, who really likes these. I try to have a dozen of these in the freezer for those mornings when we can't join him for breakfast and he's own his own (either an early launch, or we're traveling, or...). He can zap a few in the microwave, wrap them in a napkin, and eat them on the way to work. Much better than some of the fast-food breakfasts that are available. I can customize different versions according to each family member's preferences. Learning a cooking term: "Shirred" is a cooking term that means baked, especially used for baked eggs.

Do Ahead:

- Buy eggs in bulk for best prices.
- Make up dozens of these for freezing and reheating.
- Buy and process any of the ingredients for use here and with other recipes.

X1	**X2**	**x12**	
1 SERVING	2 SERVINGS	12 SERVINGS	1 2-EGG DISH PER SERVING (ABOUT ½ CUP)
1 tablespoon	2 tablespoons	¾ cup	Light cream
2	4	2 dozen	Eggs
Dashes	Dashes	repeat 12 times	Salt
Dashes	Dashes	repeat 12 times	Pepper
Dashes	Dashes	repeat 12 times	Paprika
1 tablespoon	2 tablespoons	¾ cup	Butter for dotting top of eggs (you might want to procure enough to butter dishes, too)
CUSTOMIZE OPTIONAL INGREDIENTS			
1	2	12	Bacon strips, partially cooked (see note)
¼ cup	½ cup	3 cups	Breadcrumbs, buttered
1	2	12	Slices cheese (favorite type)
¼ cup	½ cup	3 cups	Grated cheese (favorite type)
¼ cup	½ cup	3 cups	Minced or chopped ham (or corned-beef hash)
Dashes	Dashes	repeat 12 times	Ketchup [mol—my kids, more; me, less]
Dashes	Dashes	repeat 12 times	Tabasco
1 teaspoon	2 teaspoons	¼ cup	Chopped chives, parsley, or watercress

Note: The bacon will finish cooking while the eggs bake. Bacon substitutes also work well.

Steps:

1. Spray or butter individual baking dishes.
2. Pour 1 tablespoon of light cream into each dish.
3. Carefully break 2 eggs (or just one) into each dish.
4. Sprinkle with spices.
5. Dot with butter.
6. Either cover and refrigerate overnight or bake immediately.
7. Bake at 325°F for 12 to 18 minutes until the desired doneness. (Different people like hard or softer eggs.) *Note:* I remove the ones I'll be freezing at the 12-minute mark, because they will continue cooking when I reheat.
8. Enjoy some now. If you have extras, cover the dishes with plastic wrap. Set in the refrigerator to cool. Once cool, freeze until the eggs are frozen solid. Pop from the dishes. Bag. Label.
9. To serve: Remove the egg disk from the bag and place back in the dish. Either zap in the microwave for 30 seconds or heat in the oven for 5 minutes at 350°F.

Variations:

Bacon-wrapped Eggs: Between steps 1 and 2, circle a strip of bacon around the edges of the baking dish sort of like filet mignon with an egg where the steak would be.

Au Gratin Eggs: After step 1, sprinkle buttered breadcrumbs over the butter. Place a slice of cheese over the crumbs. Pour on the cream. Pour in the eggs. Sprinkle with spices, then top with grated cheese.

Hammed Up Eggs: After step 1, line the bottom of the pan with minced ham (or cubes) or corned-beef hash. Continue with step 2.

Wake Up Eggs: After step 5, pour some ketchup and a few dashes of Tabasco sauce on.

All-the-Way Eggs: Alan likes them all dressed up. That's when I line the side with a slice a bacon, the bottom with a layer of breadcrumbs, slice of cheese, ham cubes, then the eggs, then grated cheese on top.

"Husband and kids and I loved it!"—Susan Rushing

Additional Helps and Suggestions

- One of the mega-testers didn't have individual baking dishes so she tried doing one egg in a muffin tin and it didn't work. The eggs stuck and were impossible to get out.
- Jill: We tested using muffin tins with paper liners as an alternative, and it worked. The eggs baked quite well and the paper peeled away easily. We first put down a thin layer of breadcrumbs (about 1 teaspoon) in the bottom of the paper liner. Then we circled a half strip of bacon next to the

paper, and cracked 1 egg into the center. Then we dotted it with butter and poured on the cream and seasonings as usual. It came out wonderfully! The muffin tin eggs (single egg instead of double) took only 9 to 10 minutes to bake. Bethany preferred the "just-her-size" version better than the "Daddy-sized" ones.

- Jill: Also we have used regular milk instead of the cream, and it works fine.
- Jaqueline Howe and her family pronounced Elsewhere Eggs one of their favorite foods to start the day. The first time she served them (in paper liners) her three-year-old daughter, Natalie, looked wide-eyed and called everyone to the table by singing "All things are ready, come to the feast." Jaqueline switched to foil-based paper liners and found them to have much more stability. They were easy to remove from the pans with a pie server, and the liners came away from the eggs without tearing. She used buttered breadcrumbs in the bottom of the liners, and only added ¼ teaspoon of butter on top of each egg. It had plenty of flavor without greasiness. Jaqueline noted that paper liners only hold one egg, but the X1 recipe uses two, so be sure to reduce the other amounts accordingly.

Ratings

$ = 25 to 50¢ depending on how you customize it
Ease = 10
Prep-time = 10 minutes
Heating = 12 to 18 minutes
Mega-Session = 10
Equipment = individual baking dishes or ramekins

Old Dixie Breakfast

(BAKED GRITS AND SAUSAGE)

You don't have to live in the South to enjoy grits. We like grits, but they can get boring cooked the same way. Here's an option that works especially well for busy mornings.

Do Ahead:

- Buy grits in bulk for the best price.
- Buy the sausage in bulk and prepare in advance. There are healthy alternatives available.
- Buy cheese in bulk and store in small amounts ready to use in a variety of recipes.

X1 4 SERVINGS	X2 8 SERVINGS	X4 16 SERVINGS	2½ CUPS PER SERVING
2 cups	4 cups	8 cups	Water
½ cup	1 cup	2 cups	Grits
4 cups (1 lb.)	8 cups (2 lbs.)	16 cups (4 lbs.)	Grated Cheddar cheese
4	8	16	Eggs
1 cup	2 cups	4 cups	Milk
½ teaspoon	1 teaspoon	2 teaspoons	Finely chopped thyme
½ teaspoon	1 teaspoon	2 teaspoons	Finely chopped parsley
Dash	Dash	½ teaspoon	Garlic powder
2 pounds	4 pounds	8 pounds	Sausage, cooked, crumbled, drained
½ cup	1 cup	4 cups	Grated cheese for topping (optional)

Pre-Steps:

Cook the sausage. Drain, blot, and crumble.

Steps:

1. In a large pot boil the water. Use a large pot like a Dutch oven if you're doing more than one multiple. Add the grits. Stir. Return to a boil, reduce the heat, and cook 4 to 5 minutes, stirring constantly. (You don't want the grits to stick to the bottom of the pan.) The grits will become thick.
2. Add the cheese, stirring until completely melted. Remove from the heat.
3. In a separate bowl beat together the eggs, milk, thyme, parsley, and garlic powder.
4. To keep the eggs from lumping, pour a little of the hot grits mixture into the eggs and stir. Then mix all of the egg mixture back into the grits and cheese. Mix well.
5. Add the sausage and stir well.

OPTION 1: PREPARE ONE FOR EATING AND FREEZE THE REST

6. Spray 13 x 9-inch pans that can go in freezer (or use a molded shape) with nonstick spray.
7. Pour in the grits mixture, dividing evenly between the pans.
8. Bake one at 350°F for 30 minutes. (Since it is already hot, you don't have to bake it as long as when you'll pull it from the refrigerator.)
9. Cover the other pans with a heavy-duty film. Freeze.
10. Once frozen solid, pop the molded grits out and bag or completely wrap in film. Then you'll have access to your pans for other uses. Immediately continue freezing. Be sure to label the packages.
11. Thaw an Old Dixie Breakfast in the refrigerator by unwrapping it, taking care to remove all the plastic. Place in a sprayed pan (the same one you used as a mold).
12. Once thawed, bake at 350°F for 45 minutes. For an added flare, sprinkle some grated cheese over the top and then bake another 5 to 10 minutes until the cheese is melted and the casserole is hot.

OPTION 2: PREPARE ALL DIRECTLY TO FREEZE AND BAKE ON DAY OF SERVING

6. Spray 13 x 9-inch pans that can also go in freezer (or use a molded shape) with nonstick spray.
7. Pour in the grits mixture, dividing evenly between the pans.
8. Cover the other pans with a heavy-duty film. Freeze.
9. Once frozen solid, pop the molded grits out and bag or completely wrap in film. Then you'll have access to your pans for other uses. Immediately continue freezing. Be sure to label the packages.
10. Thaw an Old Dixie Breakfast in the refrigerator by unwrapping it, take care to remove all the plastic. Place in a sprayed pan (the same one you used as a mold).
11. Once thawed, bake at 350°F for 45 minutes. For an added flare, sprinkle some grated cheese over the top and then bake another 5 to 10 minutes until the cheese is melted and the casserole is hot.

Serving Ideas: This recipe looks wonderful prepared in a Bundt pan, tube pan, or in a mold. Serve this with fresh melon and home-made muffins.

Advanced Option: Though it can be tricky, you can save leftover grits from other breakfasts in a container in the freezer. Then when you have enough, you can thaw those grits, reheat, and use them in this recipe. Just take it from Step 2 above. Be very careful reheating so that the grits don't stick. I steam the grits hot enough for the cheese to melt and then proceed as above.

"We all really liked this casserole!"—Helene Brock

Additional Helps and Suggestions

- Melinda Stortenbecker made a good point: "Have cooks blot the sausage in addition to just draining it. Try out the sausage before using it in this recipe to make sure you like it." She also sprinkled additional parsley on the top before baking.

- BonnieJean Wiebe had some good ideas as well: She made one batch with sausage and one without. She said it is good either way. She also suggests using less sausage (diet reasons). She recommends setting things out the night before and cooking in the morning. She also cooked the sausage in the microwave using a stack cooker, which separates the grease.
- Jaqueline Howe thinks this casserole is excellent for lots of company. "I like Dixie Breakfast because it is one of the few breakfast casseroles I've seen that doesn't have bread in it. I usually like to fix several special breakfast breads when company comes, yet I want to have a casserole ready to feed many and avoid a time crunch. I don't like having too much bread. This is wonderful!" Jaqueline found she could use one pound of turkey sausage very well in the recipe if she pulsed the meat several times in the food processor to make it a finer grind. She also put this in her cross-shaped cake pan mold to freeze. This will be a wonderful breakfast to celebrate special days, such as Pentecost, Passover, and Resurrection Day when she serves coordinating cross buns.

Ratings

$ = 25¢—varies depending on cost of sausage
Ease = 10
Prep-time = 15 to 20 minutes
Heating = 45 minutes plus 5 to 10 more
Mega-Session = 8
Equipment = food processor to grate cheese

Corn²Bread or Double Corn Bread

This is the best recipe I've ever cooked for corn bread. A sweet grandmother gave me this recipe when I was 16. We worked side-by-side teaching knitting and needlepoint at a "Yarn Basket" store. I value the year I spent with those dozen or so grandmothers who worked there. They never made me feel stupid or naive. They just kept teaching and loving and modeled patience to me. I use this recipe for corn muffins and as a topping for the Cinco de Mayo recipe. My favorite way to prepare this recipe is Option 2 below. I make my own cornbread mix, so on my shelf I have eight jars of dry mix. The day I'm going to bake these, I open one or two jars and add the appropriate wet ingredients, bake and serve.

Do Ahead:

- Purchase cornmeal in bulk or grind popcorn to make fresh meal.
- Purchase flour in bulk or grind your own fresh.
- If you're into gardening, use your own corn.

X1	X2	X8	
6 SERVINGS	12 SERVINGS	48 SERVINGS	1 CUP (OR MUFFIN) PER SERVING
1 cup	2 cups	8 cups	Whole-wheat flour
1 cup	2 cups	8 cups	Cornmeal
¼ cup	½ cup	2 cups	Sugar (or half as much fructose)
4 teaspoons	3 tablespoons	¾ cup	Baking powder
1 teaspoon	2 teaspoons	3 tablespoons	Salt [mol]
2	4	16	Eggs
1 cup	2 cups	8 cups	Milk
3 tablespoons	⅓ cup	1½ cups	Melted butter (or oil)
1 14-ounce can	2 14-ounce cans	8 14-ounce cans	Creamed corn

Pre-Steps:

Grind flours.

Steps:

OPTION 1: MAKE AND BAKE ALL AT THE SAME TIME

1. Spray an 8-inch square pan, iron skillet, or 13 x 9-inch pan (or pans) with nonstick spray or use a Teflon® liner.
2. In a large bowl mix together the flour, cornmeal, sugar, baking powder, and salt.
3. In a separate bowl mix together the eggs, milk, melted butter, and corn.

4. Add the liquid mixture to the dry ingredients and mix well.
5. Pour the batter into the prepared pans. Bake according to the chart below.

OPTION 2: MAKE SEVERAL "MIXES" AND THEN JUST ADD WET INGREDIENTS DAY OF SERVING

1. In a large bowl mix together the flour, cornmeal, sugar, baking powder, and salt.
2. Divide into equal amounts (about 2¼ cups per container). Store in bags or jars, label.
3. In a large bowl mix together 2 eggs, 1 cup of milk, 3 tablespoons of melted butter, and 1 can of corn.
4. Place the contents of 1 package of dry ingredients in a large bowl. Add the liquid ingredients and mix well.
5. Spray an 8-inch square pan, iron skillet, or 13 x 9-inch pan with nonstick spray. Pour the batter into the prepared pans. Bake according to the chart below.

OPTION 3: MAKE MEGA-BATCH OF BATTER AND BAKE DAY OF SERVING

1. In a large bowl mix together the flour, cornmeal, sugar, baking powder, and salt.
2. In a separate bowl mix together the eggs, milk, melted butter, and corn.
3. Add the liquid mixture to the dry ingredients and mix well.
4. Divide into freezer containers, label, and freeze.
5. Thaw the batter. Bake according to the chart below.

OPTION 4: MAKE A MEGA-BATCH OF BATTER, BAKE AS MUFFINS, THEN FREEZE

1. In a large bowl mix together the flour, cornmeal, sugar, baking powder, and salt.
2. In a separate bowl mix together the eggs, milk, melted butter, and corn.
3. Add the liquid mixture to the dry ingredients and mix well.
4. Spray muffin cups with nonstick spray. Pour the batter into the prepared pans.
5. Bake according to the chart below.
6. Bag, label, and freeze.
7. Thaw, heat (the best method for heating these is steaming), and serve.

Baking Chart for a 425°F oven

(Be sure to use either muffin cup liners, spray pans with a nonstick coating, or use Teflon® sheets.)

Medium muffins/sticks	8 x 8-inch pan	Iron Skillet	13 x 9-inch pan
11 to 15 minutes	15 to 20 minutes	15 to 25 minutes	25 to 30 minutes

"Everyone loves this!"—Lauri Swanbeck

"Hubby and I both grew up with corn bread (from the South) and this is good! (And no bacon grease!) Fantastic for both kids and adults."—Sarah Hendrix

"Beautiful golden bread!"—Becky Valentine

Additional Helps and Suggestions

- Linda Bacon cautioned not to overbake. She said this corn bread is great with butter and honey. Her child was fascinated by the corn!
- Gina Pearcy liked the addition of the creamed corn. She has heard of putting sour cream in corn bread. Jill adds: You can substitute half the milk with sour cream and this recipe will work.
- Lauri Swanbeck made this batch and froze it in a plastic bag. It worked well when she thawed it out to use over the top of Cinco de Mayo recipe. She wrote of how nice it was to have the cornbread already made—she only had the meat mix to put together that night and then she could just pour the cornbread batter over it. She ground her own wheat and corn for this recipe. Her family enjoyed it. They particularly liked how moist it turned out! She thinks it would taste great with honey instead of the sugar.
- Sarah Heggie substituted rice milk for the milk.
- Michelle Manson put all the dry mix in a bag in the freezer and measured out 2¼ cups to make each batch. If you have a bug problem, follow her advice. She keeps all grains in the freezer.

Ratings

$ = 20¢ a serving—less if you grind your own flour and cornmeal
Ease = 10
Prep-time = 10 minutes—not including milling time
Heating = 1 to 30 minutes
Mega-Session = 10
Equipment = grain mill, iron skillet

Daily Bread

I have been baking homemade bread since before I was a teenager. I really liked the taste, texture, and smell of fresh-baked bread. I just couldn't stand all that kneading and waiting while it rose. I've since learned some real labor-saving techniques and have been given some wonderful pieces of equipment. Before I got a grain mill, a friend would grind the flour for me. Many health food stores sell freshly ground flour, and it does make a major difference. It isn't much more work to make the "x6" recipe (for 6 medium-sized loaves) than it is to make 1 or 2.

Do Ahead:

- Grind your own wheat or buy freshly ground.
- Make several batches and freeze the dough or baked loaves for use other times.
- Make extra loaves and make friends with your neighbors—wrap a loaf in a dishcloth, tie it up with pretty ribbon, and ring their doorbell.

Skill Mastery: There are entire books available about bread baking, so if you like baking your bread, I suggest you educate yourself.

Yeast: Use warm water (115°) to activate yeast. Add sugar or honey to the water so the yeast can feed on the sucrose. Wait until it foams in the water before pouring it into the mix. Use good yeast. Store it in the freezer or refrigerator. I've had the most success with SAF and Fermipan yeast.

Dough Enhancer: I recommend using a dough enhancer and/or extra gluten. Commercial dough-enhancer is available from food stores, bread experts, mill salesman, and health food co-ops. Or you can make it yourself.

Kneading Board: If you're kneading whole-wheat bread dough, use oil on your hands and work surface to prevent sticking. If you use more flour when you knead, you can ruin the ratios of the dough.

Rising: If you use good yeast, you shouldn't have any problems with the rising process. Living in Florida, we use our air conditioning year round and we find that 72°F isn't the best for bread dough. I place my pans on the clothes dryer while I dry a load and that works perfectly. You'll want to test the top of your dryer because you don't want the dough to get warmer than 85°F. Temperatures that high can destroy the yeast. I also purchased a portable shelf to place these pans on as I cycle them on/off the dryer. (I bake three or four x6 batches at a time and my dryer isn't that large.)

Bags: I save the bags from commercially-produced bread. I wash them easily by putting in some sudsy water, squeezing the ends with my hand, and shaking. Then release the sudsy water. Pour in clear water and rinse using the same method. Pull the bags inside out and hang to dry. Once the inside of the bag is dry, turn it so that the print is now on the outside (outside out), roll it up and store it in the freezer. When I need one, I just grab a bag. (Be careful that you don't ever use a bag inside out. You don't want the dyes/paint they use for the label to come in contact with your bread.) I save a variety of sizes from buns, loaves, and rolls. If you don't ever use store-bought bread, ask your friends to save them for you. Don't bag hot bread—wait until it cools completely before you seal it. Humidity affects texture.

X1	X2	X6	
1 LOAF	2 LOAVES	6 LOAVES	APPROXIMATELY 16 SLICES PER LOAF, OR 12 TO 16 DINNER ROLLS PER BATCH
1 cup	2 cups	6 cups	Freshly milled flour (for step 3)
1 cup	2 cups	6 cups	Warm water
1 tablespoon	1 tablespoon	2 tablespoons	Honey or sugar (pour in to the warm water)
2 teaspoons	4 teaspoons	¼ cup	Dough enhancer (optional)
2 teaspoons	4 teaspoons	¼ cup	Gluten (optional)
½ teaspoon	1 teaspoon	1-1½ tablespoons	Salt
3 tablespoons	⅓ cup	1 cup	Milk powder (optional)
2 tablespoons	¼ cup	¾ cup	Honey, applesauce, or sugar
2 tablespoons	¼ cup	¾ cup	Vegetable oil
1	1	2	Eggs (optional)
⅔ tablespoon	1⅓ tablespoons	¼ cup	Yeast (use good yeast like SAF or Fermipan)
1½ to 2 cups	3 to 4 cups	10 to 12 cups	Freshly milled flour (for step 9)

Steps:

1. Grind the flour.
2. Dissolve the yeast in warm water sweetened with 1 to 2 tablespoons of honey or sugar.
3. Mix the enhancer, gluten, salt, and milk powder into the flour for step 3.
4. In a large mixing bowl mix together the honey (or sugar or applesauce), oil, dry ingredients, and eggs. Pour in the softened yeast and sweetened water. Mix well. (I use the low setting on a DLX heavy-duty mixer.)
5. Slowly start pouring in the remaining flour. Add flour until the dough starts to leave the sides of the bowl. The dough should be slightly sticky. Don't add too much flour or the bread will be very dry. The consistency is similar to cookie dough. To test, pinch off a small amount of dough and move your fingers apart. The dough should stretch up and down.
6. Knead for 6 to 8 minutes on medium speed. If you are kneading by hand, knead for about 10 minutes.

OPTION 1: BAKE ALL THE BREAD IN SHAPES, EATING AND FREEZING SOME BAKED BREAD

7. Form into loaves, rolls, or pizza rounds. If you have quality pans, there is no need to coat or oil your pans. If you have regular pans, you'll want to oil the pans before putting in the dough.
8. Cover with a tea or drying cloth towel. Let rise for 30 to 60 minutes, until double in size.

9. Bake at 375°F for about 10 minutes until set. Then turn the oven down to 350°F for:
   - 20 minutes (for medium-sized loaves).
   - 25 minutes (for large loaves).
   - 5 to 10 minutes for dinner rolls.
   - 5 to 10 minutes for pizza rounds. (They will finish baking with the toppings.)
10. Remove from the pans immediately. Place on racks to cool. To keep crusts soft either:
    - Brush the tops with oil.
    - Spray with nonstick coating.
    - Carefully run the tops through running water (hold them sideways and work quickly).
    - Drizzle melted butter over the tops.
11. Cover the loaves until cool. (Otherwise they will dry out.)
12. Once cool, wrap in airtight containers, plastic wrap, or bags.
13. Freeze the dough in the appropriately-shaped pan or freeform (if you'll shape later) or let them rise, bake them, and then freeze the baked loaves. Wrap in waxed paper, and then place in a bag or airtight container, or wrap with plastic wrap or foil.
14. Thaw in the refrigerator. To reheat either steam, toast, or bake for a few minutes.

OPTION 2: FREEZE IN "GLOB" FORM TO SHAPE AND BAKE ANOTHER DAY

7. Divide the dough into equal portions. Shape into balls. Wrap the balls in waxed paper, then place in a bag or airtight container, or wrap with plastic wrap or foil. Freeze.
8. Thaw the dough and follow the instructions from Option 1, steps 7 through 12, or use in another recipe.

OPTION 3: FREEZE SHAPED DOUGH, THAW, AND BAKE

7. Form the dough into shapes. Place in pans, or free form. (For dinner rolls, roll out the dough into ½ cup rounds, freeze individually, and then bag.)
8. Wrap. Freeze. (If you need your pans for other uses, then remove the frozen dough from the pan and bag or rewrap.)
9. Place the dough back in the pan. Thaw in the refrigerator. Let rise.
   - You can allow it to rise in refrigerator if you have extra time. I can set one loaf in the refrigerator by 5:30 p.m. one evening and it is ready to bake at 5:30 am the next morning.
   - Or once thawed, cover with a tea or drying cloth towel. Let rise for 30 to 60 minutes, until double in size.
10. Follow the instructions for Option 1, steps 9 through 12.

Variations

Cinnamon Ring Bread: Roll the dough for 2 loaves into a large rectangle. Spread with Better Butter. Sprinkle with cinnamon/sugar mixture and raisins. Roll up jelly roll fashion. Shape into a circle. With a pair of shears (or sharp knife) cut 1-inch rings three-fourths of the way through. Tilt circles. The center of the ring should be continuous, but the outside should be these circles. It bakes beautifully. Bake flat in 375°F oven until set for about 10 minutes. Then turn the oven down to 350°F for 20 minutes (check). Drizzle with confectioners' sugar icing or sprinkle with confectioners' sugar.

Apple Ring Bread: Follow the directions for Cinnamon Ring Bread, but spread with 4 cups of applesauce before sprinkling the cinnamon and raisins.

Raisin Bread: Follow the directions for Cinnamon Ring Bread, but only use the dough for one loaf. After you've rolled the dough up jelly roll fashion, place it in an oiled loaf pan by bending it in the form of a swirl. It creates a lovely swirl and bakes nicely (bake as for a regular loaf).

Orange Cinnamon Loaf: Similar to the ring bread, spread cinnamon/sugar over rolled-out dough. Sprinkle with ½ cup of grated orange peel. Roll-up. Cut into ½-inch circles. Place the circles in a Bundt pan so the swirls are against the sides (will be visible when flipped from the pan.) Bake like the Cinnamon Ring Bread variation. Flip. In a saucepan combine 2 cups of orange juice, ½ cup of sugar, and 3 tablespoons of cornstarch, and heat until thick. Coat the loaf with orange sauce.

Double Orange Loaf: Make a double batch of orange sauce and brush half of the sauce on the rolled out dough. Sprinkle with orange peel and small bits of fresh oranges (or use canned Mandarin orange bits). Ice with the remaining orange sauce or make a confectioner's sugar-based orange icing.

Easy Italian: Use the dough for one loaf and roll out into a large rectangle. Spread with Italian dressing and sprinkle with Parmesan and mozzarella cheeses. Roll up. Brush the outside with garlic butter. Bake like a regular loaf. Once baked, brush again with garlic butter. Let it absorb, then brush again.

My Way Bread: Follow the directions for Raisin Bread, but use your favorite fillings. Here are some ideas: crushed pineapple, dried apricots, a variety of seeds, some homemade granola, pizza toppings, sandwich spreads, salad dressings.

In a Minute Pizza: Make a dozen pizza rounds (16-inch pizza disks). Bake the bread for 15 minutes (enough for it to hold its shape.) Brush them with garlic butter. Wrap tightly and freeze. During a mega-cooking session, we've cooked 6 pounds of ground meat and bagged it in 1-cup sizes. We've bagged pepperoni, pineapple, bell peppers, mushrooms, and onions in amounts for one pizza. We have poured out some of our Spaghetti Sauce (before we added the meat) to use as pizza sauce and bagged it. Instead of calling the pizza delivery service, we can pull out all these little bags, assemble our pizza round, and bake our own pizza. It is faster and much less expensive than calling those guys.

Homemade Hamburger Buns: Form Daily Bread dough into 1-cup balls. Place on oiled cookie sheets. Flatten balls with palm of your hand until they are about 1-inch thick. Let rise until they are 2-inches thick. Bake at 350°F for 20 minutes. Slice in half horizontally. If you like sesame seeds, sprinkle those on before rising.

Homemade Hot Dog Buns: I know these may sound ludicrous. Anyone health-conscious enough to make their own bread isn't going to allow their children to eat hotdogs—right?!? Well, my children and hubby like hotdogs. I know. I know. Some brands are loaded with nitrites. I buy the healthiest versions I can afford, give my family extra doses of Vitamin C, realize that I'm not perfect, and ask an extra blessing on the food. The children smile. You can make the buns yourself. Use the Daily Bread dough, about 1 cup of dough per bun. Roll the dough into 1 x 6-inch cylinders—you know, using the play-dough snake technique we all mastered at age four. Place these cylinders side-by-side in an oiled pan so that when they rise, they have no where to go but up.

- **You-Slice-'Ems:** Bake in 375°F oven for 5 minutes. Turn oven down to 350°F and bake an additional 15 to 20 minutes. (Check them.) They don't look as neat and uniform as the commercial ones, but they taste a lot better. Slice in half horizontally.
- **Hole-in-the-Buns:** Place well-oiled wooden dowels (the size of a hotdog) in the middle of each cylinder so the dough with rise around the dowel. Let rise until double. Bake at 375°F for 5 minutes. Turn the oven down to 350°F and bake an additional 15 to 20 minutes. (Check them.) Remove them from the pan, slide out the dowels, and slide in the hotdogs. They aren't what you're used to, but they are delicious. Of course, this would all be much easier is some ingenious person marketed hot dog bun pans. I can see them in my mind, but . . . .
- **Hanging Dogs:** The other method if you don't have dowels, is to form the "hollow-area" by using wadded up foil. Make hotdog shaped foil. Space them across your pan. Drape dough over shapes. They rise by expanding down over the foil. Bake as for You-Slice-'Ems.

Unique Shapes Bread: Be creative with your bread. You can sculpt with it. My children love for me to give them some dough to play with. They have been very inventive. Note: Most of these can be shaped, frozen, thawed, then baked, or shaped, baked, then served or frozen. Here are some ideas.

- **Bread Braids:** Make bread braids by dividing the dough into thirds, rolling into ropes, and braiding the ropes. Add eggs to the dough to do this, and brush the top of the dough with beaten egg before baking.
- **Animal Shapes:** Using a combination of circle and oblong shaped pieces, you can make bunny rabbits, giraffes, teddy bears, or caterpillars. Decorate with icing, raisins, or ribbon.
- **Play Shapes:** With a little maneuvering you can turn several oblongs into an airplane shape, or a choo-choo train (bake some mini rectangles and place them one after the other in choo-choo train fashion).

Dinner Rolls:

- **Clover leaves:** Roll the dough into marble-sized circles. Place 3 circles in an oiled muffin cup. As it rises it will form a tri-sectioned dinner roll.
- **Knots:** Roll the dough into a rope and tie the rope into a knot.
- **Crescents:** Roll out into a circle. Brush with melted butter. Cut the circle into 16 wedges. Roll up the wedges into croissant-shaped rolls.
- **Fans:** Roll the dough out ¼-inch thick. Brush with melted butter. Cut the dough into 2-inch

squares. Place 4 squares side-by-side in a muffin tin. They will fan out as they rise and bake beautifully.

- **Corkscrews:** Roll enough dough to make a roll into 12-inch long strips or ropes. Wrap each strip around a greased clothespin or dowel (the old fashioned ones work best) so the edges touch. Bake. Slide out the clothespin and you have corkscrew-looking rolls.

Bread Baskets: Turn your muffin tin upside down and oil the bottom of the pan. Press ½ to 1 cup of dough over the cup. Let rise. Bake as you would for Dinner Rolls. They will make a mini-bread basket. Fill with barbecue beef, chicken à la King, tuna salad, or your favorite filling. Enjoy. Or use a larger bowl to make a salad-sized bread bowl.

Bread Dough Enhancer

A dear friend, Karen Jones, gave me this recipe to help bread dough rise faster and bake better.

4 cups	Powdered milk
¾ cup	Lecithin granules
3 heaping tablespoons	Vitamin C powder
2 tablespoons	Ground ginger
3 tablespoons	Cornstarch

1. In a large bowl mix all of the ingredients until well blended.
2. Store in airtight containers. It can store on your pantry shelf.
3. To the dough for each loaf of bread add 2 teaspoons of enhancer at the same time as the flour. (I use ¼ cup of this enhancer to each batch of bread I make for 6 loaves' worth of dough. It makes dough easier to handle, rise better, and bake well.]

"I thought this would be hard, but it was fun and tastes great."—Patricia Hastings
"This is an excellent wheat recipe!"—Pam Bianco
"I really enjoyed this recipe—loads of great tasting and looking bread in less than three hours."—Lauren Down

Additional Helps and Suggestions

- Pam Geyer had never used wheat gluten or dough enhancer when baking whole wheat bread. She said they make a real difference in the rising time and the volume.
- Althea Underwood recommended letting the dough rest before forming loaves. She said the "x6" recipe really worked in her 25 year-old mixer.
- Becky Turner used bread flour instead of grinding her own. Her results were still fine! It yielded four 9 x 13-inch pizza crusts, 8 small pizza rounds, and 2 cinnamon rings.

- Pam Bianco used a breadmaker and said it worked very well. It had excellent flavor and texture.
- Lauren Down's dough mixing went very quickly with the mixer. She used the mixer to knead the dough and it was wonderful. While she worked with the dough, the remainder began to dry out—maybe a damp cloth to cover (or plastic wrap) would help. The braids were beautiful. She topped one with sesame seeds (after brushing with egg) and it was great.
- Joan Parker cooked her pizza crusts from raw dough and it took 10 minutes each. She said the rolls ("fan" type) were very nice.
- As breadmaking becomes more popular I've taught many ladies how to make bread and work out the kinks in their current processes. So, I have learned a great deal about common errors. The most important clarification I can give from all that experience is to go light with the flour. Rarely has any one of my students thought I added enough flour to the dough when I stopped adding ingredients and started kneading. They think dough should be dry, but then they end up with a hard, dense loaf. Instead, my dough is very sticky with a density between cake batter and cookie dough. My bread comes out light and fluffy. One lady who attended one of my classes couldn't believe the texture, and told how she had invested in a flour mill and quality kneading machine. she had been making bread that was extremely hard, but her family ate it because it was "healthy" and real whole wheat bread was like that. Or so they thought. They were delighted to know that she could make very healthy, whole-wheat bread that was fluffy, light, and delicious. It is almost impossible to knead sticky dough by hand, so invest in a quality machine that kneads dough for you. I have an electric kneader (my DLX—approximately $500) and a hand-crank machine (Dough-maker—approximately $75, available from country store-type catalogs such as Lehman's).

Ratings

$ = 5¢ per serving (depends on flour used)
Ease = 6
Prep-time = 3 hours
Heating = 15 to 30 minutes
Mega-Session = 10
Equipment = bread dough kneader or heavy-duty mixer, grain mill, any specially shaped pans

Dough-Knots

Homemade doughnuts are so good. Once you've eaten these, you'll never go back to store-bought again. So, I'll warn you first, these are addictive. I make them a couple times a year and I have to make a mega-batch. This is a rather time-consuming recipe, so I plan to make these when I have some time or have a video I have to watch or tape to listen to. Yes, I realize they are fried. But for a couple times a year, they are worth it. If we ate these everyday, I'd be huge and our arteries would clog. Use the best oil you can afford to minimize the absorbable fats. Even so, I think mine are better than the store-bought ones. I can control the fat I use and monitor the freshness of the oil.

Do Ahead:

- Make Mega-mix or buy baking mix in bulk.
- Buy any of the ingredients in bulk to use in several recipes.
- Make a mega-batch of these, take as food gifts to neighbors (they will love you), or freeze for further breakfasts.

X1	**X2**	**X8**	
12 DOUGHNUTS	24 DOUGHNUTS	96 DOUGHNUTS	2 TO 3 DOUGHNUTS PER SERVING
2 cups	4 cups	16 cups	Mega-Mix (page 256) or baking mix
2 tablespoons	¼ cup	1 cup	Sugar, fructose, or sucanat
¼ teaspoon	½ teaspoon	2 teaspoons	Ground cinnamon
¼ teaspoon	½ teaspoon	2 teaspoons	Grated nutmeg
1	2	8	Eggs
¼ cup	½ cup	2 cups	Milk
1 teaspoon	2 teaspoons	3 tablespoons	Vanilla extract

Steps:

1. In a large bowl mix the Mega-Mix, sugar, cinnamon, and nutmeg. Fluff with a wire whisk.
2. In the bowl of an electric mixer combine the eggs, milk, and vanilla and beat until blended.
3. Add the dry ingredients to the liquid mixture.
4. Knead until smooth (about 5 minutes by machine or 10 minutes by hand).
5. In a fryer or Dutch oven heat 3 to 4 inches of oil to approximately 375°F.
5. While the oil is heating, roll out the dough to about ¼-inch thick. Cut into "doughnuts" or other fun shapes. Our kids get really creative.
6. Make certain a responsible person is manning the hot oil and the little ones don't get too close. You don't want any burns. We assembly-line this process with one of us at the cooker and others rolling and cutting. It is a fun time with the whole family involved.
7. Cook the dough-knots in hot oil for approximately 30 seconds on each side.
8. Drain.
9. Glaze or dust if desired (see below)

Toppings:

1 cup	2 cups	2 to 4 cups	Confectioners' sugar (optional)
1 cup	2 cups	2 to 4 cups	Cinnamon/sugar mixture (optional)

Place the confectioners' sugar or cinnamon/sugar mixture in a paper bag or plastic container with a tight seal. Or try some of both. While the dough-knots are still hot, drop them in the sugar or cinnamon/sugar. Shake. Remove the dough-knots to a serving platter. Continue for the whole batch, adding more toppings if you've been generous on the first batches.

When we have more than we need, we freeze these individually, and then bag.

Thaw and enjoy. Or steam to heat, or eat straight from the freezer. My children prefer them frozen or chilled. They thaw quickly.

Cinnamon-sugar mixture: Mix together 1 cup of sugar and 3 to 4 tablespoons of cinnamon. This ratio works for us. I often substitute granulated fructose for the sugar.

"10's for family, company, and ministry."—Julie McWright

Additional Helps and Suggestions

- You can make a mega-batch of the dough, and cook just enough to eat at that time. Continue to roll out and cut the other doughnuts. Place on cookie sheets and freeze them. Once they are frozen, bag them and label the bags. Then on another day when you don't have much time, you can cook them conveniently. Take as many as you need out of the freezer bag and thaw in an airtight container in the refrigerator. The next morning start the oil. It takes some time for it to get hot enough. Play it safe. If you have little ones guard the oil. When it is hot enough, drop in the thawed donut dough. Cook as above. It only takes minutes and you'll have fresh homemade donuts. Again, the biggest time factor is getting the oil hot, so plan to do something nearby while it heats.
- This dough is soft, purposefully—that's what gives the finished donuts such a good texture. These are a wonderful alternative to store-bought donuts and are healthier.
- Dorothy Hunsberger did not like adding the confectioners' sugar—that made them too sweet for her. So, if you have done a good job of weaning your family off really sweet things (like Dorothy has), then just serve them plain dough-knots.

Ratings

$ = 30¢
Ease = 6
Prep-time = 30 to 60 minutes
Heating = 1 minute
Mega-Session = 1—We do this as its own mega-session. It is too much to try to tackle during a full mega-cooking™ session.
Equipment = rolling pin, dough mixer, cookie cutters or donut cutters

Many Muffins Mix

Fresh-baked muffins are wonderful, aren't they. But I don't always have the time to make them from scratch. I make a mega-batch of dry muffin mix and divide it into jars for storage. Then on the day of baking, I simply add the wet ingredients, plus any special flavorings and bake. I like to have dozens of these homemade mixes on the shelf, ready for quick muffins for breakfast, snacks, or a bread with dinner.

This mix makes enough for 10 batches.

Do Ahead:

- Either buy flour in bulk or mill your own from wheat berries.
- Buy restaurant-sized container of baking powder (preferably one that is aluminum-free).
- Prepare the added ingredients (e.g., dehydrate fruit or grate cheese).

DAY 1: MAKE THE MIX

20 cups	Fresh whole wheat flour (see suggestion below for alternatives; soft white works best)
2½ cups	Sugar or 1 cup of fructose
¾ cup	Baking powder
1½ tablespoons	Salt

In a large bowl mix all of the ingredients with a large wire whisk or very clean fingers. Divide into 10 equal parts—approximately 2½ cups each. Either bag or jar the mix. (I vacuum seal the mix in jars.) Store dry. If there is freezer room, store the bags in the freezer. If you find your family consumes more than this amount, then double the amount in each bag or jar. Be certain to double the liquid ingredients on the day of serving.

I put about 4¼ cups in each jar for our family, making dozens of mixes ready to use. I've found I can't mix much more at a time myself and get an even distribution of ingredients. It is so easy, you can make several batches in a matter of minutes when you have the ingredients out and ready to measure.

DAY OF USE: FOR ONE 2½ CUP BAG OR JAR:

1 cup	Milk
⅓ cup	Oil
1	Egg

1. In a large bowl beat together the milk, oil, and egg. If adding a dehydrated optional ingredient, let it soak in the liquid mixture for 10 minutes.
2. Add the dry muffin mix. The batter will be thick and lumpy.
3. Prepare muffin cups by spraying with nonstick coating or line with paper muffin cups.

4. Fill the cups three-fourths full.
5. Bake at 350°F for 15 minutes.

Options:
Either add these ingredients to the dry mix for storing or add the "single" amount to the batter on day of baking. If the "added" ingredient is completely dry, you can add it to the dry mix at time of storage. If it has any moisture or juice, add it in single amounts the day of baking. These ingredients can be added individually or combined for added flavor. For instance, cheese and bacon go well together as do apples, cinnamon, and raisins. This list is just a start to get your imagination going. You could add different seeds, many different kinds of fruits, or various meat bits.

Single	Bulk Added to dry mix	
¼ cup	2 cups	Cinnamon-sugar mixture (8 parts sugar to 1 part cinnamon) or sprinkle on batter for a "coffee-cake" look
½ cup	5 cups	Raisins
½ cup	NO	Diced apple (moist) (use apple juice in place of the milk and add ¼ cup milk solids)
½ cup	5 cups	Dehydrated apple pieces
2 tablespoons	1 cup	Grated orange peel (when mixing, use orange juice instead of the milk and add ¼ cup milk solids)
¼ cup	2 cups	Grated cheese (store mix in freezer, not on shelf) (quite a few types of cheeses work well)
¼ cup	2 cups	Bacon bits (dry and dehydrated)
¼ cup	NO	Cooked and crumbled bacon
½ cup	5 cups	Dehydrated berries (try a variety from blueberry to strawberry to mulberry)
½ cup	NO	Fresh berries
½ cup	5 cups	Dehydrated peaches (small pieces)
½ cup	NO	Fresh peaches (small pieces)
½ cup (approx.)	NO	Jam (*Note:* fill the muffin cup halfway, add a teaspoon of jam, then pour in remaining batter)
½ cup	5 cups	Dehydrated pineapple bits (substitute pineapple juice for the milk and add ¼ cup milk solids)
½ cup	NO	Pineapple bits, fresh (substitute pineapple juice for the milk and add ¼ cup milk solids)
¼ cup	2½ cups	Poppy seeds, sunflower seeds, or a combination of edible seeds

Additional ideas for more flavorings: Add to the wet batter (2½ cup dry mix amount)
Bog Muffins: Add ¾ cup of fresh cranberries.

Date Nut Muffins: Add ½ cup of dates and ½ cup of chopped nuts to batter.

Lemon Tea Muffins: Add 1 teaspoon of lemon rind and 1 tablespoon of lemon juice to the batter. Top the baked muffins with a glaze made of 1 cup of confectioners' sugar and 2 tablespoons of lemon juice.

Banana Muffins: Add 1 cup of mashed bananas and ½ cup of chopped nuts. Reduce the milk to ¾ cup.

Apricot Muffins: Add ½ cup of chopped dried apricots or 1 cup of fresh apricots. Add ¼ cup of milk solids, and substitute apricot nectar for the milk. (Optional: add ½ cup of chopped pecans.)

Meaty Muffins: Add ½ cup of cooked ground meat and ½ cup of grated cheese. (Optional: add some chilies for extra spice.)

More Explanation: You can be as creative and inventive, as you want to be. There are two different basic dry-mix versions: one uses milk in the batter but no milk solids in the dry mix. The other uses juice, which requires adding milk solids to the dry mix—2½ cups for 10 batches or ¼ cup for a single-batch.

Here are some of my family's favorite combinations:

The ingredients have been modified; follow the basic assembling directions above.

You'll note that when we substitute a juice for the milk in the wet batter, we need to add milk solids to the mix. You can either add that to the whole dry mix (then use 2½ cups) or you can just add ¼ cup to the wet batter. Modify these recipes accordingly.

For ease you can specify "w/milk solids" or "w/o milk solids" on the dry mix batch.

You can also adapt each of these combinations to ones that you add the custom flavors on day of serving. The amounts for custom flavors are listed in brackets for you.

You can add seeds and/or nuts to any of them.

Apple Oatmeal Muffins: Use this for the dry mix and follow directions above:

10 cups	Whole wheat flour
5 cups	Oats
5 cups	All-purpose flour (unbleached is preferable, but regular will do)
4 cups	Sugar
2½ cups	Milk solids
¼ cup	Cinnamon (mol to taste) [1 teaspoon]
1 teaspoon	Nutmeg [⅛ teaspoon]

¾ cup	Baking powder
1½ tablespoons	Salt
5 cups	Raisins [½ cup]

Then to each 2½ cup jar amount add:

1 cup	Apple juice (or ½ cup juice and 1 cup applesauce)
⅓ cup	Oil
1	Egg

Orange Corn Muffins: Use this for the dry mix and follow directions above:

10 cups	Whole wheat flour
5 cups	Cornmeal
5 cups	All-purpose flour (unbleached is preferable, but regular will do)
2½ cups	Milk solids
2½ to 5 cups	Sugar
	Peel of ¼ orange, grated [1 teaspoon]
¾ cup	Baking powder
1½ tablespoons	Salt

Then to each 2 ½ cup jar amount add:

1 cup	Orange juice
⅓ cup	Oil
1	Egg
½ to 1 cup	Orange pieces (optional)

Bacon Cheese Muffins: Use this for the dry mix and follow directions above:

10 cups	Whole wheat flour
5 cups	Soy, oat, or bean flour (bean flour is made from grinding dry beans through a grain mill; if it is not available, or for convenience, use either whole-wheat or white)
5 cups	All-purpose flour (unbleached is preferable, but regular will do)
2½ to 5 cups	Sugar
¾ cup	Baking powder
1½ tablespoons	Salt

Then to each 2½ cup jar amount add:

1 cup	Milk
⅓ cup	Oil
1	Egg
¼ cup	Grated cheese
¼ to ½ cup	Bacon bits (fresh or dehydrated)

Blueberry Morning Muffins: Use this for the dry mix and follow directions above:

15 cups	Whole wheat flour
5 cups	All-purpose flour (unbleached is preferable, but regular will do)
2½ to 5 cups	Sugar
¾ cup	Baking powder
1½ tablespoons	Salt

Then to each 2½ cup jar amount add:

1 cup	Milk
⅓ cup	Oil
1	Egg
½ to 1 cup	Blueberries, drained

Peachy-Good Muffins: Use this for the dry mix and follow directions above:

10 cups	Whole wheat flour
5 cups	Oat flour or whole-wheat
5 cups	All-purpose flour (unbleached is preferable, but regular will do)
4 cups	Sugar
2½ cups	Milk solids
¾ cup	Baking powder
1½ tablespoons	Salt
5 cups	Raisins (optional) [½ cup] and/or almonds

Then to each 2½ cup jar amount add:

1 cup peach nectar

⅓ cup oil

1 egg
½ to 1 cups diced peaches

Pumpkin Muffins: (same dry mix as for Peachy-good Muffins)

10 cups	Whole wheat flour
5 cups	Oat flour or whole-wheat
5 cups	All-purpose flour (unbleached is preferable, but regular will do)
4 cups	Sugar
2½ cups	Milk solids
¾ cup	Baking powder
1½ tablespoons	Salt
2 tablespoons	Cinnamon
1 teaspoon	Nutmeg
5 cups	Raisins (optional) [½ cup]

Then to each 2½ cup jar amount add

1 cup	Mashed pumpkin
⅓ cup	Oil
1	Egg
½ cup	Milk

"Husband loves them and wants them daily."—BonnieJean Wiebe

Additional Helps and Suggestions

- BonnieJean Wiebe mixed all dry ingredients by placing them in a 32-cup plastic bowl, popping on the lid, and shaking the mixture—all while she was cooking bacon for a meat loaf. She used fructose and used a combination flour: two-thirds (67%) unbleached and one-third (33%) whole wheat. She's thinking about adding chocolate chips or carob chips.
- Ruth Brown suggested adding dry milk to this recipe; or perhaps another grain or two like cornflour, or oatmeal flour, or soy to jazz up the flavor.
- I'll be honest—I couldn't figure out the mixed results we were getting on this recipe. Some loved it! (75%) And others (25%) said it needed flavor and it was bland. I was stumped. We think the muffins are so good that we don't even need to add jelly. I know it's a good recipe, so I've been experimenting and discovered that the flour used makes a big difference. I use fresh-ground whole-wheat. When I tried a batch with just plain white flour, I thought it needed some jazzing up, too. Here are some more ideas: add ¼ cup of milk solids to the basic mix if you aren't using whole wheat flour. Then use a fruit juice as the liquid that corresponds to the extra ingredients. For

example, use apple juice in the recipe with apple pieces, cinnamon, and raisins. Also, you can add more sugar (up to double the amount) and the recipe will work—I realize some people need that extra sweetness for something to be tasty. Also, experiment just as BonnieJean and Ruth suggested—make a multi-grain muffin using different flours in combinations.

- To increase the grains and give a slight crunch to your muffins, add ½ cup of millet (people grade) to the dry muffin mix. Millet is a wonderful grain (you may have noticed it's a principle "seed" in bird-feed mix) available in some grocery and health food stores. You can mill it for a good flour, or use it in the "seed" to add texture.

Ratings

$ = 10¢ (depending on variation)
Ease = 9
Prep-time = 15 minutes
Heating = 15 minutes
Mega-Session = 3—This works better as its own mega-session.
Equipment = grain mill to grind your own flour (but not necessary)

Mega-Mix

There is some quirk to my personality that makes me want to improve any recipe. In this case, I've improved on a recipe I first presented in my book, Dinner's in the Freezer!TM *That recipe is good, and I still use it in that form, but for some applications I've found this Mega-Mix works better. It is also a little bit easier to process and make up. I've reduced the shortening, and so reduced the hydrogenated oil. Since you're making the mix yourself, you can customize it if your family has allergies. Quite a few families can't eat wheat, so they can use oat flour or quinoa or a combination of other whole grains.*

Do Ahead:

- Grind the flour. *Note:* Five pounds of wheat berries will make 5 pounds of flour.
- Purchase as many of the ingredients in bulk as possible for the best price.
- Make mega-batches and store in airtight containers for use in several recipes.

About flour: I've tried numerous combinations of flour types. Though it isn't the healthiest alternative, my favorite combination is half white and half whole-wheat flour. How I'll use the mix determines what flour I'll use, such as a combination of rye and wheat for making sandwiches like Rubens. I've used oat and white (or whole-wheat) for some muffins and rolls. Experiment with your favorite.

About baking powder: Use double-acting baking powder, the aluminum-free type if possible.

About sugar: I use whole-cane sugar that hasn't been stripped or dyed. But you might not like the taste. Try it first before you make a whole bunch. Once your family is used to it, it is a great alternative to white sugar. The recipe works without the sugar, but not as well. Sugar is needed in some recipes for the chemical reaction in the baking. And this is really a small amount of sugar for the size of the batch. If your family has a sweet tooth, you'll want to double the amount of sugar in the base recipe. If one of your objectives is to wean them off sugar, then slowly, over the span of months, start reducing the sugar in recipes. See Topics section about weaning.

About storage: I store these mixes in vacuumed sealed jars, well labeled so that I don't accidentally use cake mix for pancakes (though that might be delicious). For quick reference, tape the recipes and processing instructions on the inside of a cabinet. Or place the mix in storage bags and freeze.

1 Mega-Batch

5 pounds	Flour
2½ cups	Milk solids (dry milk flakes)
¾ cup	Baking powder (double–acting)
1 tablespoon	Real Salt (or use 3 tablespoons regular table salt)
2 tablespoons	Cream of tartar
½ cup	Sugar
3 cups	Vegetable oil (I prefer Canola for this recipe)
2 cups	Vegetable shortening

Steps:

1. In a large bowl combine the flour, milk solids, baking powder, salt, cream of tartar, and sugar, and stir to mix.
2. Gradually pour the oil over the dry ingredients. Using a dinner spoon, scatter spoon-sized pieces of shortening over dry ingredients. Using a pastry knife or your fingers. Mix the shortening into the dry ingredients until it resembles coarse cornmeal.

OPTION 1: STORE AS MEGA-MIX AND ADD ADDITIONAL INGREDIENTS AT TIME OF BAKING

3. Divide the mix into 3-cup amounts and place in resealable freezer bags and freeze or vacuum seal in jars.
4. Use the mix as you would biscuit mix for a variety of recipes (see below and index).

OPTION 2: FIX THE MIX UP BY ADDING OTHER INGREDIENTS AND STORE

3. Add the other dry ingredients from the recipes below to the mix.
4. Place in resealable freezer bags and freeze or vacuum seal in jars. Label.
5. Use the mix by adding the liquid ingredients and process as the recipe indicates.

Southern Biscuits: To 3 cups of mix add ½ cup of water or juice (delicious with apple juice). Knead. Roll out, cut, and bake at 450°F for 10 minutes. Note: this is a healthy version of the rich traditional style. If you want a more traditional biscuit, add ¼ cup of sugar to the recipe and ¼ cup (½ stick) butter. You may have to add a little more flour as you knead it to "stop the stickies." You can also make it "richer" by using ½ cup of milk instead of the juice or water.

Pancakes or Waffles: To 3 cups of mix add 1 egg, 1½ cups of water or juice (experiment with different flavors). Blend. Use as you would any pancake batter. For a richer pancake or waffle, use milk for the liquid.

Pooh's Yeast Rolls: Dissolve 1 tablespoon of active yeast into 1 cup of warm water sweetened with 1 tablespoon of sugar. Allow to foam. Pour the dissolved yeast into the 3 cups of mix. Beat vigorously. Knead with additional flour until smooth. Roll into a circle. Cut the circle into 16 wedges. Beginning with a wide side roll each toward the point. Place on a greased cookie sheet and cover with a towel. Let rise until double, about 1 hour. Bake at 400°F for 10 to 13 minutes until golden brown. Brush the tops with melted butter. Makes 16 rolls.

Italian Bread Sticks: Follow the directions for Pooh's Yeast Rolls, but instead of rolling the dough into a circle, cut it into 16 strips and roll into pencil-like logs about 8 to 10 inches long. Roll each in garlic butter, then Parmesan cheese. Bake at 400°F for 15 minutes. Serve. If you like them crisp, don't remove the rolls from the oven: just turn the oven off and let the bread sticks sit there for 15 more minutes. (This works well for a gas oven—when you turn it off, the heat source is immediately cut-off and all you have is the residual warmth in the oven. When you turn an electric oven off, the element doesn't stop putting out heat immediately. It takes time for the coil to lose the heat built up in it. So, watch it.) You may want to remove the bread sticks after 5 minutes, or remove them immediately, let the element cool for bit, and then return to the warm oven. You don't want heat as much as you want warmth. Too much heat and they will burn, not just turn crispy. This achieves the rock-like ones that are so popular. Makes 16 bread sticks.

Pineapple Upside Down Cake: This is my son Reed's favorite breakfast. But of course, you can serve it as a dessert. Place pineapple rings in the bottom of a 13 x 9-inch baking pan. Sprinkle with ½ to 1 cup of brown sugar or sucanat (depending on how voracious your sweet tooth is). For the cake batter, combine 3 cups of mix, 1½ cups of sugar, 2 eggs, 1½ cups milk, and 1 tablespoon of vanilla extract. Blend for 1 to 2 minutes until smooth. Pour the cake batter over the pineapple. Bake at 350°F for 30 to 35 minutes until a knife inserted in the center comes out dry. Invert at once and serve. *Note:* This cake batter can be used for simple yellow cake and icing or as a coffeecake (top with a streusel topping: flour, cinnamon, brown sugar, soft butter).

Orange Cake: Follow the batter recipe for Pineapple Upside Cake, but use orange juice instead of milk and add 3 tablespoons of grated orange peel. Top with orange/coconut icing. (Or make it Pineapple Cake using crushed pineapple and icing.)

Buttons and Bows: To 3 cups of mix add 3 tablespoons of sugar, 2 teaspoons of nutmeg, and ½ teaspoon of cinnamon. Add 2 eggs and ½ cup of milk. Mix the ingredients well. Knead 5 to 10 times. Roll the dough ½-inch thick. Cut with a donut cutter, but twist the shape so that it forms a bow (sideways figure 8). The buttons are the donut holes. Place on cookie sheets and bake at 400°F for 8 minutes. Immediately coat in melted butter and sprinkle with cinnamon/sugar mixture.

Grilled Pockets: To 3 cups of mix add 1 cup of milk (or chicken or beef broth). Knead with additional flour until smooth. Roll out until ¼-inch thick. Cut into 4-inch squares. Load with sandwich fillings (see below). Fold over and seal with a fork. Butter the pastry and cook on a grill until golden brown, or bake at 400°F for 8 minutes, or place 1 square in sandwich maker machine, fill, top with another square, and grill according to the appliance directions. You can make these sandwiches with sliced bread; just cut off the crusts and follow the same directions (except check the oven after 5 minutes). Here are some ideas.

- **Chicken Salad Pockets:** Use chicken broth for the liquid in the pastry, and fill with chicken salad.
- **Pizza Pockets:** Fill with cheese, pepperoni, and some pizza sauce.
- **Beef Stroganoff Pockets:** Use beef broth for the liquid in the dough, and fill with leftover beef stroganoff.
- **Tuna Melt Pockets:** Use tuna juice and milk for the liquid in the pastry, and fill with tuna and cheese.
- **Veggie Pockets:** Use vegetable juice instead of milk for the liquid in the pastry; fill with sprouts, mushrooms, and zucchini.

- **Chili Pockets:** Fill with leftover chili and some grated Cheddar cheese.
- **Ham and Cheese Pockets:** Fill with ham slices and mixed cheese.

Oven-baked Chicken: Toss together 3 cups of Mega-Mix, 2 tablespoons of salt, 1 teaspoon of pepper, and 2 tablespoons of paprika. Clean 9 pounds of chicken pieces. Roll the chicken in raw, beaten egg. Shake the chicken with the seasoned Mega-Mix until evenly coated. Melt ½ cup (1 stick) of butter in an oblong pan. Place the chicken in a single layer in the butter. Bake at 425°F for 45 minutes. (*Note:* it takes about 1 cup of the seasoned Mega-Mix per 3 pounds of chicken, depending on how thickly you coat the chicken. If you only make one chicken at a time, divide it into 3 equal portions to use at different times.)

About the Pineapple Upside Down Cake: "All loved it. Beautiful. Easy."—Nora St. Laurent
"I really like this recipe!"—Kathie Wright

Additional Helps and Suggestions

- Nora St. Laurent tested several options with this recipe: "Baking the pineapple upside down cake was so easy and it looked so great! It was nice to make something like this from scratch, pay less than boxed mix, and have it taste so good." It gave her confidence in her cooking skills. She was pleased that the yeast rolls were so easy. The yeast foamed well and it rose great, too. It wasn't a bad experience like she's encountered with other bread recipes. They looked so nice, too. Her kids loved them and her husband was impressed.
- Dorothy Hunsberger suggested trying different shapes with the yeast rolls.
- Kathie Wright didn't have vacuum sealing equipment so she froze the mix in freezer bags.

Ratings

$ = 5¢
Ease = 9
Prep-time = 10 to 20 minutes
Heating = 10 to 45 minutes (depends on option)
Mega-Session = 10
Equipment = big bowl, vacuum sealer

Serendipity Seed Bread

While running errands one day we decided to drop by and visit with an author friend and pick up a few of her books to show off at an upcoming speaking engagement. Her house smelled wonderful. She was baking some "Sunflower Bread," so we sampled some. I immediately asked for the recipe. Jamie Pritchett makes this in her bread machine. I've mega-adjusted it and make it using a DLX (heavy-duty mixer) to knead, then I bake it in my own pans. She was also cleaning out her closet and gave me several new outfits. I don't believe there are such things as coincidences—the timing was too perfect. I had just gone through my children's closets and had given away more than a hundred outfits to other friends with younger children (some that morning). What a treat! I like recycling nice clothes among friends. I taught the children the meaning of serendipity, because that was indeed a serendipitous morning.

Do Ahead:

- Bulk purchase as many ingredients as possible.
- Make a mega-batch of dough and freeze some for later baking.
- Buy flour in bulk or grind your own.

X1 1 LOAF	X2 2 LOAVES	X4 4 LOAVES	
3 tablespoons	⅓ cup	¾ cup	Yeast
1⅓ cups	2⅔ cups	5⅓ cups	Water
3 tablespoons	⅓ cup	⅔ cup	Honey
⅔ cup	1⅓ cups	2⅔ cups	Whole wheat flour
3 cups	6 cups	12 cups	Bread flour
⅔ cup	1⅓ cups	2⅔ cups	Oats
1 teaspoon	2 teaspoons	4 teaspoons	Salt
2 tablespoons	¼ cup	½ cup	Poppy seeds [mol]
2 tablespoons	¼ cup	½ cup	Sesame seeds [mol]
⅔ cup	1⅓ cups	2⅔ cups	Sunflower seeds (shelled and unsalted) [mol]
3 tablespoons	⅓ cup	⅔ cup	Vegetable oil
⅔ cup	1⅓ cups	2⅔ cups	Raisins

Steps:

1. Dissolve the yeast in water. Add a few tablespoons of the honey. Let it foam.
2. In a large bowl fluff or stir together the flours, oats, and salt.
3. In a separate bowl mix the seeds together. Set aside.
4. Measure the oil and honey in the same container, with the oil going in first. (This keeps the honey from sticking to the measuring cup and helps pour quickly.)
5. In a large mixing bowl mix together the dissolved yeast, oil, and honey.
6. Add the flour gradually.

7. Once it starts to leave the sides of the bowl, pour in the seeds.
8. Knead for 8 minutes until smooth to activate the gluten.
9. Form into balls for rolls. Because the dough has a heavy texture, it is better suited to rolls than loaves. Freeze and bake another day or allow to rise and bake all on day one.
10. Allow the rolls to rise until double.
11. Bake at 325°F for 20 minutes.
12. Freeze any extras. Heat by steaming for a few minutes.

Note: If you are using a bread machine, follow the directions as to the order for adding ingredients. Add the seeds and raisins at the end of the beating time (1st or 2nd) so they don't get broken.

"I have decided that this is a wonderful breakfast bread!"—Jean Dominquez

Additional Helps and Suggestions

- Jean Dominquez stressed using warm water for the dough and greasing pans well. (*Jill:* I use a Teflon® sheet and have great results.) Jean used white raisins and suggested increasing those to 1 full cup per batch.
- Sandra Ross didn't like using the different seeds all in one bread. She suggested making the bread with only one type of seed per batch.
- Esther DeGeus made a good point: she left the raisins out because her family doesn't care for raisins, but she thinks the flavor would have been improved by their sweetness. She's right. This is a "health-nut" type recipe. The raisins serve to coddle our sweet tooth. If you omit the raisins, compensate by adding a sweetener like more honey or sugar (watch out for consistency). Or serve it with a sweet jelly, honey, or butter.
- You can make a mega-batch of these. Form them into balls and freeze individually. Once frozen, move them to a bag. You can then thaw them, let them rise, and bake on another day.

Ratings

$ = 50¢—due to cost of seeds
Ease = 5
Prep-time = 2 hours—including rising time
Heating = 20 minutes
Mega-Session = 4—make these a separate day
Equipment = bread machine, or mixer that can knead dough for you

SOUPS

Italy and India Soup

(CURRY BROCCOLI SOUP)

Since I'm trying to make my dishes healthier, when a base recipe calls for sautéing in butter, I don't. For this recipe you could sauté the onion in lots of butter before proceeding with step one (if you can afford the calories and fat). This recipe brings the two countries' prime exports together for a delicious taste sensation.

Do Ahead:

- Buy broccoli in bulk and use in a variety of recipes, or store in various forms.
- Purchase as many ingredients in bulk as possible for best prices.
- Make the soup concentrate ahead and freeze for other dinners.

X1	**X2**	**X4**	
4 SERVINGS	8 SERVINGS	16 SERVINGS	2 CUPS PER SERVING
2 pounds	4 pounds	8 pounds	Broccoli
1	2	4	Onions, chopped
6 cups	12 cups	24 cups	Chicken broth
1 teaspoons	2 teaspoons	4 teaspoons	Curry powder (your choice of hot or mild) [mol]
½ cup	1 cup	2 cups	Light cream (needed day of serving)
¼ cup	½ cup	1 cup	Grated cheese (as garnish, see Diana's suggestion below)
Dashes	Dashes	Dashes	Salt and pepper to taste (or do this at the table.)

Steps:

1. Clean and trim the broccoli. Cut off the lower part of the stems and peel the hard surface. Cut into small (1- to 2-inch) pieces. Save a few sprigs for garnishes. (Individually freeze some and bag for other times.)
2. Steam the broccoli and onions in chicken broth seasoned with curry powder until tender.
3. Remove from the stove and place in the refrigerator to cool.
4. In a blender or food processor purée the cooked broccoli/broth mixture in batches until smooth.

OPTION 1: MAKE ONE BATCH FOR THE FIRST NIGHT AND FREEZE THE REST FOR OTHER TIMES

5. Divide the mixture into meal-sized amounts.
6. Return one meal portion to the saucepan and begin heating.

7. Add the cream and heat thoroughly.
8. Serve hot. Garnish with a sprig of broccoli.
9. Season with salt and pepper at the table.
10. Bag the remaining meal portions and freeze using the bag-in-box method. Label. Once frozen solid, remove the box and pack the soup concentrate with already frozen items.
11. For the next meal, thaw one portion in the refrigerator.
12. In a saucepan begin heating the soup mixture.
13. Add the cream and heat thoroughly.
14. Serve hot. Garnish with a sprig of broccoli.
15. Season with salt and pepper at the table.

OPTION 2: MAKE ALL DURING A MEGA-COOK SESSION AND FREEZE FOR OTHER TIMES

5. Divide the mixture into meal-sized amounts.
6. Bag the meal portions. Freeze using the bag-in-box method. Label. Once frozen solid, remove the box and pack the soup concentrate with already frozen items.
7. Thaw one meal portion in the refrigerator.
8. In a saucepan begin heating the soup mixture.
9. Add the cream and heat thoroughly.
10. Serve hot. Garnish with a sprig of broccoli.
11. Season with salt and pepper at the table.

"Little effort—tastes great!"—Diana Harrison

Additional Helps and Suggestions

- Diana Harrison added a little more curry powder and a little salt, pepper, and garlic powder. She also added Cheddar and Monterey Jack cheese. Everyone liked it—even her very picky 8-year-old. She served it with homemade muffins.
- Remember, when freezing soup, freeze the concentrate. Don't waste freezer space on water or extra liquids. You can always dilute it to the consistency you want when you reheat.

Ratings

$ = 25¢
Ease = 10
Prep-time = 20 minutes
Heating = 10 minutes
Mega-Session = 10
Equipment = blender

Texas Star Chili

I never realized there was an art to chili making until we moved to Texas. There, chili is a matter of state pride and family recipes are honored with chili cook-offs. I listened, learned, and adapted. We laugh because we are still on the mild side of chili making. When Bethany Kay was born a sweet lady, a fifth generation Texan, made us a batch of chili. She apologized to me for the chili, "Jill, I know you are nursing and I wanted to play it safe so I only added about a tenth of the spices I normally add for my family. I hope it isn't too bland." It was the hottest chili I have ever had in my life. If one-tenth is volcanic, her "normal" must be thermo-nuclear. This is a basic chili, but if you like volcanic to nuclear versions, you can triple (3x), quadruple(4x), or septantiguple (70x) the spices.

Do Ahead:

- Purchase the chicken or turkey in bulk. Cook and dice in advance.
- Buy a mega-size package of beans.
- Make a huge batch of this soup and freeze for other meals.

X1	X2	X10	
8 SERVINGS	16 SERVINGS	80 SERVINGS	1 CUP PER SERVING
1 cup	2 cups	10 cups	Kidney beans (see note)
1 pound	2 pounds	10 pounds	Ground meat or combination of stew meat
½ teaspoon	1 teaspoon	2 tablespoons	Cilantro
½ teaspoon	1 teaspoon	2 tablespoons	Powdered kelp (optional)
½ teaspoon	1 teaspoon	2 tablespoons	Chili powder
½ teaspoon	1 teaspoon	2 tablespoons	Salt
Dashes	¼ teaspoon	2 teaspoons	Pepper (white pepper if you have it)
Dashes	¼ teaspoon	2 teaspoons	Dried red pepper
½ cup	1 cup	5 cups	Grated onions
½ cup	1 cup	5 cups	Grated bell peppers
1 20-ounce can	2 20-ounce cans	1 6-pound, 10-ounce) can	Stewed tomatoes, chopped (or fresh tomatoes)
½ cup	1 cup	5 cups	Grated carrots
Dashes	¼ teaspoon	2 teaspoons	Hot pepper sauce

Steps:

1. Sort and rinse the beans. Soak the beans overnight in water. Drain. *Note:* To save time, you may purchase canned beans. Reduce the cooking time to 1 hour.
2. In a large pot cook the beans in water to 3 inches above the beans. Bring the beans to a boil. Cover and simmer for 2 hours or until tender. Check every 30 minutes to make sure the beans have plenty of water. (Remember, do not add anything salty until the beans are tender.)
3. In a small bowl mix the cilantro, kelp, chili powder, salt, pepper, and red pepper.

4. Add the onions, bell peppers, tomatoes, carrots, hot pepper sauce, and spices to the beans.
5. Remove the meat from the cooled chicken and dice. Add the meat to the beans.

OPTION 1: SERVE SOME NOW AND FREEZE THE REST FOR ANOTHER TIME

6. Serve with a dollop of sour cream and 1 tablespoon each of chopped white and green onion.
7. Place the pot with the remaining portions in the refrigerator to cool. Once cool, bag using the bag-in-box method.
8. Thaw. Reheat on the stovetop or in the microwave.

OPTION 2: MAKE DURING A MEGA-COOKING SESSION

[Tag team cooking the beans and poultry for this and other recipes]

6. Follow steps 8 through 9 above.

Mexi-ghetti: Use this chili (or your favorite recipe) instead of regular spaghetti sauce with noodles. It makes a fun change of pace. Serve with chopped onions and grated cheese.

Additional Helps and Suggestions

- This is a good basic chili recipe. You can spice it up as much as you want to. We use it as a topper for nachos and hotdogs, in tortillas and as an option for taco night.
- You may add pieces of cooked carrots to the chili for added color, texture, and nutrients without distracting from the Tex-Mex character.

Ratings

$ = 20¢
Ease = 10
Prep-time = 3 hours—not including overnight soaking
Heating = 5 minutes
Mega-Session = 10
Equipment = Dutch oven

White Chili

This variation on the old standard red chili is quite delicious and a nice change of pace. Alan and I have weekly date nights and we get ideas from many professional chefs. This white chili is the result of experimenting after being served white chili at half-a-dozen restaurants. We took what we liked in each version and made one that is not only very tasty, but one that a home cook can definitely make.

Do Ahead:

- Purchase chicken or turkey in bulk. Cook and dice in advance.
- Buy a mega-size package of beans.
- Make a huge batch of chili and freeze for other meals.

X1	X2	X10	
6 SERVINGS	12 SERVINGS	60 SERVINGS	1 CUP PER SERVING
1 cup	2 cups	10 cups	Great northern beans
1 pound	2 pounds	10 pounds	Chicken or turkey
½ teaspoon	1 teaspoon	2 tablespoons	Cilantro
½ teaspoon	1 teaspoon	2 tablespoons	Powdered kelp (optional)
½ teaspoon	1 teaspoon	2 tablespoons	Salt
Dashes	¼ teaspoon	2 teaspoons	Pepper (white pepper if you have it)
½ teaspoon	1 teaspoon	2 tablespoons	Chili powder
½ cup	1 cup	5 cups	Grated onion
½ cup	1 cup	5 cups	Grated bell peppers
½ cup	1 cup	5 cups	Grated carrots

Steps:

1. Sort and rinse the beans. Soak the beans overnight in water. Drain.
2. Rinse the chicken and place in a Dutch oven (for the x10, I use my 16-quart pot). Cover with water and bring to a boil. Cover and let simmer for 1 hour. Remove the chicken and reserve the broth. Place chicken in the refrigerator to cool.
3. Cook the beans in the chicken broth. This will give the beans a wonderful flavor. Bring the beans to a boil. Cover and simmer for 2 hours or until tender.
4. In a small bowl combine the cilantro, kelp, salt, pepper, and chili powder.
5. Add the onions, bell peppers, carrots, and spices to the beans.
6. Remove the meat from the cooled chicken and dice. Add the meat to the beans.

OPTION 1: SERVE SOME NOW AND FREEZE THE REST FOR ANOTHER TIME

7. Serve hot.

8. Place the pot in the refrigerator to cool. Once cool, bag using the bag-in-box method.
9. Thaw. Reheat on stovetop or in microwave.

OPTION 2: MAKE DURING MEGA-COOKING SESSION

[Tag team cooking the beans and poultry for this and other recipes]

7. Follow steps 8 through 9 above.

Serving Suggestion: We serve this with a dollop of sour cream sprinkled with both white and green onion pieces, then a dash of paprika sprinkled over the top. Yummy and pleasing to the eye.

Additional Helps and Suggestions

• You can save time by using canned beans, then it only needs to simmer for 1 hour.

Ratings

$ = 30¢
Ease = 7
Prep-time = 20 minutes
Heating = 2 to 3 hours
Mega-Session = 10
Equipment = food processor helps with the chopping

Aunt Kay's Lunch

My sister served this to my children one day when we were visiting and they really liked it. It has now become one of my standard recipes. It is so easy and fun they use the tortilla chips as silverware. I like it better when it's been frozen because the flavors really have time to blend. You can vary this according to your "hot" tolerance. You can upgrade to HOT taco seasoning. I also add a little picante sauce to my plate.

Do ahead:

- Purchase meat in bulk and pre-cook assembly-line style.
- Purchase corn in bulk.
- Purchase chips in bulk and store. Or buy the store brand for much less. Watch the salt content.
- Purchase taco seasoning in the restaurant-sized container or make your own.
- Make your own taco seasoning in mega-quanity and use for other recipes as well.

X1 4 SERVINGS	**X2** 8 SERVINGS	**X8** 32 SERVINGS	
1 pound	2 pounds	8 pounds	Ground meat (cooked)
2 tablespoons	¼ cup	1 cup	Taco seasoning [mol]
1 17-ounce can	2 17-ounce cans	1 6-pound 10-ounce can	Kernel corn (or use fresh or frozen)
1 bag	2 bags	1 mega-bag	Taco or tortilla chips

OPTION 1: COOK FROM START, SERVE SOME, AND SAVE REST FOR OTHER MEALS

1. In a large skillet cook the meat with the seasoning at one time. Drain the fat.
2. Add the corn and heat thoroughly. It only takes a few minutes in a skillet or microwave.
3. Serve some hot at this time with chips. (See suggestions below for more serving ideas.)
4. Divide, bag, label, and freeze extra amounts for use other days.
5. Thaw. Heat. Serve with chips. (See suggestions below for more serving ideas.)

OPTION 2: COOK DURING A MEGA-SESSION, USING INGREDIENTS THAT ARE ALREADY PREPARED

1. Pre-cook mega-amounts of ground meat and store in the refrigerator for use during assembly.
2. Measure the meat and sprinkle and toss with seasoning.
3. Add the corn and mix gently.
4. Heat thoroughly for serving now. (See suggestions below for more serving ideas.)
5. Divide, bag, label, freeze extra amounts for use other days.
6. Thaw. Heat. Serve with chips. (See suggestions below for more serving ideas.)

OPTION 3: MAKE FROM ALREADY COOKED PLAIN GROUND MEAT FROM THE FREEZER

Note: The flavor of the meat won't be as intense with this method, but it is still good. This way you can store dozens of "plain meat" packages to use in various recipes.

1. Pre-cook mega-amounts of ground meat.
2. Divide into 1-pound packages, label, and freeze.
3. Thaw as many packages as you need for a meal.
4. Sprinkle and toss with seasoning.
5. Add the corn and mix gently.
7. Heat thoroughly for serving now. (See suggestions below for more serving ideas.)

OPTION 4: MAKE THIS RECIPE FROM PRE-COOKED AND SEASONED GROUND MEAT FROM THE FREEZER

1. Cook a large quantity of ground meat with the seasoning.
2. Divide into meal-sized portions, label (be certain to distinguish this seasoned ground meat from any plain packages), and freeze.
3) Thaw as many packages as you need for a meal.
4. Add the corn and heat on the stove, in a skillet, or in the microwave for a few minutes.
5. Serve with chips. (See suggestions below for more serving ideas.)

Note: This is not a really healthy recipe, but it is tasty and children will eat it and ask for seconds! You can make it as healthy as possible by:

- Draining the excess fat.
- Using ground turkey or a meat substitute.
- Using baked chips instead of fried.
- Making your own chips.
- Making your own seasoning.

"My whole family loved it!"—Paula Farris

"It's so easy. It should appeal to most everyone."—Devin Vaughn

"I made the "x2" recipe and my husband brought my hungry cousin home with him. We ate it all! Ward thought it would be better with grated cheese, but when we added it, the cheese didn't make much difference."—Bretta Ogburn

"My son loved this recipe so much that he asked to have it for breakfast."—Melinda Morgan

Additional Helps and Suggestions

- Bretta Ogburn sent her recipe for making her own taco seasoning. See below.
- Devin Vaughn served this with extra salsa and grated cheese at the table.
- Lynn Hoxmeier suggested using it as a starter for a tamale pie. All you have to do is add tamales, tomato sauce, olives, and cheese.
- Sheryl Hartzell added 2½ ounces of taco seasoning to make the meal zesty, but not too overpowering. She used ground sirloin and there wasn't any fat to drain. She was able to get it for $1.99 per pound on sale.

- Cherry Martin made a vegetarian version using a vegetarian taco mix (Natural Touch brand Taco Mix, found in health food stores). She served the warm mixture over shredded lettuce with the chips on the side. She topped the "meat" mix with plain yogurt and salsa. She also recommended using fat-free chips. She will use this recipe as a "mainstay" for quick and easy meals. She said if she made this recipe with meat, she'd use ground turkey (98% fat free) or buy cutlets and grind.
- Paula Farris noted that in Arizona they refer to taco chips as tortilla chips. (Jill: so now you westerners will know what we southerners are talking about.)
- Jill adds: Make your own chips quickly by cutting a soft tortilla into wedges and baking at 400° for 5 to 10 mintes until crispy.
- Jill adds: Make a mega-batch of "Bretta's Taco Seasoning." Store in an airtight jar and use throughout the year for many recipes.

Bretta's Taco Seasoning Mix

X1	X4	X20	
2 teaspoons	3 tablespoons	¾ cup	Chili powder
1½ teaspoons	2 tablespoons	¾ cup	Paprika
1½ teaspoons	2 tablespoons	½ cup	Cumin
½ teaspoon	2 teaspoons	3 tablespoons	Salt
1 teaspoon	4 teaspoons	½ cup	Onion powder
1 teaspoon	4 teaspoons	½ cup	Garlic powder

Note: The portions are not exact multiples. I rounded to the nearest standard size for ease of measuring and the mix is still great and easy. If you want the exact taste of the "x1," then do precise measurements.

1. In a medium bowl mix the ingredients together well.
2. Store in airtight containers. Label. Use in many recipes.

Ratings

$ = 50¢ to $1.00 per serving depending grade of meat. *Note:* my children like this and will eat four servings if I let them.
Ease = 1
Prep-time = 15 to 20 minutes
Heating = 5 minutes or less in the microwave
Mega-Session = 10 (Works perfectly during a mega-session, but it so easy that you can do multiple-batches often.)
Equipment = nothing special, maybe an electric skillet

Beef Footballs

Not only are these Beef "footballs" delicious, but they look great. This is a good company dinner. Please feel free to rename this recipe. Stuart, our sports fan, named these because they look like footballs. Please note this probably is the most expensive, and one of the most difficult, recipes in this book—some would call it more of a gourmet recipe. I realize that. But I know sometimes you want to include a "fancy" dish. For most of the testers, this recipe would be done only for special occasions. By mega-batching you can make many meals and then have a fancy meal ready for another time. I would never go to all this trouble each time I wanted to eat a nice meal. By combining steps and assembly-line preparing, you only double your time spent in preparation instead of quadrupling it.

Do Ahead:

- Buy meat in bulk to get the best price.
- Buy rice in bulk at bargain prices.
- Make your own gravy, or use a mix (homemade or store-bought).

X1 4 "FOOTBALLS"	**X2** 8 "FOOTBALLS"	**X8** 32 "FOOTBALLS"	
1 teaspoon	2 teaspoons	3 tablespoons	Salt
¼ teaspoon	½ teaspoon	2 teaspoons	Pepper
¼ teaspoon	½ teaspoon	2 teaspoons	Sage
¼ teaspoon	½ teaspoon	2 teaspoons	Garlic salt
¼ teaspoon	½ teaspoon	2 teaspoons	Tarragon
1 pound	2 pounds	8 pounds	Round steak (buy the best quality you can afford)
1 cup	2 cups	8 cups	Cooked wild rice
½ cup	1 cup	4 cups	Onions (and/or carrots, mushrooms, celery)
2 cups	4 cups	16 cups	Gravy (approximately; to marinate footballs during freezing, see how to make gravy on page 303)

Steps:

1. In a small bowl mix all the spices together.
2. Pound the steak until ¼-inch thick. Season with half of the spice mixture. (Bang repeatedly with a meat mallet.) This step is very important to tenderize the meat.
3. Pound the steaks again until about ⅛-thick. Season with the remaining spice mixture.
4. Cut the meat into 4 to 5-inch squares. (Approximate according to the shape of the cut of meat. Don't waste any.)
5. Add the onions to the wild rice. *Optional:* Also add diced carrots, mushrooms, and/or celery.
6. Spoon about ¼ cup of mix on each meat square.

7. Roll up each square and tie. The ties make them look more like footballs. Use the same method for tying as for a full roast, just in miniature.
8. In a skillet brown all the sides of each "football". If you prefer use a nonstick surface so you won't need to add any oil.
9. Remove the footballs from the skillet. Make gravy from the pan drippings or use a mix. (Please see Topics section for tips on making gravy.)
10. Bag the footballs (as many as you need for one meal in each bag) and pour gravy into the bag over the footballs.
11. Label the bags. Freeze.
12. Thaw in the refrigerator.
13. Place the beef footballs in an ovenproof dish covered with nonstick spray or use Teflon® sheets. Set the gravy aside for serving. Pour water or beef bouillon on the footballs until they are covered.
14. Bake at 350°F for 1 hour and 30 minutes until tender. (Check the water level—you might have to add more water or bouillon.)
15. Heat the gravy.
16. Serve with gravy.

Save the drippings from cooking to make more gravy for other recipes—this way homemade gravy is available in the freezer for those days when there isn't time to make it fresh. Either freeze drippings with a note (to make gravy) or after dinner make the gravy and freeze.

While the meat roll-ups (footballs) are freezing, the flavors are blending and the gravy is tenderizing the meat.

Luau Beef

I like this variation better than the original, but then I enjoy the taste of pineapple. Please read about Pineapple in the Topics section, and read the Additional Helps and Suggestions below to understand why fesh pineapple juice is important for this recipe. It makes a major difference on the outcome of the recipe. The basic intructions are the same as for Beef Footballs, with exceptions noted below. In addition to the same ingredient list above, add these or note substitutions. You can omit onions and other vegetables, if you prefer.

X1	X2	X8	
4 "FOOTBALLS"	8 "FOOTBALLS"	32 "FOOTBALLS"	
¼ cup	½ cup	4 cups	Fresh pineapple (cut in small pieces)
2 cups	4 cups	16 cups	Pineapple juice (fresh or canned) to make pineapple gravy—use instead of beef gravy
2 cups	4 cups	16 cups	Fresh pineapple juice instead of water or bouillon for the actual cooking

2 cups	4 cups	16 cups	Pineapple juice (fresh or canned) to use in cooking rice (vary this amount according to your rice/water ratio)

Follow the same steps as for Beef Footballs with these exceptions:

Pre-step: Cook the rice in pineapple juice instead of water.

1-4. Same as above.

5. If desired, add the onions, carrots, mushrooms, and celery.
6. Spread the pineapple pieces directly onto the meat. Then place about ¼ cup of the rice on each meat square.

7-8. Same as above.

9. Remove the footballs from the skillet. Make gravy from the pan drippings using pineapple juice instead of water, or use a mix. (Please see Topics section for tips on making gravy.)

10-12. Same as above.

13. Place the footballs in an ovenproof dish coated with nonstick spray or use Teflon® sheets. Set the gravy aside for serving. Pour fresh pineapple juice over the meat until completely covered. (To save money you can use a mixture of half fresh juice and half water.)
14. Bake at 350°F for 1 hour or until tender. (Check the juice level—add more juice).
15. Heat the pineapple gravy.
16. Serve the Luau Beef with gravy.

Variation:

Add crushed fresh pineapple to the wild rice. To freeze, bag the roll-ups with pineapple juice reheat and serve with pineapple gravy made from drippings. Pineapple juice is a natural meat tenderizer. I find with this version the meat is tender and done after only 1 hour of baking.

"We enjoyed it!"—Lynn Hoxmeier

Additional Helps and Suggestions

- Lynn Hoxmeier didn't have any cotton string, so she used skewers.
- Paula Farris thought the footballs were cute, but for time and convenience will make the recipe with pieces of meat and call it "Beef Supreme." She used toothpicks as skewers, but warns about the toothpicks punching holes into a plastic bag. To accomodate she advises storing the meat in plastic bowls instead of bags.
- One tester substituted onions for the pineapple in the Luau Beef and her meat was tough. Let me explain why that happens. The pineapple serves as a meat tenderizer. Use natural juice. If you use canned pineapple juice or fruit, the enzyme action won't work. You have to use fresh pineapple to get all the tenderizing benefits. Please read the section on Pineapple in Topics.
- Kris Hulsey said she'd only make this as a cooking lesson because of the number of steps. She thought it was good for the children to help (e.g., pounding, rolling, tying, etc.), but she warns it is a lot of work.

Ratings

$ = $2 to $3 per serving—very expensive
Ease = 10—This is one of the most difficult recipes in this book.
Prep-time = 1 hour (at least)
Heating = 1 hour and 30 minutes
Mega-Session = 9—I recommend making this recipe all by itself as a multiple batch, but do try to buy all the ingredients during a mega-shop to hold down the costs
Equipment = String, skewers, or toothpicks, meat mallet or pounder

Chicken for All Seasons

(GRILLED CHICKEN BREASTS)

One of my favorite mega-methods of meal preparation is to grill dozens of pounds of boneless chicken breasts, freeze them individually, and then use them in a variety of recipes on other days. Alan and I have eaten at dozens of restaurants that use this idea. They start with a basic grilled chicken breast and use various toppings to expand their menus. Many of the "topping-style" recipes are very easy to assemble. My sons can make every one of these dishes and I like that. We can plan on a grilled chicken breast meal a week and yet, with all the variations, we don't have a repeat meal but once every two months. I'll make many of the sauces in bulk, then divide and freeze them. That way, on the day of serving, we just heat up the chicken, add the vegetables (or other ingredients), and pour on the sauce. Some of these dishes can be ready for eating within 15 minutes (not including thawing time). Note about thawing: *If you are cooking only one or two of the breasts reduce the thawing time and check after 4 to 5 minutes.*

Do Ahead:

- Purchase chicken breasts in bulk.
- Remove the bones yourself for big savings.
- Grill the boneless breasts for use later.

X1	X2	X8	
8 SERVINGS	16 SERVINGS	64 SERVINGS	1 6-OUNCE BREAST PER SERVING
3 pounds (8)	6 pounds (16)	24 pounds (64)	Boneless chicken breasts

Note: When I buy chicken breasts in bulk from the grocer supply company, I can choose either 4-ounce or 6-ounce boneless chicken breasts. Since I know my family has big appetites, I always go with 6-ounce. If you choose the smaller size you will get more servings per pound. Since you'll be working with the same weight of chicken, the other ingredients will not change in most instances. There are a few exceptions, such as when you need a slice of bacon for each breast. For your convenience, both pound and count numbers are provided. Since you'll be pulling frozen, grilled chicken breasts from the freezer, knowing the count will make the work easier. The count calculations are figured on the 6-ounce size, so you will need to make adjustments for the 4-ounce size.

Steps:

If you buy boneless chicken breasts, obviously you'd skip down to step 5. For whole chickens:

1. Rinse the chicken well in water.
2. Cut the chicken into standard pieces.
3. Remove the bones from the breast pieces.
4. Use the remaining chicken pieces for other recipes (salads, soups, and casseroles) by either freezing in individual bags, or boil and freeze the broth and meat, or use in recipes during a mega-cooking™ session.

5. *Optional:* In a shallow bowl combine ½ cup of soy sauce, ½ cup of water, teaspoon of ground ginger, and ¼ cup teriyaki sauce (multiply amounts as needed) or Italian dressing. Marinate the chicken breasts in the mixture.
6. Grill the chicken over medium hot flames until cooked through, but not overcooked. It usually takes us an average of 10 minutes on each side. (If you marinated some of the breasts, be sure to keep them separated when grilling.) You also might want to cook some by wrapping in foil and letting them heat that way—it works well for some applications when you don't need the "decorative striping."
7. Freeze individually. If you marinated some of the breasts, be certain to label well. Either
   a. bag each breast in a separate freezer bag
   b. wrap each breast individually in foil or heavy-duty plastic, or
   c. place the breasts on cookie sheets or cardboard covered with plastic wrap and freeze. Once frozen solid, bag together. You can then pull out one grilled breast or half-a-dozen.
8. Use the breasts in any of the following recipes or any of your own creations.

Chicken Parmigiana

(or as my kids call it "Pizza Chicken")

Though this recipe is great with non-marinated chicken breasts, it is even more delicious with grilled breasts that were marinated in Italian dressing.

X1	**X2**	**X8**	
8 SERVINGS	16 SERVINGS	64 SERVINGS	1 6-OUNCE BREAST PER SERVING
3 pounds (8)	6 pounds (16)	24 pounds (64)	Boneless chicken breasts
1 cup	2 cups	8 cups	Pizza sauce (see Spaghetti Sauce recipe, page 357)
1 cup	2 cups	8 cups	Grated mozzarella cheese
½ cup	1 cup	4 cups	Grated Parmesan cheese

Steps:
1. Thaw the grilled chicken breasts in the refrigerator overnight or defrost in the microwave for about 10 to 15 minutes.
2. Place the chicken breasts in a 13 x 9-inch baking pan that has been coated with nonstick spray.
3. Brush pizza sauce over the breasts.
4. Sprinkle mozzarella cheese on top.
5. Bake at 350°F for 5 minutes.
6. Sprinkle Parmesan cheese on top.
7. Bake an additional 5 minutes until the cheese is melted and the meat is hot.
8. Serve hot. A great side dish for this is Noodles Alfredo.

Note: You can also use slices of turkey breast meat for most of these recipes and it works quite well. If you don't overcook the turkey, you can slice it thick and then grill it for just a few minutes to give it a wonderful flavor and that "striped" look that says "yummy."

Garden-Fresh Chicken

If you have pre-grilled the chicken, this recipe can be made up in very little time. You can pre-make this sauce for use later. I use grilled chicken that I marinated in a soy-sauce mix. Depending on your situation, you could prepare and freeze the celery, peppers, and pea pods ahead and then add them just before cooking. I like to use fresh tomatoes for this recipe—it does make a difference. This meal is very light—not much sauce. If you like a lot of sauce, you'll want to double the amounts.

X1	**X2**	**X8**	
8 SERVINGS	16 SERVINGS	64 SERVINGS	1 6-OUNCE BREAST PER SERVING
3 pounds (8)	6 pounds (16)	24 pounds (64)	Boneless chicken breasts
3 cups	6 cups	24 cups	Chicken broth
¼ cup	½ cup	2 cups	Cornstarch
¼ teaspoon	½ teaspoon	2 teaspoons	Garlic powder
⅛ teaspoon	¼ teaspoon	1 teaspoon	Ground ginger
2 tablespoons	¼ cup	1 cup	Soy sauce
2 cups	4 cups	16 cups	Sliced green pepper
2 cups	4 cups	16 cups	Sliced tomato
1 cup	2 cups	8 cups	Snow pea pods
1 cup	2 cups	8 cups	Chopped celery
1 cup	2 cups	8 cups	Scallions (or use half that amount of green onions, chopped)

1. Thaw the grilled chicken breasts in the refrigerator overnight or in the microwave on defrost for about 10 to 15 minutes.
2. Cut the chicken breasts into strips, then into 1-inch cubes.
3. Make the sauce: Combine one-third of the cold chicken broth and cornstarch and blend until the cornstarch is completely dissolved.
4. In a small bowl mix together the garlic powder and ginger.
5. In a saucepan combine the remaining chicken broth with the garlic powder and ginger mixture. Add the soy sauce. Bring to a boil. Reduce the heat to medium high, and pour in the cornstarch and broth mixture. Stir constantly, cooking over medium heat until thick and translucent, stirring frequently. Remove from the heat and set aside.
6. Prepare the chicken and vegetables: In a nonstick skillet skillet (or regular skillet with a few tablespoons of oil) stir-fry the chicken pieces and vegetables until warm. You want them to be

crispy-tender. Pour the sauce over the chicken and serve. (Or serve the sauce on the side—some children and adults might not like the sauce.)

7. Serve over a bed of rice.

Orange Stir-fry Chicken

This recipe is similar to the Garden-Fresh Chicken so I make sure to serve these a few weeks apart. The sauce can be mega-prepared, divided, and thawed for use. Then you just assemble the ingredients on the day of serving. To add some crunch, add sliced water chestnuts or almonds during step 5.

X1	**X2**	**X8**	
8 SERVINGS	16 SERVINGS	64 SERVINGS	1 6-OUNCE BREAST PER SERVING
3 pounds (8)	6 pounds (16)	24 pounds (64)	Boneless chicken breasts
¼ cup	½ cup	2 cups	Cornstarch
2 cups	4 cups	16 cups	Orange juice
¼ cup	½ cup	2 cups	Sugar or honey
¼ cup	½ cup	2 cups	Soy sauce
2 Tablespoons	¼ cup	1 cups	Grated orange rind [mol]
¼ teaspoons	½ teaspoons	2 teaspoons	Ground ginger
2 cups	4 cups	16 cups	Orange sections (or use canned Mandarin)
			cooked rice
1	2	8	Green onions, chopped for taste and garnish

1. Thaw the grilled chicken breasts in the refrigerator overnight or defrost in the microwave for about 10 to 15 minutes.
2. Make the sauce: Dissolve the cornstarch in one-fourth of the cold orange juice. Set aside.
3. In a saucepan heat the remaining orange juice with the honey, soy sauce, rind, and ginger. Reduce the heat to medium high and stir in the cornstarch and orange juice mixture. Cook over medium heat until thick and translucent, stirring frequently. Remove from the heat and set aside.
4. Cut the chicken breasts into 1-inch cubes (or serve the breasts whole).
5. In a nonstick skillet (or a regular skillet with a few tablespoons of oil) heat the chicken.
6. Toss in the oranges and cook for 2 to 3 minutes.
7. Pour in the sauce (or serve on the side).
8. Serve over rice. Sprinkle with raw chopped green onions.

Chicken Fajitas (and Beef Fajitas)

My dear husband loves fajitas, so I try to keep fajita fixings ready to heat in the freezer all the time. You can either make your own tortillas or buy them in bulk very inexpensively. I also like to keep some beef strips grilled and cut into slices to serve, that way guests can choose between chicken or beef or a combination of both.

X1	**X2**	**X8**	
8 SERVINGS	16 SERVINGS	64 SERVINGS	1 6-OUNCE BREAST PER SERVING
3 pounds (8)	6 pounds (16)	24 pounds (64)	Boneless chicken breasts
3 pounds	6 pounds	24 pounds	Beef strip steak, grilled (optional)
½ cup	1 cup	4 cups	Chopped bell peppers
½ cup	1 cup	4 cups	Chopped onion
½ cup	1 cup	4 cups	Salsa
½ cup	1 cup	4 cups	Sour cream or plain yogurt
1 cup	2 cups	8 cups	Thinly sliced lettuce
6 to 12	12 to 24	48 to 96	Tortillas shells

1. Thaw the grilled chicken breasts (and beef) in the refrigerator overnight or defrost in the microwave for about 10 to 15 minutes.
2. Cut the chicken and beef into strips.
3. In a skillet with a few tablespoons of oil. Sauté the peppers and onions. Add the grilled chicken and heat through.
4. Serve the chicken and beef, cooked vegetables, salsa, sour cream, and lettuce in separate bowls and let diners assemble their own fajitas.

Denna's Fajita Marinade

Denna C. Flickner, one of my sweet mega-testers, sent in this recipe with her evaluation of Chicken Fajitas. It adds a good flavor, just perfect for that Tex-Mex recipe. The recipe amounts she sent were for "x4" so I've added that column and given you the amounts for the other multiples.

X1	**X2**	**X4**	**X8**	
¼ teaspoon	½ teaspoon	1 teaspoon	2 teaspoons	Chili powder
¼ teaspoon	½ teaspoon	1 teaspoon	2 teaspoons	Garlic
⅛ teaspoon	¼ teaspoon	½ teaspoon	1 teaspoon	Ground cumin
¼ cup	¼ cup	½ cup	1 cup	Lime or juice (lime is preferred for a more authentic Tex-Mex taste)

1. In a small bowl combine the chili powder, garlic, and cumin.
2. Add the spices to the lime juice.
3. Pour the marinade over grilled and sliced chicken breasts.
4. Freeze.
5. Reheat in an iron skillet with sliced onions and vegetables.

(*Alternate method:* Make a triple batch of marinade and soak raw sliced chicken overnight. Then grill, freeze, and reheat.)

Grilled Chicken Crêpes

Some good cooks avoid making crêpes because it seems like so much work. I agree that I don't have the time to make crêpes—that's if I made them on the day of serving. Instead I like to make a mega-batch and freeze them individually (separated by sheets of waxed paper). Then on the day of serving I just thaw out some chicken, some sauce, some frozen peas, and some crêpes. I simply have to heat and assemble. I have a meal—which would have otherwise taken me more than an hour to prepare—ready to eat in less than 15 minutes.

X1	**X2**	**X8**	
8 SERVINGS	16 SERVINGS	64 SERVINGS	1 6-OUNCE BREAST PER SERVING
3 pounds (8)	6 pounds (16)	24 pounds (64)	Boneless chicken breasts
2 cups	4 cups	16 cups	Beige Sauce (your favorite variation, see page 362)
1 cups	2 cups	8 cups	Frozen green peas, cooked
6 to 12	12 to 24	48 to 96	Crepes, warm

1. Thaw the grilled chicken breasts in the refrigerator overnight or defrost in the microwave for about 10 to 15 minutes.
2. Cut into bite-sized pieces.
3. Either make Beige Sauce now, or thaw previously made sauce.
4. Heat the sauce, and add the cooked green peas and chicken.
5. Place ½ cup of chicken sauce inside each crepe, and roll up.
6. Set the filled crêpes side-by-side in a casserole dish. Top with any remaining sauce.
7. Bake at 350°F for 5 to 10 minutes until soft and bubbly.
8. Serve hot. Great with fresh fruit.

Grilled Chicken Salad

This salad is so easy to make and very portable, wonderful to take to luncheons. I can thaw out just one chicken breast and make two wonderful salads (if you like more meat, then it would make only one salad).

X1	**X2**	**X8**	
2 SERVINGS	4 SERVINGS	16 SERVINGS	
1	2	8	Grilled boneless chicken breasts
1 to 2 cups	2 to 4 cups	8 to 16 cups	Lettuce, torn (mixture of lettuces: endive, romaine, iceberg, etc.)
1 cup	2 cups	8 cups	Raw spinach leaves
¼ cup	½ cup	2 cups	Chopped onions
1	2	8	Celery ribs, chopped
1	2	8	Carrots, chopped
1	2	8	Green onions, chopped
1	2	8	Cloves of garlic, minced (or use garlic powder)
¼ cup	½ cup	2 cups	Sliced mushrooms
1 cup	2 cups	8 cups	Orange slices (or use mandarin oranges)
¼ to ½ cup	½ to 1 cup	4 to 8 cups	Salad dressing (try orange or Honey Mustard, see page 385)

1. Thaw the grilled chicken breasts in the refrigerator overnight or defrost in the microwave for about 10 to 15 minutes.
2. Wash the salad greens. Either spin or pat dry.
3. In a large salad bowl toss together the salad greens and other vegetables.
4. Cut the chicken breasts into strips or chunks.
5. Top the salad greens with chicken pieces and oranges. Serve with dressing on the side. Optional: Sprinkle with some coconut or nuts.
6. Serve with chilled white grapes. Also, it is wonderful to serve this in a bread bowl. See instructions on page 245.

   Note: To make a quick orange dressing: use a basic Italian dressing recipe (or mix) but substitute orange juice for the water or vinegar and add 1 teaspoon of orange zest per cup of dressing.

Bring 'em Hungry Chicken

We've had versions of this recipe in several restaurants. It is very quick to prepare, one reason it is so popular for grill-type restaurants to serve.

X1	X2	X8	
8 SERVINGS	16 SERVINGS	64 SERVINGS	1 6-OUNCE BREAST PER SERVING
3 pounds (8)	6 pounds (16)	24 pounds (64)	Boneless chicken breasts
1 cup	2 cups	8 cups	Sliced fresh mushrooms or canned (optional)
3 slices	6 slices	24 slices	Ham or ham substitute (½ slice per breast)
12 slices	24 slices	96 slices	Bacon (2 slices per breast; please see note from Carol Irby at end of recipe)
6 slices	12 slices	48 slices	Swiss cheese (1 slice per breast)
1 cup	2 cups	8 cups	Honey-mustard dressing or sauce (see page 385)

1. Thaw the grilled chicken breasts (and any other ingredients, as applicable) in the refrigerator overnight or defrost in the microwave for about 10 to15 minutes.
2. Arrange the breasts in a 13 x 9-inch baking pan.
3. Top each breast with some mushrooms (optional), then layer on ham, bacon strips, and cheese.
4. Bake at 350°F for 10 minutes until the cheese is melted and the meat is hot.
5. Serve with honey-mustard dressing or sauce on the side.

Grilled Pineapple Chicken

Next time you grill, throw on some pineapple rings. Freeze them individually to use in this recipe. I make up batches of this pineapple sauce for use in a variety of recipes. If you like sugar, you might want to add 2 tablespoons of sugar to each cup of pineapple juice. Since we're trying to reduce sugar consumption, we've found that we like this with just the natural sweetness of the juice. If you aren't sure about how to cook with pineapple, please review in the Topics section.

X1	X2	X8	
8 SERVINGS	16 SERVINGS	64 SERVINGS	1 6-OUNCE BREAST PER SERVING
3 pounds (8)	6 pounds (16)	24 pounds (64)	Boneless chicken breasts
1 20-ounce can	2 20-ounce cans	8 20-ounce cans	Pineapple rings
1 to 2 cups	2 to 4 cups	8 to 16 cups	Pineapple sauce
			Cornstarch (see step 3)

1. Thaw the grilled chicken breasts in the refrigerator overnight or defrost in the microwave for about 10 to 15 minutes.

2. If you haven't already grilled the pineapple rings you can do that now, or just put them under the broiler for a few minutes.
3. Make the pineapple sauce: To each cup of cold pineapple juice add 3 tablespoons of cornstarch. Cook until thick.
4. Arrange the breasts out in a 13 x 9-inch baking pan.
5. Pour the sauce over the breasts. Top with grilled or ungrilled pineapple rings. Pour the sauce over the breasts.
6. Bake at 350°F for 10 to 15 minutes until the meat is hot.

Rancheros Chicken

This is a quick South-of-the-border meal. So easy to prepare the kids can do it. You can cook the beans ahead and have them frozen in 1-cup amounts that only need to be thawed, or you can buy these in a can.

X1	X2	X8	
8 SERVINGS	16 SERVINGS	64 SERVINGS	1 6-OUNCE BREAST PER SERVING
3 pounds (8)	6 pounds (16)	24 pounds (64)	Boneless chicken breasts
1 cup	2 cups	8 cups	Black beans (cooked)
1 cup	2 cups	8 cups	Bell pepper strips (any color)
1 cup	2 cups	8 cups	Onion rings
1 cup	2 cups	8 cups	Salsa

1. Thaw the grilled chicken breasts in the refrigerator overnight or defrost in the microwave for about 10 to 15 minutes.
2. Arrange the breasts in a 13 x 9-inch baking pan.
3. Spoon black beans, peppers, and onions over the chicken breasts.
4. Top with salsa.
5. Bake at 350°F for 10 to 15 minutes until the meat is hot, or bake in the microwave covered for 4 to 5 minutes (depending on the oven).

Tapioca Apricot Chicken

I realize this may sound strange if your only experience with tapioca is pudding. However, it is a wonderful thickener that adds a different flavor to sauces.

X1	X2	X8	
8 SERVINGS	16 SERVINGS	64 SERVINGS	1 6-OUNCE BREAST PER SERVING
3 pounds (8)	6 pounds (16)	24 pounds (64)	Boneless chicken breasts

1 tablespoon	2 tablespoons	½ cup	Quick-cooking tapioca
1 cup	2 cups	8 cups	Apple juice concentrate
¼ cup	½ cup	2 cups	Dijon-style mustard
1 teaspoon	2 teaspoons	8 teaspoons	Ground ginger
1 cup	2 cups	8 cups	Dried apricots
⅓ cup	⅔ cups	2⅔ cups	Sliced almonds (optional)

Pre-step: If you are using frozen apple juice concentrate, allow it to thaw completely before using in step 2.

Steps:
1. Thaw the grilled chicken breasts in the refrigerator overnight or defrost in the microwave for about 10 to 15 minutes.
2. Make the apricot sauce: In a bowl dissolve the tapioca in the apple juice concentrate. Let sit for at least 5 minutes.
3. Stir in the mustard and ginger until smooth. Stir in the apricots.
4. Lay chicken breasts in a flat baking dish.
5. Cover with apricot sauce.
6. Bake at 350°F for 10 to 15 minutes or in the microwave, covered for 4 to 5 minutes (depending on the oven).
7. Sprinkle with almonds.

Chicken Cacciatore

This is one meal that Alan and I and the older children like, but Bethany and Trent don't. I simply place the vegetabe topping on twelve chicken breasts and leave four blank, then proceed—that way everyone is happy.

X1	**X2**	**X8**	
8 SERVINGS	16 SERVINGS	64 SERVINGS	1 6-OUNCE BREAST PER SERVING
3 pounds (8)	6 pounds (16)	24 pounds (64)	Boneless chicken breasts
1 cup	2 cups	8 cups	Meatless spaghetti sauce (or pizza sauce)
½ cup	1 cup	4 cups	Tomato paste
1	2	8	Cloves garlic, minced (or use garlic powder)
1 cup	2 cups	8 cups	Sliced fresh mushrooms (canned is okay)
1 cup	2 cups	8 cups	Bell pepper strips (any color)
1 cup	2 cups	8 cups	Onion rings
½ cup	1 cup	4 cups	Black olives, pitted, and sliced
			Cooked rice or noodles

1. Thaw the grilled chicken breasts in the refrigerator overnight or defrost in the microwave for about 10 to 15 minutes.
2. Arrange the breasts in a single layer in a sprayed 13 x 9-inch pan (if needed use 2 pans).
3. In a large bowl mix the spaghetti sauce and tomato paste together. Add in garlic.
4. In a separate bowl mix together the mushrooms, peppers, onions, the olives.
5. Distribute the vegetable mixture over the breasts.
6. Pour or spoon spaghetti sauce over the vegetables.
7. Bake at 350°F for 15 minutes until hot, or microwave covered for about 5 minutes.
8. Serve hot with rice or noodles.

Flash BBQ Chicken

I appreciate "real" barbecued chicken, but sometimes I just don't have the time. I can serve a pretty good substitute by thawing out some grilled breasts and coating them with barbecue sauce and baking for 15 minutes. Delicious. This barbecue sauce is good for several recipes. Or, of course, you can use your favorite store-bought version. I like to make batches of this sauce for use at other times.

X1	**X2**	**X8**	
8 SERVINGS	16 SERVINGS	64 SERVINGS	1 6-OUNCE BREAST PER SERVING
3 pounds (8)	6 pounds (16)	24 pounds (64)	Boneless chicken breasts
½ cup	1 cup	4 cups	Lemon juice
½ cup	1 cup	4 cups	Cider vinegar [mol] (white will work but gives a slightly different flavor)
½ cup	1 cup	4 cups	Honey
¼ cup	½ cup	2 cups	Worcestershire sauce
1 cup	2 cups	8 cups	Tomato paste (or use ketchup—will make the sauce thinner)
¼ cup	½ cup	2 cups	Chili sauce
1 teaspoon	2 teaspoons	8 teaspoons	Dry mustard
Dash	Dashes	¼ teaspoon	Hot sauce (optional, only if you like hot sauce)

1. Thaw the grilled chicken breasts in the refrigerator overnight or defrost in the microwave for about 10 to 15 minutes.
2. Meanwhile, make the barbecue sauce. In a saucepan mix all of the ingredients (except the chicken) and bring to a boil. Reduce the heat and simmer for 45 to 60 minutes until the sauce is thick and will coat a spoon.
3. Arrange the chicken breasts in a 13 x 9-inch baking pan and coat with barbecue sauce. Bake at 375°F for 15 to 20 minutes.
4. Serve hot with corn and baked French fries.

About Chicken Parmaigiana: "It's a keeper."—Suzi Walters.
"We loved it."—Carol Irby
About Bring 'em Hungry Chicken: "Yummy! This was my favorite."—Cathy Robrock.
About Orange Stir-fry Chicken: "Big hit with the children and their friends."—Denna C. Flickner
About all chicken recipes: "Everybody loves them—All 10's!"—Carol Irby
"Picky husband loved it!"—Denna C. Flickner.

Additional Helps and Suggestions

- Cheryl Beasley's family didn't like the barbecue sauce because they thought it had too much vinegar flavor. Some families loved it. Jill: I'd recommend you test the sauce first before you "ruin" a batch of chicken. You know your family's taste preferences. If they don't like vinegar (it is tangy), then add just a small amount. We add the vinegar for the acid affect in the recipe. The intense taste of vinegar will fade with more heat and longer exposure to heat (45 to 60 minutes usually does the trick, but depending on many different factors, it might take longer.) Lemon juice also gives the same chemical reaction and a different flavor if you were to double its amount.
- Carol Irby cooked 15 pounds of boneless chicken breasts and used them for the various recipes and just by themselves. An excellent idea.
- Denna C. Flickner not only provided the Fajitas marinade recipe, but recomended watching the temperature on the coals. The sugar in the fruit (used with some of the recipes) tends to burn easily. She froze raw breasts with the marinade, thawed the breasts, discarded the marinade, and then grilled. For the Orange Stir-Fry she commented: "I wanted to use this for a lunch recipe, so I tried making the sauce and freezing it. The sauce freezes and thaws just fine, but add the oranges after thawing." She used canned mandarins. (Jill adds: Good point. If you freeze the mandarins in the sauce, you get "mush.") With the Flash BBQ Chicken, she broiled the chicken and baked it to see if her family had a preference. They liked the broiled better, but baked was fine.
- Carol Irby also found that her bacon had to be at least half-cooked before she put it on the chicken. She broiled hers for 2 minutes at the end and it crisped everything nicely. They skipped the mushrooms and substituted Monterey Jack cheese.
- Jill adds about the bacon in Bring 'em Hungry: Depending on how thick your slices of bacon are, you might want to pre-cook. You don't want to eat undercooked pork. We use a turkey bacon substitute and it doesn't need to be pre-cooked. It is best to cook pork bacon to half-done, then put it on the chicken. The 10 minutes in the oven should complete the cooking process. Broiling does give you a nice crisp finish, so you can broil it for the last 2 minutes (as Carol suggests), or just let it bake for a softer texture.
- These were some of the most popular recipes ever tested. Families loved the taste but also how easy the recipes are to do. To hold down the cost, contact a local grocery wholesaler and inquire about buying a whole box of breasts direct. They usually come in 6- or 4-ounce sizes—at affordable prices. Remember you're only paying for the meat, so it will be somewhat more than the price per pound of whole chickens, but with whole chickens about one-fourth to one-third of the weight is bone, cartilage, and other inedible "stuff." So, compare the price per pound and I think you'll be pleasantly surprised. It is worth the few extra cents a pound to buy them already de-boned and ready-to-cook.

- If you want the decorative stripping on our food, but can't grill, cook the breasts (or other food items), heat a wood-handled ice pick on a hot burner, and burn stripes into the chicken by pressing the hot ice pick down on the item. Be careful. This is not a task for little ones. It only takes seconds to do and it looks so tasty.
- *Note:* In recipes that cook the meat more, I don't fully cook the meat on the grill—because then it would become overcooked. Do fully cook chicken that will go in salads or in recipes that will not require any additional cooking. Label well. Don't ever eat less than fully cooked chicken.
- When I calculated the servings, I used a standard 6-ounce breast. If you buy 4-ounce pieces, your servings will be 12 for x1, 24 for x2, and 96 for x8. You need to take into consideration your family's appetites. Four ounces of chicken might meet some diet guidelines, but would leave a teenage boy still hungry. So you might want to consider using 2 to 3 servings per person.

Ratings
$ = $1.00 (That is a rough estimate because of all the different variables as to price per pound and toppings)
Ease = 1
Prep-time = 20 minutes (not including marinating)
Heating = 5 to 10 minutes depending on option
Mega-Session = 1 (my mainstay!)
Equipment = Grill (indoor or outdoor), kitchen shears (to cut Fajitas)

Cinco de Mayo

We learned a whole new appreciation for the Mexican culture and cuisine while we were living in Texas. One of the big holidays there is May 5 (when the Mexican Americans celebrated the 1862 defeat of French troops at the Battle of Puebla). The Spanish call it Cinco de Mayo (translated the fifth of May). We came up with this recipe and named it according to their holiday. Trent loves this and will eat thirds, though he still picks out the olives. We have fun with this meal and decorate the table with a 50-cent Sarapai that I bought at a flea market and an artificial cactus centerpiece—and to really get in to the "fiesta" feel of the meal, we play a Mariachi band CD. We serve this with fresh fruit and a garden-green tossed salad. For a special dessert, make homemade Sopapillias.

Do Ahead:

- Purchase ground meat and sausage in bulk and precook.
- Plan to make another recipe that calls for black olives so you can split the #10 can, or dehydrate or freeze the other half of the olives for future use (such as on pizzas).
- Purchase the onions in bulk and prepare in advance.
- Either pre-make the Corn2Bread mix or batter (see page 237).
- Buy Cheddar cheese in bulk and freeze in ½ cup amounts for topping on day of serving.

X1 6 SERVINGS	**X2** 12 SERVINGS	**X15 (yields us 8 meals)** 90 SERVINGS	
1 pound	2 pounds	15 pounds	Ground beef (or turkey or portion of both), cooked
¼ pound	½ pound	3 pounds	Ground sausage (we use good old Southern style), cooked
			Corn2Bread batter (see below for multiples)
⅛ cup	¼ cup	2 cups	Chopped onion [mol] (raw or steamed, not sautéed)
½ clove	1 clove	5 clove	Garlic [mol] (mashed or grated)
16 ounces	32 ounces	1 6-pound, 10-ounce can	Stewed tomatoes or equivalent fresh or home-canned
12 ounces	24 ounces	1 6-pound, 10-ounce can	Kernel corn or equivalent fresh or home-canned
1 6-ounce can	1 12-ounce can	6 12-ounce cans	Tomato paste
1 teaspoon	2 teaspoons	¼ cup	Chili powder [mol] (depending on your taste for HOT)
½ teaspoon	1 teaspoon	1 tablespoon	Salt [mol]
¼ cup	½ cup	½ 6-pound, 10-ounce can	Pitted black olives sliced or pieces

Pre-steps:

Cook the ground beef and sausage.

Steps:

1. In a large bowl mix all of the ingredients.
2. Divide into meal-sized portions. [We cook this in our 13 x 9-inch glass casserole dish. The "meat" layer is about 2" thick. That translates to filling a quart freezer bag as full as we can.] You'll need to adjust this for your family's appetite.
3. Label. Freeze.

For serving:

4. Thaw.
5. Spray a pan with nonstick coating. Layer the meat base in the pan.
6. Prepare the Corn²Bread from scratch (see page 237) (see chart below for multiples of recipe for each sized dish), or add liquid ingredients to the Corn²Bread mix you've previously prepared, or use previously prepared Corn²Bread batter.
7. Pour the Corn²Bread batter (or your favorite cornbread batter) over the top of the meat. (Use any extra batter to make muffins, or freeze the batter and use for the next time you bake this recipe.)
8. Bake at 350°F. See chart below for baking time. (You'll need to adjust if you use a different cornbread recipe or a non-standard pan. Bake this dish according to the time of your cornbread recipe.)
9. While it is still hot from the oven, sprinkle the top with Cheddar cheese and garnish with a few dashes of paprika.

8 x 8	13 x 9	15 x 10	Casserole dish
¼ cup	½ cup	1 cup	Cheddar cheese for topping
Dashes	Dashes	Dashes	Paprika
X½	X1	X2	Corn²Bread (see page 000 for recipe) for topping
12-15 minutes	20-30 minutes	30-35 minutes	Approximate baking time if using Corn²Bread recipe

"Very nice looking dish, lots of color. Wow! Just mix it all together!"—Linda Bacon

Additional Helps and Suggestions

- Michelle Manson left out the sausage because it was $3 a pound. She used all ground chuck at only 78¢ a pound. I agree with her. I wouldn't pay $3 a pound for sausage either. Even with that substitution she said it was a keeper!

- Joanna Baker omitted the black olives from the recipe and added a 4-ounce can of green chilies to the Corn²Bread recipe (diced and drained). She told us, "Originally from Texas, we like food that has a Tex-Mex flair. The chilies added to the cornbread provide the extra heat we like. My husband added some picante sauce at the table." (They buy picante sauce by the gallon from a wholesale club.) She also used a Pampered Chef® batter bowl. She could see that all the cornmeal was mixed and then pour the mixture easily.
- Gina Pearcy's husband likes spicy food, so he used more chili powder. She said that this is a good, warm, recipe for a rainy day.
- Becky Valentine liked that the onions were still crunchy. (Jill: I do, too), but her children prefer no onions or black olives. They also served it with salsa. (Jill: We do, too).
- When you have some family members that like a recipe with an ingredient and others who don't, mega-cooking™ is perfect for you. Just mix a batch (without the onions and black olives), bag and store half of it (labeling well), then add the onions and black olives to the remainer, label, and store. You can then make up two 8x8 inch pans (one for younger children and one for everyone else) or carefully make one end of a larger pan the onion-free side, then dish out carefully. We do this with several of our recipes. We make "Trent's corner" and then are careful not to give him any of the recipe with "off-limits" food for him. By mega-cooking this way, you don't have to cook separate recipes every day for everyone on a special diet or with particular likes and dislikes, and Mom and Dad don't have to go without the flavors they like for the next 15 years, always only eating food the kids will eat, too (that's carrying devotion to children too far!).

Ratings
$ = $1.00
Ease = 9
Prep-time = 15 minutes
Heating = 12 to 35 minutes—Depending on size dish—check it at the half-way point and adjust time accordingly.
Mega-Session = 10
Equipment = Food processor to cut up the vegetables.

CIO

(CHICKEN IN ORANGE)

Chicken in Orange, protecting your children from the scum of starvation, riding the galaxy of hunger pangs. It is your first, last and one of many lines of defense against that all-too-often repeated declaration, "We're starving." This is not a recipe I cook during a mega-cooking™ weekend because of the marinating and oven time.

Do Ahead:

- Buy the freshest orange juice you can afford or squeeze your own.
- Purchase chicken legs in bulk at the best price.
- Marinate the chicken in orange juice.

X1 6 SERVINGS	X2 12 SERVINGS	X4 24 SERVINGS	
5 pounds	10 pounds	20 pounds	Chicken legs (thighs and drumsticks)
2 quarts	1 gallon	2 gallons	Orange juice
2 tablespoons	¼ cup	½ cup	Tarragon
1 tablespoon	2 tablespoons	¼ cup	Nutmeg
1 tablespoon	2 tablespoons	¼ cup	Salt
1 teaspoon	2 teaspoons	4 teaspoons	Pepper
¼ cup	½ cup	1 cup	Cornstarch
1 cup	2 cups	4 cups	Cold water

Steps:

1. Remove the skin from the chicken. Cut away all accessible fat. Clean well.
2. Place the chicken in a large container that has a sealable lid. Pour orange juice over the chicken until completely submerged.
3. Marinate at least 12 hours.
4. Remove the chicken from the orange juice as you work. While you work on the chicken, store the juice in the refrigerator. Don't allow the chicken or juice to stay out at room temperature. Don't let anyone drink this juice, either, since it's been on raw chicken.
5. Spray baking pans with nonstick spray or use Teflon® sheets. I use several 15 x 10 x 4-inch baking dishes ("oven to freezer to microwave" type).
6. Mix together all the spices.
7. Rub the spices into the meaty-side of each thigh and leg.
6. Place the chicken pieces spiced side up in single layer in the pans.
7. Pour the marinating juice over the chicken. *Note:* Since some of my family like a crispy chicken, I make certain that some pieces are arranged so that the chicken isn't completely submerged. The exposed areas will become crisp as they cook. If you completely submerge the chicken during the

baking, the chicken will be soft and tender. As the chicken cooks, the drippings will add to the orange juice. So be certain as you pour in the juice to leave at least 1 to 2 inches of room for drippings.

8. Bake at 350°F for 1 hour. (If you are managing several pans, you'll want to rotate shelves halfway through the baking.)
9. Remove the chicken from the juice and arrange as much as you'll need for a dinner on a serving platter with fresh orange slices for garnish. *Suggestion:* Place the chicken on a bed of cooked rice.
10. Make the gravy: Pour all excess marinade and drippings into a Dutch oven. Bring to a boil. Boil for 3 minutes.
11. While the marinade is boiling, mix together the cornstarch and cold water until the cornstarch is completely dissolved. (This is easy in a shaker.)
12. Slowly pour the cornstarch/water mixture into the boiling marinade a little at a time, stirring constantly.
12. Continue pouring and stirring over medium heat until the sauce is translucent and thick.
13. Pour some over the chicken for garnish and serve the rest of the gravy (proportional) on the side.
14. Bag the extra chicken in meal-sized portions, pouring in either half or one fourth (depending on which multiple you used) of the gravy into the bag with the chicken.
15. Label and freeze.
16. Thaw in the refrigerator. Place the chicken and gravy back in the baking dish and heat at 350°F for 20 to 30 minutes until hot. Follow the serving directions above.

Note: Unlike most of these recipes, this one really doesn't do well with any of the other options of preparation. The only other suitable method is to bag the fresh chicken slices, spiced as above, with the fresh orange juice. It will marinate as it freezes. Then you'd thaw and bake as usual.

"Everyone loved this recipe 'crispy' style. The sauce was great and a big hit over rice. Husband raved!"—Bretta Ogburn
"Very easy and tasty!"—Kris Hulsey

Additional Helps and Suggestions

- Kris Hulsey suggested substituting ginger for the tarragon sometimes. Also 2 of her children liked it, and one did not. So, be advised that it does have a special flavor that might not appeal to all children.
- Bretta Ogburn needed to bake her chicken an additional 15 minutes. So, check the chicken. The size of the pan (chicken spread out or stacked up) and the size of the chicken pieces will affect the baking time. She also said it looks lovely garnished with oranges. She felt the cost of these ingredients were very reasonable.
- We buy our chicken quarters in bulk from a grocery supply company and pay less than half the grocery-store price.
- If you like this blend of spices, consider making a batch of the spice blend. Jar and label it. Then

whenever you want to make CIO, you already have the blend ready. It saves some time. You could also use this blend on chicken for the grill or on fish. Be creative. You can make many variations of spice blends as you find combinations you like.

Ratings

$ = 50¢ (The cost is low because we are buying mega-amounts of chicken at one time)
Ease = 10
Prep-time = 20 to 30 minutes, not including marinating time
Heating = 1 hour
Mega-Session = 10
Equipment = nothing extraordinary

Cluck and Shuck

Yummy. After working with this recipe, I learned that the way my family eats, it wasn't worth the extra time to make neat layers for "show." I simply make a mega-mix and bag it then spoon the mix into a casserole dish and design the bell peppers neatly for appearance. It tastes the same either way. Options 1 and 2 are for those who mega-cook many recipes at a time and need to manage their freezing capacity. If you are multi-batching then option Four works the best. Plan to eat one of the recipes that day, and freeze the others. Your freezer should have no problem removing that little amount of extra heat.

Do Ahead:

- Make a mega-batch of Beige Sauce to go in several recipes.
- Buy and prepare corn in bulk.
- Buy chicken in bulk and prepare ahead, or substitute turkey meat.

X1 6 SERVINGS	X2 12 SERVINGS	X8 48 SERVINGS	
1 cup	2 cups	8 cups	Beige Sauce, basic version (see page 362)
1 cup	2 cups	8 cups	Light cream or half and half
3	6	24	Eggs, beaten
2 cups	4 cups	16 cups [mol]	Diced cooked chicken or turkey
3 cups	6 cups	24 cups	Kernel corn, fresh or canned (drained)
½ cup	1 cups	4 cups	Breadcrumbs
1	2	4 to 8	Green peppers

Pre-steps:

Make Beige Sauce. Cook and dice the poultry. Make breadcrumbs.

Steps:

OPTION 1: COLD ASSEMBLY, FREEZING, COOKING DAY OF SERVING (MIXED-BAG STYLE)

1. In a mega-sized mixing bowl combine the Beige Sauce, cream, and eggs, and mix well.
2. Add the chicken and corn.
3. Mix gently but thoroughly.
4. Divide, bag, label, and freeze.
5. Thaw.
6. Place ingredients in a casserole dish sprayed with nonstick coating or lined with a Teflon® sheet.
7. Sprinkle breadcrumbs over the casserole and arrange pepper rings on top.
8. Bake uncovered at 350° for 1 hour.

OPTION 2: COLD ASSEMBLY, FREEZING, COOKING DAY OF SERVING (ARRANGED-NEATLY STYLE)

1. In a large mixing bowl combine the Beige Sauce, cream, and eggs.
2. Spray mold(s), or line dish(es) with heavy-duty plastic film.
3. Make alternating layers of chicken and corn in the dishes.
4. Pour the liquid mixture over the chicken and corn.
5. Label, freeze.
6. Once frozen solid, remove from the mold or dish. Immediately rewrap or bag. Resume freezing.
7. Thaw.
8. Place the ingredients in an ovenproof casserole dish spraed with nonstick coating.
9. Sprinkle with breadcrumbs and arrange pepper rings on top.
10. Bake uncovered at 350° for 1 hour.

OPTION 3: HOT OR COLD ASSEMBLY, COOKING AHEAD, AND REHEATING DAY OF SERVING

(When capacity of freezer isn't an issue.)

1. In a large mixing bowl combine the Beige Sauce, cream, and eggs.
2. Spray mold(s) or dish(es) with a nonstick coating.
3. Make alternating layers of chicken and corn in dishes.
4. Pour the liquid mixture over the chicken and corn.
5. Bake at 350°F for 45 minutes.
6. If appearance doesn't matter, simply bag or wrap the ingredients in meal-sized portions. Label. Freeze.
7. If appearance does matter, wrap the entire dish in wrap and freeze. Once frozen solid, remove from the dish and immediately bag and continue freezing.
8. Thaw. Garnish as in Option 1 above, and reheat at 350°F for 20 to 30 minutes.

OPTION 4: MEGA-COOKING™ DINNERS, EATING ONE, AND FREEZING THE REST FOR ANOTHER TIME

1-4. Follow steps 1 through 4 in Option 3.

5. Bake for 1 hour at 350°F. Serve and enjoy.
6. Don't garnish the other and bake the remaining casserole(s) without garnish for only 45 minutes at 350°F.
7. If appearance doesn't matter, simply bag or wrap the ingredients in meal-sized portions. Label. Freeze.
8. If appearance does matter, wrap the entire dish in wrap and freeze. Once frozen solid, remove from the dish and immediately bag and continue freezing.
9. Thaw. Garnish as in Option 1 above, and reheat at 350°F for 20 to 30 minutes.

"All 10's"—Tamara Grim

Additional Helps and Suggestions

- Julie McWright used turkey instead of chicken and gave it an overall rating of 10.
- Cheryl Lewis preferred to cut up the peppers and mix them throughout the recipe. She also added extra flavor with salt, pepper, and some garlic, onions, or lemon pepper.
- Dorothy Hunsberger used her own home frozen corn, substituted 2% milk instead of the light cream, and left out the green peppers. She gave it an overall rating of 10.

Ratings

$ = 75¢
Ease = 9
Prep-time = 20 to 30 minutes for a mega-batch (5 minutes during a mega-session and the ingredients are ready for assembly)
Heating = 45 to 60 minutes (depending on option)
Mega-Session = 10
Equipment = kitchen shears to cut up meat

Combat Rations

My dad said that he remembers basic training for the Army well—they ate a lot of chipped beef on toast. So much so, that my mom, in deference to my Dad, rarely served it. Now as an adult, I've changed the old recipe for a healthier version. In addition to a great breakfast, this recipe makes a good lunch or an easy dinner. When I have the ingredients ready in advance, lunchtime is quick. You can freeze a mega-batch of sauce with the poultry and peas to reheat and serve over toast.

Do ahead:

- Purchase chicken in bulk, cook, and dice.
- Make basic Beige Sauce (medium thickness).
- Purchase or make bread in bulk for toast.

X1	X2	X8	
4 SERVINGS	8 SERVINGS	32 SERVINGS	
2 cups	4 cups	16 cups	Beige Sauce (see page 362)
1	2	8	Eggs, beaten
1 teaspoon	2 teaspoon	2 tablespoons	Parsley
½ cup	1cup	4 cups	Cooked peas (I use the bright green type for color)
1 cup	2 cups	8 cups	Chopped cooked chicken or turkey
¼ teaspoon	½ teaspoon	2 teaspoons	Paprika (as garnish if desired)

Pre-steps:

If you haven't already made the sauce and cooked and diced the poultry meat, do that.

Steps:

1. In a saucepan heat together the Beige Sauce, eggs, parsley, peas, and turkey meat over low to medium heat.
2. Make toast.
3. Serve the turkey sauce poured over the toast.
4. Garnish with paprika.

Substitutes:

You can substitute dried beef slices and have the All-American staple: Chipped Beef on Toast.

"Enjoyable!"—Marsha Hedges

Additional Helps and Suggestions

- Marsha Hedges said that her kids hate peas (they eat them anyway), but they liked this recipe. She also suggested that if you are on a special diet you could use a milk substitute.

- Nancy Rasmussen mentioned serving it over rice or potatoes to make it more a dinner meal. She said, "It was good with rice as well as toast."
- Jana Hoffman doubled the amount of peas and added some more Beige Sauce. She said her whole family loved it except her 8 year-old. Also, she used a crockpot to bake her turkey. (This recipe could be heated slowly in the crockpot if you preferred.)
- I like to pull out separate packages of frozen Beige Sauce and cooked diced meat (pulled out day ahead to thaw), then add the other ingredients and heat in the microwave for a quick lunch. Even so, you can make up the whole sauce including eggs, peas, parsley, meat, and sauce, and freeze it. Then thaw, heat on the stovetop or in the microwave, and serve.

Ratings

$ = 50¢ or less depending on how much you have to pay for the meat
Ease = 10
Prep-time = 5 minutes (using prepared sauce and already cooked and diced chicken)
Heating = 5 to 8 minutes on stovetop, 3 to 4 in microwave
Mega-Session = 10
Equipment = kitchen shears help when cutting up the meat

Cordon Bleu Casserole

Yes, I like traditional Chicken Cordon Bleu (see below), but for an easier and more economical version, try this recipe, It has basically the same taste—it is just easier to prepare and is more suitable for covered-dish dinners and family-times. It freezes very well.

Do ahead:

- Purchase as many ingredients as possible in bulk.
- Assembly-line process ingredients for this and for other recipes.

X1 6 SERVINGS	X2 12 SERVINGS	X4 24 SERVINGS	X8 48 SERVINGS	
1 pound	2 pounds	4 pounds	8 pounds	Ham
2 pounds	4 pounds	8 pounds	16 pounds	Turkey
½ cup	1 cup	2 cups	4 cups	Chopped onions (green onions add color)
4 cups	8 cups	16 cups	32 cups	Beige Sauce (see page 362) (regular or thin version)
1 teaspoon	2 teaspoons	4 teaspoons	3 tablespoons	Nutmeg
1 tablespoon	2 tablespoons	¼ cup	½ cup	Dill weed
4 cups	8 cups	16 cups	32 cups	Breadcrumbs (or bread cubes)
2 cups	4 cups	8 cups	16 cups	Grated cheese (Swiss is traditional)

Steps:

1. Chop the ham and turkey into bite-sized cubes.
2. Make the basic Beige Sauce. Add the onions. Stir in the nutmeg and dill weed.

OPTION 1: MAKE IN "GLOB" FORM, FREEZE, AND THEN BAKE DAY OF SERVING

3. Either use bags or plastic containers. Place bags inside boxes with the edges lapped over the side. (See instructions on page 117 for more bag-in-box details.)
4. Place half of the breadcrumbs and all of the meat cubes into the container or bag. Pour in the seasoned Beige Sauce.
5. Seal containers. Freeze.
6. Thaw in the refrigerator.
7. Spray a 13 x 9-inch casserole dish with nonstick spray. Pour the casserole into the prepared pan..
8. Sprinkle on half of the grated cheese. Top with the remaining breadcrumbs and cheese.
9. Bake at 350°F oven for 30 minutes until the cheese is melted and the casserole is bubbly.

OPTION 2: FREEZE IN SHAPED FORM, AND BAKE DAY OF SERVING

3. Either use metal pans or line glass pans with waxed paper or foil. Spray the pans with nonstick spray.
4. Arrange half of the breadcrumbs or cubes on the bottom of the pans.
5. Arrange meat cubes over the breadcrumbs. Pour in the seasoned Beige Sauce.
6. Top with half of the cheese. Then half of the breadcrumbs, then the remaining cheese.
7. Cover pans either with lid, plastic wrap, or foil. Freeze. Once frozen solid, remove from pans and either wrap or bag.
8. Remove wrapping; place back in pan (sprayed). Thaw in refrigerator, covered.
9. Bake in 350°F oven for 30 minutes until cheese is melted and ingredients are bubbly.

OPTION 3: BAKE COMPLETELY, FREEZE, AND THEN REHEAT

3. Spray pans with nonstick coating, or line with waxed paper or foil or use Teflon® sheets.
4. Arrange half of the breadcrumbs or cubes on the bottom of the pans.
5. Arrange meat cubes over the breadcrumbs. Pour in the seasoned Beige Sauce.
6. Top with half of the cheese. Then half of the breadcrumbs, then the remaining cheese.
7. Bake at 350°F for 30 minutes until the cheese is melted and the casserole is bubbly.
8. If desired serve one now.
9. Freeze the remaining (or all) casseroles. Remove from the pans. Continue freezing.
10. Thaw. Serve thawed or reheat by placing back in the pan and warming at 325°F for 15 to 20 minutes or reheat in the microwave oven.

Traditional Chicken Cordon Bleu

You can make traditional Chicken Cordon Bleu ahead and freeze it, then bake it the day of serving. This provides a more relaxed time before the meal. Don't write off this recipe because you had a lousy Cordon Bleu at a banquet. Homemade is so much better. This is a shorthand version that works well.

For each chicken breast you'll need ½ slice of ham, ½ slice of Swiss cheese, an egg/milk mixture and ½ cup of breadcrumbs.

Steps:

1. Between sheets of waxed paper, flatten boneless chicken breasts to ¼ -inch thickness.
2. Brush with egg/milk mixture.
3. Place a half-slice of ham and a half-slice of cheese on each piece of chicken.
4. Wrap up the chicken jelly roll fashion. Tuck the ends under and fasten with toothpicks.
5. Coat the chicken with more egg/milk mixture. Roll in breadcrumbs.
6. Wrap in waxed paper individually. Place in freezer bags. Label. Freeze.

7. Thaw. Pan fry in a skillet with ½-inch of oil for about 20 minutes. Drain and serve with chicken gravy.

"Great to do ahead; fancy; good-tasting!"—Robin Wood

Additional Helps and Suggestions

- Nancy Rasmussen used crushed crackers instead of the breadcrumbs and she only had half of the amount listed. She was surprised that it still came out great. She said it looked great and was easy! She liked that it was high in protein and fairly low in fat.
- Marsha Hedges made the sauce too thick so the casserole came out dry. So she added three times the amount of the sauce it called for. The small amount of the recipe leftover made a nice lunch treat. She loves the Beige Sauce recipe. She added parsley, onion powder, celery seed, and chives to the sauce. It's a great substitute for cream of celery soups. She gave it all 10's.
- Jill adds: The mega-testing of these recipes was a major help. On the test recipe I didn't specify the thickness of sauce to make. Marsha caught that mistake. I use the thin sauce and it soaks into the breadcrumbles and gives the meat a delicious flavor. Also, I like to add a little garnish to it by making the glob form (Option 1), spreading it in the pan, then sprinkling a few cracker crumbs and some fresh grated cheese on top to make it look great.
- This is one of Alan's favorite next-day lunches. It warms up great in the microwave at his office.
- The flavor is really determined by the ham. When we used the honey-baked ham, this was sweet. With a ham substitute, it has a different, but good, flavor also.
- Since the breadcrumbs/cubes don't have to look great (they are all mixed up with the sauce), I use the heels and crusts leftover from Scalloped Pineapple (page 403). So, I always try to make these recipes at the same time.
- Every year Alan's company gives us a ham. Instead of just getting two meals from it, I can use it in recipes (like this one) and stretch one ham into 20 to 30 meals!

Ratings

$ = 75¢ to $1.50 serving (a lot depends on price of ham and turkey meat)
Ease = 10
Prep-time = 15 to 30 minutes (depending on how much you were able to do ahead)
Heating = 30 minutes
Mega-Session = 10
Equipment = kitchen shears to cut up the bread and meat, Teflon® sheets to make clean-up easy

Count Stroganov Beef (Beef Stroganoff)

The story goes that a French chef who wanted to win the patronage of Count Paul Stroganov, a Russian aristocrat, created this dish. The dish became very popular especially when the Russian nobility fled their homeland. I've cooked this dish several different ways. The budget/quick method involved simply opening a can of cream of mushroom soup and a can of golden mushroom soup into two pounds of cooked, crumbled ground meat. My family likes this (printed here) version the best—of course, it is more expensive and some more work. But I agree with them it is delicious. By mega-cooking it, we can have it even on nights when I don't have time to cook. We serve this over cooked rice, noodles, or in bread or biscuit baskets.

Do ahead:

- Purchase, cook, and chop meat in bulk.
- Purchase any of the ingredients in bulk.
- Make mega-batches of the "bestest gravy" for use in several recipes including this one.

X1 6 SERVINGS	X2 12 SERVINGS	X8 48 SERVINGS	
1 pound	2 pounds	8 pounds	Stew meat
3 cups	6 cups	24 cups	Bestest Gravy in the World (recipe follows)
1 cup	2 cups	8 cups	Chopped onion
1 cups	2 cups	8 cups	Mushroom pieces
8 ounces	16 ounces	64 ounces	Sour cream (or plain yogurt)

1. In a skillet cook the stew meat in the large chunks as they come from the butcher. If you use a coated skillet, you shouldn't have to use any oil. If you feel you must, use a little oil. Brown the meat well. Leave the drippings for gravy (see below.)
2. Store the meat in the refrigerator to cool.
3. When cool, cut into ¼- to ½-inch cubes with kitchen shears.
4. Make gravy using skillet drippings (see below).

OPTION 1: MAKE BASE, FREEZE, AND FINISH ON DAY OF SERVING (THE BEST TASTE AND CONSISTENCY FOR A REASONABLE AMOUNT OF WORK ON THE DAY OF SERVING)

5. Add the onions and mushroom to the gravy.
6. Stir in the meat pieces.
7. Divide, label, and freeze using the bag-in-box method.
8. Thaw.
9. Heat in the microwave for about 5 minutes.
10. Fold in 8 ounces of sour cream per batch. Stir until well blended.
11. Heat an additional 2 minutes.
12. Serve hot over rice, noodles, or in individual bread baskets.

OPTION 2: MAKE COMPLETE, FREEZE, AND HEAT ON DAY OF SERVING. (A GOOD TASTE AND CONSISTENCY AND THE LEAST AMOUNT OF WORK ON THE DAY OF SERVING)

1. Add the onions, mushrooms, and sour cream to the gravy.
2. Stir in the meat pieces.
3. Divide, label, and freeze using the bag-in-box method.
4. Thaw.
5. Heat in the microwave for about 5 to 7 minutes.
6. Serve hot over rice, noodles, or in individual bread baskets.

OPTION 3: COOK MEAT FOR USE IN SEVERAL RECIPES AND MAKE A MEGA-BATCH OF GRAVY (A GREAT TASTE AND CONSISTENCY, BUT MORE WORK ON DAY OF SERVING)

1. Freez the meat cubes in separate bags for use in this and other recipes.
2. Freeze the gravy in batch-sized amounts—use the bag-in-box method since this is so liquid.
3. At least one day ahead of time, thaw a package of meat and gravy.
4. Add the meat, onions, mushrooms and sour cream to thawed gravy.
5. Heat on stovetop or in the microwave until bubbly. Stir often.
6. Serve hot over rice, noodles, or in individual bread baskets.

Bestest Beef Gravy in the World

(or so Bethany said when she was tiny)

This gravy is delicious. Yes, it is rich, but as long as you don't eat it every day, it shouldn't be a major problem. I use it for stews, with roasts, in homemade potpies, and in Count Stroganov Beef. Whenever I cook quality beef, I either take the time to make up as much gravy as I can, or I scrape the pan and save all the drippings for use another time. Freeze the drippings in ice cube trays. The two-ounce size works great for so many applications. This same technique can be used to make chicken gravy as well

X1 3 SERVINGS	**X2** 6 SERVINGS	**X8** 24 SERVINGS	
2 ounces	4 ounces	16 ounces	Beef drippings
2 cups	4 cups	16 cups	Milk
¼ cup	½ cup	2 cups	Butter
¼ cup	½ cup	2 cups	All-purpose flour
½ teaspoon	1 teaspoon	4 teaspoons	Kitchen Bouquet®
Dashes	Dashes	teaspoons	Salt and pepper to taste

Pre-step:

When you cook a roast, stew meat, fajita meat, or brown any beef, pour about ½ to 1 cup of water into the pan and scrape up all the drippings. The water should become so thick you can't see through it. One mistake some cooks make is to use too much water so this is more of a broth.

OPTION 1: STORE THE PAN LIQUID FOR ANOTHER DAY

2. Pour the pan liquid into 2 ounce ice cube trays.
3. Freeze.
4. Once solidly frozen, pop out of the tray, bag, and label.
5. Thaw as many cubes as needed to make gravy.
6. In a saucepan melt the butter.
7. Stir the flour into the butter until heated through and the flour leaves the side of the pan.
8. Carefully stir the pan liquid into the flour. Don't let it clump. This should be hot.
8. Slowly add the milk. Making certain to blend well.
10. Heat about 5 to 10 minutes until thickened (depending on how much you're making and the quality of your pan).
11. Stir in the Kitchen Bouquet®.
12. Season with salt and pepper to taste.
13. Serve with the meal.

OPTION 2: MAKE GRAVY THAT DAY AND FREEZE EXTRA

2. In a large saucepan melt the butter.
3. Stir the flour into the butter until heated through and the flour leaves the side of the pan.
4. Carefully stir the pan liquid into the flour. Don't let it clump. This should be hot.
5. Slowly add the milk. making certain to blend well.
6. Heat about 5 to 10 minutes until thickened (depending on how much you're making and the quality of your pan).
7. Stir in the Kitchen Bouquet®.
8. Season with salt and pepper to taste.
9. Serve with the meal. Freeze the extra for use in other recipes.
10. When you reheat it you, you need to stir. You might have to add a little more milk to get the consistency you want.

Additional Helps and Suggestions

- Please read the roux and beurre manié enteries in the Topics section to learn more about gravy and sauce making.
- Re-cap about the gravy:—Adding raw flour into a hot mixture is a sure way to have a lump battle. Instead I'm suspending the flour in the butter, then adding the roux and milk. This process is very similar to making Beige Sauce, because, I'm basically making Beige Sauce, flavored with beef drippings and Kitchen Bouquet®.

- Following these directions will produce a sauce that freezes well and is delicious and creamy when reheated. To cut calories, some cooks will want to substitute water for the milk in the gravy. It works, but it isn't as good as this. The water-version separates and needs more sour cream added at serving—so you've defeated any calorie and fat savings you had at first.

Ratings
\$ = \$2
Ease = 6
Prep-time = 30 to 60 minutes, depending on how experienced you are at making the gravy, etc.
Heating = 5 minutes
Mega-Session = 10
Equipment = kitchen shears

Deutsche Brats

(GERMAN DINNER)

This recipes freezes wonderfully. It is one of the few potato dishes I've found that does freeze well. In fact, it usually tastes better after being frozen. The "trick" is to use fresh potatoes. You can take the time and make this quite attractive by arranging the bottom layer of the potatoes and apples in a pattern, then carefully turn the casserole out on a plate—beautiful! Or you can do it the way I do most of the time, dump it out of the freezer bag and bake. It really is delicious reheated. We slice the potatoes very thin.

Do ahead:

- Purchase potatoes in bulk and pre-process. (Dehydrate extra to make scalloped potatoes later.)
- Purchase apples in bulk and pre-process. (We use apples in a variety of recipes.)
- Purchase onions in bulk and pre-process.

X1 6 SERVINGS	X5 12 SERVINGS	X10 60 SERVINGS	
1 pound	5 pounds	10 pounds	Fresh potatoes, washed and sliced (peeled if desired—I don't)
2 to 3 (1 lb)	10 to 15 (5 lbs)	20 to 30 (10 lbs)	Apples, sliced (or a 6-pound 10-ounce can of prepared apples)
3 ounces	1 pound	2 pounds	German bratwurst, thinly sliced (we don't use much, 2 pounds is plenty for our tastes. If you are into meat, use more. This recipe is even great without meat at all.)
1 cup	5 cups	10 cups	Chopped or sliced raw onions [mol]

Pre-steps:

If you haven't pre-processed the onions, potatoes, and apples, do that now. Slice the bratwurst. I use kitchen shears to save labor and time.

Steps:

Note: Depending on how many deep casserole dishes you have, you can either build the casseroles in dishes or directly into freezer bags.

1. Prepare a deep casserole dish by spraying with nonstick spray or lining with a Teflon® sheet.
2. Layer in one-fourth of the potatoes, one-third of the apples, then one-third of the bratwurst, and one-third of the onions.
3. Repeat step 2 twice to make 3 complete layers.
4. Make a final layer of potatoes on top.

5. Cover one casserole and bake at 350°F for 30 minutes. Remove the cover for the last 5 minutes to give a textured top crust.
6. For the remaining casseroles, here are some alternatives:
   a) If you used dishes, wrap them in heavy-duty wrap (I prefer Reynolds 914 Film, restaurant quality). Once these are frozen solid, pop the frozen casserole out and bag or rewrap with more film—do not allow thawing. Label and return to the freezer immediately. If you used bags, label and freeze.
   b) Line the dishes with a large (at least five times larger than the size of the dish) piece of film across the bottom and up the sides. Layer the ingredients, and seal the plastic. Make certain that it is well covered and sealed. Every bit of the surface should have at least a double layer of film. This method works well when it is done perfectly. As soon as the casserole freezes solid it will pop-out easily and you'll be able to reuse the dish. I still recommend wrapping it a second time. The problem with this is that if you don't keep the film smooth, it will fill in crevices between the food and can be a safety hazard if you don't remove every bit of it before cooking.
   c) Build the layers in a freezer bag using the bag-in-box method. They won't come out as "molded" but they taste the same and it makes very little difference for some dinners. I usually use this alternative. We simply thaw a bag of ingredients, carefully move them to a prepared pan, and bake by the same method.
7. There are different ways to cook the ingredients depending on how much time you have the day of serving:

OPTION 1: THAW AND BAKE

A. Thaw. Place the ingredients in a casserole dish that has been sprayed with a nonstick coating or lined with a Teflon® sheet. Be careful to remove all bits of film, if necessary.
B. *Optional, but preferred method:* Place a heavy pan (like a cast iron skillet) over the ingredients to weigh them down. You can cook this without the skillet, it just doesn't come out as "molded" in appearance.
C. Bake uncovered for 30 minutes at 350°F.

OPTION 2: DON'T THAW, BUT BAKE FROM FROZEN STATE

A. Prepare the casserole dish with a nonstick method.
B. Cover and bake at 300°F for 45 minutes.
C. Remove the lid and bake for 15 minutes more. (This is an average; depending on how deep your casserole dish is, you may need to adjust the time.)

OPTION 3: DON'T THAW, BUT COOK IN CROCK POT ALL DAY LONG

A. In the morning, place the frozen ingredients in a crock pot. Set on simmer.
B. You can serve it hot for dinner, but it won't have the same texture on the top.
C. If you want the crunchy texture, remove the ingredients from the crock pot and place in a prepared casserole dish. Bake at 350°F for 10 to 15 minutes.

"Very quick and easy. Great for mega-cooking™."—Debbie China

Additional Helps and Suggestions

- Sara Jean Dagen was able to buy an apple slicer/corer for $1 at one of those dollar stores. They really make the work easier. She wrote, "Seems low fat—even my husband commented." She pointed out and I agree that it doesn't look great. "I'd be nervous about serving it—tastes good, but it didn't even appeal to me until I smelled it cooking!" So, I'll warn you it is a "unique" recipe. It tastes wonderful and smells wonderful, but is different. Please test it first to see if you like it. Many families truly appreciate it once they taste it.
- You can vary the amount of meat. Some families want more (and need more) meat, so just double or triple the amount of bratwurst.
- Regarding freezing potatoes: they are tricky. They work in this recipe because the apples and onions "marinate" them.
- You can also add layers of sauerkraut. Alan and I really like this version, but the children don't like the sour taste as well. Sometimes I make half one way and half the other and label them accordingly, (adult version and kiddy version).

Ratings

$ = $1
Ease = 6-8 (depending if you have an apple slicer/corer)
Prep-time = 20 to 30 minutes
Heating = 20 minutes
Mega-Session = 10
Equipment = apple corer/slicer really helps (several models available—we have one that also peels. It works like a cork-screw and peels the apples at the same time it cores and slice them.)

Dueling Chickens

(SPICY BAKED CHICKEN)

These chickens are delicious. I serve them with curried rice, fresh vegetables, steaming fresh-baked bread, crispy tossed salad, and a luxurious, yet not too caloric, dessert. We have fun with this meal and play Dixieland jazz music and "dueling banjos." The seasonings really make this dish very flavorful—the long time in the freezer helps. Of course, if you don't need two chickens, just halve the recipe and make one-chicken dinners. I like to make several dinners worth of chickens, all stuffed and ready to bake. You have two options: to pre-bake these chickens and then freeze, or to freeze them raw and bake on the day of serving.

Do ahead:

- Buy the chickens in bulk to save money.
- Buy spices in bulk or harvest your own.
- Buy onions and garlic in bulk.

X1	**X2 (my base-line)**	**X 8**	
4 SERVINGS	8 SERVINGS	64 SERVINGS	
1	2	8	Chickens: roasters (fresh, not frozen) approximately 4½ pounds each
1 to 2	2 to 4	8 to 16	Onions, raw, quartered
2 to 4 cloves	4 to 8 cloves	16 to 32 cloves	Garlic (or equivalent)
1 tablespoon	2 tablespoons	½ cup	Dill [mol]
1 tablespoon	2 tablespoons	½ cup	Cilantro [mol]
½ tablespoon	1 tablespoon	¼ cup	Caraway seek [mol]
2 tablespoons	¼ cup	1 cup	Oregano [mol] coarsely ground
1-2 tablespoons	⅛ to ¼ cup	½-1 cup	Cajun blackened fish seasoning
½-1 tablespoon	1-2 tablespoons	¼-½ cup	Louisiana hot sauce
1 8 x 8	2 13 x 9	2 15 x 10 or 4 13 x 9	Pans (I prefer glass pans for this recipes for more even baking)

OPTION 1: PRECOOKING THE CHICKENS, THEN FREEZING:

1. Wash the chickens in water, and drain. Separate the giblets and trim fat.
2. Spray a baking dish with nonstick spray. Place the roasters breast side up in the pan. Stuff each bird with fresh onions and garlic.
3. Mix the dry spices together and rub into the flesh of the chickens. (You can remove the skin, but be sure to wrap in foil to bake.)
4. Quickly and carefully sprinkle Louisiana hot sauce on the chicken. (You don't want any area too concentrated with the sauce—Ohhwhee! That's hot!)

5. Bake at 350°F for approximately 15 to 20 minutes per pound per chicken. Example: If you used 4½ pound birds, you bake them for 1 to 1½ hours (or adjust to your oven). You don't want to cook them completely because you'll finish the last few minutes of baking when you reheat.
6. Check halfway through the baking process. Marinate with juices, if desired. Tent foil, if necessary to prevent the edges becoming too crisp.
7. Bag, label, and freeze.
8. Thaw in the refrigerator (allow 24 to 48 hours). Do not thaw at room temperature. Spray a baking dish with nonstick spray and reheat for 20 to 30 minutes.

OPTION 2: PREPARING CHICKEN, FREEZING, THEN COOKING

1. Wash the chickens in water, and drain. Separate the giblets, and trim fat.
2. Spray a baking dish with nonstick spray. Place the roasters breast side up in the pan. Stuff each bird with fresh onions and garlic.
3. Mix the dry spices together and rub into the flesh of the chickens. (You can remove the skin, but be sure to wrap in foil to bake)
4. Quickly and carefully sprinkle Louisiana hot sauce on the chicken. (You don't want any area too concentrated with the sauce—Ohhwhee! That's hot!)
5. Bag the chickens, label, and freeze.
6. Thaw in the refrigerator (allow 24 to 48 hours) Do not thaw at room temperature.
8. Bake at 350°F for approximately 20 minutes per pound per chicken. Example: If you used 4½ pound birds, you bake them for 1½ hours (or adjust to your oven).
9. Check halfway through the baking process. Marinate with pan juices, if desired. Tent foil, if necessary to prevent the edges becoming too dark.
10. Enjoy.

"Very quick and easy to prepare"—multiple chickens real quick.—Debbie China
"Affordable with great results. Low fat—high flavor. We loved it and our Texas friends really liked it. Leftovers were enjoyed."—Tina W. Cook
"Excellent!"—Judy Clark

Additional Helps and Suggestions

- Judy Clark commented: "Smells sooo good when it's cooking! Make sure you serve one that night so you are not left wanting. I love cooking whole chickens in advance—and this recipe is great! I take the whole cooked, frozen chicken and drop it in the crockpot on low in the morning. At dinnertime, you have a juicy, hot chicken with flavor and skin texture that you can't get if it isn't prebaked (or grilled.) This recipe worked excellent that way.
- Tracey Cavender said it was a little spicy for her family. She and her husband enjoyed it. They did leave off the hot sauce. She thought families with young children should consider this—and thought it might not be the best choice for them.
- Tina W. Cook's testing packet arrived late so she told us: " There wasn't a lot of time—so friends of ours had dinner and I fixed 2 roasted chickens (1 dueling and 1 oregano/garlic); 2 rice dishes

(1 brown rice and 1 Curried Rice—see page 391). There were obviously leftovers and the dueling chicken and curried rice froze well! I think it tasted better after freezing!"

- Tina W. Cook also suggested: "Bake the chicken upside down (breast down). This keeps the breast from being so dried out. The fat from the back will help keep breast moist. This is particularly important when the skin has been removed! I also left the skin on the wings so they wouldn't get so dry."
- Sara Jean Dagen said she may try to adjust it to pieces of chicken—perhaps lay pieces on onion and garlic and coat individual pieces. (She hates cutting up chicken to serve it—deboning it is okay, but not pretty!) She also made the good point that whole chicken is not cheap. She could buy one already cooked from her grocery store for the same price as the raw one.
- Jill adds: To hold down the cost of this recipe, buy your chicken directly from a distributor or grocery wholesaler. You'll have to buy 6 to 12 (or more depending on the package sizes). But you can mass-prepare them as in this recipe and have great chicken for less than half the price of the ones pre-cooked at the grocery store.

Ratings

$ = $1.50 to $2.00 (It is so good that a serving is a LOT)
Ease = 8
Prep-time = 15 to 30 minutes
Heating = 1 to 1½ hours for initial baking. Reheating only a few minutes in microwave or 20 minutes in oven.
Mega-Session = 10
Equipment = crockpot for reheating, garlic press

Flying Fish

(TUNA PUFFS)

On our morning walks, we enjoy watching the activity in the water. At one of the small bridges, we watch the fish jump out of the water to catch the insects on the surface. Our children are always fascinated about some of the fish's ability to "fly" for so long over the water. Not only do we enjoy watching fish, we do enjoy eating our share. Living on an island in Florida, we are able to buy fish directly from the fisherman. Even if you don't have such wonderful access to fish, you should make seafood a regular part of your diet—the health benefits are worth the cost. We make these "tuna puffs," though, from canned tuna (or I use fish left over from another meal). By using decorative molds (personal Bundt pan molds), this meal is very attractive. I serve these Flying Fish puffs with homemade clam chowder (as a gravy) or with a cocktail sauce.

Do ahead:

- Purchase tuna in bulk (or substitute your favorite cooked and flaked fish).
- Purchase produce in bulk for the best price.
- Make soft breadcrumbs ahead and use in several recipes, or freeze for future use.

X1	**X2**	**X4**	
4 SERVINGS	8 SERVINGS	16 SERVINGS	
1 cup	2 cups	4 cups	Milk
½ cup	1 cup	2 cups	Breadcrumbs (soft, not hard)
1 tablespoon	2 tablespoons	¼ cup	Prepared mustard
1 tablespoon	2 tablespoon	¼ cup	Finely chopped onion
½ teaspoon	1 teaspoon	2 teaspoons	Salt [mol]
½ cup	1 cup	2 cups	Tuna, flaked and drained
2	4	8	Eggs, beaten

Note: When you've mixed this correctly, it will have the consistency of muffin batter. It will pour, but slowly. The "x1" recipe should yield 4 custard-cups worth, 6 standard muffins, 4 mini-Bundt pan shapes, or 12 mini-muffins. Adjust the baking time accordingly.

Steps:

1. In a large saucepan or Dutch oven slowly heat the milk with the breadcrumbs, mustard, onion, and salt. Cook over medium heat for 5 minutes.
2. Remove from the heat and add the tuna fish and eggs. Blend well.

OPTION 1: MAKE MIX, FREEZE IN "GLOB" FORM FOR SHAPING ON BAKING DAY

3. Divide into meal-sized amounts.
4. Bag, label, and freeze.

5. Thaw.
6. Pour into muffin tins or molds. (I use a mini-Bundt pan for the mold.) Fill about two-thirds full.
7. Bake at 350°F for 45 minutes.

OPTION 2: FREEZE IN SHAPE AND BAKE DAY OF SERVING

3. Spray muffin tins or molds with nonstick spray. Pour the batter into the prepared muffin cups until about two-thirds full.
4. Wrap the entire dish in heavy-duty film.
5. Freeze.
6. As soon as the muffins are frozen solid, pop out of the mold and bag or rewrap. Work quickly; you don't want them to thaw. Continue freezing until use.
7. Place the frozen shapes back in their molds.
8. Thaw.
9. Bake at 350°F for 45 minutes.

OPTION 3: FORM AND BAKE, THEN FREEZE AND SIMPLY RE-HEAT [SINCE YOU'LL BE BAKING IN THE MOLDS, THE MOLDS HAVE TO BE OVEN-READY]

3. Spray muffin tins or molds with nonstick spray. Pour the batter into the prepared muffin cups until about two-thirds full.
4. Bake at 350°F for 45 minutes.
5. Enjoy serving for dinner that night and freeze the rest, or bag and freeze them all. Be careful not to break the shape. Carefully place them in a large bag on a cookie sheet or flat piece of cardboard. Slide the cardboard with bagged loaf onto a freezer shelf, making certain it is level. Once it is frozen solid, it can be moved around in the freezer and packed tightly with other food. (I don't use a "flimsy" shape mold, but one that is more substantial—with thick walls.)
6. To serve: Remove from the bag and place on a shallow baking dish sprayed with nonstick spray. Heat at 350°F for 15 to 20 minutes.

"My kids gobbled them up"—Lisa Fisher

Additional Helps and Suggestions

- Jenny Goff added a little garlic powder and gave it an overall rating of 10. She liked that they are very cheap to make.
- Please adjust the time. I don't make them very large so they will bake evenly. Since they continue cooking a little once your remove them from the oven, the center doesn't have to be completely cooked. That's why I like the miniature Bundt pan molds—the center is hollow and these bake perfectly. If you use regular muffin tins, don't let the edges get too crispy.
- Also, baking the puffs in a metal pan works well. However, you can use custard cups. Place the cups in a bain (water bath). Set the custard cups in another pan and pour water into the pan being

careful not to get any water in the cups or on the batter. Water helps control the baking temperature and assures more even baking—especially important for any molds that have more than a 3-inch diameter. See Topics for explanation about bain marie.

- I don't recommend baking these as a loaf or in a larger mold. It won't cook evenly throughout. Don't use anything with a diameter of more than 5 inches, and then for 3 to 5 inch molds, only fill about 2 inches deep.

Ratings

$ = 10¢
Ease = 10
Prep-time = 20 minutes
Heating = 45 minutes
Mega-Session = 10
Equipment = food processor to chop produce, any special baking pans (e.g., mini-Bundt pan or mini-muffins)

Green Eggs and Ham and Turkey and Beef and Chicken and . . .

I'm always trying to jazz up leftovers. I happened upon this recipe while rummaging through my freezer. I had quite a few little bags of leftover meat from previous mega-cooking sessions, such as turkey meat, sausage, Canadian bacon, whatever. My precious daughter, Bethany Kay, had been asking me to come up with a recipe called "Green Eggs and Ham," so, I played around and came up with this. I mega-prepare the ingredients, but assemble on the day of cooking, though you could mega-cook it ahead.

Do ahead:

- Purchase, cook, and dice meat in bulk. Store in cup-sized amounts in the freezer.
- Whenever your bread starts to stale, freeze it for use in recipes rather than throwing it away.
- Buy milk and eggs in bulk for the best price.

X1 6 SERVINGS	X2 12 SERVINGS	X4 24 SERVINGS	
2 cups	4 cups	8 cups	Milk
8	16	32	Eggs
¼ teaspoon	½ teaspoon	1 teaspoon	Green food coloring (or as needed; see Note 1)
4 cups	8 cups	16 cups	Bread cubes, 1-inch
4 cups	8 cups	16 cups	Chopped meat (use a variety of meats)

OPTION 1: MAKE MIX, FREEZE IN "GLOB" FORM FOR SHAPING DAY OF BAKING (NOT AS ATTRACTIVE AS THE LAYERED VERSIONS, BUT STILL TASTY)

1. In a large bowl mix together the milk, eggs, and food coloring. Add a little food coloring at a time until you get the shade of green you like.
2. Soak the breadcrumbs in the egg mixture.
3. Add the meat.
4. Divide into meal-sized amounts.
5. Bag, label, and freeze.
6. Thaw.
7. Spray a 13 x 9-inch pan with nonstick spray. Press the thawed mixture into the pan.
8. Bake at 350°F for 45 minutes.

OPTION 2: FREEZE IN SHAPE AND BAKE DAY OF SERVING

1. In a large bowl mix together the milk, eggs, and food coloring. Add a little food coloring at a time until you get the shade of green you like
2. Spray pan(s) with nonstick spray. Layer the bread cubes on the bottom of the pan.
3. Layer meat over the bread cubes.

4. Pour the egg mixture over the meat.
5. Freeze.
6. As soon as it is frozen solid, pop out of mold and bag or rewrap. Do this quickly; you don't want it to thaw. Continue freezing until use.
7. Place the frozen shape back in the mold.
8 Bake at 350°F for 45 minutes.

OPTION 3: FORM AND BAKE, THEN FREEZE AND SIMPLY RE-HEAT (SINCE YOU'LL BE BAKING IN THESE MOLDS, THEY HAVE TO BE OVEN-READY)

1. In a large bowl mix together the milk, eggs, and food coloring. Add a little food coloring at a time until you get the shade of green you like.
2. Spray pan(s) with nonstick spray or using Teflon® liners. Layer the bread cubes on the bottom of the pan.
3. Layer meat over the bread cubes.
4. Pour the egg mixture over the meat.
5. Bake at 350°F for 45 minutes.
6. Enjoy one for dinner that night and freeze the rest, or bag and freeze them all. Once frozen solid, remove from the pan, rewrap, and continue freezing.
7. Spray the mold with nonstick spray. Remove the dish from the bag an place back in the mold.
8. Bake at 350° for 15 to 20 minutes.

Note 1: For those who need to stay away from food coloring, use cooked, chopped, pureed spinach as needed to achieve the desired color green.
Note 2: You can use any kind of leftover bread: dinner rolls, sandwich slices, French, what ever you have.
Note 3: I don't make these ahead, I keep the ingredients in the freezer ready to assemble and then mix it up fresh the day of baking. This works for breakfast, lunch, or an easy dinner.

"My family loved this recipe."—Jessica Maher

Additional Helps and Suggestions

- Jessica Maher said she made this recipe with breakfast sausage. One morning they used maple syrup on it and it tasted just like French toast with sausage. One night they had it for dinner with fresh fruit. Her kids really like it. For those on special diets she suggested using an egg substitute, low-fat milk, and turkey meat or a soy meat substitute.
- Jill adds: If the name of this recipe doesn't sound good to you, I understand. Call it something else. Of course, you can omit the green coloring. But for those of us who have read some of Dr. Seuss' books so many times we have them memorized, this recipe really excites the little ones—a dish all their own!

Ratings

$ = 10¢ (but since I'm using left-overs, it's as if it is "free food")
Ease = 10
Prep-time = 20 minutes (depending on how much chopping you have to do)
Heating = 45 minutes (reheating 15 to 20)
Mega-Session = 8 (it does well, but I like to use leftovers another day)
Equipment = nothing extra, kitchen shears would speed any chopping of meat

Ham Rolls

The seemingly difficult task of grinding cooked ham might make this recipe seem out of reach for the average cook. Not every kitchen has a meat grinder. If you can't grind the cooked ham, then simply chop it finely—into the tiniest pieces possible. If you have a food processor run the meat through the grater or use a metal blade on the dish-type of food processor. This looks great. I like to slice these logs into disks and serve with a homemade cheese sauce.

Do ahead:

- Purchase ham in bulk and use in a variety of recipes.
- Buy any of the ingredients in bulk quantities.
- Make mega-batches of this recipe and freeze for later use.

X1	X2	X4	
6 SERVINGS	12 SERVINGS	24 SERVINGS	
2 tablespoons	¼ cup	½ cup	Butter, softened
2 tablespoons	¼ cup	½ cup	Prepared mustard
1 cup	2 cups	4 cups	Ground cooked ham (see Note 1) [mol]
2 cups	4 cups	8 cups	Flour
4 teaspoons	3 tablespoons	⅓ cup	Baking powder
½ teaspoons	1 teaspoons	2 teaspoons	Salt [mol]
¼ cup	½ cup	1 cup	Butter, softened
¾ cup	1½ cups	3 cups	Milk

Steps:

1. In a medium bowl mix 2 tablespoons (or ¼ or ½ cup) of butter and the mustard together until creamy.
2. Mix the butter/mustard into the ham. Refrigerate until use in an airtight container.
3. Fluff (or sift) together the flour, baking powder and salt.
4. Cut in ¼ cup (or ½ or 1 cup) of buter until the size of small peas.
5. Add milk until a soft dough forms.
6. Knead the dough a few minutes until smooth. (I use my heavy-duty mixer for the mixing and kneading.)
7. Roll out the dough to a ¼-inch thickness on a floured surface into a 16-inch square. (If you're making mega-batches, you'll want to do this round robin with as much dough as you can comfortably handle. When I do x4, I divide the dough into fourths, work one ball, and refrigerate the other 3 balls until use.)
8. Spread with a proportional amount of ham mixture.
9. Roll up jelly roll fashion.

OPTION 1: BAKE ALL, FREEZE, AND REHEAT THE DAY OF SERVING

10. On a baking sheet that has been sprayed with nonstick spray, place the ham rolls raw edge down. (You can bake 2 on a jelly roll pan side-by-side. Leave space in between for rising. If necessary, cut apart with a serrated knife.)
11. Bake at 425° for 15 to 20 minutes.
12. Serve one with Cheese Sauce (see page 363) if desired.
13. Refrigerate extra ham rolls.
14. Once the ham rolls are cool, either wrap in plastic or bag. Freeze on a flat surface (place the bag or plastic wrap on a cookie sheet or piece of cardboard). Once frozen solid, pack it tightly with other food.
15. Place on a cookie sheet to thaw in the refrigerator. Remove all packaging.
16. Bake at 350°F for 10 to 15 minutes.
17. Serve with Cheese Sauce (see page 363).

OPTION 2: BAKE ONE, FREEZE THE REST TO BAKE ON DAY OF SERVING

10. On a baking sheet that has been sprayed with nonstick coating place one ham roll raw edge down.
11. Bake at 425° for 15 to 20 minutes.
12. Serve one with Cheese Sauce (see page 363).
13. Wrap the other rolls individually in waxed paper, then bag or wrap in plastic wrap.
14. Freeze on a flat surface. (Place the bag or plastic wrap on a cookie sheet or piece of cardboard.) Once frozen solid, pack it tightly with other food.
15. Place on a cookie sheet to thaw in the refrigerator. Remove all packaging.
16. Bake at 425°F for 15 to 20 minutes.
17. Serve with Cheese Sauce (see page 363).

OPTION 3: FREEZE ALL TO BAKE ON OTHER DAYS

10. Wrap each roll individually in waxed paper, then bag or wrap in plastic wrap. Label.
11. Freeze on a flat surface (place the bag or plastic wrap on a cookie sheet or piece of cardboard). Once frozen solid, pack it tightly with other food.
12. Place on a cookie sheet to thaw in the refrigerator. Remove all packaging.
13. Bake at 425°F for 15 to 20 minutes.
14. Serve with Cheese Sauce (see page 363).

Note 1: I recommend half Dijon and half yellow mustard. You can use all one type, or mix your favorites.
Note 2: The mustard-ham mixture is great on sandwiches. Freeze leftovers (or make extra) in ½ cup portions. Thaw and spread on bread.

"So easy and quick! Kids could even make this."—Cheryl Lewis

Additional Helps and Suggestions

- Dorothy Hunsberger used turkey ham instead of regular ham and rated 10 for taste. She also suggested that some might want more meat (as much as double). Adjust the recipe to suit your needs. It will work with more or less meat.
- Cheryl Lewis suggested this would be wonderful with cooked sausage as the filler and topped with gravy.
- Tamara Grim said one loaf by itself wasn't enough for a meal for her family of six, so she served it with a couple of side dishes.

Ratings

$ = 50¢
Ease = 8
Prep-time = 30 minutes
Heating = 15 to 20 minutes
Mega-Session = 8
Equipment = meat grinder, food processor are helps with the meat chopping

Harvest Bird

(BAKED CHICKEN AND ACORN SQUASH)

As I mentioned before, I plan mega-cooking to coincide with seasonal harvests. But because I'm mega-cooking and freezing, we can enjoy a Fall Harvest meal in the middle of Winter or in Spring. Plan to make this recipe in the fall when squash is plentiful and cheap. You might want to prepare summer peaches to team up with this recipe later when squash is harvesting. If you manage your own garden, you can often time harvests to your preferences.

Do ahead:

- Buy squash in season to use in this recipe and freeze or dehydrate for other recipes.
- Buy chicken in bulk for the best price.
- Prepare your own cling peaches by buying in season.

X1 4 SERVINGS	X2 8 SERVINGS	X6 24 SERVINGS	
2	4	12	Small acorn squash
4	8	24	Chicken legs or quarters
2 tablespoons	¼ cup	¾ cup	Cooking oil
4 cloves	8 cloves	10 cloves	Garlic (unpeeled)
¼ cup	½ cup	1½ cups	Brown sugar
1 teaspoon	2 teaspoons	2 tablespoons	Salt
1 teaspoon	2 teaspoons	2 tablespoons	Rosemary leaves
1 16-ounce can	1 32-ounce can	1 6-pound, 10-ounce can	Sliced cling peaches

Steps:

1. Clean, seed, and cut the acorn squash into 1 to 2 inch chunks. If you bought quality squash and washed it well, you shouldn't have to peel it.
2. Clean the chicken. Remove the skin and fat (if desired).
3. Toss the acorn squash pieces with oil and garlic.
4. Arrange the chicken, squash (see Additional Helps, below, about when to add squash), and garlic in the bottom of a casserole pan.
5. In a small bowl, mix together the brown sugar, salt, and rosemary.
6. Sprinkle the chicken and squash with the sugar mixture.
7. Bake at 400°F for 1 hour. Check every 15 minutes and baste with drippings.
8. If there is any fat, skim and discard.
9. Add the peaches and juice to the chicken.

OPTION 1: MAKE ONE FOR DINNER THE FIRST NIGHT AND FREEZE THE REST FOR OTHER EVENINGS

10. Place extra pans of chicken with peaches in the refrigerator to cool.
11. Bake one pan an additional 15 minutes. Serve.
12. Once cool, bag the other meals in freezer bags (use bag-in-box method) or place in airtight containers. Label. Freeze.
13. Thaw.
14. Place in an ovenproof pan and bake at 400°F for 15 minutes.

OPTION 2: PREPARE ALL DURING A MEGA-COOKING SESSION AND FREEZE ALL TO COMPLETE BAKING OTHER TIMES

10. Set the pans in the refrigerator to cool.
11. Once cool, bag the meals in freezer bags (use bag-in-box method) or place in airtight containers. Label. Freeze.
12. Thaw.
13. Place in an ovenproof pan and bake at 400°F for 15 minutes.

"10"—Janice Miller
"The peaches really add to this—only trouble is, the kids ate them all up!"—Michele Nielsen

Additional Helps and Suggestions

- With this recipe we add the peaches near the end of the baking for two reasons: 1) the peaches will turn to mush if you bake them for an hour and 15 minutes and 2) the peach juice will overwhelm all the other flavors and everything will taste too peachy.
- Michele Nielsen recommended cooking the chicken for 15 to 30 minutes before adding the squash. She thought the squash was too soft. I agree with Michele.
- We like firm vegetables. I trained my children to prefer "raw" rather than "well-done." So, I don't add the squash until the 30-minute point of the chicken baking, and they are still firm after 45 minutes. So, adjust according to your family's preference. (Most families liked the squash soft.)
- Squash are tough to cut. If it is too difficult for you, here's another method. Put the whole squash (washed first) in the microwave and cook for 3 to 5 minutes on high. It shouldn't cook the squash, but will soften it. Once it is cool enough to handle, cut it up. If you "pre-cook" it this way, you'll definitely want to add it later in the chicken cooking process.

Ratings

$ = 75¢ to $1.00 depending if you can buy the chicken in bulk
Ease = 8
Prep-time = 30 minutes
Heating = 1 hour and 15 minutes (reheating 15 minutes)
Mega-Session = 10
Equipment = nothing extra

Honolulu Chicken

I enjoy shopping in used bookstores and have collected quite a few old cookbooks. The most I've ever paid for a used cookbook was $18.00 (my usual price is one dollar) but this book, Hawaiian and Pacific Foods, *published in 1943 by M. Barrows and Company, was exceptional. The first 126 pages were filled with narrative about the unique cooking style of the Pacific. It was a "cookbook," not just a recipe book. Katherine Bazore, who wrote the book before Hawaii was a state, introduced the haoles on the mainland to this delicious cuisine. (Pronounced "howly," haole is a term for any member of the Caucasian race or for non-Hawaiians.) After reading it, I played around in the kitchen and made my haole version of grilled chicken. It is one of my all time favorite recipes—we do the "x8" batch.*

Do ahead:

- Purchase, marinate and grill chicken in bulk.
- Purchase any of the ingredients in bulk.
- Make a mega-batch of the sauce for use in this recipe and others (it is great as a dip for egg rolls).

X1 5 SERVINGS	**X2** 10 SERVINGS	**X4** 20 SERVINGS	**X8** 40 SERVINGS	
5	10	20	40	Chicken breasts or half-breasts (de-boned) [mol]
2½ cups	5 cups	10 cups	20 cups	Pineapple juice (use as much from drained pineapple and use additional to make this amount)
2½ tablespoons	⅓ cup	⅔ cup	1⅓ cups	Chicken bouillon (quality, not those salt cubes)
¼ cup	½ cup	1 cup	2 cups	Cornstarch
2 cups	4 cups	8 cups	16 cups	Cider vinegar [mol]
1 cup	2 cups	4 cups	8 cups	Sugar (if using fructose or sucanat, use half the quanity)
2½ tablespoons	⅓ cup	⅔ cup	1⅓ cups	Soy sauce
½ teaspoon	1 teaspoon	2 teaspoons	4 teaspoons	Ground ginger
2 20-ounce cans	4 20-ounce cans	1 6-pound 10-ounce cans	2 6-pound 10-ounce cans	Pineapple rings or chunks
3	6	12	18 to 24	Large bell peppers, cut into strips or rings

Depending on how much meat your family eats in ratio to other ingredients, you can vary the size of the chicken breasts. Some families are big meat eaters and will want to use whole breasts and some will use smaller, 4-ounce breast fillets.

Prepare Chicken Strips:

1. Place the chicken and pineapple juice in an airtight container and marinate in the refrigerator overnight.
2. Grill the chicken breasts. Reserve the marinade for making sauce. Store in the refrigerator until needed.
3. Cut the grilled chicken breasts into strips.

Prepare Sauce:

4. In a large saucepan or Dutch oven boil the pineapple juice for at least 5 minutes to kill any bacteria.
5. Dissolve the bouillon cubes in the boiling pineapple juice.
6. In a separate container dissolve the cornstarch in vinegar. (Using a shaker makes this easier.)
7. Pour the vinegar into the pineapple juice. Add the soy sauce. Continue cooking over medium heat.
8. Mix the ginger into the sugar and stir into the hot juice mixture.
9. Stir until the mixture is thick and transparent.

Arrange Ingredients and Bake:

10. Layer the chicken breasts in a 13 x 9-inch baking dish .
11. Pour the sauce over the chicken.
12. Bake at 350°F for 30 minutes.
13. Arrange the pineapple rings or chunks and bell peppers over the chicken.
14. Bake at 350°F an additional 30 minutes.
15. Serve over a bed of rice. Taking a few extra minutes, you can arrange the dish to look spectacular.

OPTION 1: PRE-GRILL THE CHICKEN, FREEZE THE JUICE, AND ASSEMBLE THE DAY OF SERVING

1. Follow steps 1 through 3 above, and then freeze the chicken in meal-sized amounts in bags. You can freeze the chicken in the juice or separately. Be certain to use the bag-in-a-box method with the juice.
2. Thaw the meat and juice.
3. Follow steps 4 through 15 above.

OPTION 2: MAKE THE COMPLETED MEAL AND FREEZE READY TO HEAT

1. Follow steps 1 through 14 above.
2. Place the ingredients in bags (use bag-in-box method) or plastic containers. Label. Freeze.
3. Thaw.
4. Place in an ovenproof dish.
5. Bake at 350°F for 20 minutes until the ingredients are bubbly.
6. Follow step 15 above.

"We thought it was great! (Two of her four children thought it was a little too sweet.)"—Jenny Goff

Additional Helps and Suggestions

- Jenny Goff also tried this recipe with leg quarters and it was very good—not quite as good as with boneless chicken, but almost.
- Jessica Mader used the leftover chicken over a green salad for lunch. She also had a good point: She normally mega-cooks but made only "x1" of this recipe to test to see if they liked it. She said the next time they will make "x4." Remember to test recipes before you make a whole lot, so you don't get "stuck."
- One tester didn't like that much bell pepper. So, if you aren't a pepper fan, please reduce that amount. (I try to include a lot of vegetables in my recipes, but I realize that one of my children picks out the peppers.) So adjust for your family's preferences. Reducing the amount of peppers will not affect the sauce or chemical balance.)
- Colleen Finley substituted sucanat for the sugar.
- Lisa Fisher asked for another way to cook the chicken (bless their hearts, they grilled this recipe outside when there was snow on the ground!) You can pan fry them in a little bit of oil. To give them that wonderful "grilled" look use a heated ice pick (See Topics section for how-to).
- You can buy chicken breasts directly from the wholesale grocer. They come in 4-ounce and 6-ounce sizes. Or you can make your own by cutting up boned breasts or whole chickens.
- Also since the chicken doesn't require the meat tenderizing enzyme reaction of the pineapple juice (as tough beef would), I use the less expensive canned pineapple juice for the flavor.
- Read about vinegar in the Topic sections to be sure this isn't too vinegary for you. This definitely has a sweet and sour taste.

Ratings

$ = $1.00 (depending on price of chicken)
Ease = 7
Prep-time = 30 minutes (varies especially if you are deboning your chicken)
Heating = 1 hour
Mega-Session = 10
Equipment = grill

Instant Thanksgiving

Basically, this recipe is a "Thanksgiving-less" turkey or chicken and dressing recipe. It's a way of having the delicious flavor of poultry and dressing, but on an ordinary Tuesday. See below for a "left-over" version.

Do Ahead:

- Purchase, cook, and dice chicken or turkey in bulk.
- Either make your own bread and cube, or buy bread in bulk and cube.
- Make you own broth or buy in bulk.

X1 8 SERVINGS	X2 16 SERVINGS	X8 64 SERVINGS	
¼ cup	½ cup	2 cups	Butter (for dressing)
1 teaspoon	2 teaspoons	3 tablespoons	Sage
1 teaspoon	2 teaspoons	3 tablespoons	Poultry seasoning
2 tablespoons	¼ cup	1 cup	Finely chopped parsley
6 cups	12 cups	48 cups	Bread cubes (or crumbs)
½ cup	1 cup	4 cups	Butter (for gravy)
¾ cup	1½ cups	6 cups	All-purpose flour
6 cups	12 cups	3 gallons	Broth (fat skimmed off)
2 pounds	4 pounds	16 pounds	Poultry, cooked and cubed (chicken or turkey)

Steps:

1. In a saucepan melt the butter (for dressing). Add the sage, poultry seasoning, and parsley.
2. Place the bread cubes in a large bowl.
3. Pour the seasoned butter over the bread cubes and toss. Set aside.
4. In a skillet melt the butter (for gravy) and blend in the flour. Slowly add the broth and stir until thickened over medium heat.
5. Add the chopped meat to the gravy. Mix well.

OPTION 1: MAKE MIX, FREEZE IN "GLOB" FORM FOR SHAPING DAY OF BAKING

This version will not have the defined layers of the other options. Though it doesn't look as good, it tastes the same.

6. Mix the gravy and dressing together.
7. Divide into meal-sized amounts.
8. Bag, label, and freeze.
9. Thaw.
10. Spray a 13 x 9-inch pan with nonstick spray and place the mixture in the pan.
11. Bake at 350°F for 30 to 40 minutes.

OPTION 2: FREEZE "LAYERS" SEPARATELY AND ASSEMBLE DAY OF BAKING.

6. Divide the bread cubes into equal portions. Bag, label, and freeze.
7. Divide the meat and gravy mixture into equal portions. Bag, label, and freeze.
8. Thaw out a bag of dressing and a bag of meat and gravy.
9. Spray a 13 x 9-inch baking dish with nonstick spray. Place half of the dressings on the bottom of the pan.
10. Pour all of the meat and gravy over the dressing.
11. Top with the remaining dressing.
12. Bake at 350°F for 30 to 40 minutes.

OPTION 3: FORM AND BAKE, THEN FREEZE AND RE-HEAT

Since you'll be baking in these molds, they have to be oven-ready.

6. Spray as many pans as you need with nonstick spray.
7. Place half of the dressing on the bottom(s) of the pan(s).
8. Pour all of the meat and gravy over the dressing among the pan(s).
9. Top with the remaining dressing.
10. Bake at 350°F for 30 to 40 minutes.
11. Enjoy one for dinner. Cover the remainig casseroles with plastic and freeze. Once frozen solid, Pop it out of the dish and bag or rewrap.
12. To serve: Remove from the bag and place in a dish. That has been sprayed with nonstick spray. Bake at 350°F for 15 to 20 minutes.

Thanksgiving Anytime Casserole

You can make a "leftover" version after the holidays. Instead of serving turkey and dressing every meal after the big holiday dinner (until your whole family doesn't want to see it again for another whole year), prepare this casserole from Thanksgiving leftovers, freeze it and then serve in a few months. They'll love you for it.

Using your leftover dressing, gravy, and turkey, follow any of the options above for freezing and reheating. This is one delicious way to have a "mock-banquet" on any old day. The meat stays moist because it is being frozen with its gravy.

"Great! Easy. My husband asked for this a second time this week!"—Jean Dominquez

Additional Helps and Suggestions

- I'll be honest, this recipe received mixed reviews from the mega-testers. My husband loves it. I read and re-read the comments and made some adjustments. I think the big difference is the quality and amount of bread used.
- Jean Dominquez's husband named this recipe. I had been calling it "Scalloped Chicken." They felt that sounded like something kids wouldn't want to eat.

- Sandra Ross recommended using your own stuffing recipe. Jill: I suggest that you leave the stuffing a bit dry, otherwise the gravy will make the casserole too soupy.
- Suzy Richards suggested putting the dressing only on the top of the chicken. The bottom layer came out too "mushy." You could also reduce the amount of butter and use more bread.
- Melanie Fierro brought up a good point: Be sure to skim the fat off the chicken broth, otherwise the gravy will be too greasy.

Ratings
$ = 50¢
Ease = 8
Prep-time = 15 minutes
Heating = 30 to 40 minutes
Mega-Session = 8
Equipment = food processor to chop up produce

J.J.'s Prayer Casserole

(TATER TOT DINNER)

Starter Recipe—If you've never mega-cooked, this is the best place to start.

J.J. Howe is quite a hostess. It seems almost half the times I call my long-distance friend, she has house guests—guests that come for a week at a time. She has learned to mega-cook and this is one of her most popular recipes to serve to other families with small children. She served it to us on one of our visits, and my children insisted I learn how to make it. She calls it her prayer casserole because she prays for friends while she makes it up. What a blessing it would be on her life if everyone who makes this says a prayer for J.J.

Do Ahead:

- Buy meat in bulk to save money and then cook it at one time for this and other recipes.
- Purchase large cans of soup or make your own.
- Buy any of the produce in bulk and mega-process.
- Check with a wholesaler about buying the potato nuggets at cut-rate prices.

X1 4 TO 6 SERVINGS	X2 8 TO 12 SERVINGS	X4 16 TO 24 SERVINGS	X8 32 TO 48 SERVINGS	
2 cups (1 lb)	4 cups (2 lbs)	8 cups (4 lbs)	16 cups (8 lbs)	Ground meat
¼ cup	½ cup	1 cup	2 cups	Minced onions
1 cup	2 cups	4 cups	8 cups	Diced celery [mol]
1½ cups or 1 can	3 cups or 2 cans	6 cups or 4 cans	12 cups or 8 cans	"Cream of _____ soup" concentrate (your favorite commercial soup or homemade, see page 364)
2 cups	4 cups	8 cups	16 cups	Grated cheese (combination or your favorite)
1 pound	2 pounds	4 pounds	8 pounds	Frozen potato nuggets (tater tots)
8-inch square or 9-inch round	9 x 13 or 2 8-inch square or 9-inch rounds	Twice of x2	Quadruple of x2	

Pre-step for all options:

1. If you are making your own soup, make it ahead or while you are browning the meat.
2. Process the produce: cut the celery and mince the onion. Grate the cheese (if applicable).

OPTION 1: SINGLE BATCH

3. In a large skillet brown the meat, onion, and celery. Drain.
4. Stir in the soup.
5. Spray a casserole dish with nonstick spray. Pour the mixture into the prepared casserole dish.
6. Cover the top with the grated cheese.
7. Top with the nuggets.
8. Bake (uncovered) at 400°F for 40 minutes.

OPTION 2: MULTI-BATCHING (BAKE ONE NOW AND FREEZE REST FOR LATER BAKING)

3. In a large skillet brown the meat. Drain.
4. Stir in raw onion and celery.
5. Stir in soup.
6. In one casserole dish, pour in a proportional amount of mixture (e.g., if you are making the x4 amount, you'd pour in one-fourth of the mixture).
7. Cover the top with grated cheese.
8. Top with potato nuggets.
9. Bake uncovered at 400°F for 40 minutes. While it is baking you can complete steps 1 and 2 with the remaining meat mixture.
10. Divide the remaining mixture into bags, label, and freeze.
11. Divide the cheese into proportional amounts, label and freeze.
12. If needed, divide the nuggets, label, and freeze.
13. Store the bags near each other in the freezer for convenience. (You might want to even rubber band or tape bags of meat, cheese, and nuggets together.)
14. The day before you want to serve this, take out one package of cheese and one package of meat and allow them to thaw in the refrigerator. Keep the potato nuggets in the freezer, but set them within easy reach.
15. Spray a casserole dish with nonstick spray. Arrange the layers in the dish. Pour in the meat/soup mixture. Cover with cheese.
16. Pull out the potato nuggets and place on top of the cheese.
17. Bake uncovered at 400°F for 40 minutes.

OPTION 3: MULTI-BATCHING (BAKE ALL OF THEM, EAT ONE NOW, FREEZE THE OTHERS FOR LATER REHEATING)

3. Follow steps 3 through 5 in Option 2.
4. Spray as many casserole dishes as you need with nonstick spray.
5. Using assembly-line techniques, fill the dishes. Pour the meat mixture into each dish. Then cover each with the cheese. Then top with the nuggets.
6. Bake all of them at 400°F for 30 minutes. (If they won't all fit in the oven at once, cover the ones waiting to bake and refrigerate until they go in the oven.)
7 If you want to serve one that night, bake one casserole for an additional 10 minutes.
8. Cover the casseroles with airtight lids or use foil or plastic wrap.

9. Place the partially baked casseroles in the refrigerator to cool. When they are no longer hot, place them in the freezer.
10. Once they are frozen solid, you can pop them out of their pans (so you can use the pans for other recipes). Wrap them in foil, plastic wrap, or put in freezer bags. Label well.
11. To serve: Remove the wrap from one of the casseroles and replace it in its freezer dish.
    a) Cover with foil, plastic wrap, or an airtight lid. Thaw in the refrigerator overnight. Place the casserole in a cold oven 20 minutes before you want to serve it. Turn the oven on to 400°F and bake for 15 minutes. It should be wonderfully hot and ready. If you have a "hot" or quick oven, check it after 10 minutes. If it isn't ready at 15 minutes, give it another 5 minutes.
    b) At least 1 hour before you wish to serve it, place a casserole in a cold oven and turn it on to 300°F. Bake for 1 hour or until hot throughout. *Note:* If you're making a double-batch in a 13 x 9-inch dish, then allow at least an additional 30 minutes for baking from the frozen state.

OPTION FOUR: PREPARING THIS DURING A MEGA-SESSION

3. Chop and mince all the produce in quantity for this and other recipes. Treat onions with Brown Away (if desired). Store in airtight containers in the refrigerator.
4. Brown the meat for this and other recipes. Store in airtight containers in the refrigerator.
5. Make a large batch of "Cream of Soup" for this and other recipes. Store in airtight containers in the refrigerator.
6. Grate cheese (if applicable). Store in airtight containers in the refrigerator.
7. Assemble casseroles. In a large bin, bowl, or pot (don't worry all the ingredients are cold, so you can use any clean container), combine the appropriate amounts of meat, onions, celery, and soup. For example, out of the container of onions, just measure out 1 cup (if you're doing "x4") minced onion and add it to the meat mixture, then go to the celery container, etc.]
8. Follow the same directions as for multi-batching. (Option 2 works best for a mega-session, because you don't have to worry about the extra heat.)

Additional Helps and Suggestions

- Yes, I wrote this intentionally as a beginner's recipe, giving more details than for other recipes. Once you begin to understand how these techniques work, you'll be able to work the recipes with ease.
- *Note:* For Options 1 through 4 it is not necessary to cook the onions or celery. They work much better in recipes where they will be frozen if you add them in raw.
- I usually just grate onions and use them even in recipes like this that call for minced. I use a fine grate that works well for the onions for texture and flavor.
- About buying the cheese: Weight of cheese depends on which cheese you choose. I didn't state the amount in weight because it depends on how fine you grate and the type of cheese. As a guide, I've found that 3 pounds of Cheddar cheese will yield me about 9 cups grated. More dense cheese will yield less in volume (heavy cheese gives you fewer cups per pound). Less dense cheese (like swiss or mozzarella) will yield more cups per pound. Read the label and make adjustments. For this recipe,

I like to use a blend of several different cheeses. Since we like a little zip to our food, I'll add Monterey Jack with jalapeño peppers to one batch or to one side of the dish. It gives this recipe a different flavor.

- This recipe makes a great lunch or an easy dinner. Because of the size and appetites of my family, x2 is one meal's worth. The x2 amount fits perfectly in a 13 x 9-inch casserole dish. The x1 works in an 8-inch square or an 8 or 9-inch round dish.
- About the soup: use your favorite flavor of "cream of soup." Some good ones are mushroom (golden or regular), celery, asparagus, chicken, or for a slightly different flavor try a creamed fish/seafood version. I like to make my own using a basic Beige Sauce, adding the flavoring I like. For this recipe, I make mixed-vegetable soup using whatever vegetables I have on hand, and adding some vegetable powder. (I dehydrate vegetables, then when they are completely dry, use a hand-held chopper to turn the pieces into a powder.) You can buy broth powders at grocery and health-food stores. See directions for "Cream of" soups on page 364. If you are just starting to mega-cook, make it easy on yourself and use a commercial soup. If using commercial soup, instead of opening two cans of soup, you can use one of the larger 26-ounce cans. It's not an exact doubling, but it's close enough—especially if it saves you money. With many mega-cooking™ recipes, you can alter the ingredients up or down to fit standard sizes and the recipe isn't hurt. The time to be precise is with baked goods like muffins or cakes.

Ratings

$ = 75¢
Ease = 10
Prep-time = 20 minutes—depending if you make your own soup or not
Heating = 40 minutes
Mega-Session = 10
Equipment = nothing extraordinary though a food processor does help when you are chopping lots of produce

Martian Corn Craters

My little girl loves cornbread. Since I like to please my family, I played around in the kitchen until I finalized this version for her. And, yes, I do serve it with Corn²Bread (see page 237). When we were perfecting this recipe the news was filled with press briefings and news of the Pathfinder's results. We watched the discovery of Yogi and Mini Matterhorn. This recipe seemed to fit in well with that study. I just didn't dye it red—we don't need any additives.

Do Ahead:

- Purchase and prepare any of the ingredients in bulk to save time and money.
- Assembly-line process as much of the preparation as possible.

X1	X2	X8	
6 SERVINGS	12 SERVINGS	48 SERVINGS	2 4-OUNCE CUSTARD CUPS PER SERVING
2 tablespoons	¼ cup	1 cup	Salad oil (as healthy as you can afford)
½ cup	1 cup	4 cups	Finely chopped onion
3 tablespoons	⅓ cup	1½ cups	Flour
2 cups (1 pint)	4 cups (1 quart)	16 cups (1 gallon)	Milk
½ pound	1 pound	4 pounds	Ham, cooked and chopped into small cubes (or use a ham substitute)
6	12	48	Eggs
2 cups (1 pint)	4 cups (1 quart)	16 cups (1 gallon)	Half and half
1 teaspoon	2 teaspoons	3 tablespoons	Sugar (if using fructose, you may use half the amount)
1 teaspoon	2 teaspoons	3 tablespoons	Salt
1 cup	2 cups	8 cups	Kernel corn (canned works fine)

Steps:

1. In a skillet heat the oil and lightly sauté the onion. Stir in the flour. Gradually add the milk and continue as with any basic white (beige) sauce, stirring until thick.
2. In a large bowl beat together the eggs and half and half. Mix in the sugar and salt.
3. In a large bowl or pot mix together the white sauce, egg mixture, corn, and ham.

OPTION 1: MAKE MIX AND FREEZE IN "GLOB" FORM FOR SHAPING DAY OF BAKING

4. Since the mix is so liquid, use the bag-in-a-box method for freezing.
5. Divide into meal-sized amounts.
6. Bag, label, and freeze.
7. Thaw.
8. Pour into ramekin or custard cups.

9. Place the cups in a casserole dish. Carefully pour water in the large dish about half way up the sides of the custard cups as for a bain marie.
10. Bake at 350°F for 35 minutes.

OPTION 2: FREEZE IN SHAPE AND BAKE DAY OF SERVING [YOU CAN USE PLASTIC MOLDS FOR FREEZING]

4. Spray custard cups with nonstick spray. (Make certain they can be used in the freezer as well as in the oven.)
5. Pour the mix into cups.
6. Cover with a piece of heavy film.
7. Freeze. Make certain the cup is level.
8. Once they are frozen solid, remove from their cups and bag. Continue freezing.
9. To serve: Place each frozen crater back into its ramekin (spray first with nonstick spray).
10. Thaw.
11. Place the cups in a casserole dish. Carefully pour water in the large dish about half way up the sides of the custard cups as for a bain marie.
12. Bake at 350°F for 35 minutes.

OPTION 3: FORM AND BAKE, THEN FREEZE AND SIMPLY RE-HEAT [SINCE YOU'LL BE BAKING IN THESE MOLDS, THEY HAVE TO BE OVEN-READY]

4. Spray custard cups with nonstick spray. (Make certain they can be used in the freezer as well as in the oven.)
5. Pour the mix into cups.
6. Place the cups in a casserole dish. Carefully pour water in the large dish about half way up the side of the custard cups as for a bain marie.
7. Bake at 350°F for 35 minutes.
8. Enjoy some for dinner that night and freeze the rest or freeze all of them for future use.
9. Cover each baked crater with a piece of film. Freeze. Make certain the cup is level.
10. Once they are frozen solid, remove from their cups and bag. Continue freezing.
11. To serve: Place each frozen crater back into its ramekin (spray first with nonstick spray).
12. Heat and serve. You can bake them from the frozen state at 300°F for 30 minutes (depending on the size of your custard cups); from a thawed state at 350°F for 15 minutes; or in the microwave (keep a piece of suitable plastic over the top to keep the steam in). Microwaving time will vary depending on your oven, but as an average 5 minutes on medium will heat it through.

Jill's Favorite Option: Since I don't have many custard cups, I make the mix, freeze it in the "glob" form, and then bake these the day of serving. If you use Option 1, it fits great into a mega-session weekend plan.

"Very good."—Helene Brock

Additional Helps and Suggestions

- One of my testers asked me to come up with an alternative baking method for those who don't have custard cups. I've been experimenting, but the quality isn't acceptable to me with any other method. When using large casserole dishes, the outside edges cook before the middle is done. An alternative, though I was not very pleased with the appearance, is to use paper liners in muffin tins. Then you'd only need to bake it for 20 minutes. Set the whole muffin tin in a bain marie (water bath) as above. To prevent a scalding water burn, use a turkey baster to remove the hot water from the pan. Also, if the custard cups might slide around when moving the pan in and out of the oven, try placing a thin tea towel (or nonstick shelving material) in the larger pan, and then add the water and custard cups. This prevents the cups from sliding or tipping.
- If you are doing a mega-session, then use just a basic Beige Sauce (see page 362; make a mega-batch for use in this and other recipes) and add the onion at the time of assembly. Simple.

Ratings

$ = 35¢
Ease = 6—because of the different bowls used and having to make a white (beige) sauce
Prep-time = 20 minutes
Heating = 35 minutes
Mega-Session = 10
Equipment = custard cups

Mega-Tasty Meat Loaf

I'll admit this recipe was not easy for me to write, but so many people have asked me for my meat loaf recipe that I decided to include it in this book. The reason that I struggled is because I didn't have a meat loaf recipe. I started the same way, but I'd add whatever I had on hand. This variation is the one the family said was best. I'm also including ways you can customize it or give yourselves a change. I form three meat loaves in my ring molds and the rest we make freeform (a combination of Options One and Two). The basic recipe is a general all-American version—oatmeal and all. See the alternatives for making meat loaves with personalities.

Do ahead:

- Purchase meat in bulk for best price. Call and get bids first.
- Tag this process on to other meat recipes.
- Make a dozen or so meat loaves and freeze for baking another day.
- Buy and cook lots of bacon for this and other recipes (good substitutes are available for special diets).

X1 1 LOAF	X2 2 LOAVES	X8 8 LOAVES	
1 tablespoon	2 tablespoons	½ cup	Chopped parsley
1 tablespoon	2 tablespoons	½ cup	Oregano flakes
1 tablespoon	2 tablespoons	½ cup	Chopped chives
½ teaspoon	1 teaspoon	4 teaspoons	Tarragon
½ teaspoon	1 teaspoon	4 teaspoons	Salt [mol]
½ teaspoon	1 teaspoon	4 teaspoons	Pepper [mol]
½ teaspoon	1 teaspoon	4 teaspoons	Kelp powder
½ teaspoon	1 teaspoon	4 teaspoons	Thyme
1 pound	2 pounds	8 pounds	Ground beef (best you can afford)
1 pound	2 pounds	8 pounds	Ground turkey
½ pound	1 pound	4 pounds	Ground sausage (your favorite)
1 cup	2 cups	8 cups	Cooked oatmeal
2	3	16	Eggs (whole) [mol]
1 12-ounce can	2 12-ounce cans	1 6-pound, 10-ounce can	Tomato paste (or use homemade)
½ cup	1 cup	4 cups	Chopped onions
½ cup	1 cup	4 cups	Chopped bell peppers
½ teaspoon	1 teaspoon	4 teaspoons	Worcestershire sauce
½ pound	1 pound	4 pounds	Bacon, cooked and crumbled (optional)

Pre-steps:

Cook the bacon (in the microwave or in a skillet). Drain and crumble. Cook the oatmeal (or use leftovers). To add extra richness, cook the oatmeal in milk instead of water. Cool in the refrigerator.

Steps:

1. In a small bowl toss together all dry spices: parsley, oregano, chives, tarragon, salt, pepper, kelp, and thyme. Set aside.
2. In a huge bowl, drum, or clean sink, combine all of the ground meat together. (The best way I know is with fingers and strong arms, so Alan does this for me. To be considerate, I do allow the meat to sit out for an hour to remove the chill. It is hard to "goosh" when your hands are cold. As he mixes, I pour in the other ingredients.)
3. Add the cooled oatmeal. Continue mixing.
4. Add the eggs and mix well.
5. Add the tomato paste, onions, and bell peppers, and mix until smooth.
6. Sprinkle in the spices and Worcestershire sauce. I do this as he gooshes so we get a more even distribution. (Please note that x8 is a lot of food to move around.)
7. Add the bacon bits and mix evenly.

OPTION 1: FORM LOAVES AND FREEZE, BAKE ON DAY OF SERVING

8. If you are doing this all yourself, have sheets of waxed paper ready to use. It is very difficult to tear off sheets of waxed paper when your hands are covered in meat loaf mix.
9. Form the mix into loaves on waxed paper. We shape all the meat loaves so that we know we've distributed the mix evenly. (You could measure out about 8 cups of mix each. Depending on the ingredients you included, the volume will differ.)
10. Wrap freeform loaves in waxed paper, then, in either aluminum foil or plastic wrap, place flat in the freezer. Freeze solid. Once frozen solid, pack tightly with the other food. (Wrap in waxed paper first because the tomato sauce will react with the aluminum foil, plus it is very difficult to remove plastic wrap from a frozen meat loaf. The waxed paper solves both these problems.
11. Thaw the meat loaf in the refrigerator by placing on a flat plate and covering with plastic or placing in an airtight container.
12. Place the thawed meat loaf on a rack in a shallow baking dish. Bake at 350°F for 1 hour. (This works for meat loaves formed with about 8 cups of mix. If you vary the size of your meat loaves up or down, adjust the time for baking accordingly).

OPTION 2: FREEZE IN MOLDS AND BAKE ON DAY OF SERVING

8. Divide the meat loaf into plastic molds. (Plastic salad molds work nicely. The ring-shaped plastic separates easily from the molded mix, making a very attractive meat loaf.)
9. Freeze solid. Once frozen solid, pop it out of the mold and bag or wrap. Continue freezing.
10. Place the molded loaf in a flat dish. (A quiche pan works perfectly.) Thaw in the refrigerator overnight.
11. Bake at 350°F for 1 hour or according to the size of your loaf.

OPTION 3: FREEZE IN "GLOB" FORM AND SHAPE, THEN BAKE ON DAY OF SERVING

8. Divide the meat loaf mix into equal portions.
9. Either bag (use bag-in-box method) or place in airtight plastic containers. Label. Freeze.
10. Thaw in the bag or container in the refrigerator.
11. Once thawed, shape on a shallow baking dish.
12. Bake at 350°F for 1 hour or according to the size of your loaf.

OPTION FOUR: SHAPE AND BAKE LOAVES AND SIMPLY REHEAT ON DAY OF SERVING

8. Spray several baking dishes or line with aluminum foil for easy clean up.
9. Shape meat loaves and place in baking dishes. Since you'll be mega-baking, you can squeeze two loaves side-by-side on a standard 13 x 9-inch baking pan.
10. Bake at 350°F for 45 minutes (if you'll be completing the baking another day. If you want to use these as-is—for sandwiches or other dishes—then bake the whole hour.)
11. Cool in the refrigerator.
12. Wrap. Label. Freeze.
13. To reheat, thaw, then bake at 350°F for 15 minutes.

Alternatives:

Salsa Meat Loaf: Use salsa instead of tomato paste. Add cilantro to the dry spices (same amount as parsley).

Roquefort Meat Loaf: Use blue cheese or Roquefort dressing instead of the tomato paste. Add Parmesan cheese (same amounts as the bell pepper).

Risotto Meat Loaf: Double the amount of oregano. Substitute cooked rice for the oatmeal. Add Parmesan cheese (same amounts as the bell pepper). Pour Italian dressing over it as it bakes. Serve with Noodles Alfredo or a bowl of risotto rice.

Dressed-up Meat Loaf: Substitute dry stuffing mix soaked in milk or broth for the oatmeal (same amount of liquid as oatmeal recipe calls for—the stuffing mix should completely absorb the liquid.) It may sound odd, but try adding a can of whole-berry cranberry sauce—it is delicious.

Wonderland Meat Loaf: Add mushrooms (same amount as bell peppers). Alice ate mushrooms to grow and shrink. You could complete the theme by adding oysters, as in The Walrus and the Carpenter. (My children won't eat oysters, so I don't include them; you could also substitute clams.)

Crunch and Munch Meat Loaf: Substitute corn flakes for the oatmeal. Add equal amounts of crispy rice cereal. Don't soak. Make a "crust" with crushed corn flakes by rolling the shaped meat loaves in flakes and some crispy rice cereal before baking or freezing. Bake as usual. Depending on your children's tastes, they might like this even more if you double the amount of cereal added.

"Very easy."—Linnea Rein
"Taste for an adult: '10.'"—BonnieJean P. Wiebe

Additional Helps and Suggestions

- BonnieJean P. Wiebe had a good idea: She mixed her meat loaf in her sink. First, she put a baggie over the drain cover and placed it back in the sink. That sealed the cover, so the meat never touched the drain itself. That helped with clean-up and was a good solution for any sanitation concerns.
- Linnea Rein had a great idea: Use a 6-ounce can of tomato paste and add ½ cup of unsweetened applesauce. Omit the thyme and tarragon.
- This is one recipe we make every mega-cook, because it fits so well into a mega-session. Let me walk you through it so you can make the variations easily. I set out 8 large containers (dish tubs, upside down cake takers, punch bowls, whatever I have). You might want to label each bowl so you can remember easily. We then throw in the ingredients. For example, we'll put 2 pounds (approximately, I don't measure exactly, I just "eyeball" it) of ground beef into each bowl. Then 2 pounds of ground turkey. Then 1 pound of sausage. We then only add the oatmeal to the variations that call for oatmeal (not Risotto, Dressed Up, or Crunch and Munch). We dump the cereal into the one for Crunch and Munch, the dressing into the Dressed Up, and the cooked rice into the Risotto. We continue like this for each ingredient. Then when all the ingredients are in their corresponding containers, Alan "gooshes" each one and bags it after labeling it properly. He moves to the next one. It takes us about an hour to get all the ingredients in the bowls. Then it takes him an hour to goosh, bag, and label all of them. But then we have 32 meatloves in the freezer, ready to thaw and bake—and they have eight different flavors. I wouldn't recommend you start at this level, but if you can follow the logic, you'll see that it is a good use of time. It's very efficient and not really very complicated.
- Even if you already have a favorite meat loaf recipe, you can use these same mega-processing ideas to make your work more efficient and time-saving. Also, you might want to try some of these variations with your recipe.
- One tester said that cooking the bacon was the most time-consuming part of this recipe. You can omit the bacon, or cook it while you're working on something else. Use the microwave and work in cycles. While a trayful is cooking, work on another recipe or another aspect of this recipe.

Ratings

$ = 45¢—depending on variation
Ease = 6
Prep-time = 1 to 2 hours for a huge batch and multiple variations
Heating = 1 hour
Mega-Session = 10—this recipe is ideal for a mega-session or for mega-batching
Equipment = large containers for mixing, large grill/skillet to cook bacon

Pirozhki

(SMALL MEAT-FILLED PASTRIES)

These little pastries work well for a snack, appetizer, covered dish item, buffet item, or as a main course. If we use these for a main course, I serve them with a hearty soup. To stay in the Russian-mode, serve with cabbage-based soup. Pirozhkis are some work to make. That's why I like to make a mega-batch and keep them in the freezer for a variety of purposes. I never know when Alan's going to have a "Oh, honey, we're having a party tomorrow at the office and I said I'd bring . . ." If you don't have the time to make all the pastries at one time, you can freeze the dough in balls (to be rolled out another time) or in circles (ready for filling). The filling also freezes well.

Do Ahead:

- Bulk purchase as many of the ingredients as you are able.
- Assembly-line cook the ground meat for this and several other recipes.
- Make X8 of the pastry and use for this and other recipes (it freezes well).

Pastry

X1	**X2**	**X8**	
4 SERVINGS	8 SERVINGS	32 SERVINGS	8 TO 10 PIROZHKIS PER SERVING
¾ cup	1½ cups	6 cups	Butter, softened
2 cups	4 cups	16 cups	Flour
1 teaspoon	2 teaspoons	3 tablespoons	Salt
½ cup	1 cup	4 cups	sour cream

Steps:

1. Mix the flour and salt together.
2. Cut the butter into the flour until it is the size of small peas.
3. Stir in the sour cream.
4. Mold the dough into balls (4, 8, 32 for x1, x2, and x8 respectively).

OPTION 1: MAKE ALL THE PASTRIES AT ONE TIME

5. Place the balls in an airtight container and refrigerate. Make the filling now and freeze, or make it on the day of baking.
6. Remove one ball at a time. Keep the rest in the refrigerator. Repeat the process until you've made as many as you need.
7. Roll the dough out to ⅛-inch thickness. Cut with a 3-inch circle. (I get between 8 and 10 per rolled out ball or circle.)
8. Fold one side of the pastry circle over the filling. Bring over the two sides and seal the top. It looks like a round envelope. To seal, you'll want to dampen your fingertips and press gently.
9. Prepare cookie sheets by spraying them with nonstick spray or use Teflon® sheet.

10. Place stuffed pirozhkis, seam-side down on cookie sheets.
11. Bake at 400°F for 15 to 20 minutes.
12. Serve. Freeze extra pirozhkis on cookie sheets covered with plastic wrap. Once completely frozen, slide them off the cookie sheet and into a bag. Since they were frozen individually, you can thaw and serve as many as you need for a given occasion.
13. Reheat by baking at 350°F for 10 minutes.

OPTION 2: STORE THE PASTRY DOUGH IN BALL FORM FOR USE AT ANOTHER TIME

5. Freeze balls in airtight bags. Label.
6. Thaw as many bags as you need and follow directions above.

OPTION 3: STORE THE PASTRY CIRCLES FOR FILLING ANOTHER TIME

5. Place the balls in an airtight container and refrigerate. Make filling (see below).
6. Remove one ball at a time. Keep the rest in the refrigerator. Repeat the process until you've made as many as you need.
7. Room the dough out to ⅛-inch thickness. Cut with a 3-inch circle.
8. Using a teaspoon or melon ball scoop, place a scoop of filling in the middle of each circle.
9. Lay pastry circles on waxed paper and freeze. Assembly-line this process using several trays or cardboard flats. While rolling out new circles, freeze a batch. It doesn't take long to freeze.
10. When the circles are completely frozen, place them in containers. Label. Continue freezing until use.
11. Remove as many circles as you need. Thaw flat on waxed paper.
12. Follow filling and baking instructions above.

Filling

X1	X2	X8	
½ pound	1 pound	4 pounds	Ground meat, cooked and crumbled
½ cup	1 cup	4 cups	Onion, finely chopped
2	3	16	Eggs, hard-cooked and chopped
1 teaspoon	2 teaspoons	3 tablespoons	Parsley flakes
1 teaspoon	2 teaspoons	3 tablespoons	Dill weed [mol] adjust to family's preferences
½ teaspoon	1 teaspoon	4 teaspoons	Salt
Dash	½ teaspoon	4 teaspoons	Pepper

Steps:

1. In a small bowl mix the spices and herbs together.
2. Sprinkle the spices/herbs over the meat. Toss.
3. Stir in the eggs and onions.

FILLING OPTION 1: MAKE ALL THE PASTRIES AT ONE TIME

4. Place filling in airtight container in the refrigerator and remove a cupful at a time to use as you make the pirozhkis.
5. Follow directions above.

FILLING OPTION 2: STORE THE FILLING FOR USE ANOTHER TIME

1. Divide the filling into one-cup amounts.
2. Bag, label, and freeze.
3. Thaw and use in processing as described above in Pastry Options Two or Three above.

Serving Suggestion: If I serve these as an appetizer or on a buffet, I make several different sauces to serve with these. My favorites with this recipe are Honey Mustard sauce (see page 385), apricot sauce, and as odd it may sound, just good old American BBQ sauce.

"We all loved them."—Patricia A. Hastings
"Even my son, 'Mr. Picky,' had seconds."—Lauren Down

ADDITIONAL HELPS AND SUGGESTIONS

- Patricia Hastings found that it goes a lot smoother if you make the dough balls and filling earlier in the morning. Then at about 4:30 or 5:00 P.M. have the kids help seal them into little bundles. Her 5 year-old had a ball doing this with her. She also liked that you probably already have these ingredients in your home.
- Pam Bianco served Pirozhkis with spaghetti sauce over them. She froze the remainder to microwave and serve to her husband after work for a snack. She substituted evaporated milk for the sour cream in the pastry.
- Lauren Down used the "x2" recipe. She did the meat during a mega-session, but rolled the pastry the next day. Filling and folding takes the longest time, but it sure is worth it. Her "x2" recipe yielded 72 pirozhkis. They had some for dinner and she saved the rest for a dinner party. She plans to try making some with sausage.
- Becky Turner said they were very good, but that they did need a dipping sauce. Also, she said that dill isn't a favorite with her family. So, if your family doesn't like dill, leave it out or substitute a spice they do like.
- Cindy Munger's son had these with other fillings in Russia. She said a variety of fillings would be fun. So, you can be as creative as you like with this basic recipe. She used game meat for filling.
- For special diets, you can omit the eggs in the filling and it still is delicious.
- Joan Parker used a pastry blender for the dough. She also used a cookie dough dropper for the filling.

Ratings

$ = 5¢—per pirozhki
Ease = 5—lots of work, but worth it

Prep-time = 1 to 2 hours—depending on how many you are making
Heating = 15 to 20 minutes
Mega-Session = 8—make filling during a mega-session, but give yourself more time to make them—finish up on another day
Equipment = mixer to make dough, pastry cutter

Porkie Pines

I wasn't ready for the response I received for this meal. The children all gave two thumbs up. Trent, who is my difficult to please eater, really likes these. I think they are his favorite meal. So, if Trent likes these, other children will, too. I originally got the idea from some friends in Amish country in Pennsylvania. We adjusted the ingredients to our liking, mega-batched, and added it to our "include every time list." Because of the "jagged edges" from rice, they look (if you use your imagination) like rolled up porcupines, or as baby Bethany said, "Porkie pines."

Do Ahead:

- Buy the ground meat in bulk. (Keep in raw state, do not pre-cook.)
- Buy rice in bulk. (We buy several types and make our own rice medley.)
- Buy and prepare the vegetables in bulk.

X1 Makes 10	X2 Makes 20	X8 Makes 80	
1 pound	2 pounds	8 pounds	Ground meat (beef or turkey or . . .)
4 slices	8 slices	1 loaf	Bread (of course, the better the bread, the better this recipe is.)
1	2	8	Eggs, beaten
1 cup	2 cups	8 cups	Milk (your choice of grade)
1 cup	2 cups	8 cups	Chopped onions
2 ribs	4 ribs	1 stalk	Celery, chopped (optional)
2	4	8 to 16	Carrots, chopped (optional)
¼ cup	½ cup	2 cups	Uncooked rice
1 teaspoon	2 teaspoons	3 tablespoons	Salt [mol]

Pre-steps:

Prepare the vegetables. Keep in raw form. Do not precook. Make homemade whole bread, if you desire. Or this works well for hard, or less than fresh bread.

Steps:

1. In a large bowl crumble the bread and soak in milk.
2. Add the beaten egg to the milk/bread mixture.
3. Mix in the remaining other ingredients. (Very similar to "gooshing" meat loaves.)
4. Shape into 2½-inch meatballs (between the sizes of golf and tennis balls). (You can vary this size according to your family's preferences, just adjust the cooking time accordingly.)
5. Lay the meatballs so they don't touch each other on plastic wrap-lined cookie sheet(s). Gently cover with a layer of plastic wrap (film) and freeze.
6. When the meatballs are frozen solid, rewrap/bag them all in one big bag or rewrap/bag them in

meal-sized portions. Because you froze them individually, you can reach in the bag and pull out just the number you need for dinner. (Same method we use for grapes, see page 118)

Serving

2 to 4 cups	4 to 8 cups	16 to 32 cups	Tomato juice or vegetable juice (I use a generic brand of popular juice made from 8 vegetables.)

7. Thaw as many meatballs as you need for the meal. Lay them in a shallow oven pan (2 to 3 inches deep) that you have prepared with a nonstick method. Pour 1 cup of juice over the meatballs. (Ratio 1 cup of juice per 4 meatballs.) The juice should come at least half way up the side of the meatballs.
8. Bake uncovered at 350°F for 1 hour and 30 minutes.

Alternative way to pre-prepare: Instead of freezing the raw meatballs, you can pre-bake (same directions as Steps 7 and 8) all of them at one time, then freeze them in meal-sized portions in their "vegetable juice gravy." Then thaw and simply re-heat either by microwave or oven. I prefer the freezing-raw method because when I mega-cook so many recipes at one time, I try to minimize the amount of heat to remove from my food. I'm having to balance out the demand on my freezer's ability to "freeze" so many entrees at one time. I just remember to serve on a day I'm home and have 1½ hours before dinner for them to bake. It is a trade-off between saving time or electricity. If you're only mega-cooking one recipe at a time, then either method would work well.

"The whole family loved this! A winner at our house! We'll be using this recipe regularly!"—Lauri Swanbeck

Additional Helps and Suggestions

- Lauri Swanbeck used a food processor to finely chop the onions, which helps to get the onion into recipes unnoticed by finicky children. Works great!
- Linda Bacon grinds her own chicken breasts or turkey.
- Lynn Nelson felt there was too much bread in it, so the meatballs were very soft. Otherwise, good! (Jill: we experimented and found that the type of bread you use does really change this recipe. When I use my homemade "Daily bread" it comes out perfectly. If you are using off-the-shelf white, you might want to reduce the bread and milk.)
- Sarah Heggie used brown rice and found it works as well as white rice. She also used rice milk instead of regular milk. She experimented using a combination of TVP and ground beef.
- Joanna Bakers' family has always preferred her oatmeal meat loaf to her bread crumb loaf—so she assumed the same for this recipe. They loved it. She's not sure about the difference in cost—bread versus oatmeal—but the difference in taste and texture makes the difference for her family. Also, she found that she needed more vegetable juice to cover half way up the meatballs. (Jill: You'll have to adjust that figure according to your pan. I like to use more because we then use it as "gravy" over a side dish of rice.)

Ratings
$ = 50¢
Ease = 8
Prep-time = 30 minutes
Heating = 1 hour and 30 minutes
Mega-Session = 10
Equipment = food processor to chop up vegetables helps

Puffed Stuff

Like so many of the other recipes in this book, this one can be pre-prepared in several different ways. My favorite method to fit in with a mega-cooking weekend is Options 1 or 2. But if I choose to make this recipe on an "as-I-cook" method, then Option 3 works best. Use the option that works best with your lifestyle, keeping in mind the amount of storage space you have and the size of your equipment and dishes. You could bake this as one large puff, but I've found that it doesn't freeze and reheat as well as it does if I make individual puffs. Use either muffin tins or individual molds. This meal looks so good with a little creative presentation that you'll want to serve it to company.

Do Ahead:

- Purchase, cook, and crumble ground meat in bulk.
- Purchase any of the other ingredients in bulk.
- Make soft breadcrumbs ahead and use in several recipes, or freeze for future use.

X1	X2	X8	
18 PUFFS	36 PUFFS	144 PUFFS	2 PUFFS PER SERVING
2 cups	4 cups	16 cups	All-purpose flour
1 tablespoon	2 tablespoons	½ cup	Baking powder
1 teaspoon	2 teaspoons	3 tablespoons	Salt [mol]
¼ teaspoon	½ teaspoon	2 teaspoons	Pepper [mol]
2 cups	4 cups	16 cups	Beaten eggs
2 cups (1 pint)	4 cups (1 quart)	16 cups (1 gallon)	Milk
3 tablespoons	⅓ cup	1½ cups	Butter, melted
1 pound	2 pounds	8 pounds	Ground meat, cooked and crumbled (beef, turkey, ham, chicken, sausage, or a combination
1 cup	2 cups	8 cups	Diced carrots

Steps:

1. In a large bowl whisk together the flour, baking powder, salt, and pepper.
2. In a separate bowl beat together the eggs, milk, and melted butter. (For the larger batches, you'll want to use your mixer.)
3. Add the egg mixture to the flour mixture.
4. Add the cooked meat and carrots.

OPTION 1: MAKE MIX, FREEZE IN "GLOB" FORM FOR SHAPING DAY OF BAKING

5. Divide into meal-sized amounts.
6. Bag, label, and freeze.
7. Thaw.

8. Press into sprayed molds or muffin tins.
9. Bake at 350°F for 25 minutes.

OPTION 2: FREEZE IN SHAPE AND BAKE DAY OF SERVING [YOU CAN USE PLASTIC MOLDS FOR FREEZING.]

5. Press into sprayed molds or muffin tins.
6. Wrap the entire dish in heavy-duty film.
4. Freeze.
7. As soon as it is frozen solid, pop out of the mold and bag or rewrap. Do this quickly; you don't want it to thaw. Continue freezing until use. Once frozen, bag dozens of puffs together. When you're ready to use them, you can pull out as many as you need.
8. On the day of serving spray the mold with nonstick spray. Remove the puffs from freezer and replace in the mold.
9. Bake at 350°F for 25 minutes.

OPTION 3: FORM AND BAKE, THEN FREEZE AND SIMPLY RE-HEAT [SINCE YOU'LL BE BAKING IN THESE MOLDS, THEY HAVE TO BE OVEN-READY.]

5. Press into sprayed molds or muffin tin.
6. Bake at 350°F for 25 minutes.
7. Enjoy one for dinner that night and freeze the rest, or bag and freeze them all. Be careful not to break the shape. I carefully place them in a large bag that I have placed on a cookie sheet or flat piece of cardboard. I slide the cardboard with bagged puffs onto a freezer shelf. Making certain it is level. Once it is frozen solid, I can move it around in the freezer and pack it tightly with other food.
8. To serve: Remove from the bag and place on a shallow baking dish (spray it first). Heat at 350°F for 10 to 15 minutes.

Note about Option 3: It could turn out dry if over-cooked or not handled properly. If you use this option, be sure to serve it with a delicious sauce like Holidays Sauce (see page 375) or sweet and sour sauce, or a delicious home-made gravy—which, of course, you can pre-make months ahead.

> "This was a huge hit with the children, which inspired me that it would be a great way to get more vegetables in them."—Amy Beatty
> "We all loved this! WOW! So easy to make and the leftovers are great for lunch the next day."—Sandy Farrar

Additional Helps and Suggestions

- Kellie Coombs remarked that the "batter" is soupy! She's right. Don't expect a "meat loaf" type batter. It will pour. She also found that her husband doesn't like the "meat" taste. She liked it, as did her son and daughter. She's going to try it with sausage.

- Amy Beatty suggested that it would work well without the meat as a side dish with lots of veggies or as a vegetarian entrée.
- Sandy Farrar will also try this recipe using a frozen mixed vegetable in place of the carrots. They used chicken as the meat. They may also try chicken with broccoli (like a chicken casserole). She used Mrs. Dash as a seasoning.

Ratings

$ = 25¢
Ease = 10
Prep-time = 15 minutes
Heating = 25 minutes
Mega-Session = 10
Equipment = muffin tins

Rosa's Con Pollo

(YELLOW RICE AND CHICKEN)

Yellow rice and chicken is one of our family's favorites. I didn't really learn how to make it until we moved to Central America, where it is a staple. Each family we met had their own version. This recipe is a little bit of this family's and a little bit of that family's. In Latin America, the dish is called Arozas con Pollo. We renamed it to honor Rosa, a maid that became a Christian sister. This recipe is very easy and tasty. The "trick" is steaming it after it has been frozen. (Pollo is pronounced "poh-l'yoh.")

Do Ahead:

- Purchase, cook, and dice turkey in bulk to use in this and other recipes.
- Purchase as many of the other ingredients in bulk as possible.
- Assembly-line process the preparing of produce with other recipes.

X1 6 SERVINGS	X3 18 SERVINGS	X6 36 SERVINGS	
3 cups	6 to 9 cups	9 to 18 cups	Diced cooked turkey [mol] or chicken
1	2	3	Onions, chopped [mol]
1	2	3	Bell peppers, chopped (any color, or mixed)
1 large can	2 large cans	1 6-pound, 10-ounce) can	Kernel corn, or equivalent fresh or frozen
1 1-pound pkg.	3 1-pound pkgs.	6 1-pound pkgs.	Yellow rice (saffron included; see note)
1 cup	2 cups	3 cups	Chopped or sliced black olives (optional)
1 4-ounce jar	2 4-ounce jars	3 4-ounce jars	Pimiento pieces (optional)
2 tablespoons	6 tablespoons	12 tablespoons	Lemon juice
1 cup	3 cups	6 cups	Breadcrumbs [mol]

Note: MSG is not acceptable to me or to many families, so read the package of yellow rice carefully. Some manufacturers use MSG as a flavoring. There are several alternatives:

1. Buy a healthful brand that doesn't contain MSG. (As more and more of us refuse MSG, manufacturers will remove it.)
2. Make your own mix using saffron. Add 1 to 2 teaspoons per multiple (1 to 2; 3 to 6; 6 to 12).
3. Make your own mix using turmeric (less expensive than saffron). Add 1 to 2 teaspoons per multiple (1 to 2; 3 to 6; 6 to 12). Healthy, whole grain rice works great in this recipe. Change the ingredient amounts to x 1: 2 cups, x3: 6 cups, x6: 12 cups of whole grain rice. The amount of water that works well for steaming is 3 cups, 9 cups, 18 cups.

Steps:

1. Prepare the meat: bake, chop turkey meat, or debone chicken.
2. Chop the onions and bell peppers. Steam them, if your family prefers them soft. Remember, onions and peppers freeze better in their "raw" state.
3. Prepare the corn, if using fresh or frozen.
4. In a large pot cook the rice according to the package instructions. If you have leftover broth from the poultry, use it and add water to equal the required amount.
5. Open cans. Chop the olives, if necessary. (Chopped olives are usually cheaper.)
6. Add the chicken, onions, peppers, corn, olives, pimiento, lemon juice, and breadcrumbs.
7. Serve.

FOR MULTIPLE BATCHES:

8. Divide the remaining rice into meal-sized portions. Label. Freeze using the Bag-in-Box method.
9. Thaw in the refrigerator.
10. You can heat this using several methods:
    a. The best heating method for this and most rice dishes is to steam it back to "life." First, thaw the rice in the refrigerator overnight. Then place the rice in a steamer and heat through. (See below.) Be sure to monitor the water level.
    b. Thaw the rice in the refrigerator overnight. Cook in the microwave for 10 to 20 minutes on medium high, covered. Check after 10 minutes. This method is not quite as good as steaming.
    c. You can bake it, but it will dry out some, so add some water, and cover before baking.
    d. Steam the dish directly out of the freezer without thawing. It will take 30 to 45 minutes, depending on how large a block it is. Fluff it with a fork every 10 minutes so the cooked rice is moved to the side, leaving the frozen block exposed to the steam.

Additional Helps and Suggestions

- Tricia Watts added a few cloves of minced garlic.
- Melanie Fierro suggests that you top it with sliced green, red, and or yellow peppers to make a more attractive presentation.
- I buy a 6-pound, 10-ounce (#10) can of olives to use for this and several recipes (such as pizza). It is less expensive this way.
- I now have a wonderful countertop steamer, and I think it is my favorite kitchen aid. I use it more than I do the microwave oven. If you don't have a steamer appliance, you can rig one: Put the rice mix in a metal colander. Pour water into a Dutch oven to just below the bottom level of the colander. Place the colander over the water. Cover. You're making a "double boiler homemade steamer." Bring the water to a boil. The steam will fluff the rice back up. It's so easy Reed could cook this when he was 10 years old. It only takes about 5 to 10 minutes for the dish to be hot and fluffy.
- This is one of the easiest recipes we make. It is the most popular one for giving as a ministry meal for other families. You can alternate the extra ingredients (corn, pimiento, olives).

- As for side dishes, I like to serve it with homemade bread or tortillas, fresh fruit cup, and leafy green salad. I also like to serve this with a bean soup for the first course.

Ratings

$ = 50¢ (varies if you use turmeric, saffron, or packages; when I use whole grain rice and turmeric the cost goes down to 35¢

Ease = 10

Prep-time = Approximately one hour (depending on the rice you use and if youy have a food processor to help with the chopping)

Heating = 5 to 10 minutes

Mega-Session = 10

Equipment = Rice cooker would make this much easier; at least rig up a steamer system with a Dutch oven and colander

Seven Layer Dinner

This dish, though similar to other casseroles, has a distinctive style. Depending on the mold you use and how artfully you arrange the layers, it can be quite attractive. You can use your favorite ground meat or ground meat substitute. It works well for vegetarian meat-substitutes.

Do Ahead:

- Buy vegetables in bulk.
- Chop or slice vegetables assembly-line style.
- Buy ground meat or meat substitute in bulk.

X1 4 SERVINGS	X2 8 SERVINGS	X4 16 SERVINGS	X8 32 SERVINGS	
2 cups	4 cups	8 cups	16 cups	Sliced raw potatoes (use fresh)
2 cups	4 cups	8 cups	16 cups	Sliced carrots
½ cup	2 cups	4 cups	4 cups	Chopped celery [mol]
1 pounds	2 pounds	4 pounds	8 pounds	Ground meat (raw)
½ cup	1 cup	2 cups	4 cups	Diced onions
1 cup	2 cups	4 cups	8 cups	Green peppers (diced)
2 teaspoons	4 teaspoons	3 tablespoons	¼ cup	Salt [mol]
¼ teaspoon	½ teaspoon	1 teaspoon	2 teaspoons	Pepper
2 cups	4 cups	8 cups	1 6-pound 10-ounce can	Canned tomatoes (or fresh or home-canned)

Pre-steps:

Chop or slice the vegetables.

Steps:

1. Blanch the potatoes if you're going to freeze this recipe unbaked. (See below.)
2. Spray a mold or casserole dish with nonstick spray. (I use a variety of 2 to 3 quart molds to shape this dinner.) Or use a regular casserole dish lined with a Teflon® liner.
3. Line the bottom of the mold with potatoes.
4. Layer in this order: carrots, celery, hamburger, onion, green pepper.
5. Sprinkle salt and pepper on each layer as you build.
6. Pour the tomatoes over the mixture in the dish.
7. Freeze each mold. Once it is frozen solid, pop out and bag or wrap in heavy-duty film.

8. Thaw. Either place in the same mold (if it is ovenproof) or on a flat casserole dish/sheet. It should retain the shape of the mold.
9. Bake at 350°F for 2 hours.

Alternate method: Bake several casseroles all at one time, then freeze. Simply warm up casserole on day of serving. (Similar to method for Porkie Pines—see page 344.)

To blanch for this recipe: Place the potatoes in boiling water for 2 to 3 minutes. Remove the potatoes and place in ice water. This one step will give the potatoes a much better texture after you freeze and bake it. Note: For the best taste, bake the recipe using the alternate method and then simply reheat.

Alternative to blanching: You can use slices of previously baked potatoes. Bake (or microwave) the potatoes until halfway done. The potatoes will finish cooking through when you bake it. You can use fully baked potatoes (leftovers) in this recipe. Just be careful that you don't over-handle them so that they turn to mush.

Note: You'll want to treat the potatoes with brown away, if you are mega-processing lots of them and they will be exposed to the air for more than 15 minutes before they go into this recipe.

Note: You have to use fresh potatoes for freezing. Please see the Topics section for more details.

"Very easy!"—Lauri Swanbeck
"Nice to be loaded with veggies! Very easy to put together when mega-cooking."—Linda Bacon
"A big hit here! Will definitely be repeated!"—Leslie L. Smith

Additional Helps and Suggestions

- Lauri Swanbeck offered some good alternatives: Instead of ground beef, she used "LightLife Gimme Lean," which is a soy substitute. She used dehydrated onions and green peppers. Since her family doesn't care for cooked celery, they had celery sticks with the casserole instead. She suggested using half diced tomatoes and half tomato sauce.
- Sarah Hendrix suggested using a slight amount of ketchup in the meat layer if you like a more "meat loafy" version. Otherwise, the veggies were still flavorful and colorful. She served this entrée with Corn^2 Bread. "Yum!"

Ratings

$ = 50¢
Ease = 8
Prep-time = 20 to 30 minutes
Heating = 2 hours or 20 to 30 minutes for reheating
Mega-Session = 9
Equipment = food processor to help with cutting vegetables

S.O.S.

(SWEET POTATOES, ORANGE JUICE, AND SAUSAGE)

One year I had an overabundance of sweet potatoes, and played around with different ways to prepare them. I especially wanted some recipes that would make good lunches for the children (simple and easy to reheat). I served this for lunch one day after they had completed a unit study on Marconi, and before they took a bite they wanted to know what it was. When I told them it was sweet potatoes, orange juice, and sausage, they responded immediately with "S.O.S!" It has been one of their favorite lunches ever since.

Do ahead:

- Buy sweet potatoes by the bushel for great prices.
- Make lots of mashed sweet potatoes and freeze for side dishes.
- Make soft breadcrumbs ahead and use in several recipes, or freeze for future use.

X1 4 SERVINGS	X2 8 SERVINGS	X4 16 SERVINGS	
4	8	16	Sweet potatoes (medium-sized)
1 pound	2 pounds	4 pounds	Cocktail sausages
¼ cup	½ cup	1 cup	Orange juice
1 tablespoon	2 tablespoons	¼ cups	Brown sugar (optional)
2 tablespoons	¼ cup	½ cup	Butter
½ teaspoon	1 teaspoon	2 teaspoons	Salt

Steps:

1. Peel the sweet potatoes, and cut in large pieces.
2. Place sweet potatoes in a pot of water and boil for 10 to 15 minutes until soft.
3. Bake the sausages at 350°F for 10 minutes. Drain off any fat.
3. Mash the sweet potatoes with the orange juice, brown sugar, butter, and salt.
4. Add the cooked sausages.
5. Divide into meal-sized portions.

OPTION 1: FREEZE ALL FOR BAKING AND SERVING ANOTHER DAY

6. Store, label, freeze. (I use the bag-in-box-method.)
7. Thaw.
8. Pour into a casserole dish that has been sprayed with nonstick spray.
9. Bake at 350°F for 30 minutes until bubbly hot.

OPTION 2: BAKE ONE FOR DINNER AND FREEZE THE REST

6. Pour one dinner's worth into a casserole dish that has been sprayed with nonstick spray.

7. Bake at 350°F for 30 minutes until bubbly hot.
8. Store, label, and freeze the rest for other meals. (I use the bag-in-box-method.)
7. Thaw.
8. Pour into a casserole dish that has been sprayed with nonstick spray.
9. Bake at 350°F for 30 minutes until bubbly hot.

Note: I've written the above recipe according to popular American diet choices, but please note that we omit the sugar or butter and find it to be just as delicious. We've adjusted our taste buds so that we "jazz dishes up" by reducing or eliminating sugar and fat. Of course, you can "dull it down" by adding sweeteners and fat.

Sassy Sausage

X1	X2	X4	
4 SERVINGS	8 SERVINGS	16 SERVINGS	
4	8	16	Sweet potatoes (medium-sized)
1 tablespoon	2 tablespoons	¼ cups	Brown sugar (optional)
½ teaspoon	1 teaspoon	2 teaspoons	Salt
1 pound	2 pounds	4 pounds	Cocktail sausages
¼ teaspoon	½ teaspoon	1 teaspoon	Cinnamon
½ cup	1 cup	2 cups	Chunky applesauce

Steps:

Follow the directions for S.O.S., but substitute applesauce for the orange juice and add cinnamon.

"Dear husband and I love it with homemade bread!"—Kellie Coombs

Additional Helps and Suggestions

- Kellie Coombs used pineapple instead of applesauce in the Sassy Sausage. What a delicious idea! She did say that her kids didn't like it at all. It's the texture, not the taste. (Jill: My children like this, but I can see how it might not appeal to all children. This is one that adults rate very high!)

Ratings

$ = 45¢
Ease = 9
Prep-time = 20 minutes
Heating = 30 minutes
Mega-Session = 10
Equipment = mixer to help you mash potatoes

Spaghetti Sauce

I didn't include a recipe for spaghetti sauce in Dinner's in the Freezer!™ *because I figured most people already knew how to make it and they had their favorite versions. However, since then I've received so many letters from readers who want my recipe that I thought I'd include it here. There are dozens of recipes I use this basic spaghetti sauce in. I always make a mega-pot full. I have to laugh because on our honeymoon we stayed a few nights in a private condominium in the Florida Keys. Since it had a fully-equipped kitchen, I though I'd impress Alan with my culinary skill. We bought groceries. I made spaghetti. But of course I knew how to make it for a family of six, not a couple. We ate spaghetti-sauced dishes for days. Ah, if he only knew that was the start of mega-cooking . . . or is it that the honeymoon has never ended?*

Do ahead:

- Purchase as many ingredients as possible in bulk.
- Make the mega-batch and freeze sauce for use with dozens of recipes.
- Really go all out and process your own tomatoes.
- Team this recipe up with others during a mega-cooking weekend.

X1 MAKES 4 CUPS	**X2** MAKES 8 CUPS	**Mega-batch (x20)** MAKES ALMOST 4 GALLONS	
1 15-ounce can	2 15-ounce cans	2 6-pound 10-ounce cans	Tomato sauce
1 6-ounce can	1 12-ounce can	1 6-pound 10-ounce can	Tomato paste
2 tablespoons	¼ cup	2 cups	"Spicy Spaghetti Seasoning" (see note)
1 tablespoon	2 tablespoons	1 cup	Dried oregano
¼ cup	½ cup	5 cups	Chopped onions
¼ cup	½ cup	5 cups	Chopped bell peppers
¼ cup	½ cup	5 cups	Mushrooms
1 clove	2 cloves	20 cloves	Garlic, whole, just peeled
1 pound	2 pounds	20 pounds	Ground meat (combination of turkey and beef)

Note: If you can't find Tone's Presti's Spicy Spaghetti Seasoning at a wholesale club or restaurant supplier, make your own by combining dehydrated onions and bell peppers, garlic, basil, and parsley.

Steps:

1. In a Dutch oven stir together the tomato sauce and paste, and sprinkle in the spagetti seasoning and oregano. Stir well.
2. Add the onions, bell peppers, mushrooms, and garlic.
3. Bring to boiling over medium heat. Remember, tomato-based sauces have a very low boiling point, so stir often.

4. Reduce the heat to simmer.
5. Cover. Allow to simmer for 1 hour. (I pour some sauce off at this stage for pizza sauce, label, and freeze.)
6. Add the meat and simmer for 2 to 3 hours, stirring every 15 minutes.
7. Divide. Label. Freeze using the bag-in-box method.
8. Thaw. Heat in the microwave or on the stovetop by adding 1 cup of water to every 8 cups of sauce (or more water if you like thinner sauce).
9. Use in a variety of recipes.

Use for:

Spaghetti Sauce and Noodles: Boil noodles and toss with sauce. Serve with grated Parmesan cheese.

Spaghetti Noodle Casserole: Use leftover spaghetti sauce and noodles and place in a sprayed 13 x 9-inch pan. Cover with grated Parmesan and mozzarella cheeses. Heat until the cheeses melt. Delicious.

Mission Trip Lasagna: Add 3 cups of water to every 8 cups of spaghetti sauce. Then use your favorite lasagna recipe. Here's how to adapt it: Don't pre-cook the lasagna noodles. Rinse them in water and build your layers, alternating between noodles, sauce, and cheeses. We like to add some cooked vegetables (carrots, squash, etc.). Freeze. The noodles will absorb that extra water and then soften when you bake it. This method really saves work and you don't have to burn your fingers working with hot noodles.

Manicotti: Stuff manicotti shells with a mixture of half this sauce and half cheese and additional water (4:1 ratio). You don't need to boil the shells. They'll absorb the moisture from the sauce. Freeze. Bake in a casserole dish covered with more of this sauce diluted with water at the rate of 4 cups sauce to 1 cup water.

Pizza Sauce: See Step 5 above and use for Pizzas in a Minute, Personal Pizzas, and Pizza Turnovers recipes.

> "My dear husband is very picky about sauces and this is his favorite of the made at home variety!"—Becky Turner
> "I may never buy another jar of commercial spaghetti sauce!"—Pam Geyer
> "My family thought it was better than storebought and I have a very picky eater."—Suzi Walters.
> "My kids liked it—Quite a compliment because they have refused commercial spaghetti sauce over the last year."—Deborah Wilson

Additional Helps and Suggestions

- Susan L. Mehl said she could cut the simmer time by 1 hour and she added the meat immediately to the sauce.

- Becky Turner processed the cooked ground beef in the food processor for a few seconds. When added to the sauce it made the sauce seem much meatier. It's amazing.
- Carol Irby used only 10 pounds of ground meat and she added 12 cups of water. (Jill: I only add water to it when I'm reheating it or using in a recipe that I'll need a more liquid sauce. I don't want to waste freezer space on water.)
- Patricia Hastings used tomatoes that she grew herself and froze for later use!
- Suzi Walters had some good suggestions: Make a batch of sauce with Italian sausage, another with chicken, and another with hamburger before labeling and freezing. They added some olives to some of their sauce.
- Jill: The base recipe is a thick sauce concentrate. I dilute it with water depending on the application. For pizza sauce we use it straight; for lasagna we dilute at 8:3 ratio; for manicotti, 4:1 ratio; for regular spaghetti and noodles, 8:1 ratio.
- I buy a 6-pound, 10-ounce (#10) can of mushroom pieces, use half in this recipe, and freeze the rest in ½ cup amounts for use on pizza and in other recipes like Mushroom Turnovers (page 397).

Ratings

$ = 25¢
Ease = 8
Prep-time = 3 to 4 hours
Heating = 5 minutes
Mega-Session = 10
Equipment = large pot

Twenty-Third Psalm Pie

This recipe is a variation of an old Scottish dish, Shepherd's Pie. Children really enjoy this and it is very easy to prepare. Experiment with different meat: ground beef, ground turkey, chopped stew meat, etc.

Do ahead:

- Purchase and prepare (chop or grate) onions and carrots in bulk.
- Prepare homemade tomato soup (for possible use in several recipes or as a first course).
- Buy ground meat and cook in bulk.

X1 4 SERVINGS	X3 12 SERVINGS	X6 24 SERVINGS	
3 tablespoons	½ cup	1 cup	Chopped or grated onions
2 cups (1 lb)	6 cups (3 lbs)	12 cups (6 lbs)	Cooked and crumbled meat [mol]
⅔ cups	2 cups	4 cups	Sliced or cubed cooked carrots
1 cups	4 cups	6 cups	Tomato soup concentrate (canned or homemade)
Dash	1 teaspoons	2 teaspoons	Tabasco sauce [mol]
2 cups	6 cups	12 cups	Mashed potatoes (homemade is better, but instant will also be good)
Dash	Dash	Dash	Paprika for decoration and flavor

Pre-steps:

Grate or chop the onions (no need to sauté or cook). Cook the meat. Peel, chop or slice the carrots. Cook the carrots. (Options: boil for approximately. 4 to 5 minutes (until just barely softened), microwave with a little water 3 to 5 minutes, or steam for 5 minutes). This step is optional. Some families prefer their carrots heartier than others do. The baking will soften them up quite a bit. I've found for my own family that I don't have to pre-cook the carrots for freezer-batches.

Prepare homemade tomato soup, chill or use canned version. *Note:* One can of tomato soup concentrate equals about 1 cup. This recipe requires concentrated soup, so do not dilute.

Steps:

1. In a large bowl gently mix together all ingredients except the mashed potatoes and paprika. Be careful not to crush the carrots.
2. Divide into meal-sized portions.
3. Store, label, and freeze.

Serving:

Method I: Thaw. Place the meat mixture in a casserole dish. Place the mashed potatoes on top of the meat mixture. Sprinkle with paprika. Bake at 350°F for 20 minutes.

Method 2: Place the frozen meat mixture in a casserole dish. Bake at 300°F for 30 minutes. Top with mashed potatoes. Bake at 350°F an additional 10 minutes.

Method 3: Place the frozen meat mixture in a casserole dish. Cover with plastic film. Microwave on "thaw" for 30 minutes until thawed. Cook on high for approximately 1 minute per half-cup. Spoon on the potatoes, sprinkle with paprika, and microwave an additional 3 minutes. Serve.

Tips: Freeze the meat mixture in the shape of the casserole dish for easier heating on serving day. Sculpt or funnel the mashed potatoes on top of the meat mix in a pleasing pattern—you can make it look very fancy.

"Everyone liked it."—Dee Kimmel

Additional Helps and Suggestions

- Dee Kimmel likes to use her microwave, especially in the summer to keep the kitchen heat down.
- Patricia Peoples is diabetic and said that this recipe was O.K. She had some options: adding green beans and using "tomato and rice" soup.
- I don't recommend any other options for this recipe. The best way to go is to make the meat mix and then add the mashed potatoes on the day of serving. If you want to make this and serve it all on the same day, then skip steps 2 and 3. Place the meat mixture in the prepared casserole dish, top with the mashed potatoes, dust with paprika, and bake at 350°F for 20 minutes.

Ratings

$ = .50¢
Ease = 10
Prep-time = 20 to 30 minutes
Heating = 30 minutes
Mega-Session = 10
Equipment = food processor to help you chop vegetables

SAUCES, BUTTERS, AND SYRUPS

Beige Sauce

(BASIC "WHITE" SAUCE)

Basic white sauce is the start or beginning of so many recipes that knowing how to make it is fundamental to "from-scratch" cooks. Since I use whole-wheat flour, my sauce doesn't come out "white." It is more of a "beige" color. It might take your sensibilities a little while to adjust to beige sauce, but it is worth the journey out of your comfort zone. Because we like a thick, almost pudding-like white sauce, I almost always make the thick version. (See note about soups.)

Do ahead:

- Buy wheat in bulk or grind your own.
- Make mega-batches of this and freeze it in 1 to 2 cup portions for use in dozens of recipes.
- Vary this basic recipe as needed and freeze the variations.

X1	**X2**	**X8**	
4 SERVINGS	8 SERVINGS	32 SERVINGS	½ CUP SERVINGS
2 tablespoons	¼ cup	1 cup	Whole wheat flour
½ teaspoon	1 teaspoon	1 tablespoon	Salt
Dash	⅛ teaspoon	½ teaspoon	Pepper
2 tablespoons	¼ cup	1 cup	Butter (real butter, not any substitutes)
2 cups	4 cups	16 cups	Milk

Steps:

1. In a large bowl mix the flour, salt, and pepper.
2. In a saucepan (for x8 use a Dutch oven) melt the butter (don't let it burn) over medium or low heat. Don't remove the pan from the burner.
3. Stir the flour mixture into the hot butter. It will clump together and leave the edges of the pan.
4. Slowly pour in the milk and stir.
5. Cook, stirring constantly, until thickened, about 5 to 8 minutes.
6. Use in a recipe; or divide, label, and freeze for later use.

Variations: Add any of the following to the basic recipe (details to follow). If they are "dry ingredients," add to the flour/salt/pepper mixture before adding to the butter. If it is a "wet ingredient," add as the sauce thickens. Any of these can be used with the medium (above), thin, or thick versions.

X1	X2	X8	
¼ cup	½ cup	2 cups	Finely chopped onions
¼ cup	½ cup	2 cups	Chopped fresh tomatoes
1½ teaspoons	3 teaspoons	¼ cup	Curry powder (as hot as you like it)
⅛ teaspoon	¼ teaspoon	1 teaspoon	Ground ginger
1 teaspoon	2 teaspoons	3 tablespoons	Lemon juice
1 tablespoon	2 tablespoons	½ cup	Fresh cut dillweed
1 teaspoon	2 teaspoons	3 tablespoons	Dried dillweed
1½ teaspoons	3 teaspoons	¼ cup	Prepared horseradish (mol, depending on how much bite you want it to have)
¼ cup	½ cup	4 cups	Freshly chopped parsley
1 cup	2 cups	8 cups	Grated Cheddar cheese
¼ teaspoon	½ teaspoon	2 teaspoons	Dry mustard
¼ teaspoon	½ teaspoon	2 teaspoons	Each: basil, sage, tarragon, and rosemary
1 cup	2 cups	8 cup	Grated cheese, (your favorite. I use a mixture of Cheddar, mozzarella, and Jack), optional

Onion Sauce: Add onions as the butter melts. Proceed as above.

Tomato Serving Sauce: Add tomatoes as it thickens, after you've added the milk. Proceed as above.

Curry Sauce: Mix curry powder and ginger into the flour before adding to the butter. Proceed as above.

Dill Sauce: Stir in either fresh or dried dillweed and lemon juice into the butter/flour mixture before adding the milk. Proceed as above.

Horseradish Sauce: Stir in horseradish with the flour and add to melted butter. Proceed as above.

Parsley Sauce: Add parsley after step 5 above, when the sauce is "finished."

Cheddar Cheese Sauce: Just as the sauce finishes, stir in Cheddar cheese and dry mustard. Stir until completely melted. Serve.

Mixed Cheese Sauce: Just as the sauce finishes, stir in cheeses. Stir until completely melted. Serve.

Thin Beige Sauce

This would make more of a "soupy" sauce. Follow the same steps as above.

X1	X2	X8	
Makes 2 cups	Makes 4¼ cups	Makes 17 cups	
1 tablespoon	2 tablespoons	½ cup	Butter (real butter, not any substitutes)
1 tablespoon	2 tablespoons	½ cup	Flour
½ teaspoon	1 teaspoon	1 tablespoon	Salt
Dash	⅛ teaspoon	½ teaspoon	Pepper
2 cups	4 cups	16 cups	Milk

Thick Beige Sauce

More of a very thick gravy-like sauce. Follow the same steps as above.

X1	X2	X8	
3 tablespoons	⅓ cup	1½ cups	Butter (real butter, not any substitutes)
3 tablespoons	⅓ cup	1½ cups	Flour
½ teaspoon	1 teaspoon	1 tablespoon	Salt
Dash	⅛ teaspoon	½ teaspoon	Pepper
2 cups	4 cups	16 cups	Milk

Note about using white (beige) sauce as starter for soups: To freeze the soup and then use it as concentrate, make the thick beige sauce, then add water or milk the day of serving to make it more the consistency of soup. However, if serving the soup that day, make the thin beige sauce.

Creamed Soup

Make basic Beige Sauce (above).

Cream of Chicken Soup

As the sauce gently boils, sprinkle in powdered broth (I use a wonderful powder purchased through a co-op—rather than the salty bouillon cube available at many grocery stores.) Because I'm using a high quality broth, I use ½ cup of the powder for a mega-batch. You'll have to taste the soup to determine the potency of your broth. Remember: add little amounts. You can always add more, you can't remove it once it's mixed in. I also sprinkle in about 1 cup of finely diced turkey or chicken.

Option: For a more pronounced chicken flavor, use chicken broth for half of the milk: 8 cups of milk and 8 cups of broth.

This recipe is so delicious, I have even served it reheated from the freezer to company and they raved!

Cream of Vegetable Soup
Follow the same steps as for Cream of Chicken except use vegetable broth instead of chicken broth and sprinkle in chopped steamed vegetables. You can make:

Cream of Mushroom—add chopped mushrooms (you may substitute 1 or 2 cup(s) of mushroom juice for 1 or 2 cup(s) of milk if you're using canned mushrooms rather than fresh.

Cream of Asparagus—same as with mushroom, except use fresh or canned asparagus.

Cream of Corn—same as with mushrooms, except use fresh or canned corn (no chopping needed) and add a couple of cans of creamed corn.

Cream of your choice—same principles apply.

Extras: For those who want to add more flavor or to jazz up the soups, add some steamed onions, celery, or bell peppers to the soup. Warning: Some children don't like the added flavorings, so taste it first.

Cream of Tomato Soup
Follow the same steps as for Cream of Chicken Soup except add one small can of tomato sauce. Stir.

"Good! We used it for another recipe."—Nancy Rasmussen

Additional Helps and Suggestions
- Nancy Rasmussen noted that because of the use of butter (expense and nutrition) she only gave this recipe an 8/9 rating, but added that it really made it have a good flavor.
- Cheryl Lewis said she'd try using cornstarch or arrowroot flour in place of the flour. (Please see Topics section for an explanation about thickening agents.)
- Pamela Evans used powered milk. She added the milk solids to the flour and then added the water.
- Depending on my plans for the soup, I'll spice it up or down. If it is to be used in a recipe that calls for a "can of cream of ______" soup, I'll make just the basic recipe. If I'm making the soup as a first course, I'll jazz it up with "extras."
- These soups freeze well. I make the mega-batch and then divide and store the soup in freezer bags (formed in a leftover box to make a "soup brick"—the Bag-in-Box method).
- My favorite powdered broth is made by Frontier Herbs and is available at some grocery stores and co-ops. Tone's is available at most grocery stores. It has more flavorings than I usually like to use, but it makes a tasty soup. Of course, you can make your own broth powder via a dehydrator. I dehydrate my vegetables, then once they are completely dry, I chop them very fine into a powder using a blender. This powder is loaded with flavor and it's a great way to use up leftover vegetables.
- Once when we were mega-shopping, my supply of large cans of cream of _____ soups weren't available. To complete my menu and cooking I would have had to buy $26 worth of small cans. I

refused to pay that price. I figured if "they" could make cream of mushroom soup, so could I. So I started experimenting. The soups I've made are tastier than the canned, much less expensive, and only have the ingredients that I put in—no additives or preservatives or colorings or . . . . I like to keep a stock of soups in the freezer ready for sauces, casseroles, or as a first or second course. By adding cheese, I have a delicious cheese sauce for vegetables or potatoes. Many of these adaptations are in this book (above), while some are available in *Dinner's in the Freezer!™*

- Several of the mega-testers told me that it took them longer than 5 to 8 minutes for the sauce to thicken. One lady told me it took as long as 12 to 15 minutes. A single batch for me thickens up nicely in 5 minutes (a mega-batch in about 8 minutes) so I researched the issue and have added more information in the Topics section. Briefly—factors that affect the thickening are the type of flour used (whole-wheat in contrast to white), the quality of the pan, and the temperature. I use fresh whole-wheat flour, a top-of-the-line pan (that dispenses heat wonderfully) and medium heat, and the butter and flour are hot when I add the milk. (I did the same recipe in a lower-quality pan and it took me 8 minutes for the single recipe). I never remove it from the heat until it is thickened. I stir to disperse the heat evenly and to keep it from clumping.
- As I state in several places throughout the book, I use real butter. I don't like the way margarine tastes, cooks, or treats my body. I do often substitute Better Butter Spread (see page 370) for butter in most all of my recipes, except this one. It comes out too thin. You can experiment using oil for the butter in these recipes. It will affect the flavor, but it is an option you might prefer for health and economic reasons. Also note that using salted or unsalted butter will affect the taste. If you don't like salt, use unsalted butter and perhaps even reduce the salt in the recipe.

Ratings

$ = 10¢

Ease = 10—very basic recipe.

Prep-time = 15 minutes

Heating = 5 minutes

Mega-Session = 10 (We make "x8" or "x16" of the basic recipe and then use in dozens of recipes)

Equipment = Quality pots, wire whisk makes it easier to blend

Sauce with an Attitude

This variation of a basic white sauce has a zing. It makes a great starter for several recipes like Breakfast Pizza and some soups. It is also great on vegetables. Depending on which mustard you use, the sauce takes on a different flavor. My personal favorite variation is to use Dijon-type mustard for that added zip. I make up the "x8" batch, use what I need for that meal, and then freeze the rest in 2-cup amounts for later use. Adding cheese is optional and will make a different sauce. For use in other recipes in this book, see the index.

Do Ahead:

- Purchase all the other ingredients in bulk as you are able.
- Grate cheese if necessary.
- Make the sauce ahead and freeze for later use. It works for a variety of recipes.

X1 MAKES 2½ CUPS	X2 MAKES 5 CUPS	X8 MAKES 22 CUPS	
2 tablespoons	¼ cup	1 cup	Butter
2 tablespoons	¼ cup	1 cup	Flour
½ teaspoon	1 teaspoon	3 tablespoons	Salt
Dash	⅛ teaspoon	1 teaspoon	Pepper
½ teaspoon	1 teaspoon	1 tablespoon	Paprika
2 cups (1 pint)	4 cups (1 quart)	16 cups (1 gallon)	Milk
Dash	⅛ teaspoon	1 teaspoon	Tabasco
⅛ teaspoon	¼ teaspoon	1 teaspoon	Worcestershire sauce
1½ teaspoon	3 teaspoons	¼ cup	Prepared mustard
¼ cups	½ cups	4 cups	Grated cheese (your favorite, or mixture of Cheddar, mozzarella, and Monterey Jack) (optional)

Steps:

1. In a saucepan (for x8 use a Dutch oven) melt the butter (don't let it burn).
2. While the butter is melting, in a medium bowl mix the flour, salt, pepper, and paprika.
3. Stir the flour mixture into the butter. It should clump together and leave the edges of the pan.
4. Slowly pour in the milk and stir. Continue cooking over medium heat.
5. Stir and cook continuously until thickened, about 5 to 8 minutes.
6. In a small bowl mix together the Tabasco sauce, Worcestershire sauce, and mustard.
7. Add the mustard mixture to the thickened sauce and blend well.
8. If desired, stir in the cheese until smooth.
9. Use in a recipe or divide, label, and freeze for later use.

Variation: Once in a while, you'll need a really thick sauce that is more like a pudding. In that case, just double the amount of butter and flour. It will come out very thick.

Dragon Sauce

(reprinted here from *Dinner's in the Freezer!*™ with a few improvements)

We like the eggroll sauces served in restaurants. Some grocers carry a similar brand of duck sauce. However, it is expensive and loaded with sugar, MSG, and other additives. So I started experimenting with peaches. It paid off. This sauce is made with the leftover peach nectar from canned peaches. Because we aren't adding colorings it won't be the pretty peach or "red-dish" color like the store versions.

3 cups	Peach nectar/juice (syrup from canned peaches. Pineapple, apricot and/or plum juice/syrup also works well.)
3 tablespoons	Cornstarch (mol, more for a thicker sauce, less for a thinner sauce—we like a very thick sauce and use ⅓ cup)
¼ cup	Fructose or ½ cup sugar (optional)
¼ cup	Vinegar
1-2 tablespoons	Soy sauce
½ cup	Puréed peaches (optional)

1. In a shaker jar mix the cornstarch and 1 cup of the juice until the cornstarch is completely dissolved.
2. In a saucepan mix together the remaining juice and other ingredients.
3. Cook over medium heat until boiling.
4. Pour in the dissolved cornstarch and juice.
5. Stir constantly until thick and transparent, about 3 to 4 minutes.
6. Serve.
7. Freeze the remainder in meal-sized portions (or using ice cube trays)
8. Thaw and heat. (*Note:* Add a little water if necessary during reheating to reach the desired consistency.)

Note: I like to buy the 6-pound, 10-ounce can of peaches, make a cobbler, and reserve the syrup to use for this sauce. To make it extra rich blend some of the peaches until semi-liquid with small peach pieces visible. Add the purée to the sauce. This goes well with egg rolls, or over chicken and duckling. It's even delicious over rice.

About Sauce with an Attitude: "I loved the sauce."—Pam Jensen
About Dragon Sauce: "My kids thought it was great!"—Pam Geyer

Additional Helps and Suggestions

- Pam Jensen didn't have any Tabasco sauce so she substituted jalapeño pepper juice.
- Pam Geyer liked the Dragon Sauce with chicken nuggets! She said for an adult it was a little on the sweet side.
- You can certainly reduce the sugar in the recipe. I found that different brands of peaches affect the taste. Some peach processors add extra sugar in their canning process. If your peaches have sugar added, you shouldn't need to add any to this recipe.
- The Dragon Sauce will thicken in the refrigerator. If you are reheating it, plan on adding some extra water to reach the desired consistency.

Ratings

$ = 5¢
Ease = 8
Prep-time = 15 minutes
Heating = 5 minutes
Mega-Session = 7—I make sauces up another day and then use them with other recipes as I need them.
Equipment = whisk

Better Butter Spread

I was making my own "health-butter" by blending 1 cup of oil with 1 cup of soft butter (room temperature). Then I met Terri Metcalf at a Michigan homeschool convention. She was running her Nutriflex booth, educating ladies about flour and other health issues. Before I was scheduled to give a workshop, I was able to chat with Terri. I could have talked with her all day—she was a wealth of information. For instance, she told me of an even "better butter." She gave me permission to use the basic recipe. I've had fun making special spreads and experimenting with freezing it. You can substitute Better Butter Spread in any recipe in this book that calls for butter.

Do Ahead:

- Purchase all of the ingredients in bulk for the best prices.
- Make mega-batches and freeze for use in dozens of recipes.
- Tag team this in your blender when you make Daily Bread.

X1 Makes 2 cups	X2 Makes 4 cups	X8 Makes 16 cups	
½ cup	1 cup	4 cups	Water
½ cup	1 cup	4 cups	Canola oil
1 tablespoon	2 tablespoons	½ cup	Liquid lecithin
½ pound	1 pound	4 pounds	Butter, softened to room temperature

Steps:

1. In a blender pitcher, combine the water, oil, and lecithin.
2. Blend on high until the consistency of mayonnaise. Don't over blend.
3. Add the butter and blend well.

OPTION 1: MAKE A SINGLE BATCH FOR CURRENT USE

4. Refrigerate in a covered container. It will be the consistency of tub-margarine after refrigeration.

OPTION 2: MAKE MEGA-BATCHES AND FREEZE EXTRA FOR OTHER RECIPES

4. Repeat steps 1 through 3 until you've made as many batches as you need. (*Note:* My blender isn't large enough to make more than "x2" at a time.) Refrigerate in covered containers.
5. After the Better Butter Spread is set, you can freeze it.
6. Thaw in the refrigerator and use just as you would tub margarine or soft butter in recipes.

OPTION 3: MAKE BUTTER MEDALLIONS

4. After the Better Butter is set, push small amounts into a plastic candy mold (available at craft stores) or partially fill ice cube trays (it'll make a simple shape, but still nice). Freeze. Pop out and bag for later use. Then just before serving dinner, place this on the table, like a 5–star

restaurant with custom butter molds. They melt quickly, so we use a silver butter dish that has been in my family since the 1800's. It is made especially for this purpose. It has a glass tray for butter and a well for ice. You can find treasures like these in stores—many people don't know how to use them. Alternatively, make your own by placing a plate over a dish filled with ice.

The benefits of this recipe are: It tastes like butter, yet is more economical. It spreads easily right from the refrigerator. It is lower in total fat, saturated fat, cholesterol, and calories than regular butter. It contains no trans-fatty acids like margarine does.

Variations: (These amounts are for "x1." Adjust for larger batches.)

Honey Better Butter: Before you refrigerate (after step 4), stir in 1 cup of honey. This is delicious on hot toast.

Garlic Better Butter: Before you refrigerate (after step 4), stir in 1 teaspoon of garlic extract (juice).

Orange Better Butter: Use orange juice instead of the water. After step 4, stir in 1 tablespoon of grated orange peel.

Lemon Better Butter: Use ¼ cup lemon juice and ¼ cup water. After step 4, stir in 1 tablespoon of grated lemon peel.

Cinnamon Better Butter: After step 4, stir in cinnamon/sugar mixture (per batch: 1 tablespoon of cinnamon, 1 cup of confectioner's sugar).

Maple Better Butter: After step 4, stir in ¼ to ½ cup of maple syrup. Great on pancakes.

Herbed Better Butter: After step 4, add 1 tablespoon of (or a combination of): chives, parsley, sesame seeds.

Cheese Better Butter: After step 4, add ¼ cup of grated cheese.

Fruity Better Butter: After step 4, add ¼ cup of your favorite fruit preserves.

"Very easy!"—Cynthia Fisher

Additional Helps and Suggestions

- Terri Houchin noted that the thickening stage happens all of a sudden. It took her by surprise. She said that it was thinner than she expected at first, but it thickened up in the refrigerator.
- Cynthia Fisher orders lecithin through a catalog, so it's something she keeps in stock. She considered the cinnamon butter less attractive than regular butter—yet, she gave it a 10 rating for taste.

- Jill adds: Even if you don't want to make the Better Butter, you can flavor regular butter or margarine by following the same suggestions above and mixing with room temperature butter or margarine.
- I find it very easy to combine making Better Butter with making Daily Bread. I first make a batch of Better Butter and store it. Then instead of immediately cleaning out the blender pitcher, I pour in the warm water for the bread recipe and pulse a few times, then use that "buttery water" in the bread recipe. It rinses the blender well and doesn't waste any of the butter. The blender is much easier to clean, and the bread is a tad bit more creamy. I include this example to encourage you to think through many of the steps you take in the kitchen that could be combined or tag-teamed so clean up is easier or you don't waste ingredients. Much of mega-cooking™ works because we are combining steps to minimize workload and maximize ingredients.

Ratings

$ = 5¢ per 1 tablespoon serving (approximately); there are so many variables. It depends on where you buy your ingredients.
Ease = 9
Prep-time = 10 minutes
Heating = none
Mega-Session = 9 (good to make lots to then use in other recipes)
Equipment = a good blender

Brown Away

Some fruit changes color once it is cut. This isn't an aspect of the pigment, is due to the cut flesh being exposed to oxygen. The chemicals react with the oxygen and form a brown "polymer." Not very attractive. To stop this you have to either reduce any exposure to oxygen or stop that enzyme reaction by coating fruit with something like mayonnaise as in a salad or dip, or treating the surface with an acid such as citrus juice, apple juice, and some dressings, or use this Brown Away.

We keep a batch of this in a standard spray bottle. We spray all of our produce as we process it because we are processing so much (hundreds of pounds) and it is exposed to air before we get it into a recipe (the coating stage).

One other thing you can do with some produce is to immediately soak in water. It stops the air exposure. This is effective when working with potatoes. I still like to add some juice and food grade (35%) hydrogen peroxide to that water bath. There are commercial products that work well, also.

We have learned a great deal about food chemistry because of our special needs son and because we write cookbooks. One fascinating "ingredient" we've been studying is hydrogen peroxide (H_2O_2). It is in many raw foods. But as soon as some of them are processed, the hydrogen peroxide is lost. For instance, H_2O_2 is in fresh squeezed orange juice, but the pasteurizing process removes it and it definitely isn't prevalent in reconstituted versions. Hydrogen peroxide works as a great agent for keeping foods fresh and slowly down the browning process. We first learned of food grade (35%) hydrogen peroxide from some Amish families when I was speaking in Lancaster County, Pennsylvania. We have read several books and pamphlets and encourage you to research this important chemical if you're interested in health issues and food chemistry.

Considering all of the above, here is our new and improved Brown Away recipe:

X1	**X2**	**X4**	
Makes 1 cup	Makes 2 cups	Makes 4¼ cups	
1 cup	2 cups	4 cups	Water (purest you can afford)
1 tablespoon	2 tablespoons	4 tablespoons	Lemon juice
1 teaspoon	2 teaspoons	4 teaspoons	Food grade (35%) hydrogen peroxide (optional) Read safety issues, below, before buying

Steps:

1. Mix all the ingredients together.
2. Store in a spray bottle.
3. Spray any fruit or vegetables to slow the browning process.

Safety issues: Please note that you have to be very careful with food grade (35%) hydrogen peroxide. Keep it locked up in a freezer. Only store it in childproof containers. Diluted as in this recipe, it is beneficial. But if a child were to swallow it, there could be horrible effects. Treat it with respect. Ask your supplier about their advice for safety. Read the label and follow directions carefully. You could use off-the-shelf 3% grade—the "preserving" effect won't be as profound, but it will help some.

We buy our food grade (35%) hydrogen peroxide from a health food store or co-op. One quart has lasted us for years. We and other people use it for other applications such as mouth swishes, topical lotions, and swimming pool water purification alternatives.

Holidays Sauce

Though I've tried for years, I don't think it is possible to mega-cook and freeze Hollandaise sauce. The ingredients just don't freeze. Hollandaise sauce is so delicious and is used on so many recipes that I had to come up with a freeze-able substitute. This recipe is it. It has a similar flavor, a slightly different consistency, but you can mega-cook it, so it is worth the adjustment. Please note that you can't substitute faux-butter or margarine. Only real butter freezes well and makes this a smooth sauce.

Do Ahead:

- Buy flour in bulk or grind your own.
- Make mega-batches of this and freeze it in 1 to 2 cup portions for use in dozens of recipes.
- Make your own lemon juice from a box of lemons you can purchase at cut-rate prices.

X1	**X2**	**X8**	
Makes 2½ cups	Makes 5 cups	Makes 20 cups	
3 tablespoons	⅓ cup	1½ cups	Butter (real butter, no substitutes)
3 tablespoons	⅓ cup	1½ cups	All-purpose flour (though I rarely recommend it, this is one time I do use white flour)
2 cups (1 pint)	4 cups (1 quart)	16 cups (1 gallon)	Milk
3 tablespoons	⅓ cup	1½ cups	Lemon juice
2	4	16	Egg yolks (beaten)

Steps:

1. In a saucepan (for x8 use a Dutch oven) melt the butter (don't let it burn).
2. While the butter is melting, in a bowl beat together the lemon juice and eggs until creamy yellow in color.
4. Stir the flour into the butter. It will clump together and should leave the edges of the pan.
5. Slowly pour in a little milk and stir. Continue cooking over medium heat.
6. Slowly pour in a little of the lemon/egg mixture and stir. Continue cooking over medium heat.
7. Alternate between the milk and egg mixture until you've added all the liquids.
8. Cook, stirring constantly, until thickened about 5 to 8 minutes.
9. Use in a recipe or divide, label, and freeze for later use.
10. Reheat in the microwave or on the stovetop, stirring often.

Warning: This is one of the "trickiest" recipes I make. Dedicate your full attention to it. I don't make this recipe when I'm in the middle of half-a-dozen projects. I really watch it because:

- I don't want the eggs to scramble in the hot mixture. (Blend well.)
- I don't want the lemon to separate the milk.
- I don't want the sauce to stick on the bottom of the pan.
- I do want it all to blend well and be creamy.

Serving Suggestions: Serve over vegetables. Decorate with some boiled egg bits as a garnish. Serve as gravy on the side. Excellent with fish.

Variations: Again, these are mega-versions of the standards. The standard recipes are very complicated and almost impossible to make ahead, much less freeze. Though these recipes aren't as "chef-quality"as the originals, they are good and do-able for the mega-cook. Serve these sauces over vegetables or with meat dishes. The Mousseline is great with fish.

Do Ahead Béarnaise Sauce: In addition to the Holidays Sauce above:

X1 MAKES 2¾ CUPS	X2 MAKES 5½ CUPS	X8 MAKES 21 CUPS	
3 tablespoons	⅓ cup	1½ cups	White wine vinegar
2 teaspoons	4 teaspoons	⅓ cup	Minced green onion
½ teaspoon	1 teaspoon	4 teaspoons	Pepper (coarsely ground)
1 teaspoon	2 teaspoons	3 tablespoons	Tarragon [mol to taste]

Steps:

Prepare the Holidays Sauce to step 6. In a saucepan combine the vinegar, onion, and pepper. Bring to a boil over medium heat. Reduce the heat to simmer and allow to reduce to about half the liquid. Strain off the liquid. Add the tarragon. Add this mixture to the sauce and resume with step 7.

Quick Mousseline Sauce: Make the Holidays Sauce as described above. Once it is cooled (either thawed from freezer, or cooled before freezing), fold in:

X1 MAKES 3½ CUPS	X2 MAKES 7 CUPS	X8 MAKES 28 CUPS	
1 cup	2 cups	8 cups	Whipped cream

Note: Make the Holidays sauce ahead, and then add the whipped cream right before serving.

Eggs Benedictine

Just as in the other recipes, this is not the same as its famous name-sake, Eggs Benedict, but our family has come to appreciate it even more. Also, it is so much easier that we have it more often than we would if I had to do it from scratch.

Do Ahead:

- Make Holidays Sauce, freeze, then thaw for this recipe.

- Purchase any of the ingredients in bulk for savings.
- Package breakfast-sized portions ready to assemble
- Make your own English muffins from scratch. (Recipe in *Dinner's in the Freezer!™)*

X1	**X2**	**X8**	
1 SERVING	2 SERVINGS	8 SERVINGS	
½	1	4	English Muffins
1	2	8	Slices Canadian Bacon, cooked
1	2	8	Pineapple rings, optional
1	2	8	Poached eggs
½ cup	1 cup	4 cups	Holidays Sauce (above)

Steps:
1. On each English muffin half, layer a slice of bacon, pineapple ring, and poached egg. Cover with sauce.
2. Place under the broiler for a couple of minutes.
3. Serve.

Note: To poach eggs quickly, place 2 tablespoons of water in a microwave-safe dish and gently slide an egg into the water. Cook at medium power for 2 minutes. Perfect. Before I had the poaching pan (made especially for this purpose), I used a muffin pan to poach 6 eggs at a time. Adjust the time according to the dish you use.

"I thought this was delicious served with broccoli and salmon patties."—Pam Geyer

Additional Helps and Suggestions
- Pam Geyer said that for freeze-able "Hollandaise" sauce this is terrific!

Ratings
$ = 5¢
Ease = 2
Prep-time = 15 minutes
Heating = 2 to 3 minutes
Mega-Session = 5 (I prefer to do this at another time and then use with other recipes mega-cooked)
Equipment = wire whisk

Love-Sweet Syrup

As much as I enjoy the taste of maple syrup, I realize that 1) real maple syrup is very expensive, 2) many of the store-brand syrups are mostly sugar-water, and 3) we don't need to start the day with a sugar-rush. So, I make my own syrup with ingredients that are friendlier to our lifestyle. Serve this syrup hot over pancakes, waffles, French toast, or some of the recipes in this book. It even works well over ice cream and cheesecake (but don't tell my hips).

Do Ahead:

- Purchase juice in bulk for the best prices. You can order the concentrate cans from a grocery supply in cases for a fraction of the retail price.
- Make a mega-batch and freeze in meal-sized portions for later use.

X1	X2	X4	
Makes 3 cups	Makes 6 cups	Makes 12 cups	
2 tablespoons	¼ cup	½ cup	Cornstarch
2 cups	4 cups	8 cups	Cold water (as pure as you can afford)
1 12-ounce can	2 12-ounce cans	4 12-ounce cans	Frozen apple juice concentrate
½ teaspoon	1 teaspoon	4 teaspoons	Maple extract [mol]

Steps:

1. Mix the cornstarch in one-fourth of the cold water until completly dissolved. I use a shaker to mix it well.
2. In a large saucepan combine the juice, remaining water, and the water/cornstarch solution and place over medium heat. (For a quicker version see Suggestions, below.)
3. Cook, stirring constantly, until it thickens and becomes clear.
4. Once it is as thick as syrup, add the maple extract.
5. Either serve hot immediately or divide, store, and freeze. (Let it cool in the refrigerator, then pour into plastic freezer bags and place the bags in a box to shape as it freezes. Once it is frozen solid, remove the bag from the box and continue freezing.)
6. To use: Remove a bag from the freezer and let it thaw overnight. The next morning either heat it in the microwave or on the stovetop. If necessary, add more water to make it the desired consistency.

Version using quality ready to drink juice (my favorite of the two versions).

X1	X2	X4	
3 cups	6 cups	12 cups	Apple juice (see note)
2 tablespoons	¼ cup	½ cup	Cornstarch

½ cup	1 cup	4 cups	Cold water (as pure as you can afford)
½ teaspoon	1 teaspoon	4 teaspoons	Maple extract [mol]

Steps:

1. Mix the cornstarch in the cold water until completely dissolved. I use a shaker to mix it well.
2. In a large pot, combine the juice, and the water/cornstarch solution, and place over medium heat.
3. Cook, stirring constantly, until it thickens and becomes clear.
4. Once it is as thick as syrup, add the maple extract.
5. Either serve hot immediately or divide, store, freeze. (Let it cool in the refrigerator, then pour into plastic freezer bags and place the bags in a box to shape as it freezes. Once it is frozen solid, remove the bag from the box and continue freezing.)
6. To use: Remove a bag from the freezer and let it thaw overnight. The next morning either heat it in the microwave or on the stovetop. If necessary add more water to make it the desired consistency.

Note: Buy thick juice you cannot see through. If your grocery doesn't carry "real" juice, you can buy it from a co-op or health food store. Avoid juice that is diluted with water or "contains" fruit juice.

Variations: Try a variety of juices. I've found that the "maple extract" only works well with the apple version, so omit it with other flavors. Try cranberry juice, peach nectar, orange juice, pineapple juice, or grape juice. You may also make blueberry, strawberry, or plum juice in a blender, adding water as needed. Leave the fruit bits in—it is delicious that way. Try your favorite fruit juice, but do a single batch to see if you like it before you make mega-batches of it.

"This was delicious!"—Linda Bacon

Additional Helps and Suggestions

- Michelle Manson froze the syrup in an ice cube tray, them transferred them to a plastic bag in the freezer. She can just take out as many cubes as she needs and heat them in the microwave.
- Sarah Heggie suggested an optional honey or sweetener ingredient listed for those whose families have a "sweet tooth" like hers: Add granulated sugar to the mix as it thickens. (x1: 2 tablespoons to ¼ cup); (x2: ¼ cup to ½ cup); (x4: ½ cup to 1 cup), according to how sweet your tooth is.
- Linda Bacon said, "This was delicious! We usually do use maple syrup but I think this is less expensive and lower in calories. We all enjoyed it on our Saturday morning pancakes! I'm going to try the cranberry juice option next." She just defrosted it for 5 minutes in the microwave.
- Lynn Nelson made her version using good quality grape juice. (Jill adds: It can work as a non-alcoholic alternative to some wine sauces. You might want to alter it somewhat, getting ideas from wine-based sauces.)
- *Quick Method:* It does take a long time to thicken. Some of the families said it took a good 15 minutes after reaching boiling. What can affect that time is how well your pan disperses heat. I've tested

with several different pans and it does make a big difference. Here's my current method, but it is tricky—I heat the juice to boiling, then add in the dissolved cornstarch. It thickens very quickly. You have to be careful because if you blink, it will clump and give you lumps. If you can stay with it and stir constantly, this method will save a good 10 minutes. The slow method should work every time even for inexperienced cooks. For more on how sauces work, see the Topics section.

- Of all my recipes this is the one I've made the most. We use variations of this syrup as a sauce on meat, with appetizers, as the "spread" on sandwiches, and as a dip for eggrolls, as well as on many breakfast foods. It is good to spread on crêpes and then roll them up for a great snack. If you make it a little thicker, it can serve as a healthier alternative to jelly on some breads.

Ratings

$ = 5¢ (depends on quality of juice)
Ease = 7
Prep-time = 10 to 20 minutes
Heating = 3 to 5 in microwave
Mega-Session = 4 (though I use this recipe with ingredients I bought mega-shopping, I choose to make it another day and make a mega-batch)
Equipment = a good sauce pan, a blender or quality juicer for making fresh juices (if applicable)

Mega-Mayonnaise and Mayonnaise-based Dressings

Making dressing each day is a hassle. There are plenty of better things to do. So I make mega-batches of the dressing, store some in the refrigerator for immediate use, and then freeze the rest for another time. Admittedly, the frozen-then-thawed versions aren't as tasty as fresh, but I think they are just as good as store-bought versions. I've learned how to make a freeze-able mayonnaise and how to revive it. If possible with the mayonnaise, use either plastic, wooden, or glass bowls and spoons. Metal and mayonnaise are not friends. The whole-egg version of the mayonnaise is lower in calories and more heart-friendly, and though it won't taste as rich as the yolk-only version it is also a little easier. Please do not make a mega-batch the fist time you try this recipe. Start slow. Make x1 or x2 to see if you like it and can handle the special care required.

Warning: *This is a very difficult recipe. But if for health reasons you need to make your food from scratch, it is an option. Again, this is not for the novice cook. It may take several tries to work out the recipe to fit your tastes. Also, please note that it doesn't look as clean and white as store-bought. It is more natural, and natural food isn't always as attractive as that which has been dyed. Read about proper care and handling of eggs and the CDC's warning about raw eggs in the Topics section. If your eggs aren't 100% clear of any salmonella bacteria, then buy a commercial mayonnaise and use it for the following dressing recipes.*

Do Ahead:

- Make mega-batches of dressing, store some in the refrigerator for immediate use, and freeze the rest.
- Buy as many ingredients as possible in bulk for best prices.
- Make a mega-batch and use immediately in a mega-recipe.
- Plan to make "Clouds" or some other egg white recipe the same day.
- Or purchase store-brand mayonnaise or salad dressing/sandwich spread to make the other dressing recipes.

X1 MAKES 2½ CUPS	**X2** MAKES 5 CUPS	**X6** MAKES 15 CUPS	
2	4	12	Egg yolks or half that amount with whole eggs
2 tablespoons	¼ cup	¾ cup	Lemon juice (as fresh as possible) or vinegar
½ teaspoon	1 teaspoon	1 tablespoon	Salt
2 cups	4 cups	12 cups	Vegetable oil (use the healthiest you can afford)
1 teaspoon	2 teaspoons	2 Tablespoons	Dry mustard
Dash	¼ teaspoon	1½ teaspoons	Paprika [mol]
3 drops	6 drops	⅓ teaspoon	Hot sauce

Steps:

1. Set the eggs out at least 30 minutes before using. One trick of mayo is to make sure the eggs and oil are the same temperature.
2. With a mixer, beat the egg yolks on high until thick and lemon colored.

3. Beat in half of the lemon juice and salt.
4. Add the oil, one drop at a time, until you've added 2 to 3 tablespoons. Slowly drizzle in the remaining oil, still beating on high. (If you go too fast, it will not work. Slowly, slowly, slowly. I had the kids time me and it took 3 minutes to add 1 cup. So this isn't a quick recipe.) The mixture will begin to thicken. If you add too much, it becomes thinner and becomes runny. After adding about three-fourths of the oil, watch very carefully and stop when the desired consistency is achieved.
5. Again, slowly add the remaining lemon juice. Continue beating until thick.
6. Add the remaining ingredients, stirring well.
7. Immediately pour into glass containers with airtight lids (such as glass jars) up to 1-inch from the threading. Place a circle of plastic wrap on the surface of the mayonnaise. Don't let the plastic interfere with the seal of the lid. Top with the lid and use a vacuum sealer to close. Do not let the mayonnaise touch metal, if at all possible.
8. Store one portion in refrigerator for up to one week (double-check it).
9. Use some for other types of dressings.
10. Store other jars in the freezer.
11. To revive, thaw in the refrigerator. Pour the mayo into a blender and blend on high with ½ cup of plain yogurt or sour cream to each cup of mayo until creamy again. (This makes a less salty, healthier version that has a great zing—especially if you use low calorie yogurt or sour cream.)

Note: You can substitute store-bought mayonnaise for any of the following recipes. Experiment with sandwich spread also as a substitute. For a slightly different flavor, use half plain yogurt and half mayonnaise in the recipes. Remember to make a single batch to see if you like the new taste first before you make a mega-batch.

Speedy Island Dressing

X1 MAKES 1½ CUPS	**X2** MAKES 3 CUPS	**X6** MAKES 8¼ CUPS	
1 cup	2 cups	6 cups	Mega-Mayonnaise (fresh, not frozen or thawed) (or use a combination of half yogurt and half commercial mayonnaise or sandwich spread)
¼ cup	½ cup	1½ cups	Ketchup
¼ teaspoon	½ teaspoon	1 tablespoon	Garlic powder
¼ cup	½ cup	¾ cup	Pickle relish

Steps:

1. Mix all of the above ingredients.
2. Store as in Mega-Mayonnaise above.

Traditional Thousand Island Dressing

Worth the extra effort.

X1	X2	X6	
Makes 2 cups	Makes 4 cups	Makes 12 cups	
1 cup	2 cups	6 cups	Mega-Mayonnaise (fresh, not frozen or thawed)
½ cup	1 cup	3 cups	Chili sauce
1 tablespoon	2 tablespoons	⅓ cup	Honey
¼ cup	½ cup	¾ to 1½ cups	Chopped pimiento-stuffed olives
2 tablespoons	¼ cup	¾ cup	Finely chopped green peppers
2 tablespoons	¼ cup	¾ cup	Finely chopped onion
12	24	¼ cup	Capers [optional]

Steps:

1. In a large bowl mix the Mega-Mayonnaise and chili sauce.
2. Stir in the honey.
3. In a separate bowl mix the remaining ingredients. Stir into mayonnaise mixture.
4. Pour into glass jars and follow the freezing and storing procedure as described for Mega-Mayonnaise .
5. Chill at least 1 hour before using on salad or in other dishes like Rueben sandwiches.

Russian Dressing

X1	X2	X6	
Makes 1 cup	Makes 2 cups	Makes 6 cups	
⅔ cup	1⅓ cups	4 cups	Mega-Mayonnaise (fresh, not frozen or thawed)
⅓ cup	⅔ cup	2 cups	Chili sauce
¼ cup	½ cup	1½ cups	Dill pickle (chopped) or pickle relish
⅛ teaspoon	¼ teaspoon	¾ teaspoon	Dry mustard
⅛ teaspoon	¼ teaspoon	¾ teaspoon	Onion powder
⅛ teaspoon	¼ teaspoon	¾ teaspoon	Pepper

Steps:

1. In a large bowl combine all ingredients.
2. Pour into glass jars and follow the freezing and storing procedure as described for Mega-Mayonnaise.
3. Use for a variety of applications and salads. Suggestion: Brush this sauce onto skinless chicken and bake.

Cucumber Dressing

X1	X2	X6	
MAKES 1½ CUP	MAKES 3 CUPS	MAKES 9 CUPS	
1 cup	2 cups	6 cups	Mega-Mayonnaise (fresh, not frozen or thawed)
½ cup	1 cup	3 cups	Peeled, seeded, finely chopped cucumbers
¼ teaspoon	½ teaspoon	1½ teaspoons	Cayenne pepper

Steps:

1. In a large bowl combine the cucumber and other ingredients. Mix well.
2. Pour into glass jars and follow the freezing and storing procedure as described for Mega-Mayonnaise.

Green Goddess Dressing

X1	X2	X6	
MAKES 1¼ CUP	MAKES 2½ CUPS	MAKES 7½ CUPS	
⅓ cup	⅔ cup	2 cups	Chopped fresh parsley
1 cup	2 cups	6 cups	Mega-Mayonnaise (fresh, not frozen or thawed)
⅓ cup	⅔ cup	2 cups	Chopped chives
3 tablespoons	⅓ cup	1 cup	Tarragon vinegar
1 tablespoon	2 tablespoons	⅓ cup	Anchovy paste
⅛ teaspoon	¼ teaspoon	1 teaspoons	Salt
1 clove	2 cloves	6 cloves	Garlic, crushed

Steps:

1. In a blender process the parsley for 1 minute.
2. Measure the fine parsley into equal amounts according to how many batches you are making. Depending on the capacity of the blender, you'll may need to do this recipe round-robin style.
3. In the blender combine the parsley and remaining ingredients for one batch.
4. Blend until smooth.
5. Repeat the process if needed to make as many batches as you want.
7. Pour into glass jars and follow the freezing and storing procedure as described for Mega-Mayonnaise.

Buttermilk Dressing

X1 Makes 1½ cup	X2 Makes 3 cups	X6 Makes 9 cups	
1 tablespoon	2 tablespoons	⅓ cup	Parsley flakes
½ teaspoon	1 teaspoon	1 tablespoon	Onion powder
¼ teaspoon	½ teaspoon	½ tablespoons	Garlic powder
¼ teaspoon	½ teaspoon	1½ teaspoons	White pepper
⅛ teaspoon	¼ teaspoon	¾ teaspoon	Salt
1 cup	2 cups	6 cups	Mega-Mayonnaise (fresh, not frozen or thawed)
½ cup	1 cup	3 cups	Buttermilk

Steps:

1. In a small bowl combine the parsley, onion powder, garlic powder, pepper, and salt.
2. In a separate bowl mix the buttermilk into the Mega-Mayonnaise.
3. Stir the spice mixture throughout the mayonnaise mixture.
4. Store as for Mega-Mayonnaise above, except if serving some for that day, please allow it to chill for at least 5 hours.

Honey Mustard Dressing

X1 Makes 1½ cup	X2 Makes 3 cups	X6 Makes 9 cups	
1 cup	2 cups	6 cups	Mega-Mayonnaise (fresh, not frozen or thawed)
¼ cup	½ cups	1½ cups	Dijon mustard (or half and half with yellow mustard)
¼ cup	½ cup	1½ cups	Honey

Steps:

1. In a medium bowl combine all of the ingredients.
2. Store as for Mega-Mayonnaise.
3. Use as a dip or in a variety of recipes. If it is too thick for salad, then add milk slowly and whip.

About Buttermilk Dressing: "This is much better than [commercial brand] dressing and no MSG headache afterwards. A real winner!"—Denna C. Flickner

About Mega-Mayonnaise and Buttermilk Dressing: "Excellent recipe—very tasty. My family loved this one!"—Pam Bianco

Additional Helps and Suggestions

- Cindy Munger, who has to keep foods low-fat for her husband, replaced the mayonnaise in the Speedy Island dressing with ½ cup of yogurt and ½ cup of Miracle Whip® brand salad dressing. She also substituted a scant teaspoon of dill for the pickle relish (they don't eat pickles). She had the great idea of using a multi-cup measure with spout so she could pour it into her jar. She rated it a "10" for adult taste. She also recommended including instructions for how to culture buttermilk at home, so look in the Topics section for the how-to. It helps hold the cost down.
- Denna C. Flickner pointed out that the capers really add the touch that makes the Traditional Thousand Island Dressing worth the time. She also noted that the yolk-only version of the Mega-Mayonnaise tastes much better than the whole egg version. (I agree!).
- I learned a lot from Lauren Down. Here's what she had to say about making the Mega-Mayonnnaise and Honey Mustard Dressing—"During the last of the mixing, the mayo began to breakdown. After an additional 5 mintues of mixing, no better. Rather than waste the mayo, I tried a salad dressing recipe and mixed it with a wire whip—it blended beautifully and tastes great. The mayo may not look great but it is still useful. At the end of the mixing, my mixer was overheating and slowing down, which may have caused the problem. The mayo looked something like sour milk with curd in it but it still made a lovely, smooth salad dressing. Great way to reclaim an 'oops'!"
- Pam Bianco had the wonderful idea of using an infant's medicine syringe to drip the oil in very slowly. She also added: "I think it would be helpful to note in the instructions not to expect very white mayonnaise. Also it looked very much like mayonnaise from the store until I added the last ½ cup of oil. It made it very runny and grainy—it felt like too much oil." She's right. When the mayonnaise looks right, stop. Depending on the size and type of eggs, the oil amount will vary. She added that it did thicken in the refrigerator. So, if the mayo is runny, chill it for a few hours.
- One tester forgot to let the eggs sit out and become the same temperature as the oil and it was runny—even after sitting overnight. The reason that happens is because the egg yolk (actually the lecithin present in the yolk) works as an emulsifier. It really isn't that complicated, but basically it has to do with changing the electrical charge of the molecules of the different substances. We know oil and water don't mix. So, the yolk "holds" the oil. If you add too much oil, it breaks that bond and collapses, causing runny sauce. One solution is to place an egg in a separate bowl and add a little of the runny mayonnaise to the yolk, then more mayonnaise to the yolk, until it is all blended. That should "fix" any runny problems. Do not just add one more egg yolk to the mayonnaise. That won't work. By adding mayonnaise to the yolk, you get a higher lecithin ratio. For an interesting science experiment, try it the other way—the yolk will not help and oil will still be separating. (Cold "paralyzes" the egg's emulsifying action.)
- Althea Underwood added the dry mustard at the end, but it was lumpy and left lumps in the mayonnaise. I hadn't thought of that. Be sure to check dry mustard and mash it with the back of a spoon if necessary to get rid of any lumps. It should be a fine powder as you sprinkle it in.
- Kathie Wright, bless her heart, tried this recipe with a hand mixer. She had to hold the mixer, turn bowl, and drizzle oil—she needed three hands. She highly recommended using a standing mixer. I agree, I wouldn't try it without one. Some food processors work great and even have a "mayo" attachment (it drizzles the oil for you).

Ratings

$ = 10¢

Ease = 1

Prep-time = 20 to 30 minutes

Heating = none

Mega-Session = 0 (though you will want to use some of these recipes for other meals, it is to much work to attempt during a mega-session. You might want to make this a week ahead of a mega-session, so you can then use it in upcoming recipes.)

Equipment = standing mixer

SIDE DISHES

Accordion Potatoes

There are not many ways to freeze potatoes and have them come out delicious. The trick is to use fresh potatoes. The fresher the better. This works because of the marinating process that goes on during the freezing. These potatoes fan out like accordions and are as delicious as they look. Buy the type and size of potatoes that suit your family's tastes and appetites. These measurements and baking times are figured for an average potato—approximately 6 inches long, 3 inches wide. If your potatoes vary greatly from that size, adjust the baking time and ingredients accordingly.

Do Ahead:

- Buy potatoes in bulk for a terrific price. Or grow your own. Potatoes are surprisingly easy to grow.
- Scrub the potatoes. Use some in this recipe, the rest in other recipes—cut and dehydrate or cut and freeze. But process them the day of purchase if at all possible.
- Make your own Italian dressing for use in many recipes.

X1	X2	X8	
4 SERVINGS	8 SERVINGS	32 SERVINGS	1 POTATO PER SERVING
4	8	32	Potatoes (as uniform in size as you can manage)
1 cup	2 cups	8 cups	Italian dressing
¼ cup	½ cup	2 cups	Grated Cheddar cheese
2 tablespoons	¼ cup	1 cup	Grated Parmesan cheese
2 to 4 tablespoons	¼ to ½ cup	½ to 1 cup	Combination of chopped herbs or vegetables (tiny bits) such as parsley, chives, thyme, sage, green onions, etc., optional

Steps:

1. Clean the potatoes well. Scrub with a stiff brush to not only clean off dirt, but to soften tough skin.
2. Cut the potatoes into thin slices, but not all the way through. Use the handles of 2 wooden spoons placed beside the potatoes to help keep from cutting through.
3. Spray a baking dish with a nonstick spray or use a Teflon® liner.
4. Place the potatoes in the dish. Fan out the potatoes as much as possible without breaking any of the disks from the base.
5. Drizzle one-fourth of the Italian dressing over the potatoes.
6. Bake at 425°F for 15 minutes.

7. Open the oven, pull out the potatoes, and drizzle one-fourth of the Italian dressing over the potatoes.
8. Bake an additional 15 minutes.
9. Repeat steps 7 and 8 twice more—until you've used all the dressing, and potatoes have baked 1 hour.

OPTION 1: PREPARE SOME TO SERVE IMMEDIATELY AND FREEZE THE EXTRAS

10. Remove the potatoes from the baking dishes, except those you'll eat for that meal. Place the remaining potatoes in the refrigerator to cool.
11. Sprinkle those you'll be eating with the cheeses (and any additional herbs). Bake an additional 10 to 15 minutes until the cheese is melted and the potatoes are fully soft.
12. After dinner, the other potatoes should be cool enough to handle. Wrap them individually in plastic wrap or bag them carefully together. (Be careful to keep the attractive fan shape intact.) Do not drain, keep all dressing with the potatoes. That extra liquid will help keep the potatoes from drying out while freezing.
13. Freeze.
14. Thaw as many potatoes as you need. Bake as in step 11 above.

OPTION 2: FREEZE THEM ALL AT ONE TIME (THAWING AHEAD METHOD)

10. Wrap each potato individually in plastic wrap or bag them carefully together. (Be careful to keep the attractive fan shape intact.) Do not drain, keep all dressing with the potatoes. That extra liquid will help to keep the potatoes from drying out while freezing. Label and freeze them.
11. Later, in preparing dinner, thaw as many potatoes as you need.
12. Sprinkle the potatoes with the cheeses (and any additional herbs). Bake at 425° for an additional 10 to 15 minutes until the cheese is melted and the potatoes are fully soft and hot.

OPTION 3: FREEZE THEM ALL AT ONE TIME (RE-BAKING FROM FROZEN STATE)

You'll need an extra ¼ cup of Italian dressing for each potato with this method.

10. Repeat step 1 in option 2.
11. Remove as many potatoes as you need for a meal from the freezer. Spray a dish with nonstick spray or use a Teflon® liner.
12. Place the potatoes in the prepared dish. Bake at 300° for 30 minutes.
13. Pour an additional ¼ cup of dressing over each potato. Bake another 15 minutes.
14. Sprinkle the potatoes with the cheeses (and any additional herbs). Bake at 400°F an additional 10 to 15 minutes until the cheese is melted and the potatoes are fully soft and hot.

"I was surprised at how good the frozen ones tasted—I couldn't tell much difference between reheated and fresh."—Michele Nielsen

"This has become a family favorite with all five of my "tasting committee."—Mrs. Hieyoung

Additional Helps and Suggestions

- Dee Kimmel suggested saving time by starting the cooking process in the microwave.
- Patricia Peoples suggested using a cooking spray if your family doesn't like Italian dressing.
- Jill adds: Adjust the time for baking if you use smaller or larger potatoes. For the basic recipe, I used potatoes that were 5 to 6 inches in length and about 3 to 4 inches in diameter.

Ratings

$ = 10¢—low-budget—especially if you make your own dressing and buy potatoes in bulk
Ease = 9—Once you get the hang of cutting the potatoes, it goes smoothly. One mega-tester told us her 10-year-old prepared this recipe.
Prep-time = 2 to 3 minutes per potato
Heating = 1 hour 15 minutes
Mega-Session = 10
Equipment = wooden spoons, good sharp knife, glass baking dish

Curried Rice

Rice is so easy to make that I don't make up batches of cooked rice and freeze it. If I have any leftover rice, I do freeze it for future use. How I use this recipe is to make up the rice mix, store it ready to cook and then steam it the day I'll eat it. It is so easy to mix-up and it saves time on those days when you are rushed. Please review the section in the book about cooking rice.

Do Ahead:

- Purchase all of the ingredients in bulk.
- Purchase and process the onion and corn in bulk. Dehydrate extras.
- Since I have to budget my freezer space, I use dehydrated onion and corn, and I store this rice mix in an airtight jar in my cupboard.
- Clean and dry the rice. (See Note.)

X1	X2	X8	
6 SERVINGS	12 SERVINGS	48 SERVINGS	1 CUP PER SERVING
⅛ teaspoon	¼ teaspoon	1 teaspoon	Gumbo filé (spice), optional
⅛ teaspoon	¼ teaspoon	1 teaspoon	Turmeric
½ teaspoon	1 teaspoon	4 teaspoons	Kelp powder (sold with the spices), optional
1 tablespoon	2 tablespoons	½ cup	Chicken broth concentrate (powder form)
1 teaspoon	2 teaspoons	3 tablespoons	Curry powder
2 cups	4 cups	16 cups	Raw rice, clean and dry (my favorite is Basmati)
½ cup	1 cup	4 cups	Kernel corn, fresh, chopped, or frozen (If you're using dehydrated ingredients, use half of those amounts)
½ cup	1 cup	4 cups	Finely chopped onion (If you're using dehydrated ingredients, use half of those amounts]
3 cups	6 cups	24 cups	Water (you might have to adjust this amount depending on which type of rice you use)

Note: Rice is dirty. and should be washed before you use it. If you're making rice to be steamed immediately, rinse it several times and then use it. But since I want to store this rice mix dry, I rinse the rice at least three times and then spread it out on tea towels to completely dry. I don't want any moisture on it so that, when I'm ready to use the rice, it is ready to cook.

OPTION 1: MAKE MIX FOR DRY STORAGE AND STEAM THE DAY YOU'LL EAT IT

1. In a small bowl mix the filé, turmeric, kelp powder, chicken broth concentrate, and curry powder.
2. In a large bowl sprinkle the spice mixture over the rice. Toss so that the spices are spread as evenly as possible among the rice.

3. Toss in the corn and onions.
2. Divide into meal-sized amounts (3 cups each for our family).
3. Label and store. I store rice mixes in jars, sealed airtight.
4. On the day of serving, pour the rice into a steamer pan with 3 cups of water.
5. Steam for 40 minutes.

OPTION 2: MAKE MIX FOR FREEZING AND STEAMING THE DAY YOU'LL EAT IT

1. In a small bowl mix the filé, turmeric, kelp powder, chicken broth concentrate, and curry powder.
2. In a large bowl sprinkle the spice mixture over the rice. Toss so that the spices are spread as evenly as possible among the rice.
3. Toss in the corn and onions.
4. Divide into meal-sized amounts (3 cups each for our family).
5. Label and store. You can place in labeled bags and then into your freezer.
6. On the day of serving, pour frozen raw rice into steamer pan with 3 cups water.
7. Steam for 45 minutes.

OPTION 3: MAKE RICE AHEAD AND JUST REHEAT DAY OF SERVING

1. In a small bowl mix the file, turmeric, kelp powder, chicken broth concentrate, and curry powder.
2. In a large bowl sprinkle the spice mixture over the rice. Toss so that the spices are spread as evenly as possible among the rice.
3. Toss in the corn and onions.
4. Begin a round-robin process of cooking the rice. For each 3 cups of rice mix use 3 cups of water.
5. When the rice finishes cooking, label and store in the freezer in meal-sized portions
6. On the day of serving, re-steam about 20 minutes to heat through.

I highly recommend you use a steamer or rice cooker to cook your rice. It is my favorite appliance—and I don't say that easily. Until I purchased my steamer, I rigged one—using a Dutch oven, lid and a metal colander.

"Super-delicious. Lovely and smelled great!"—Tina W. Cook

Additional Helps and Suggestions

- Tina W. Cook used brown rice because at the time her store didn't have Basmati. Everyone in her family felt it was a delightful change from plain brown rice (rice with seasoning and onions, etc.) with or without gravy as usually served.
- Karen B. Collins tossed the rice with almonds and stirred in some chicken pieces.
- Sara J. Dagen cooked the rice in the microwave using a Tupperware® steamer.
- If you can't find kelp at a reasonable price and easily, just leave it out. Also, some of our testers had trouble finding gumbo filé. It might be in your store under the label sassafras. That's all gumbo file is—ground sassafras.

- I don't recommend cooking this recipe just on a pot on the stove. Please rig up a steamer. As soon as you have the money, go buy a steamer and use it to heat and cook much of your food. Steamers can be as low as $15 in some stores. Shop around for the best model you can afford.

Ratings

$ = 20¢
Ease = 9
Prep-time = 20 to 30 minutes—including the washing of the rice but not the drying time
Heating = average 40 minutes
Mega-Session = 10—the mix
Equipment = steamer—either an electric appliance, bamboo stove top version, home-made colander in a Dutch oven version, or microwave type

Garden Rice Medley

(SIDE DISH OR VEGETARIAN ENTRÉE)

Some meals are as attractive as they are tasty. This is one of them. You can make a mega-batch of this dish and completely bake the meals and then simply reheat at serving. Or bake it partially, freeze the ingredients, and complete the baking at time of serving.

Do Ahead:

- Purchase as many of the ingredients in bulk as possible.
- Assembly-line process as many of the fresh vegetables as possible for this and other recipes.
- Dehydrate or freeze any extra vegetables or use on pizza, salads, soups or other recipes.

X1	**X2**	**X4**	
12 SERVINGS	24 SERVINGS	48 SERVINGS	1 CUP PER SERVING
1 cup	2 cups	4 cups	Chopped onions
1 cup	2 cups	4 cups	Chopped bell pepper (use a variety of colors, if possible)
¼ cup	½ cup	2 cups	Butter (optional)
¾ cup	1½ cups	3 cups	Water
2½ cups	5 cups	10 cups	Chicken broth (concentrate, undiluted)
3 tablespoons	⅓ cup	¾ cup	Tomato paste
½ teaspoon	1 teaspoon	2 teaspoons	Black pepper
¼ teaspoon	½ teaspoon	1 teaspoon	Dried, ground Saffron (optional)
Dash	¼ teaspoon	½ teaspoon	Worcestershire sauce
1½ cups	3 cups	6 cups	Long grain rice, uncooked
2 cups	4 cups	8 cups	Chopped tomatoes
1 pound	2 pounds	4 pounds	Broccoli
½ pound	1 pound	2 pounds	Zucchini
2 cups	4 cups	8 cups	Frozen green peas [mol]
6	12	24	Asparagus spears (fresh or frozen) [mol]

Steps:

1. Process the vegetables: wash, core (if necessary), and chop into 1-inch pieces.
2. If you like sautéed onions, sauté the onions and bell peppers in the butter to soften. I don't like the extra fat, so I just steam the vegetables for a few minutes with water to soften. I use a steamer, but a microwave-colander system works well also.
3. In a Dutch oven mix together the water, broth, tomato paste, pepper, saffron, and Worcestershire sauce.

4. Add the rice, onions, bell peppers, and tomato. Bring to a boil. Remove from the heat.
5. Place in an ovenproof dish. Bake at 350°F for 30 minutes.
6. Stir in the cut broccoli, zucchini, green peas, and asparagus spears.

OPTION 1: MAKE ONE DISH FOR DINING THE FIRST NIGHT AND FREEZE THE REST FOR FINAL COOKING ANOTHER DAY.

7. Divide the mixture into meal-sized portions. Set one meal's worth in a baking dish.
8. Freeze the rest using the bag-in-box method. Remember to label.
9. Continue baking the rice for tonight covered for 45 minutes until the liquid is completely absorbed, the rice is tender, and the vegetables are tender-crisp.
10. To finish the other dinners, thaw, place in an ovenproof container, and follow step 9 (prior step).

OPTION 2: MAKE ALL DURING A MEGA-COOKING™ SESSION AND FREEZE ALL FOR OTHER NIGHTS

7. Divide the mixture into meal-sized portions. Freeze using the bag-in-box method. Remember to label.
8. To finish the other dinners, thaw, place in an ovenproof container, and bake the rice covered for 45 minutes until the liquid is completely absorbed, the rice is tender, and the vegetables are tender-crisp.

OPTION 3: COMPLETELY BAKE THE ENTREES AHEAD AND SIMPLY REHEAT DAY OF SERVING

7. Continue to baking the rice covered for 45 minutes until the liquid is completely absorbed, rice is tender, and vegetables are tender-crisp.
8. Divide the rice into meal-sized portions.
9. Freeze using the bag-in-box method. Remember to label.
10. To reheat: Thaw a bag. Use a steamer to reheat. If you don't have a steamer, make one using a metal colander and Dutch oven. (See instructions on page 59).

"We loved this dish!"—Colleen Finley
"My children gobbled this up—they asked for it at lunch with sandwiches. At dinner—it was so pretty."—Jessica Mader

Additional Helps and Suggestions

- Jessica Mader said that it was a very pretty presentation, especially if you use red, green, and yellow peppers.
- Jenny Goff added a little garlic powder and Lowery seasoning salt and gave it a "10" for taste for an adult. (Two of her children didn't like the zucchini.)
- To hold down the cost you can omit the asparagus. Sometimes it is expensive. I try to time this recipe when I can get good asparagus at "gleaning" prices. The reason asparagus is so expensive is that it is tricky to grow and usually a farmer has to wait at least three years before he has a crop to

sell. Also, it takes special handling to pick and package. If you can afford it and you like asparagus, it does add to the flavor combination.

- You can turn this recipe into an entree: Garden Chicken and Rice Medley. Simply add chunks of cooked chicken. You can then serve it hot or as a cold salad.

Ratings

$ = 40¢ (depending on price of asparagus)
Ease = 10
Prep-time = 15 to 30 minutes depending if you have a food processor to help chop the vegetables
Heating = 30 minutes plus 45 minutes (then reheating can take 10 to 15 minutes)
Mega-Session = 10
Equipment = steamer, food processor

Mushroom Turnovers

Alan arrives home from work hungry. Either we need to have an early dinner or I need to offer him a snack. These work great. I also use them for covered dish functions and on buffet tables. Of course, they make excellent appetizers. I like to make up a double x4 batch of the dough and roll out all the circles. I'll make up some of these Mushroom Turnovers, freeze some circles for filling later, and use some with other fillings. (See below.) Try some of your favorite fillings.

Do Ahead:

- Purchase and process the vegetables in bulk.
- Purchase cream cheese in bulk for the best price (use in this and other recipes).
- Make a mega-batch of the dough for this and other recipes. Freeze the dough for use later. Or make all four of the variations during one mega-batching session.

X1	X2	X4	
40 SERVINGS	80 SERVINGS	160 SERVINGS	1 TURNOVER PER SERVING
For Pastry:			
8 ounces	16 ounces	32 ounces	Cream cheese
1½ cups	3 cups	6 cups	Flour (for making the pastry)
1 cup	2 cups	4 cups	Butter, softened (or use Better Butter Spread, see page 370) [mol]
For Filling:			
½ pound	1 pound	2 pounds	Mushrooms, minced
1	2	4	Large onions, minced
¼ cup	½ cup	1 cup	Sour cream
1 teaspoon	2 teaspoons	1 tablespoon	Salt
¼ teaspoon	½ teaspoon	1 teaspoon	Dried thyme leaves
2 tablespoons	4 tablespoons	8 tablespoons	Flour (for making the filling)
1	2	2 to 4	Eggs, beaten (approximately—used for sealing edges of pastry)

Steps:

1. In the bowl of an electric mixer cream together the cream cheese, flour, and butter until smooth.
2. Form into balls (2 balls per batch), cover, and refrigerate for at least 1 hour.
3. While the pastry dough is chilling, make the filling.
4. Steam the mushrooms and onions. While still warm, add the sour cream, salt, thyme, and flour (2nd amounts). Set aside.
5. Remove 1 dough ball from the refrigerator. Roll out to ⅛-inch thickness.

6. Cut the dough with a 3-inch (or as close as possible) cookie cutter.
7. Repeat rolling out the dough and cutting to make as many 3-inch circles as possible.

OPTION 1: MAKE DOUGH AHEAD AND FREEZE CIRCLES, FREEZE FILLING, AND ASSEMBLE DAY OF SERVING

8. Cut out 3-inch waxed paper squares. Stack up pastry rounds between squares of waxed paper. Place in a bag. Freeze flat.
9. Bag the filling in equal portions, label.
10. Thaw as many circles and bags of filling as you need.
11. Place 1 teaspoon of filling in the center of each circle. Brush the edges of the dough with egg.
12. Fold over into a half circle. Press the edges together with a pastry wheel or the tines of a fork.
13. Place on an ungreased cookie sheet. Bake at 450°F for 12 to 14 minutes.

OPTION 2: MAKE THEM AHEAD, FREEZE, AND THEN BAKE THE DAY OF SERVING

8. Place 1 teaspoon of filling in the center of each circle. Brush the edges of the dough with egg.
9. Fold over so it makes the shape of a half circle. Press the edges together with a pastry wheel or the tines of a fork.
10. Cover cookie sheets or cardboard with waxed paper.
11. Place the turnovers on waxed paper with no edges touching. Freeze. Bag or wrap.
12. Remove as many turnovers as you need from the freezer.
13. Place the frozen pastries on an ungreased cookie sheet. Bake at 450°F for 16 to 20 minutes. No need to thaw.

OPTION 3: BAKE THEM AHEAD, FREEZE, AND THEN REHEAT.

8. Follow steps 11 through 13 above in Option 1.
9. Follow steps 10 through 12 above in Option 2.
10. To reheat, place on an ungreased cookie sheet. Bake at 450°F for 5 to 8 minutes. Or microwave for 1 minute for a few turnovers.

Miniature Blueberry Turnovers: Follow the recipe above for making the pastry circles, but fill with one teaspoon of blueberry pie filling. You can drizzle with a confectioner's sugar icing (1 cup sugar and 1 teaspoon milk [mol]). Or use your favorite pie filling, such as mincemeat, apple, peach, or cherry.

Pizza Turnovers: Follow the recipe above for making the pastry circles, but fill with a slice of pepperoni, a teaspoon of pizza sauce, and sprinkle with a dash of oregano. Add a few strands of grated cheese.

Catchy Turnovers: Follow the recipe above except substitute tuna fish for the mushrooms. Proceed as before.

"Excellent."—Helene Brock

Additional Helps and Suggestions

- Helene Brock used a glass for cutting the rounds. She was able to double the dough recipe and only use 1 cup of butter. The last of the flour had to be mixed in by hand. They rolled out well, cut well, and looked and tasted great. The double recipe yielded 110 three-inch circles. She also said that this recipe is not difficult, it is just time consuming.
- BonnieJean Wiebe's husband doesn't like sugar so she used sugar-free blueberry jelly by spreading it sparingly—it tastes great. She has a marble pastry board and rolling pin which she put outside in the cold—it helped with rolling this dough out.
- Linnea Rein brought up some excellent points. She found it awkward to brush the edges with egg after placing the filling on the circle, so she did it before putting filling on the circle. She's going to use a 4-inch cutter next time—there will be fewer turnovers, but less work and larger turnovers. She'll need to monitor the baking time and make adjustments. She thought the dough was very nice to work with. She wondered if a superior quality could be achieved using "⅓ less fat" cream cheese and margarine instead of butter. [Jill: Reduced fat cream cheese works well, but I can't recommend using margarine—I do recommend using Better Butter Spread (see page 370) for this recipe.]
- I buy mushroom pieces and just cut them up on a cutting board with a sharp knife. One mega-tester used her blender to mince the mushrooms and ended up with a watery filling, so we don't recommend that method. I don't use my food processor because it turns them into pate. The mushrooms are just too soft to work in a food processor. (It will slice fresh mushrooms well.) When I steam mushrooms and onions, I do it in a microwaveable colander over a plate to catch the moisture. You want the mushrooms and onions fairly dry.
- I use a 3-inch biscuit cutter to cut these and it goes very quickly. You can even dip the edges of a drinking glass in flour and use it to cut the rounds. You can vary the size of the rounds, but be sure to adjust the baking time according to the size of your rounds.
- If you have any filling leftover (it never balances out exactly for me), use it to make pocket sandwiches, or freeze it for use another day.
- When I use a Teflon® sheet, these just slide off and look wonderful. Depending on how well your oven disperses heat and which shelf you use, you'll need to watch the bottoms to keep them from over-browning. It's worth the few dollars to buy those wonderful Teflon® sheets.

Ratings

$ = 10¢
Ease = 6—easy, but time consuming
Prep-time = 1 hour or more
Heating = 12 minutes
Mega-Session = 5—I prefer to make these a separate day and then do lots with a variety of fillings.
Equipment = 3-inch round cutter, rolling pin and cloth (or board), Teflon® sheets, mixer to make dough

Red, White, and Green

(POTATO AND SPINACH CASSEROLE)

Do you get tired of plain old potatoes and rice? Here is a delicious side dish that looks good and can be prepared ahead and frozen. Please review the Topic on how to freeze potatoes. Most recipes with potatoes don't freeze well. This one does, because of the way we handle the potatoes and the ingredients that surround them.

Do Ahead:

- Buy any ingredients in bulk for the best prices.
- Prepare potatoes for a variety of recipes.
- Buy fresh spinach and process some for this recipe. Cool, then dehydrate the rest for use in soups and dressings.

X1 6 SERVINGS	X2 12 SERVINGS	x4 24 SERVINGS	
1½ pounds	3 pounds	6 pounds	Frozen, chopped spinach (or same amount of fresh cooked)
2 pounds	4 pounds	8 pounds	Baking potatoes (figure about ½ pound per potato)
2 pounds	4 pounds	8 pounds	Sweet potatoes (figure about ½ pound per potato)
½ cup	1 cup	2 cups	Chopped onion
¼ cup	½ cup	1 cup	Butter
¼ cup	½ cup	1 cup	Flour
2 teaspoons	4 teaspoons	3 tablespoons	Salt
¼ teaspoon	½ teaspoon	1 teaspoon	Pepper
2½ cups	5 cups	10 cups	Milk

Steps:

1. Thaw the spinach and pat dry, or cook fresh spinach and drain.
2. Scrub the potatoes clean. If desired, slice them very thin now before cooking.
3. Place the potatoes in a pot (Dutch oven for larger batches). Cover with water. Heat on high until boiling.
4. Cover the pot, reduce the heat, and allow to simmer for 20 to 30 minutes. The potatoes should be tender, but not soft.
5. Remove the potatoes from the pot and allow to cool in the refrigerator until you can handle them comfortably.

6. While the potatoes are cooling, make the onion sauce. If the potatoes aren't already sliced, slice them once they have cooled.
7. In a saucepan sauté the onions in butter until tender. Add the flour, salt, and pepper. (*Note:* To make this during a mega-session, make a huge batch of Basic Beige Sauce and use some of it for this recipe. Add raw, grated onions to that.)
8. Pour in the milk slowly and stir constantly while the sauce thickens over medium heat.
9. When the potatoes are cool, peel and slice into ¼-inch rings.

OPTION 1: ASSEMBLE THE INGREDIENTS, BUT BAKE ON DAY OF SERVING

10. Prepare several molds, bowls, or pans (approximately 2-quart size) for assembling the ingredients. I use some bowls the same shape as my round casserole dish.
11. Line the dishes with waxed paper for easy removal.
12. Arrange half of one batch of potatoes in the bottom of each mold, bowl, or pan.
13. Make a layer of one batch of spinach over the potatoes.
14. Pour on half of one batch of onion sauce.
15. Arrange the rest of the potatoes on top of the sauce.
16. Pour the remaining sauce over the potatoes.
17. Either put a lid on the mold, bowl, or pan, or cover with plastic wrap. Freeze.
18. Once it is frozen solid, pop out of the mold, rewrap, and label. Continue freezing until use.
19. Thaw by placing a frozen potato casserole in an ovenproof dish (with an ovenproof lid) to thaw in the refrigerator.
20. Once thawed, bake covered at 375°F for 30 minutes.
21. Remove the cover and bake 15 minutes more until brown and bubbly.

OPTION 2: BAKE ALL THE CASSEROLES AND FREEZE THEM READY TO HEAT

10. Prepare several casserole dishes by spraying with a non-stick coating. Choose dishes that have ovenproof lids or plan on using foil. If it is a glass or ceramic dish, you'll want to line it with waxed paper so you can remove the frozen ingredients more easily if you choose freezing option b on step 19 below.
11. Arrange half of one batch of potatoes in the bottom of the dish.
12. Make a layer of one batch of spinach over the potatoes.
13. Pour on half of one batch of onion sauce.
14. Arrange the rest of the potatoes on top of the sauce.
15. Pour the remaining sauce over the potatoes.
16. Bake covered at 375°F for 30 minutes.
17. If you want to enjoy a casserole on the first day, remove the lid of one of the casseroles and continue baking 15 minutes more until brown and bubbly.
18. Place the other casseroles in the refrigerator to cool.
19. Once cool, either:
    a. spoon the ingredients into a bag (you'll lose the attractive design, but it still tastes great) and freeze using the bag-in-box method. Or

b. freeze in the casserole dish. Once frozen, pop out of the dish and bag or rewrap so you can use your dish for other cooking projects. Return to the freezer.

20. Place the ingredients in an ovenproof dish. Thaw in the refrigerator. Bake uncovered at 375°F for 15 minutes.

"Very easy. Colorful!"—Tricia Watts

Additional Helps and Suggestions

- Tricia Watts preferred to boil the potatoes whole, then slice them. (Jill: I slice up lots of potatoes all at once and use in many recipes—I like this idea and will use it for several applications.)
- Suzy Richards thought the sauce was the best part, so she'll customize the recipe for her family by leaving out the sweet potatoes, using half the spinach, doubling the sauce, and adding some cheese. (Jill: I like her idea to make it a delicious version of scalloped potatoes. But I need ways to get spinach into my children, so I'll keep it as a spinach dish with potatoes.)
- Amy Beatty said: "My non-sweet-potato-eating family, especially my husband, loved this, which was a pleasant surprise. I thought they would turn their noses up".

Ratings

$ = 10 to 25¢—depending on price of potatoes
Ease = 8
Prep-time = 30 to 45 minutes
Heating = 30 minutes
Mega-Session = 9
Equipment = nothing special, food processor to cut up potatoes helps speed up processing

Scalloped Pineapple

Here's a side dish quite different from the standard mashed potatoes. Loaded with pineapple, this recipe is definitely tasty. My family loves this recipe. It is ideal for covered dish dinners and for company. Crushed pineapple works the best in the recipe, but if you can't find it, you can substitute pineapple bits. Please follow the instructions about using alternatives to sugar. We rarely use white sugar in our home, so for this recipe I use a quality substitute, only half the amount called for of sugar. Please note: I don't mean faux food or chemical substitutes like aspartame or saccharine. I use granulated fructose or cane sugar or sucanat or malt (before being processed into white sugar). In my opinion this is best using my own whole wheat bread, but if you prefer a more traditional taste, you can use store-bought bread. To really make the dollars stretch, buy several loaves of day-old bread, and make mega-batches.

Do Ahead:

- Purchase pineapple in bulk. The 6-pound, 10-ounce (#10) cans make this very economical.
- Either make your own bread and cube, or buy in bulk and cube.
- Buy eggs in bulk and use in a variety of recipes. (See page 152 about eggs.)

X1	X2	X8	
8 SERVINGS	16 SERVINGS	64 SERVINGS	¾ CUP PER SERVING
1 20-ounce can	2 20-ounce cans	1 6-pound, 10-ounce can	Crushed pineapple (or bits), undrained
1 cups	2 cups	8 cups	Sugar (or half of that of substitute)
3	6	24	Eggs, beaten well
4 cups	8 cups	32 cups	Bread, cut into 1- inch cubes (no crusts)

Note: If you are using commercial bread, figure that half a loaf (8 slices) will make 4 cups. One slice usually yields ½ cup of bread cubes. You may use crusts if desired, but it will affect the appearance.

Steps:

1. In a mega-mixing bowl dissolve the sugar in the pineapple (with its juice).
2. Beat in the eggs.
3. Stir in the bread cubes carefully until the bread is wet. The bread cubes will "marinate" and absorb the liquids as it freezes.

OPTION 1: MAKE MIX, FREEZE IN "GLOB" FORM FOR SHAPING ON BAKING DAY

4. Divide into meal-sized amounts.
5. Bag, label, and freeze.
6. Thaw.
7. Pour into a 13 x 9-inch baking dish that has been prepared with a nonstick method. Or use a decorative mold shape.
8. Bake at 350°F for 1 hour.

OPTION 2: FREEZE IN SHAPE AND BAKE DAY OF SERVING

4. Gently press into oven and freezer proof 13 x 9-inch pan(s) or use molded pan(s).
5. Wrap the entire dish in heavy-duty film.
6. Freeze.
7. As soon as it is frozen solid, pop out of the mold and bag or rewrap. Do this quickly; you don't want it to thaw. Continue freezing until use.
8. After removing the wrapping material, place the frozen ingredients back into the mold or pan.
9. Bake at 350°F for 1 hour.

OPTION 3: FORM AND BAKE, THEN FREEZE AND SIMPLY RE-HEAT (SINCE YOU'LL BE BAKING IN THESE MOLDS, THEY HAVE TO BE OVEN-READY.)

4. Gently press into oven and freezer proof 13 x 9-inch pan(s) or use molded pan(s).
3. Bake at 350°F for 1 hour.
4. If using a mold, let stand 10 minutes before removing from the mold.
5. Enjoy one for dinner that night and freeze the rest, or bag and freeze these. Be careful so you don't break the shape. I carefully place them in a large bag that I have laying on a cookie sheet or flat piece of cardboard. I slide the cardboard with bagged loaf onto a freezer shelf, making certain it is level. Once it is frozen solid, it can be packed tightly with other food. (I don't use a "flimsy" shape mold, but one that is more substantial—thick walls.)
6. To serve: Remove from the bag and place back in the pan. (Spray it first). Heat at 350°F for 15 to 20 minutes.

"My company loved it."—Melanie Thurman

Additional Helps and Suggestions

- Melanie Thurman suggested adding cinnamon to the recipe.
- Suzy Richards said it was also good cold. The browner and crispier, the better. She felt it was too sweet and is only going to use ¾ cup of sugar. (Jill: Not all pineapple is processed the same way. If your pineapple is sweetened or in syrup, then you won't need as much sugar as the recipe suggests. If you use unsweetened pineapple, you can adjust the amount of sugar to your family tastes.)
- Jean Dominquez thought it would be even better with about ½ cup of chopped nuts.
- Melanie Fierro suggested adding chopped ham to make it a main dish. Or to sweeten it up a bit, add a little sugar and marchino cherries and serve it cool with whipped cream.

Ratings

$ = 15¢
Ease = 9
Prep-time = 15 to 20 minutes
Heating = 1 hour
Mega-Session = 10
Equipment = kitchen shears to cut up the bread

DESSERTS

Clouds

These make an elegant and tasty dessert. If you have the freezer space, try to keep some of these in your freezer all the time for when you need an "instant" dessert or have to take something to a social function.

Do Ahead:

- Purchase restaurant-sized cream cheese at bargain prices.
- Make your own pie fillings and either can or freeze them.

X1	**X2**	**X6**	
10 SERVINGS	20 SERVINGS	60 SERVINGS	1 CLOUD PER SERVING
8 ounces	16 ounces	48 ounces	Cream cheese, softened
½ cup	1 cup	3 cups	Confectioners' sugar
¼ teaspoon	½ teaspoon	1½ teaspoons	Vanilla extract
1 cup	2 cups	6 cups	Heavy cream
			Pie filling or pudding

Pre-steps: Allow cream cheese to soften.

Steps:

1. In a large bowl whip the cream cheese.
2. Add the sugar (should be creamy).
3. Add the vanilla extract.
4. Gradually mix in the heavy cream.
5. Shape into 3½ inch shells. You can either shape them with a spoon, or make them more eye pleasing by using a pastry tube. (I use prepared cookie sheets and make these bowl-shaped mounds—about 6 to 8 per standard cookie sheet.)
6. Freeze on cookie sheets. Once frozen solid, you can bag these for easier storage.
7. Thaw. Top with pie filling and sprinkle with nuts or confectioners' sugar.

Warning: These are rich. But you can cut the calories somewhat by using low fat cream cheese and half and half instead of the cream.

"Fun and tasty."—Sherry Sartain

Additional Helps and Suggestions

- Sherry Sartain used a cookie cutter to fill up and shape the "clouds" into Christmas trees or snowmen. You could really get creative with this. Children love this sort of thing and have fun making them.
- Joy McKelvey filled hers with chocolate pudding—yum! She also stressed that you need waxed paper when freezing.
- Definitely use waxed paper, cooking parchment, or Teflon® sheets on your cookies sheets.

Ratings

$ = 30¢ each—not including pie filling or pudding.
Ease = 10
Prep-time = 20 minutes—plus or minus depending on how fancy you get with shaping the mounds.
Heating = none
Mega-Session = 2—best to do another day, but you can mega-shop for the ingredients.
Equipment = Electric mixer, Teflon® sheets.

Day-O "Cookies"

(OATMEAL BANANA COOKIES)

I'll take freshly baked cookies anytime compared to old stiff ones. So, with this recipe I like to make mega-batter. Bake enough for that day's snack and immediate eating. Then I freeze the batter in snack-sized amounts for later baking. We named them Day-O because that song Harry Belafonte made popular reminds us of the tropics (bananas) and the "O" also represents the oatmeal. And these "Day-O" cookies will always make them say, "And I wanta go home." Why?—to eat Mom's cookies. Also, they are made fresh each day we serve them: "Day." Please note these are not "standard" cookies. They are muffin-like on purpose. I wanted a healthier, less sweet snack for my children.

Do Ahead:

- Purchase mega-size oatmeal or oat groats and flake your own oatmeal.
- Buy bananas in bulk and mash. Bake some in breads, cookies, or freeze for later use. (If desired, treat with Brown-Away. Drain extra liquid off before freezing.)
- Buy any or all the ingredients in bulk for use in dozens of recipes. I buy restaurant-sized containers of spices and baking ingredients.
- Grind your own flour fresh for this recipe, or use some previously ground and frozen.

X1 MAKES 2+ DOZEN	**X5** MAKES 10+ DOZEN	**X10** MAKES 20+ DOZEN	
1½ cups	7½ cups	15 cups	Flour
1 teaspoon	2 tablespoons	¼ cup	Salt [mol]
_ teaspoon	1 tablespoon	2 tablespoons	Baking soda
_ teaspoon	1 tablespoon	2 tablespoons	Nutmeg
1 teaspoon	4 teaspoons	3 tablespoons	Cinnamon
_ cups	4 cups	8 cups	Shortening
½ cup	2½ cups	5 cups	Honey
1	5	10	Eggs, beaten
1 cup	5 cups	10 cups	Bananas, mashed
1 teaspoon	2 tablespoons	¼ cup	Vanilla extract
1½ cups	7½ cups	15 cups	Oats

Steps:

1. In a large bowl mix together the flour, salt, baking soda, nutmeg, and cinnamon. Fluff it together with a big wire whisk so the ingredients are evenly distributed.
2. In a large mixing bowl beat together the shortening and honey until smooth.
3. Beat the eggs and vanilla into the honey mixture.
4. Add the bananas. Mix carefully.

5. Mix flour mixture and oats with the liquid batter.
6. Refrigerate for at least 30 minutes before forming into cookies and baking.

OPTION 1: BAKE THEM ALL AND FREEZE

7. Preheat the oven to 400°F.
8. Spray cookie sheets with nonstick coating or line with Teflon® liners. Remember the "air-pans" work best and are worth any additional cost.
9. Drop dough by tablespoon about 3 inches apart onto cookie sheets.
10. Bake at 400°F for 12 to 15 minutes. They will be a beautiful golden color and your house will smell wonderful. You'll need to "round-robin" the use of cookie sheets and your oven.
11. Remove to wire racks and cool.
12. Bag and freeze.
13. Thaw and serve. (These aren't nearly as good as ones fresh out of the oven.)

OPTION 2: BAKE SOME, AND FREEZE "READY-TO-BAKE" RAW COOKIES

Day 1

7. Preheat the oven to 400°F.
8. Spray cookie sheets with nonstick coating or line with Teflon® liners for the one you'll bake and line the other ones line with waxed paper) Remember the "air-pans" work best and are worth any additional cost.
9. Drop dough by tablespoon about 3 inches apart onto cookie sheets.
10. Bake one cookie sheets worth (or as many as your family will eat at one sitting) at 400°F for 12 to 15 minutes. They will be a beautiful golden color and your house will smell wonderful.
11. Gently place film (e.g., Reynolds 914) over the raw cookies and seal the edges. Freeze each tray until the cookie dough is frozen solid.
12. Once completely frozen, remove cookies from the sheet and freeze in a bag. Immediately return to the freezer. Do not let the dough thaw. You'll need to work quickly and only pull out one tray at a time. Using this method, you'll be able to pull out one cookie or two dozen from the bag as needed to bake.

Day of 2nd serving and each subsequent serving

13. Pull as many cookies as you want to bake, place on a sprayed cookie sheet, and bake at 400°F for 12 to 15 minutes until golden brown.
14. Remove to a wire rack and cool. Enjoy.

OPTION 3: BAKE SOME, AND FREEZE BATTER FOR LATER SHAPING AND BAKING

Day 1

7. Preheat the oven to 400°F.
8. Spray cookie sheets with nonstick coating or line with Teflon® liners. Remember the "air-pans" work best and are worth any additional cost.

9. Drop the dough by tablespoon about 3 inches apart onto a cookie sheet.
10. Bake one cookie-sheet worth (or as many as your family will eat at one sitting) at 400°F for 12 to 15 minutes. They will be a beautiful golden color and your house will smell wonderful.
11. Divide the batter into snack-sized amounts and freeze in "glob" form.

Day of 2nd serving and each subsequent serving

12. Thaw the batter. Cook as in Steps 9 and 10.

Alternatives: Of course, you don't have to bake the cookies at the same time you're making the batter. Though I've never done this, you could just go straight to freezing for later baking. We have to have some right then to munch on while we work.

Note: When I use my DLX for this recipe, I can't mix all "x10" at one time in the mixing bowl.

Option 1: I collect enough ingredients to make "x10", but just make the "x5" recipe twice. Remember to accomodate the equipment you have—don't make batches too big for your bowls.

Option 2: Or I use the DLX to mix all the liquids ingredients (through step 4), and then I'll add the liquid ingredients into the flour mixture (in a huge mixing bowl) and mix by hand with a heavy-duty spoon.

Converting Recipes Note: If you want to use real butter and sugar in this recipe, use the same amount of butter as Crisco® sticks and double the amount of honey specified for the amount of sugar you'll need or use the same amount of honey required for the amount of granulated fructose you'll need. If you are substituting for one ingredient, but not both, read the following paragraphs and make adjustments.

Normally when substituting Crisco® sticks for butter you'd add an additional ¼ cup of water. But since we're using honey instead of sugar, we don't need to add the additional water. One cup of butter is equal to ¼ cup water and 1 cup of Crisco® stick (basically).

Here is the basic rule for substituting honey for sugar in a recipe: Reduce the liquids by half the amount that you are adding by using honey and increase the dry ingredients so the ratio of dry to wet stays the same. Example: If you're adding in 1 cup of honey to a recipe, reduce the wet ingredients ½ cup and add ½ cup more flour. It can get complicated, but for those with sugar sensitivities, it is well worth the adventure.

Here is the ratio for substituting butter for the Crisco® sticks only:

2 cups	9 cups	18 cups	Flour (amount slightly increased)
¾ cup	4 cups	8 cups	Butter (adds 2 cups more liquid than using Crisco® sticks did)
½ cup	2½ cups	5 cups	Honey
1	4	8	Eggs, beaten (amount slightly decreased)

Here is the ratio for substituting sugar for the honey only:

1½ cups	7½ cups	15 cups	Flour
¼ cup	4 cups	8 cups	Butter
1 cups	5 cups	10 cups	Sugar or half of that amount of granulated fructose
1	5	10	Eggs, beaten

Note: I don't do a perfect math multiplication as I increase batch amounts. That comes from experience and tasting. I also round up or down to fit my utensils and equipment without sacrificing taste or consistency.

"All 10's."—Tina Cook

"I found these quite tasty with a cup of hot coffee for breakfast or an afternoon break."—Tracey Cavender

Additional Helps and Suggestions

- Tina Cook used a melon-baller and had tiny mini-muffin style cookies. She points out that this dough does not flatten as it cooks. She is right. I developed these as a healthier alternative to the standard, really-sweet cookie. These are more "muffin" like than "cake" like. Because you bake them "drop-style" like cookies, my children call them "cookies." I'm also trying to encourage them to like more healthy food.
- Karen B. Collins likes the warm cookies best. I agree with her that they aren't nearly as good cold. They reheated theirs in the microwave and ate them as muffins for dinner with butter. She said that they were great for breakfast, too. She also suggests making them as muffin/cupcakes and ice them with a cream cheese icing. See below for Karen's recipe.
- Jill adds: Occasionally bananas are on sale for 10¢ a pound because they are starting to brown. I'll buy LOTS. We peel them, drop them in the mixer, and it mashes them for us. We then make up a batch of these "cookies" and put the other mashed bananas into ice cube trays. When they are frozen, we pop out and bag the 2-ounce cubes. We then can use those 2-ounce cubes in everything from banana bread to Smoothy-Frothies (page 209). If you don't have a heavy-duty mixer, you can mash the bananas easily with a fork, potato masher, or pastry blender (knife). To keep them from browning, we spray them with Brown Away (page 373).

Karen Collins' Cream Cheese Icing

2 teaspoons	Vanilla extract
¼ stick	Margarine
8 ounces	Cream cheese, softened
1 pound	Confectioners' sugar (10x)

1. In a medium bowl fluff the confectioners' sugar.
2. In a large bowl cream the margarine and cream cheese together.
3. Stir in the "fluffed" confectioners' sugar and vanilla.
4. Ice the "cookies"

Also there is a "sugar-free" cream cheese icing recipe in my book, *Dinner's in the Freezer!*. It is basically the same recipe as the one above but uses ¼ cup of honey instead of the confectioners' sugar.

Ratings
$ = 25¢
Ease = 8
Prep-time = 30 minutes
Heating = 12 to 15 minutes
Mega-Session = 7—We usually do these on a separate day. We do buy bananas in bulk or when they go on sale
Equipment = A nice mixer really speeds up the mixing and mashing

Japanese Fruit Pie

I've learned that it is not much more work to make 3 pies than it is to make one. So, I'm always looking for good recipes that will freeze. My Aunt Ginny sent me this recipe and she is right—it does freeze well. Note that this recipe will also make Japanese chewy bars.

Do Ahead:

- Make a mega-batch of pie pastry and freeze for use in dozens of recipes.
- Buy as many of the ingredients as possible in bulk.
- It is only a tiny bit more work to make 3 or 4 pies as it is to make one, so enjoy one today and freeze two for another evening. Or double the x3 and make 6, or really go for the gold and double the x4 and make eight—just keep in mind how many pie pans you have. I like to use metal pans for those I'll freeze because the pies will just pop out with a slight push on the bottom. It is much more difficult to get them out of a glass pie pan. I'll make a huge batter and make some pies and some snack bars—see recipes below.

X1	X2	X3	X4	
6 SERVINGS	12 SERVINGS	18 SERVINGS	24 SERVINGS	6 SLICES PER PIE (OR 10 TO 12 2-INCH SQUARE BARS PER PAN)
½ cup	1 cup	1½ cups	2 cups	Butter
¾ cup	1½ cups	2¼ cups	3 cups	Sugar
2	4	6	8	Eggs
1 teaspoon	2 teaspoons	3 teaspoons	4 teaspoons	Vinegar (white or red)
1 teaspoon	2 teaspoons	3 teaspoons	4 teaspoons	Vanilla extract
½ cup	1 cup	1½ cups	2 cups	Flaked coconut
½ cup	1 cup	1½ cups	2 cups	Raisins
½ cup	1 cup	1½ cups	2 cups	Chopped pecans
1	2	3	4	9-inch pie shell(s), unbaked

Steps:

1. In a large bowl cream the butter and sugar. (I would definitely use a mixer for x3 and x4.)
2. Add the eggs and mix well.
3. Add the vinegar and vanilla. Mix until evenly distributed.
4. Stir in the coconut, raisins, and pecans.
5. Pour into the pie shell.
6. Bake at 300°F for 50 to 55 minutes.
7. Serve and enjoy.
8. Cool the other pies in the refrigerator.

9. Once cool, wrap in plastic and freeze. Once the pies are frozen, you can pop them out and place them in a bag. Label and continue freezing.
10. To serve, thaw in the refrigerator and enjoy.
11. If you prefer this pie warm, you can either
    a) Cut each slice, place on a microwave dish and zap for 30 to 60 seconds, or
    b) Heat in the oven in a baking dish, at 300°F for 10 to 15 minutes.

Private Treats: Sometimes you need dessert for only one or two and you don't need to thaw or serve an entire pie. So, with one of the pies that has cooled in the refrigerator, I slice into six pieces. I individually freeze each piece by bagging them separately. Label and freeze. This way you can send one piece along with a lunch or have a private dessert with your spouse once the children have gone to bed.

Allergies: Since I'm allergic to nuts, I don't add pecans to the batter in step 4. I pour enough for one pie. Then add the pecans to the rest of the batter (only 1 cup) then pour the batter for the other pies. I bake them all together. I cut my pie into individual pieces and freeze as in "Private Treats" above. So when the rest of the family is having theirs with nuts, I have mine without and we're all happy. This concept of customizing for allergies works for many of the recipes. For the "allergy-free" version, freeze in single serving size, so that family member can still eat along with the rest of the family. I sometimes add ¼ cup of granola to my "private" servings to give it the texture of the nuts. It is delicious.

Tarts: You can make this pie into individual tarts, also. Adjust the baking time to about 20 minutes and check—it depends on the size of your tart pans. (Sometimes I make pastry shells in muffin tins—as an alternative to cutting the pie into pieces—there's just more pastry per piece that way.)

Japanese Chewy Bars and Japanese Granola Bars: You can make this recipe into Japanese Chewy Bars by greasing (I rarely do this) a jellyroll pan (or use a Teflon® sheet). Pour the batter (x3 or x4 recipe amount) into the jellyroll pan. Bake at 300°F for 20 to 25 minutes. Immediately cut into bars. (Be careful of the Teflon® sheet, if used.) Wrap the bars in waxed paper. Place the wax paper-wrapped bars into plastic bags and freeze. Or make Japanese Granola Bars: a variation of this recipe is to put down a thin layer (2 to 4 cups, until the entire surface is covered) of homemade granola (see page 215) on the jellyroll pan, pour the batter over that, then bake (same as for chewy bars)—another delicious snack.

"Wonderful, will definitely make this one again!"—Terri Houchin

Additional Helps and Suggestions

- Terri Houchin says, "I intend to try it with twice the coconut and omit the raisins. It's really delicious the way it is, but I'm going to try some variations for versatility's sake."

- Marcille Lytle used 1 cup of pecan meal instead of 1½ cups chopped pecans (for the x3 recipe). She always uses pecan meal instead of chopped pecans. It costs a lot less than chopped pecans. She buys 5 pounds through her co-op for $7.00 and stores it in her freezer for later use.
- About the bars, depending on how thick of a bar you like, use "x3" or "x4" amount across the jellyroll pan. (I like "x4" for a thick bar.) The time will vary slightly because of the difference in the batter. Check it after 20 minutes. If it is not ready, check it again in 5 minutes. It should be done by then. I use a Teflon® sheet now and it just comes out perfectly after 25 minutes.

Ratings

$ = 30¢—price of raisins and nuts vary so much
Ease = 10
Prep-time = 20 minutes
Heating = 50 to 55 minutes for pie, 20 to 25 for bars
Mega-Session = 10
Equipment = food processor for chopping pecans, good mixer for batter

Lemon Snow Bunnies

(LEMON SNACK BARS)

This is one of my children's favorite snack foods. It is so easy to make that I make 4 double batches at at time and freeze them in snack-sized bags. They are great for picnics or packed lunches. If I pack them directly from the freezer, they thaw by lunchtime. Please note: You make this snack in two stages: 1) the "crust" and 2) the filling on the crust.

Do Ahead:

- Purchase an entire box of lemons for a great price.
- Grate the rind and freeze for use in several recipes.
- Juice the lemons, pour into ice cube trays, and once frozen, bag the cubes for use in several recipes. (Remember the tip of heating lemons before juicing to double the amount of juice.)

STAGE 1 ("CRUST"):

X1	**X2**	**X4**	**X8**	
32 SERVINGS	64 SERVINGS	128 SERVINGS	256 SERVINGS	1 X 2-INCH BARS
½ cup	1 cup	2 cups	4 cups	Butter, softened (or Better Butter Spread, see page 370)
1⅓ cups	2⅔ cups	5 ⅓ cups	10⅔ cups	Flour
¼ cup	½ cup	1 cup	2 cups	Sugar (or half the amount of fructose)
1 8 x 8	1 13 x 9	2 13 x 9	1 15 x 10 or 2 13 x 9	Pans (I prefer glass pans for this recipes for more even baking)

1. Preheat the oven to 350°F.
2. In a large bowl combine all of the ingredients and press evenly in the pan.
3. Bake at 350°F for 15 to 20 minutes. (If necessary, switch shelves halfway through the baking.) While the crust is baking, make the topping. The crust will look dry and very lightly golden. You don't want it as dark as a pie crust—it will continue to bake with the topping.

STAGE 2 (TOPPING):

X1	**X2**	**X4**	**X8**	
2	4	8	16	Eggs (beaten)
Dash	Dashes	Dashes	Dashes	Salt (or to taste)
¾ cup	1½ cups	3 cups	6 cups	Sugar (or half as much fructose)

¼ cup	⅓ cup	1 cup	2 cups	Lemon juice
1 teaspoon	2 teaspoons	4 teaspoons	3 tablespoons	Lemon rind or zest
2 tablespoons	¼ cup	½ cup	1 cup	Flour
¼ teaspoon	½ teaspoon	1 teaspoon	2 teaspoons	Baking powder

1. In a large bowl beat the eggs and mix in the remaining ingredients.
2. Pour the "pudding" batter over the baked crusted.
3. Bake at 350° for 25 to 30 minutes. The topping should look dry with no liquid spots. Be careful not to overbake or they will become too dry and brittle. You want them to be "chewy."
4. Sprinkle with confectionsers' sugar if desired. Cool. Cut in brownie-sized bars. Package in snack-sized portions. Freeze.

"10."—Marcille Lytle

Additional Helps and Suggestions

- Leslie Gipson used lemon extract instead of the grated lemon rind and gave it a "10" for taste for both adults and children.
- Terri Houchin was able to cut the butter amount in the "x2" crust to 3 sticks and it came out overall "10". By doing that, she reduced the fat and calories.
- My son, Reed, made a mega-batch of these all by himself the day before one of our week-long trips. He wrapped each bar individually in waxed paper. He froze some overnight and keep some unfrozen. We ate the unfrozen ones the first day. The frozen ones thawed nicely and were delicious several days later. They were a great treat and saved us having to run through the drive-thru's for every stomach growl. Alan likes that they aren't messy like some snacks that leave crumbs all in the car. (Of course, we take other munchies, too.)
- Cynthia Fisher thinks it would be more nutritious with Better Butter instead of regular butter.
- If you use salted butter in this recipe, there is no need to add salt to the topping.
- To make these into a wonderfully fancy dessert, form the crust in individual tart molds (sprayed to make them non-stick). Bake for 5 to 10 minutes (depending on the size of the mold). Then add the topping. Bake for 10 to 15 minutes. (Check this because if you are making very small sizes, it will take less time.) You can also use muffin tins and then use muffin papers for easy removal. These look great and are wonderful for teas, brunches, or as an easy dessert for a buffet.
- Jill: We like to double the topping in this recipe for more of a pie-like snack. It works well. Just use the "x2" amount of topping for the "x1" crust. Bake it for about 5 mintues longer. The children love it this option so much that it's the main way I bake it now—it just makes a slightly messier snack for roadtrips.
- We've made Orange Bunnies, but substituting orange juice for the lemon juice and grated orange rind for the lemon rind—delicious! Because orange juice isn't as potent as lemon juice, use orange juice concentrate (same amount as for lemon juice) and don't dilute the concentrate.

Ratings

$ = 20¢—Much less than store-bought bars
Ease = 9-10
Prep-time = 15 minutes
Heating = 20 minutes and then 30 minutes
Mega-Session = 7—I mega-process a box of lemons during a mega-session, freeze the juice, and then another day I use that juice and make a mega-batch of these bars
Equipment = a mixer makes the blending much easier than doing it by hand; a lemon reamer helps with making the zest

Pina Colada Cookies

These cookies are so good that I'm asked for the recipe every time I serve them—and that's been for more than nineteen years. I usually make the x8 recipe, bake half the dough into cookies—serve half of those that day and freeze the other cookies for another day—and freeze the rest of the batter for baking another day. That way I'm only making a small batch of the icing each time. I like having frozen raw cookies in the freezer for those times you just need a quick snack—I can bake half-a-dozen in my toaster-oven. Freeze the leftover juice in one-half-cup amounts for use in a variety of recipes. I have made these cookies without the coconut (I was out) and they were still delicious as just "Pina Cookies."

Do Ahead:

- Buy pineapple in a 6-pound, 10-ounce (#10) can for the best price.
- Purchase any of the ingredients in bulk for use in this recipe as well as others.
- Make the dough ahead and freeze for future baking, or make mega-batches of baked cookies and freeze some for other days.

X1 40 COOKIES	X2 80 COOKIES	X8 320 COOKIES	
2 cups	4 cups	16 cups	Flour
½ tablespoon	1 tablespoon	¼ cup	Baking powder
½ teaspoon	1 teaspoon	4 teaspoons	Baking soda
¼ teaspoon	½ teaspoon	2 teaspoons	Salt
½ cup	1 cup	4 cups	Shortening (or Crisco® sticks)
½ cup	1 cup	4 cups	Granulated fructose or twice those amounts of sugar
1	2	8	Eggs (beaten)
1 teaspoon	2 teaspoons	3 tablespoons	Vanilla extract
¼ cup	½ cup	2 cups	Flaked coconut
			Pina Colada Cookie Icing (follows)
1 20-ounce	2 20-ounce cans	1 6-pound, 10-ounce can	Crushed pineapple, drained (reserve juice)

Steps:

1. In a large bowl mix the flour, baking powder, soda, and salt together. With this much flour, it is easier to use a large wire whisk to fluff the ingredients together.
2. In a separate bowl cream the shortening and sugar together. You can do this by hand, but a good mixer makes the work so much easier.
3. Add the beaten eggs and vanilla to the shortening mixture. Mix well until smooth.
4. Alternate adding the flour mixture and the pineapple until blended. (*Note:* The dough will be lumpy from the pineapple pieces.)

OPTION 1: MAKE MIX AND FREEZE IN "GLOB-FORM" FOR SHAPING AND BAKING ANOTHER DAY

5. Divide the dough into freezer bags.
6. Label and freeze. (Use bag-in-box method.) (See note above about pineapple juice.)
7. To use: thaw a bag of dough.
8. Spray a cookie pan with nonstick coating.
9. Drop the dough by rounded tablespoon. Flatten slightly. These are mounded cookies.
10. Bake at 400°F for 8 to 10 minutes until lightly golden.
11. Remove to a wire rack to cool.
12. While still warm, drizzle with pineapple icing and sprinkle with extra coconut (press into icing).

OPTION 2: FREEZE IN COOKIE SHAPES AND BAKE DAY OF SERVING

5. Line a cookie sheet or piece of cardboard with waxed paper or a Teflon® liner. (Double-check that cardboard or pan will fit flat in the freezer.)
6. Drop the dough by rounded tablespoon. Flatten slightly. These are mounded cookies.
7. Set level on the freezer shelf.
8. Once the cookie dough is completely frozen, bag the frozen disks for use later. This way you can pull out and bake one or a dozen cookies as the need arises.
10. Spray a pan with nonstick coating.
11. If the dough has thawed, bake at 400°F for 8 to 10 minutes. If they are still frozen, bake at 350°F for 12 to 15 minutes. Follow the directions above for icing, if desired.

OPTION THREE: BAKE THE COOKIES ALL THE FIRST DAY

5. Spray a cookie pan with a non-stick coating.
6. Drop dough by rounded tablespoon. Flatten slightly. These are mounded cookies.
7. Bake at 400°F for 8 to 10 minutes until lightly golden.
8. Remove to a wire rack to cool.
9. While still warm, drizzle with pineapple icing and sprinkle with extra coconut (press into icing).
10. Enjoy the cookies. If you baked more than you'll need in the next few days, the rest will freeze well for a few months. Lay the cookies on waxed paper (cookie sheet or box lid). Freeze. Once frozen solid, bag. Then you can pull out as many of the cookies as you need. They thaw very quickly. Another option: Bag a few in a small sandwich bag and freeze. Pack them with the lunches. By the time lunch rolls around, the cookies will have thawed.

Pina Colada Cookie Icing

X1	X2	X8	
4 cups	8 cups	32 cups	Sifted confectioner's sugar
2 tablespoons to ¼ cup	¼ to ½ cup	2 to 4 cups	Pineapple juice (use remainder from when you drained the can of crushed pineapple)
¼ cup	½ cup	2 to 4 cups	Flaked coconut

Steps:

1. Either shift the sugar or fluff with a wire whisk in a bowl.
2. Slowly add half of the juice and stir.
3. If the icing is too thick, then add a small amount of juice until it is a little softer than toothpaste. The heat of the cookies will cause it to run if you make the icing too thin.
4. Drizzle this icing over the warm cookies.
5. Sprinkle the coconut over the icing and press gently. Any extra icing freezes well.

Note: One trick I use a lot is to make a huge batch of icing and freeze small amounts of it in plastic bags. As I need the icing for this and other recipes, I thaw one of the bags, cut a tiny bit off one of the corner, and insto-presto—I have a pastry bag.

"The taste was great."—Linda Bond (no relation)

Additional Helps and Suggestions

- Jana Hoffman made part of the recipe with coconut and part without. They liked them best while they were still warm. (Jill: I agree.)
- Robin Wood found that they do not store well in a cookie jar. They get soggy.
- I agree with Robin, that's why I only bake as much as we'll eat on one day. Freeze the rest individually and freeze some dough. They absorb the moisture in the air and stick to each other in a cookie jar. They will taste good, but you have to scoop them with you fingers and eat "cookie globs."

Ratings

\$ = 10¢
Ease = 9
Prep-time = 20 to 30 minutes
Heating = 8 to 10 minutes
Mega-Session = 5—I prefer to make these on a separate a day, though I do go ahead and buy the ingredients in bulk and store until I need them.
Equipment = mixer for the dough, Teflon® sheet for ease of baking

Pumpkin Bread Pudding

I've learned that pumpkins cost a whole lot more the last week of October than they do the first week of November. I buy several large ones and we process the fruit for several recipes. We cut it in to cubes, boil it, mash it, and bag it. I then have enough for a year for a dollar or two. I have dozens of recipes for the pumpkin—this is one of our favorites. I also add a cup of cooked pumpkin to muffin, bread, and soup recipes. It adds color, sweetness, and fiber. You can toast the seeds for a snack or to add to granola.

Do Ahead:

- Buy pumpkins on sale November 1 or 2. They are cheap and sometimes free. Process. See details above.
- Buy bread from a day-old store for best prices.
- Buy as many other ingredients as possible in bulk.
- Make mega-batches of this recipe and follow your choice of options.
- Cut up bread cubes for this and other recipes all at one time.

X1 10 SERVINGS	X2 20 SERVINGS	X4 40 SERVINGS	2-INCH SQUARE BARS
8 slices	16 slices	32 slices	Day-old,whole-wheat bread
1 cup	2 cups	4 cups	Mashed pumpkin (canned or homemade)
2	4	8	Eggs
2 teaspoons	¼ cup	3 tablespoons	Ground cinnamon
1 teaspoons	2 teaspoons	4 teaspoons	Grated nutmeg
¼ teaspoon	½ teaspoon	1 teaspoon	Salt
⅛ teaspoon	¼ teaspoon	½ teaspoon	Ground cloves
½ cup	1 cup	2 cups	Raisins (or dates)
½ cup	1 cup	2 cups	Chopped pecans, optional
2 cups	4 cups	8 cups	Milk
⅔ cup	1⅓ cups`	2⅔ cups	Firmly packed brown sugar
1 cup	2 cups	4 cups	Whipped cream [optional]

Steps:

1. Using a pair of kitchen shears, trim the crusts from the bread. (Freeze crusts for other cooking projects). Cut each slice of bread into 3 strips and then cut each strip into 3 or 4 pieces. This should make 1-inch squares (doesn't have to be exact).
2. If you haven't prepared the pumpkin, do that now.
3. Separate the eggs and have them ready to use. Leave the egg whites out to become room temperature.
4. In a small bowl, mix spices together.

OPTION 1: FREEZE IN LOOSE FORM, POUR IN PAN AND BAKE DAY OF SERVING

5. Either use bags or plastic container. Place bags inside boxes with the edges lapped over side. (See instructions on page 117 for more details on the Bag-in-Box method.)
6. In each container, place bread cubes. Add pecans and raisins.
7. In a mixing bowl beat together the milk, pumpkin, egg yolks, brown sugar, and spices.
8. In a separate bowl beat the egg whites until stiff.
9. Fold the egg whites into the pumpkin mixture.
10. Pour the pumpkin mixture over the breadcrumbs.
11. Seal the containers. Freeze.
12. Thaw in the refrigerator.
13. Pour the pudding batter into a sprayed 2-quart shallow baking dish.
14. Bake at 350°F for 1 hour until a knife inserted in the center comes out clean.
15. Serve warm or chilled. Add a dollop of whipped topping if desired.

OPTION 2: FREEZE IN SHAPED FORM, AND BAKE DAY OF SERVING

5. Either use metal pans or line glass pans with waxed paper, foil, or a Teflon® liner. Spray pans with nonstick coating.
6. Arrange the bread cubes on the bottom of the pans.
7. Sprinkle nuts and raisins over the bread cubes.
8. Follow steps 7 through 10 above in Option 1.
9. Cover the pans with a lid, plastic wrap, or foil. Freeze. Once frozen solid, remove from the pans and either wrap or bag. Continue freezing.
10. Remove the wrapping, and place back in a sprayed pan. Thaw in the refrigerator, covered.
11. Follow steps 14 and 15 in Option 1.

OPTION THREE: BAKE COMPLETELY, FREEZE, AND THEN REHEAT

5. Spray pans with nonstick coating, or line with waxed paper or foil.
6. Follow steps 6 through 8 above in Option 2.
7. Follow step 14 in Option 1.
8. Either serve one now and freeze the rest, or freeze all.
9. Remove from the pans and wrap or bag. Continue freezing.
10. Thaw. Serve thawed or reheat by placing back in the pan and warming at 325°F for 10 minutes.

"Very rich and elegant! Fantastic."—Sandy Farrar
"This is wonderful. A great recipe!"—Kellie Coombs

Additional Helps and Suggestions

- Sandy Farrar had a wonderful idea. She's going to make it next time using raisin bread. (she'll omit additional raisins and cut back on the cinnamon.) She also said she saw no need to cut crusts off—they used the whole slice of bread. She also sprinkled some brown sugar over the top before she baked it.

- Kellie Coombs was starting to mega-cook. It took her 3 hours to make 4 mega-recipes. (Jill: That was great! That might give you an idea of how to pace yourself. Remember, no one is clocking you. Work at your own pace. The more you do this, the less time it will take.)
- If you're working a mega-session, you might want to mass-prepare lots of bread cubes or bread-crumbs. Freeze them. Then use them on another day for recipes like this one. Or go ahead and prepare it all at the same time you are doing some other bread-base recipes.
- For a review of working with egg whites, see the Topics section.

Ratings
$ = 30¢
Ease = 8
Prep-time = 30 minutes
Heating = 1 hour
Mega-Session = 8
Equipment = mixer to get good egg whites.

Sopaipillas

(MEXICAN DESSERT PUFFS)

Don't relegate this to the "only on special occasions" list just because this is an ethnic dessert. Of course, I like to serve these with a Spanish-themed meal. Nevertheless, these are so good that we like them with fried chicken meals and Count Stroganoff Beef. It is barely any more work to make the mega-batch of dough instead of the x1 amount. We only fry one dessert's worth at a time, and freeze the dough in balls for other meals. We make it a family project so making the dessert can be almost as enjoyable as eating it. We've had some of our hardest laughs as each child learned how to "shake" the "soppies." They invariably don't put the lid on tight one time and they get coated with sugar. We laugh with them, not at them, as they recover from their surprise. You pronounce "sopaipillas"—soh-pie-pee-l'yahs.

Do Ahead:

- Buy the ingredients in bulk.
- Make a mega-batch of dough. Cook some the first night, freeze the remaining dough for other times.

X1	**X2**	**X8**	
12 SERVINGS	24 SERVINGS	96 SERVINGS	3 PUFFS PER SERVING
2 cups	4 cups	16 cups	All-purpose flour
1 teaspoon	2 teaspoons	3 tablespoons	Baking powder
½ teaspoon	1 teaspoon	4 teaspoons	Salt
1 tablespoon	2 tablespoons	½ cup	Shortening
⅔ to ¾ cup	1 to 1½ cups	6 to 8 cups	Cold water
For Toppings			
⅓ cup	⅔ cup	3 cups	Honey
2 tablespoons	¼ cup	1 cup	Butter
3 tablespoons	⅓ cup	1½ cups	Sugar
¼ teaspoon	½ teaspoon	2 teaspoons	Ground cinnamon

Steps:

1. In a large bowl fluff or sift together the flour, baking powder, and salt.
2. Cut the shortening into the flour with a pastry knife or by using your heavy-duty mixer.
3. Gradually add cold water until the dough is moistened and cleans the side of the bowl. Be careful not to add too much water. You can always add a few drops more, you can't remove it.
4. Divide the dough into batch amounts and form into balls.

OPTION 1: MAKE SOME TODAY AND FREEZE OTHER BATCHES TO FRY ANOTHER DAY

5. Bag each batch amount in a freezer bag or place in an airtight container. Set one batch amount in the refrigerator to chill and freeze the other batches for another day.
6. Depending on how many soppies you will eat at one sitting, divide dough into balls.: 2 balls for "x1," 4 balls for "x2," and 16 balls for "x8.") My family will eat a double batch at one sitting. Keep the dough you aren't working on covered with a damp paper towel to prevent drying. If you work at a relaxed pace, you'll want to keep the unused dough in an airtight container in the refrigerator.
7. Begin heating the oil to 360°F degrees in a deep fat fryer, skillet, or Dutch Oven. You'll need it at least 2-inches deep.
8. Roll the dough to ¼-inch thickness. Cut into 3-inch diamonds. (Since we're all working together, one child will be rolling out dough, one will be cutting diamonds, another will be running them back and forth to me or Daddy (working the hot oil) and then one gets to do the topping. We rotate the children around the "stations.")
9. Fry 3 or 4 diamonds at a time. Turn once until puffed and golden brown. It only takes about 1 minute on each side so be careful not to overcook them.
10. Drain them well. Then place on paper towels to soak up any extra oil.
11. Make the honey butter. One of us makes the honey butter by zapping the butter and honey together in a microwaveable dish until the butter is melted. Stir well. Or you could do this on the stovetop.
12. Make the cinnamon sugar. Mix together sugar and cinnamon. (We keep a container of cinnamon/sugar available for use in dozens of recipes.)
13. Roll the puffs in honey butter, and then sprinkle with cinnamon sugar. Enjoy.
14. On other days, thaw frozen batch amounts and repeat steps 6 through 13 above.

OPTION 2: FRY ALL TODAY, EAT SOME, AND FREEZE FOR ANOTHER DAY

5. Bag each batch amount in a freezer bag or place in an airtight container. Set batches in the refrigerator to chill (see step 6 above for details).
6. Follow steps 6 through 13 above.
7. Freeze puffs individually. Once frozen, bag.
8. Thaw puffs and reheat by baking in a 350°F oven for 6 to 8 minutes.

Note: I understand that to be "proper" we're supposed to either roll them in the honey butter or sprinkle them with sugar. My children like both. You decide for your family. We use a small airtight container with ½ cup of cinnamon sugar. We place 2 to 3 puffs in it, place the lid on and then shake. This way we get a more even distribution. You could just sprinkle on the cinnamon sugar out of a shaker.

Around-the-Clock: These are not only good for dessert, but we like them for breakfast and snacks. Think of them as Mexican donuts.

"All 10's."—Lacey Farrar

Additional Helps and Suggestions

- Sandy Farrar said: "My 14 year-old daughter (Lacey) prepared and made these on taco night. She had fun and we all liked them. We froze half the recipe to use next taco night. It was an easy side dish for her to make. She also made tacos and trimmings and tamales, and refried beans. So she was busy, but able to handle it all well."

Ratings

$ = 5¢
Ease = 10
Prep-time = 20 to 30 minutes
Heating = 1 minutes
Mega-Session = 6—can make dough and freeze, but these are best eaten within hours of being fried
Equipment = deep fat fryer or deep skillet

"Strawberry Taffeta" or "Straw and Rice"

(STRAWBERRY RICE PUDDING)

This is one of those tea party-type desserts that is perfect when the ladies come over. It is delicious enough for anyone, but I have to call it Straw and Rice to get my he-man boys to eat it. Isn't it funny how a name can "change" the flavor of a dish. The best way to make this is to make your own strawberry frozen yogurt and homemade rice pudding. If you don't have the time, buy vanilla frozen yogurt and add your own strawberries. If you are really pressed for time, buy strawberry frozen yogurt and packaged rice pudding and layer in dessert glasses. You can make this days ahead and store in your freezer for serving. Though I don't make mega-batches for long term freezing, I do mega-prepare the strawberries. Note: this rice pudding recipe is good as a dessert all by itself (don't fold in the pureed strawberries if you want a plain rice pudding—just serve it in a sundae dish and sprinkle with cinnamon). You can use this quick, no added sugar version of frozen yogurt, make your own with an ice cream freezer, or purchase it from the store.

Do Ahead:

- Buy strawberries in season at great prices and mass process (dehydrate or freeze several different ways).
- Buy rice in bulk for this and other recipes.
- Buy white grape juice concentrate by the case for the best price and use as the sweetener in many recipes.

Simple Frozen Yogurt

X1	X2	
4 SERVINGS	8 SERVINGS	ABOUT 14 OUNCES PER SERVING
1 cups	2 cups	Plain vanilla yogurt
1 cups	2 cups	Frozen strawberries
1 tablespoon	2 tablespoons	White grape juice concentrate

Make Simple Frozen Yogurt

1. In a blender whip the yogurt, strawberries, and concentrate.
2. Place in an airtight container and freeze for 30 minutes. While it is freezing, make the rice pudding.
3. Place the yogurt back in the blender and whip until smooth.
4. Return to the airtight container and freeze for an additional 30 minutes.
5. Repeat steps 3 and 4 so that you've frozen the yogurt for 2 hours (4 sessions of blending and freezing).
6. You can:
   a. Enjoy it now because it is ready to eat, as it is very delicious. Or,
   b. Freeze this on popsicle sticks for a delicious, healthy snack. Or,
   c. Use it in this Strawberry Taffeta recipe.

Rice Pudding

X1	X2	
4 SERVINGS	8 SERVINGS	1 CUP PER SERVING
3 ½ cups	7 cups	Skim milk
½ cup	1 cup	Long-grain rice
4 teaspoons	3 tablespoons	Sugar or granulated fructose
½ teaspoon	1 teaspoon	Salt
¼ cup	½ cup	Puréed strawberries (cold)

Make Pudding

1. In a saucepan heat the milk, rice, sugar, and salt to boiling.
2. Reduce the heat to low and cover the pot.
3. Simmer for 50 minutes—stirring occasionally to keep it from sticking.
4. Check. The rice should be tender and the pudding creamy.
5. Place in an airtight bowl. Lay a sheet of plastic wrap directly on the surface of the pudding. Put the lid on the bowl. Refrigerate until ready to assemble the dessert.
6. Just before you're ready to serve fold in the puréed strawberries.

ADDITIONAL INGREDIENTS FOR STRAWBERRY TAFFETA

X1	X2	
1 cup	2 cups	Puréed frozen strawberries

Assemble Dessert

1. In sundae dishes (or use whatever you have, even goblets), place 2 tablespoons of puréed strawberries.
2. Add a layer of 2 tablespoons of frozen yogurt.
3. Add a layer of 2 tablespoons of rice pudding.
4. Repeat layers until you reach the top of your dish.
5. Serve immediately, or cover and freeze for serving later.

Note: I do not make the completed desserts way ahead of serving. You can freeze them for one or two days, but they aren't nearly as good. Don't freeze for much longer or the pudding becomes grainy. You can make the simple frozen yogurt days ahead.

Idea: This concept works with a variety of fruit, though the strawberry version is my favorite. Try it with blueberries, bananas, or peaches. Remember all the fruit needs to be puréed and frozen.

Section Five

Plans

Six Month Plan

(6 months or 26 weeks)

187 dinner entrees

213 side dishes [others will be fixed that day, or the entrée is an all-in one, some meals with use several side dishes (i.e., bread and potato and vegetable]

121 breakfasts (other breakfasts will be fixed that day)

122 lunches (other lunches will be made that day or we'll use leftovers from dinner)

90 desserts, snacks, or appetizers (we don't need these every day)

REPEAT PATTERN:

4 meals of any recipe (repeat every 6 weeks)

8 meals of any recipe (repeat every other month)

Vegetarian Possibilities

I realize that some of my readers are vegetarians. I also know that vegetarianism ranges from those who don't eat red meat to those who won't eat any product that comes from any animal, with many variations in between. The following list is of recipes that either are already meat-free or can be adapted by the use of meat substitutes—for some of these recipes, it is just a matter of omitting the meat. The vegetarian would need to calculate his nutrients from the entire meal, not just the adapted recipe. In other words, I have not balanced proteins in these recipes.

Crockpot Options

Wouldn't it be nice to have dinner ready when we come in the door after a rough day? By letting a crockpot slowly reheat the food all day for us, that is just what we'll have. The following recipes can be reheated in a crockpot. (In some cases, such as meat loaves, the texture will be different than if you oven-baked). If you want a more crispy crust, then you can remove it from the crockpot and bake the ingredients in an ovenproof pan uncovered for approximately 10 minutes.

Assembling Amounts

SHOPPING TO SESSION CONVERSIONS

This chart serves you with conversions between the shopping amounts of some ingredients and the pre-prepared, processed amounts. For instance, when your recipe calls for one onion, chopped, you'll need to know how much that is (out of the mass of processed onions you pre-prepared) in measured amounts.

It also has room for you to keep track of any additional ingredients that you use or any variations you find in processing.

Ingredient	Processing	Shopping Amount	Assembling Amount	Note
Bell peppers	Chopped	1 pepper	~ 1 cup	
Bell peppers	Slices	1 pepper	~ 1 cup	
Carrots	Chopped	1 carrot (3 ounce-peeled)	⅔ cup	
Celery	Sliced/chopped	1 rib	~½ cup	
Ground meat	Cooked and crumbled	1 pound	3 cups	
Onions	Chopped	1 medium onion (5.0 ounce peeled)	1¼ cup	
Potatoes	Sliced	1 medium potato (6.0 ounce peeled)	1¼ cup	
Potatoes	Sliced	1 pound (14.5 ounce peeled)	3 cups	
Poultry	Cooked and chopped	1 pound	1 cup	
Stew Meat	Cooked and cut into ½-inch pieces	1 pound	~2 cups	

Selected Bibliography

Ball Freezer Book. Muncie, IN: Ball Corporation, 1976.

Bazore, Katherine. *Hawaiian and Pacific Foods.* New York: M. Barrows and Company, 1943.

Becker, Brad and Sue Becker. *The Bread Beckers' Recipe Collection.* 1997.

Dyer, Ceil. *The Freezer Cookbook.* New York: Essandess Special Edition (a division of Simon and Schuster), 1967.

Famous Florida Chefs' Favorite Citrus Recipes. Lakeland, FL: Florida Citrus Commission, 1966.

Fowler, Sina F. and Bessie B. West. *Food for Fifty.* 3rd ed. New York: John Wiley & Sons, Inc., 1950.

General Foods Kitchens. *Frozen Foods Cookbook.* 2nd ed. New York: Random House, Inc., 1962.

Gortner, Willis A., and Frederick S. Erdman, and Nancy K. Masterman. *Principles of Food Freezing.* New York: John Wiley & Sons, Inc., 1948.

Greer, Carlotta C. and Ellen P. Gibbs. *Your Home and You.* Boston: Allyn and Bacon, Inc., 1963.

Meyer, Hazel. *Freezer Cook Book.* Philadelphia: J. B. Lippincott Company, 1970.

Ministry of Agriculture, Fisheries and Food. *The Accelerated Freeze-Drying (AFD) Method of Food Preservation.* London: Her Majesty's Stationery Office, 1961.

Larson, Kathryn and Nell B. Nichols, eds. *Farm Journal's Freezing & Canning Cookbook.* Philadelphia: Farm Journal, Inc., 1973.

Phillips, Patricia. *Pressure Cooking is Pleasure Cooking.* Eau Claire, WI: The Johnson Press, 1973.

Quat, Helen. *The Wonderful World of Freezer Cooking.* New York: Hearthside Press, 1964.

Rolfs, Shirley. *Manual for Preparation of Frozen Foods.* 1957.

Simpson, Jean I. and Demetria M. Taylor (with the technical assistance and cooperation of The Frozen Food Foundation). *The Frozen Food Cook Book.* New York: Simon and Schuster, 1948.

Spann, Donna G. *Grains of Truth.* Alexandria, VA: ASAP Printing & Mailing Co., 1998.

Sparks, Boyden. *Zero Storage in Your Home.* Garden City, NY: Doubleday, Doran & Co., 1945.

Tannahill, Reay. *Food in History.* New York: Stein and Day, 1973.

Tannenbaum, Beulah and Myra Stillman. *Understanding Food: The Chemistry of Nutrition.* New York: McGraw-Hill Book Company, Inc., 1962.

Treat, Nola and Lenore Richards. *Quantity Cookery.* Boston: Little, Brown and Company, 1951.

Tressler, Donald K., and Clifford F. Evers, and Barbara H. Evers. *Into the Freezer—and Out.* New York: The AVI Publishing Company, 1953.

Waldo, Myra. *Cooking for the Freezer.* Garden City, NY: Doubleday & Company, Inc., 1960.

Subject Index

Recipe Index